Terrorists, Victims and Society

Wiley Series in

The Psychology of Crime, Policing and Law

Series Editors

Graham Davies   and   **Ray Bull**

University of Leicester, UK   *University of Portsmouth, UK*

The Wiley series in the Psychology of Crime, Policing and Law publishes concise and integrative reviews on important emerging areas of contemporary research. The purpose of the series is not merely to present research findings in a clear and readable form, but also to bring out their implications for both practice and policy. In this way, it is hoped the series will not only be useful to psychologists but also to all those concerned with crime detection and prevention, policing, and the judicial process. Current titles of interest in the series include:

Terrorists, Victims and Society

Psychological Perspectives on Terrorism and its Consequences

Edited by

Andrew Silke
University of Leicester, UK

WILEY

Other Wiley Editorial Offices

John Wiley & Sons Inc., 111 River Street, Hoboken, NJ 07030, USA

Jossey-Bass, 989 Market Street, San Francisco, CA 94103-1741, USA

Wiley-VCH Verlag GmbH, Boschstr. 12, D-69469 Weinheim, Germany

John Wiley & Sons Australia Ltd, 33 Park Road, Milton, Queensland 4064, Australia

John Wiley & Sons (Asia) Pte Ltd, 2 Clementi Loop #02-01, Jin Xing Distripark,
Singapore 129809

John Wiley & Sons Canada Ltd, 22 Worcester Road, Etobicoke, Ontario, Canada M9W 1L1

Wiley also publishes its books in a variety of electronic formats. Some content that appears
in print may not be available in electronic books.

Library of Congress Cataloging-in-Publication Data

Terrorists, victims, and society : psychological perspectives on terrorism and its
    consequences / edited by Andrew Silke.
        p.   cm. — (Wiley series in psychology of crime, policing, and law)
    Includes bibliographical references and index.
    ISBN 0-471-49461-5 — ISBN 0-471-49462-3 (pbk. : alk. paper)
        1. Terrorism—Psychological aspects.   2. Terrorists—Psychology.   3. Victims of
terrorism—Psychology.   I. Silke, Andrew.   II. Series.
HV6431 .T554   2003
155.9′35—dc21   2002153140

British Library Cataloguing in Publication Data

A catalogue record for this book is available from the British Library

ISBN 0-471-49461-5 (hbk)
ISBN 0-471-49462-3 (pbk)

Typeset in 10/12pt Century Schoolbook by TechBooks, New Delhi, India
Printed and bound in Great Britain by The Cromwell Press, Trowbridge, Wiltshire
This book is printed on acid-free paper responsibly manufactured from sustainable forestry
in which at least two trees are planted for each one used for paper production.

Contents

About the Editor

Dr Andrew Silke (BSc Hons, AFBPsS, PhD) is a forensic psychologist who has worked both in academia and for government. He has published extensively on terrorists and terrorism in journals, books and the popular press, and his most recent book on the subject was *Terrorism Research: Trends, Achievements, Failures* published by Frank Cass (2003). He is an Honorary Senior Research Associate of the Centre for the Study of Terrorism and Political Violence at the University of St Andrews and is a Fellow of the University of Leicester. His work has taken him to Northern Ireland, the Middle East and Latin America. He is a member of the International Association for Counter-terrorism and Security Professionals and serves on the United Nations Roster of Terrorism Experts. *Email: andrew_silke@yahoo.co.uk*

About the Contributors

Dr Jacqueline Bates-Gaston, *The Northern Ireland Prison Service, Dundonald House, Belfast BT4 3SU, Northern Ireland*
Dr Jacqueline Bates-Gaston (BA, MSc, MSC, C.Psychol, AFBPsS) has worked in management development and training, employment rehabilitation and counselling, and as a Senior Lecturer in Psychology at the University of Ulster. She has been the Chief Psychologist with the Northern Ireland Prison Service for more than 11 years. During that time she has worked closely with both staff and prisoners using her occupational and forensic training and experience. She is responsible for the development and implementation of prisoner initiatives to assess and address offending behaviour. In 1991 she set up a specialised Staff Support Unit designed to meet the needs of staff traumatised by assaults and terrorist violence both inside and outside the working environment. This unit was the first of its kind in Northern Ireland. Her work has given her extensive insight and experience into how terrorists can operate in a prison environment and the psychological impact on those who work with them.

Dr Deborah Browne, *Email: debcbrowne@yahoo.co.uk*
Dr Deborah Browne has lectured in forensic psychology and has worked as a principal research officer for government. She has published papers in various academic journals and has presented at a number of national and international conferences. Previous work has included a period as consultant for the United Nation's Children's Fund (UNICEF) in Sarajevo during the Bosnian conflict. Key areas of her research interest have included the development of antisocial behaviour in children and young people, the consequences of child abuse, and psychological issues affecting foster children.

Dr John Horgan, *Department of Applied Psychology, University College Cork, Enterprise Centre, North Mall, Cork City, Republic of Ireland*
Dr John Horgan is a lecturer at the Department of Applied Psychology, University College Cork, where he teaches courses on forensic psychology and the psychology of terrorism and political violence. His work on

terrorism has been published in a variety of sources and his books include *The Future of Terrorism* (2000) and *The Psychology of Terrorism* (2003), both with Max Taylor and published by Frank Cass (London).

Dr Orla Muldoon, *School of Psychology, Queen's University Belfast, David Keir Building, 18–30 Malone Road, Belfast BT9 5BP, Northern Ireland*

Orla Muldoon (RGN, BSSc, PhD, PGCUT, C.Psychol) is a lecturer at the School of Psychology, The Queen's University of Belfast. Her research interests are in the area of applied psychology, particularly the influence of social and environmental factors on psychological and social wellbeing. She has published a number of papers on the impact of political violence. These papers have considered how young people cope with armed conflict, the impact of conflict on child adjustment and the wider effects of conflict on society. More recently she has been involved in research projects examining the role experience may play in contributing to conflict, particularly focusing on the impact of conflict experiences on social attitudes and acceptance of violence. She is a member of the British Psychological Society, International Society of Political Psychology, Association of Child Psychology and Psychiatry and the Society for the Psychological Study of Social Issues.

Professor Betty Pfefferbaum, *Department of Psychiatry and Behavioral Sciences, University of Oklahoma Health Sciences Center, PO Box 26901, WP-3470, Oklahoma City, OK 73190-3048, USA*

Betty Pfefferbaum (MD, JD) is a general and child psychiatrist and professor and chairman of the Department of Psychiatry and Behavioral Sciences at the University of Oklahoma College of Medicine where she holds the Paul and Ruth Jonas Chair. She helped plan and organise clinical services after the 1995 Oklahoma City bombing, and has treated many victims and family members and is actively engaged in research related to the bombing. She assisted in mental-health clinical and research efforts related to the 1998 United States Embassy bombings in East Africa. She has provided consultation regarding clinical and research efforts associated with the September 11, 2001 terrorist attacks. She is the director of the Terrorism and Disaster Branch of the National Child Traumatic Stress Network, a federal initiative to improve treatment and services for traumatised children.

Dr Marc Rogers, *Internet Innovation Centre, University of Manitoba, Winnipeg, Manitoba, Canada*

Dr Marc Rogers is a lecturer at the Department of Psychology at the University of Manitoba and principal researcher in the area of computer crime and cyber-terrorism. He has worked with various law-enforcement agencies and has published several articles and book chapters in the area of cyber crime and cyber deviance.

Dr Karl A. Seger, *President, Associated Corporate Consultants, Inc, 1241 Harbour View Drive, Lenoir City, TN 37772, USA*

Karl A. Seger has provided anti-terrorism consulting and training for all branches of the US military, the Departments of Justice and the Treasury, and for the Federal Emergency Management Agency. He assisted in the development of the army's terrorism counteraction programme and was the contract writer for TC19-16, *Countering Terrorism on US Army Installations*. He is the author of the *Antiterrorism Handbook* (Presidio Press, 1990) and co-author of *Computer Crime: An Investigator's Handbook* (O'Reilly & Associated, 1995). He provides security training and consulting services for government and corporate clients and has been conducting anti-terrorism training around the world for more than 20 years.

Dr Andrew Silke (*see* 'About the Editor')

Professor Ginny Sprang, *College of Social Work, University of Kentucky, Lexington, KY 40506, USA*

Ginny Sprang (PhD) is an Associate Professor at the University of Kentucky with a joint appointment to the College of Social Work, and the College of Medicine, Department of Psychiatry. She is a Principal Investigator of the Comprehensive Assessment and Training Services (CATS) project, a clinical and research project that assesses and treats traumatised children and their families. She is author of *The Many Faces of Bereavement: The Nature and Treatment of Natural, Traumatic and Stigmatized Grief* (Brunner-Routledge, 1995), and has written numerous articles on trauma, bereavement and victimisation of adults and children.

Dr Margaret Wilson, *Department of Psychology, Keynes College, The University of Kent at Canterbury, Canterbury, Kent CT2 7NP, UK*

Dr Margaret Wilson is an applied psychologist who has for many years been teaching forensic psychology in the UK. She has conducted a great deal of research on terrorist behaviour and lectured extensively on the subject worldwide. She can currently be contacted through the University of Kent at Canterbury, where she holds an honorary post.

Series Preface

The Wiley Series in the Psychology of Crime, Policing and the Law publishes integrative reviews on important emerging areas of contemporary research. The purpose of the series is not merely to present research findings in a clear and readable form, but also to bring out their implications for both practice and policy. In this way, it is hoped that the series will not only be useful to psychologists, but also to all those concerned with crime detection and prevention, policing and the judicial process.

As Andrew Silke, the editor of *Terrorism, Victims and Society: Psychological Perspectives on Terrorism and its Consequences*, makes clear, this book is no fast-buck response to the events of September 11, 2001. Rather, it represents a considered and comprehensive appraisal from a psychological perspective of the motivations and origins of terrorists, the impact of their acts on its victims, and of ways of combating terrorism. While terrorism has been repeatedly studied from the perspective of its political, ethnic or religious roots, the psychological element has frequently been ignored.

The first section of the book is given over to the debate surrounding acts of terrorism and their perpetrators. The contributors do not duck the subjective and judgemental element of the label 'terrorist'—we must remember that the resistance heroes of the Second World War were called 'terrorists' by their Nazi occupiers—but focus on the personality and behaviour of terrorists. What combination of personality traits and family and societal influences produce a terrorist? The acts themselves are frequently horrific, with violence and death meted out to all, without regard to traditional distinctions between combatants and the innocent. As the contributors emphasise, such acts are rarely random but precisely calibrated for their psychological impact: terrorists can be psychologists too. To understand, but not excuse, such behaviour is the first step to coming to terms with terrorism.

The second section is devoted to the victims of terrorism and the impact of such acts on their lives, attitudes and behaviour. As we have seen in Northern Ireland and elsewhere, terrorism can persist over generations, wrecking the lives of its victims and polarising the attitudes of whole communities. Dealing with the psychological consequences of terrorism for its victims, direct and indirect, and influencing well-established attitudes and stereotypes is a challenge dealt with in depth by the contributors to this book.

The third section is devoted to the problem of responding to terrorism from a psychological perspective. Historically, some terrorist campaigns have been successfully resisted and defeated. The problem for established authority is how to combat and suppress terrorist acts, while at the same time not increasing the sympathy of the community at large for those responsible for the original outrages. Part of that response may involve new laws and offences, police and military initiatives or political, economic and religious changes, but as our contributors emphasise, all must be carefully evaluated in terms of their perceived psychological consequences for the individuals involved and the community at large.

The editor, Andrew Silke, is well placed to bring together this important and ground-breaking series of papers. Dr Silke himself has made a significant contribution to the growing literature on psychological aspects of terrorism and its consequences. As a young researcher and at some personal risk, he conducted extensive field research in Northern Ireland, interviewing people involved in the violence, and trod the streets and lanes where acts of terror had taken place. The wealth of his knowledge and contacts are reflected in this book. It deserves to be read not merely by those interested in the academic study of terrorism but also by the politicians and law-enforcement personnel who must deal at first-hand with the consequences and perpetrators of this scourge of our age.

GRAHAM M. DAVIES
University of Leicester

Preface

In the wake of the September 11 attacks and subsequent events in Afghanistan and elsewhere, the world's attention has turned to the question of how best to tackle terrorism. This focus will fade with time—and probably quicker than many expect—but for now the issue of how best to understand and resolve terrorist conflicts dominates much public thought and activity. One clear certainty at this juncture is that there are no easy and straightforward solutions to terrorism. However, research on the subject conducted over the past three decades has helped identify some of the key issues that must be faced in tackling the problem, and has discerned some of the important features of effective counter-terrorism policies.

Many obstacles block efforts to reach a reliable understanding of terrorism and its impact. At a fundamental level there is incredible discrepancy over what the term actual means and who can fairly be described as a terrorist and who cannot. 'Terrorism' is a fiercely political word and one that is both incredibly alive and dishearteningly legion. As a term, it is far too nimble a creature for social science to be able to pin it down in anything like a reliable manner, and the result has been frustrating and unending debate in order to reach an accepted demarcation of the boundaries of the word. This has been sorely felt within the social sciences, and Poland (1988) noted correctly that this failure to agree on an acceptable definition is 'the most confounding problem in the study of terrorism'. So intractable are the various contentions that Shafritz, Gibbons and Scott (1991) concluded sombrely that 'it is unlikely that any definition will ever be generally agreed upon'.

While an agreed definition is probably as far off as ever, the needs of this volume require at least the bones of a framework for focus. A few of the chapters that follow will touch again on the subject of definition in their introductions, but overall the volume follows the relatively concise outline provided by Martha Crenshaw, a political scientist with a singular expertise in the psychology of terrorism. Crenshaw has described terrorism as 'a particular style of political violence, involving attacks on a small number of victims in order to influence a wider audience' (Crenshaw, 1992).

The events of September 11 cruelly illustrated that 'small' is a relative term. There is also dissent as to what behaviours fit comfortably within this definition. Nevertheless, the focus of this volume is very much that of what could be described as 'insurgent' terrorism. This is essentially a strategy of the weak, the use of violence 'by groups with little numerical, physical or direct political power in order to effect political or social change' (Friedland, 1992). In practical terms, 'insurgent' terrorists tend to be members of small covert groups engaged in an organised campaign of violence.

Terrorism is a complex and capacious subject, and psychological research has been conducted on many different aspects of the phenomenon, not all of which can be considered in this collection. As a field of study, terrorism is distinctive in that it is a difficult and sometimes dangerous topic to investigate, and for obvious reasons the number of people actively researching the subject has always been small. Adding to this lack of bodies on the ground are serious and persistent concerns regarding the manner and reliability of the methods used to gather and analyse most of the data currently available on the subject. As Groebel (1989) pointed out: 'Most data are either not available at all, are only fragmentary, or cannot be tested with respect to their reliability and validity. Terrorists are rarely open to direct observation and usually do not volunteer for scientific interviews' (p. 25).

The literature of terrorism is still young: almost all of the books on the topic have been written since 1968. The explosion of publications in the late 1970s has been followed by less dramatic but relatively steady growth, and although the tragic events of September 11, 2001 resulted in a flood of publications on the subject, there is no sense that the quantity reflects any improvement in quality (Alexander, 2002). This is an old problem. Schmid and Jongman (1988) noted that despite the fact that a very sizeable body of literature on terrorism has accumulated, the substance of this writing is less than impressive: 'Much of the writing in the crucial areas of terrorism research is impressionistic, superficial, and at the same time often also pretentious, venturing far-reaching generalizations on the basis of episodal evidence' (p. 177).

The study of terrorism is truly multidisciplinary and, perhaps for the better, no one discipline has been able to firmly take pre-eminence in this area of study. Researchers from fields such as political science, criminology, psychology, sociology, history, law, military and communication sciences have all contributed. However, despite this diversity of backgrounds the research itself remains plagued by a number of problems. Ariel Merari, a psychologist and writer with a keen sense of the limitations of research efforts to date, makes the following general point:

> Terrorism is a study area which is very easy to approach but very difficult to cope with in a scientific sense. Easy to approach—because it has so many

angles, touching upon all aspects of human behaviour. Difficult to cope with—because it is so diverse. As terrorism is not a discipline, there can hardly be a general theory of terrorism . . . There are few social scientists who specialise in this study area. Most contributions in this field are ephemeral. Precise and extensive factual knowledge is still grossly lacking. Much effort must still be invested in the very first stage of scientific inquiry with regard to terrorism—the collection of data (quoted in Schmid and Jongman, 1988, p. 177).

In examining the quality of research on terrorism, Schmid and Jongman (1988) noted in their review that 'there are probably few areas in the social science literature on which so much is written on the basis of so little research'. They estimated that 'as much as 80 per cent of the literature is not research-based in any rigorous sense; instead, it is too often narrative, condemnatory, and prescriptive' (p. 179). A review of recent research work found that only about 20 per cent of published articles on terrorism are providing substantially new knowledge on the subject (Silke, 2001). The rest are simply reiterating and reworking old data. Further, while the backgrounds of the researchers may be relatively diverse, there has in general been a constant shortage of investigators to carry out studies in this area. Since it first emerged as a clear and substantial topic of study, terrorism has suffered from a near-chronic lack of active researchers.

PSYCHOLOGICAL APPROACHES TO THE STUDY OF TERRORISM

Crenshaw (1990) noted that 'it is difficult to understand terrorism without psychological theory, because explaining terrorism must begin with analysing the intentions of the terrorist actor and the emotional reactions of audiences' (p. 247). Yet despite this, the number of psychologists actively researching in the area has always been very small. In 1985, Schmid and Jongman carried out a review of all available terrorism researchers. They found that just 10 per cent of this sample were psychologists (just 11 individuals). A review carried out in 2000 on the published literature on terrorism found that psychologists and psychiatrists accounted for less than 6 per cent of the research work on terrorism (Silke, 2000). So while psychology has played a role in trying to understand terrorism, it has in general been a very minor contributor and one that has arguably grown less active and vigorous with time.

According to Merari (1991), both terrorism and terrorists have been largely ignored by psychology as a discipline. This is a perception not without substance:

Until recently, the academic community paid very little attention to the phenomena of terrorism. For academic psychology, in particular, terrorism was nonexistent throughout the 1970s, a period when scores of terrorist groups were established all over the world and terrorist attacks became one of the most frequent topics of media headlines. The Psychological Abstracts, the most authoritative compendium of academic publications in psychology, listed no reference to terrorism or to related terms, such as 'hostages' or 'hijacking', until the end of 1981. . . . some psychological and psychiatric articles and books on terrorism appeared before 1982 but the articles were not published in the journals covered by the Psychological Abstracts and the books, apparently, did not deserve a mention in the opinion of the Psychological Abstracts editors. Clearly this subject remained outside the interest and attention of mainstream psychology. Although political scientists have devoted considerably greater attention to terrorism than psychologists and sociologists, on the whole the scientific community has so far allocated a very small part of its research effort to this subject—a strange attitude towards a phenomenon that is clearly one of the most common forms of violent domestic and international political conflict in our time (Merari, 1991, p. 91).

The reasons for this general neglect are not difficult to imagine. Terrorism is a violent, emotive and dangerous activity, and terrorist groups are secretive, ruthless and very dangerous organisations. The risks involved for the potential researcher are considerable: academic researchers have been threatened, kidnapped, attacked, shot, bombed and killed in their attempts to study terrorism.

Other obstacles also hinder research efforts. Many traditional methods of research struggle badly when attempts are made to apply them to the study of terrorism. Merari (1991) points out that: 'On the practical side, terrorism is a very elusive subject for research. . . . Collecting systematic standardized, reliable information for the purpose of comparisons is next to impossible. Moreover, the customary tools of psychological and sociological research are almost always inapplicable for studying terrorist groups and their individual members' (p. 89). However, Merari does note that the physical manifestations of terrorism as well as public responses to it are, in principle, much more accessible to research than the psychology and sociology of terrorists. In practice, however, even research in this area is not always easy.

Further, and despite the considerable potential, much terrorism research conducted by psychologists seems wasted, with repeated explorations of avenues already effectively exhausted by previous researchers. Many researchers seem to have only a casual and cursory awareness of other terrorism research. The dead-ends of terrorist abnormality and terrorist personality reoccur, flouting the overwhelming body of evidence to the contrary that has emerged over the past 25 years. Speculation and theorising are invaluable to the development of constructive research, however psychology's performance here borders on dereliction. The problem appears to be that too few dedicated psychologists take terrorism as their primary interest. As Merari points out, often individuals whose speciality and main interest lie elsewhere see an application for their own area in terrorism. They wade in, publish a paper or two and then depart. This leaves the few dedicated researchers to deal with a continuous supply of material espousing viewpoints and theories that serious researchers have in fact relegated years previously, as what evidence was available consistently showed such approaches to be fruitless and/or fundamentally wrong.

Despite the generally sporadic nature of psychological research on terrorism, there are nevertheless a number of areas where psychological enquiry has produced truly important findings. In particular there has been good research on the question of whether terrorists are psychologically abnormal (and the related question as to whether a terrorist personality exists). Even better work has been done on the victims of terrorism, and over the past 20 years psychologists have made enormous progress in understanding how people respond to being caught up in terrorist incidents.

THE SCOPE OF THIS VOLUME

At a time when there is an increasing sense of paranoia regarding terrorism, there is a powerful need for balanced, expert and accessible accounts of the psychology of terrorists and terrorism. This book is intended to help address this need. However, it should not be seen as a knee-jerk reaction to the tragic events of September 11. Yonah Alexander (2002) recently commented that more than 150 books on terrorism had been published in the first 12 months after the terrorist attacks on New York and Washington— roughly three new books each week. He questioned, rightly, whether the quality of this flood of printed matter would stand any test of time. This volume is hopefully somewhat better prepared for such probation.

Though published well after the September 11 attacks, work on this collection of papers began back in 1998 when I met the Series Editor for a coffee at the campus of the University of Leicester. I had already heard that Wiley had (for some time) wanted to publish a book on psychology and terrorism, but had been struggling to find someone to take on the project. I agreed to edit the book, but little appreciated then just how long it would take to bring the finished volume to fruition. From the outset, the intention was to include in one volume contributions from psychologists and psychiatrists with the 'right' backgrounds: people who had direct experience of researching terrorism; who had met actual terrorists; who had worked with the victims of terrorist violence; and who had worked to assist those tasked with the serious responsibility of combating and responding to terrorism. Needless to say, the list of potential contributors was a short one, and it took much time to gather together the various authors. The end product, though, has hopefully been worth the long wait.

Divided into three parts, the book aims to provide a holistic account of terrorism and its impact. The first general section focuses on terrorists as individuals and as groups. The contributions here attempt to provide a balanced and objective insight into the psychology of terrorists: what are their motivations, what keeps them involved in terrorist groups, and what eventually forces most to end their active involvement in terrorism. This section also tackles the special issues of terrorist hostage-taking, suicidal terrorism and the growing concern over cyber-terrorism.

The second section of the book explores the impact of terrorism. Some of the best work psychology has carried out on the subject of terrorism has focused on the issues surrounding victims, and the chapters here examine how terrorism affects both its direct and indirect casualties. The section also examines the differences between isolated incidents and long-running terrorist campaigns, the special cases of groups such as children and the increasingly sensitive role of the media.

The final section of the book focuses on the thorny questions of how best to respond to, and manage, terrorism. It is hoped that these chapters can provide some insight for those concerned with short-term tactical problems (e.g. whether or not to retaliate), as well as for those looking at the more long-term strategic questions of bringing an entire terrorist campaign to an end.

Ultimately, the focus of this book is to present a clear and succinct view of what psychological research has revealed about terrorists and terrorism. The results are often disturbing, sometimes surprising and frequently disheartening. Perhaps most worrying of all is the extent to which this current level and range of knowledge has repeatedly been ignored and overlooked by those with the responsibility of controlling terrorism. This book attempts to provide a clear, intelligent and well-informed account of what psychology has learned over the past 30 years about issues relating to terrorism. It also aims to demonstrate just how one branch of social science can provide a powerful tool for insight and guidance on one of the most challenging problems facing the modern world.

ANDREW SILKE

REFERENCES

Alexander, Y. (2002). September 11: US Reactions and Responses. Paper presented at the ESRC Conference of the St Andrews/Southampton Research Project on the Domestic Management of Terrorist Attacks, 19–20 September 2002, Southampton, UK.

Crenshaw, M. (1990). Questions to be answered, research to be done. In W. Reich (Ed.), *Origins of Terrorism*. Cambridge: Woodrow Wilson Center.

Crenshaw, M. (1992). How terrorists think: what psychology can contribute to understanding terrorism. In L. Howard (Ed.), *Terrorism: Roots, Impact, Responses* (pp. 71–80). London: Praeger.

Friedland, N. (1992). Becoming a terrorist: social and individual antecedents. In L. Howard (Ed.), *Terrorism: Roots, Impact, Responses* (pp. 81–93). London: Praeger.

Groebel, J. (1989). The problems and challenges of research on terrorism. In J. Groebel and J.H. Goldstein (Eds), *Terrorism: Psychological Perspectives* (pp. 15–38). Seville: University of Seville.

Merari, A. (1991). Academic research and government policy on terrorism. *Terrorism and Political Violence*, **3**(1), 88–102.

Poland, J.M. (1988). *Understanding Terrorism: Groups, Strategies, and Responses*. New Jersey: Prentice-Hall.

Schmid, A.P. and Jongman, A.J. (1988). *Political Terrorism*, 2nd edn. Oxford: North-Holland Publishing Company.

Shafritz, J.M., Gibbons, E.F. Jr and Scott, G.E.J. (1991). *Almanac of Modern Terrorism*. Oxford: Facts on File.

Silke, A. (2000). The road less travelled: trends in terrorism research 1990–1999. Paper presented at the International Conference on Countering Terrorism Through Enhanced International Cooperation, 22–24 September 2000, Courmayeur, Italy.

Silke, A. (2001). The devil you know: continuing problems with research on terrorism.*Terrorism and Political Violence*, **13**(4), 1–14.

PART I

The Terrorists

CHAPTER 1

The Search for the Terrorist Personality

JOHN HORGAN

University College Cork

INTRODUCTION

Wardlaw (1989) suggested that the most commonly asked question about terrorism is 'why do people become terrorists?' (p. 171). Following the September 11 attacks his sentiment was reflected in questions unwavering in their similarity, particularly 'why would they do it?' That a proper understanding of terrorist motivation remains outside our grasp is an issue that continues to sit uncomfortably within psychological research on terrorism, and continues to be tackled with embarrassingly vague references to broad typologies, fuzzy psychological processes that are as imprecise and unhelpful within contemporary psychology as anywhere else—psychoanalysis is particularly guilty post-September 11. These are often stuck onto various political science theories with little or no understanding of the psychological bases and limitations of such theories. In addition are equally imprecise and indeterminate references to broad social processes resulting in an inherent lack of any predictive utility whatsoever. We are, to paraphrase Post (1987a), still 'primitive' in our understanding of the psychology of terrorism and terrorists (p. 307).

This chapter addresses only the mostly academic issue of the 'terrorist personality', its uncomfortable presence in the literature, and its increasingly comfortable relationship with conventional wisdom and common sense—neither of which are very useful in understanding the terrorist.

Terrorists, Victims and Society: Psychological Perspectives on Terrorism and its Consequences.
Edited by Andrew Silke. © 2003 John Wiley & Sons, Ltd.

One might suspect that a naive personality debate has dissipated from the literature, but this is actually not true. In the past 12 months alone, there has been a torrent of resurgent efforts to profile the terrorist 'mind' by a slew of authors, notably psychoanalytic in tradition.

The question 'what motivates the terrorist?' has permeated behavioural research efforts since the early 1970s, mirroring the upsurge in academic interest in contemporary terrorism around that period. Despite the heterogeneity of motivation of people who become terrorists (between and within groups) and other general issues relating to terrorism, a persistent theme throughout behavioural studies reflects concerns about how the terrorist might be 'psychologically different' from the non-terrorist, or how his or her involvement in terrorism might be characterised by some special process. This approach, often oversimplified in scope, is clearly found in the contemporary literature, principally in the works of psychologists and psychiatrists who have something to say about terrorism. Merari (2000), echoing the sentiments of many researchers, noted that 'presumably, there are ... factors that differentiate terrorists from non-terrorists', with reference to 'the psychological make up of terrorists' (p. 59). A suggestion dismissed by many is that the search itself is not particularly useful at all. As Taylor (1988) and Wardlaw (1989) proclaim, psychological approaches to understanding terrorist behaviour reflect inclinations to explain extreme behaviour in 'simple psychological terms that obscure the real complexities' (p. 171).

Actually, it would be rather surprising to contemporary academic psychologists that simplistic explanations of this complex behaviour persist. This alone warrants a more critical examination of the psychological literature, as well as a discussion of alternative explanations on the nature of terrorist behaviour (explanations with much momentum in criminology and contemporary forensic psychology). Another problem to be overcome is that psychological accounts of terrorism (and, admittedly, even the valuable ones) do not yet sit easily within interdisciplinary accounts.

Crenshaw's (1990) position serves as a useful guideline along which we might begin:

> We can analyse terrorism at the level of the individual practitioner or the collective actor, the terrorist group. In turn both actors, individual and group, must be seen in relation to society as a whole. Similarly terrorism alters the behaviour of individuals, collective actors such as the terrorist organisation or the government, and societies. *The integration of these levels of analysis is a significant problem for research on terrorism* (p. 249) [emphasis added].

Assertions about terrorist behaviour derive from macro- and micro-studies within terrorism research as a whole, but of relevance to the assumptions and assertions of psychological aspects of terrorism is that its knowledge stems from (a) examinations of the individual psychology of the terrorist, and (b) evidence of how the individual's behaviour is influenced or determined by the group/organisation.

THE SEARCH FOR THE TERRORIST PERSONALITY

Terrorism and Psychopathy

Let us begin with logic. When confronted with the immediate results of terrorism, whether we like to admit it as scholars or not, our tendency to focus on the drama surrounding such brutal violence inevitably and intuitively leads us into explaining that behaviour with attribution to the person responsible. Even at that we are usually presented with sanitised accounts by the media; if we were to face the reality of a bombing, few would not be forgiven for assuming that the person responsible is in some way special, different or perhaps even abnormal. Conventional wisdom might reinforce such views when the day-to-day behavioural features of terrorist violence are considered. For example, Anderson (1994) describes the IRA's vigilante assaults as follows:

> There is the '50-50' (the victim is forced to touch his toes while a bullet is fired into his spine); 'breeze blocking' (the methodical shattering of bones by dropping flagstones or cinder blocks on joints); and the 'six pack' (shots to the knees, ankles, and elbows). Through long experience, the squads now know how to maximize suffering: injuries can be heightened by forcing a shooting victim to lie on concrete, and the most efficient way to destroy an elbow is by bringing the hand toward the shoulder and firing into the bend . . .

As a result of what terrorist acts demand of the terrorist, Cooper (1976) suggested that: 'The true terrorist must steel himself against tenderheartedness through a fierce faith in his credo or by a blessed retreat into a comforting, individual madness.' It is inevitable then, Cooper argues, that 'the political terrorist needs either a highly-insulated conscience or a certain detachment from reality' (p. 232). This theme has long been reflected in the literature. In a 1981 review of arguments that 'terrorism is driven by mental disorders', Corrado (1981) concluded that psychopathy was then the feature most prominently associated with terrorists (e.g. Cooper, 1977, 1978; Hacker, 1976; Hassel, 1977; Kellen, 1979, 1982; Pearce, 1977).

Psychopathic behaviour and many features of terrorist violence have similarities, notably in terms of how terrorists respond to their victims: if terrorists perpetuate violence often resulting in the death of non-combatants then surely they must lack empathy or remorse; this is re-inforced given their antisocial and irresponsible behaviour, and even more so when the terrorist, not content with destruction in itself, subsequently claims responsibility for the act! The tendency to ascribe explanations of outright abnormality/mental illness owing to the savagery of the be-haviour is noted by many, and even go as far as to suggest sadism (see, for example, Burton, 1978; Taylor, 1988). Empirical evidence or not, such explanations pass for plausible.

By and large, however, there remains little to support the argument that terrorists can or should be necessarily regarded as psychopathic owing to the nature of the offences committed. Cooper (1976) correctly argued that: 'The life of the true, political terrorist is a hard and lonely one' (p. 232). Without necessarily commenting otherwise on the personal motivation of terrorists, the social and personal lives of people who be-come terrorists do suffer psychologically (see Bowyer-Bell, 1979, 2000; Burton, 1978; Coogan, 1995; Jamieson, 1989, 1990a, 1990b). The ability to form close bonds may be tantamount to dealing with such pressures. An alleged Provisional IRA (PIRA) leader described to the author how his involvement in the PIRA affected not only himself but his family and Republican colleagues:

> It was . . . it was very hard. And it still is, often. Actually, I'm very lucky in the sense that my wife *shared* my [political] convictions, and the fact that she realised the depth of my involvement without knowing what I was *actually* doing, she had an understanding of what it was about, and like the fact that she had been arrested herself and strip-searched in the house at one stage she had a full understanding of what the pressures [were] that could come on her and for her own benefit, it was better not to know.

Such realities seem incompatible with the pathological egocentrici-ties consistent with psychopathic personalities. Taylor and Quayle (1994) gleaned the following remark from a terrorist leader in Northern Ireland: 'there are very few obvious what do you call them . . . psychopaths . . . they'd stand out like a sore thumb and everyone would know them' (p. 107). This reflects an organisational concern, the basis of which represents a logical argument against psychopathology notions of terrorist behaviour. Loyalty in the face of continuing hardship and unrelenting commitment to the greater ideological cause and movement are qualities that go hand in hand with being a member of an illegal, underground organisation.

Furthermore, while terrorist victims are often incidental, chosen on symbolic bases (e.g. airline passengers, soldiers), they contrast sharply with the victims of psychopathic murderers, in that rather than aspiring to 'a broader ideological context' (Taylor, 1988, p. 88) the psychopath's rea-sons are personal, fuelled and sustained by elaborate personal fantasies. Frequently the terrorist may not even experience the effects of his or her violence first-hand, for example if a bomb is left to explode minutes, hours or even weeks later.

Of course, any terrorist may find it difficult to attain complete insulation from the effects of his or her violence, at least at the beginning of his or her development. Cooper (1976) adds that '[f]ew terrorists seem to derive a real satisfaction from the harm they cause' (p. 237). Kellen (1982) supports this by reminding us that 'some terrorists do experience remorse, and we have proof of it' (p. 237) (see Burton, 1978). We ought to remember too that the view of terrorists as necessarily abnormal by virtue of the nature of their behaviour therefore ignores the processes whereby members become brutalised and more committed as a result of membership and increased psychological commitment to the group.

And more obvious issues exist, particularly if we consider the bidirectional nature of terrorist violence and extra-legal violence employed by agents of the state in counter-terrorism operations: do we also refer to the Israeli or US soldier who engages in qualitatively similar behaviour as psychopathic? In such contexts, as with the fickle and euphemistic labelling in our usage of 'terrorism', we prefer to employ different terminology and draw on different explanations.

A more alarming inconsistency within the research in this field, somewhat different in character yet revelatory of the tendency of novice terrorism researchers to ignore evidence, relates to that of judgements meriting 'psychopathy' labels in the absence of clinical diagnosis. For instance, Kellen's (1982) arguments that Carlos the Jackal was a psychopath were based on 'what he says about himself and from the exploits he stresses in his interviews' (p. 18). According to Silke (1998), Pearce's emphasis on psychopathy is based on 'secondary sources such as terrorist autobiographies, biographies and media interviews. In one case, Pearce made a diagnosis of psychopathy based mainly on an individual having tattoos on his torso' (p. 60). If, as some have suggested, we already know enough about terrorism to warrant discarding expectations of terrorist personality types, or disorders (particularly for something so obvious as psychopathy), we might surely be forgiven for wishing to explore further the basis on which such claims are made in the first place, given their persistence.

Perhaps if the opportunity ever arose to examine actual terrorists in clinical settings, there might be some evidence to link at least a few of the 'sore thumbs' with pathological disorders. In the meantime, however, there is poor evidence for the principle that psychopathy is an element of the psychology of terrorist organisations. Despite the attractiveness of the theme (and the subtlety by which this attractiveness permeates common assumptions), terrorist movements should be seen neither as organisations of necessarily psychopathic individuals because of the brutality of behaviour involved, nor likely to recruit people with psychopathic tendencies.

A DIFFERENT KIND OF TERRORIST PERSONALITY

Aside from the behavioural features associated with psychopathy, other efforts focus on similarities between terrorist behaviour and the predominant traits of personality types. A distinct body of research exists in support of the argument that the terrorist is psychologically dissimilar to non-terrorists. A characteristically positivist approach, this epitomises the majority of psychological contributions. Although some of this research is dated (a few considerably), that it persists as compelling research (in both its nature and stated findings) *and* that its conclusions are developed upon within similar kinds of analyses in the contemporary literature, warrants that it be addressed here in order that we might assert its veracity and overall worthiness.

In 1981, the West German Ministry of the Interior commissioned social scientists to examine over 220 German terrorists (Baeyer-Katte *et al.*, 1982; Jäger, Schmidtchen and Sullwold, 1982). Some terrorist leaders were typified by an extremely extraverted personality, characterised by 'unstable, uninhibited, inconsiderate, self-interested and unemotional' behaviour (see Taylor (1988) and Crenshaw's (1986) reviews in English). The second type of terrorist leader is the neurotically hostile individual who: 'rejects criticism, and is intolerant, suspicious, aggressive and defensive' (Taylor, 1988, p. 145). According to Crenshaw (1986):

> Bollinger . . . a member of the West German study team, also found that some of the terrorists he interviewed were attracted to violence—which he attributed to unconscious aggressive motives . . . the terrorist group represents an outlet for archaic aggressive tendencies, frequently rooted in youthful conflicts with stepfathers. The attraction to violence may also be a result of identification with the violent acts of father figures (a violence several individuals had actually experienced); that is, an identification with the aggressor . . . Jäger, however, found no common pattern in attitudes towards violence, neither ambivalence nor attraction . . . some individuals reported a strong prior aversion to aggression. They were conscious of a need to justify their behaviour and felt a sense of limitation.

Any results that involve such different findings by members of the same team have implications for the reliability and validity of the analyses, especially in this case given the implications that the role of the heterogeneity of terrorists might pose. For the moment, however, this lack of consensus between researchers is significant since, despite the variety of results, the analyses revealed that 'the communal life from which [the West German terrorists] emerged was extraordinarily homogenous' (Crenshaw, 1986, p. 389).

To reiterate, the initial findings of Sullwold (another team member) were associated with traits illustrative of narcissism, as later elaborated by his colleague Bollinger, and later again in the 1980s and 1990s by further authors (e.g. Pearlstein, 1991; Post, 1984, 1987a, 1987b, 1990). Crenshaw develops a discussion on the results of the German research, and states that certain emotional deficiencies blind narcissists to the negative consequences of their actions. According to Crenshaw's analysis of the findings, those displaying narcissistic tendencies might 'also possess a high tolerance for stress' (see also Lanceley, 1981, p. 28). Post (1987a, p. 308) supports the claims of the German researchers and argues:

> individuals with particular personality dispositions are drawn to terrorism. A feature in common among many terrorists is a tendency to externalise, to seek outside sources of blame for personal inadequacies . . . Bollinger found psychological dynamics resembling those found in narcissistic borderlines. He was particularly struck by the history of narcissistic wounds, which led to a deficient sense of self-esteem and inadequately integrated personalities. The terrorists he interviewed demonstrated a feature characteristic of individuals with narcissistic and borderline personalities—splitting. He found that they had split off the de-valued parts of themselves and projected them onto the establishment which then became the target of their violent aggression.

Unfortunately, methodological issues reduce the strength of the assertions from the original research. Not only were terrorists unwilling to meet the researchers (owing to the circumstances in which the interviews were taking place), but researchers also reported a lack of co-operation from local officials (Crenshaw, 1986). As if not problematic enough, Crenshaw reminds us that the researchers were of course interviewing *suspected* terrorists—apprehended but not yet convicted of offences: 'Since interviews with social science researchers did not have the status of privileged communications, the researchers could have been subpoenaed to give evidence in the cases' (p. 382). The implications of such problems should be borne in mind when examining subsequent discussions (e.g. Post and Pearlstein) that develop the conclusions based on this earlier research.

In a 1992 review, Friedland presented an overview of explanations of terrorism that refer to processes supporting the existence of some degree of distinctive characterisation of the terrorist:

> Such explanations hold . . . that the turning to terrorism may be attributed to abusive child-rearing. Gustav Morf . . . maintained that the rejection of the father and his values plays a dominant role in the making of terrorists. Robert Frank noted that terrorism is prevalent in societies where fantasies of cleanliness are prevalent. Peter Berger attributed terrorist behaviour to the sense of fulfillment and power that individuals presumably derive from absolute dedication, commitment and self-sacrifice, and from the infliction of pain and death (p. 82).

Reich (1990) also describes several similar reductionist accounts, some of historical significance, including Lombroso's attributions of explanations in terms of vitamin deficiencies to explain 'bomb-throwing' (*pellagra* in particular); psychiatrist David Hubbard who proposed faulty ear functioning as common among terrorists; and most impressively of all: 'Paul Mandel, a biochemist...having studied the inhibitory effects of gamma-aminobutyric acid (GABA) and serotonin on violence in rats, extrapolated his findings to terrorism.' These are hardly convincing arguments, with obvious criticisms of them pointing to non-existent predictive utility and utterly circular reasoning (Friedland, 1992).

In the context of a scientific study of behaviour (which implies at least a sense of rigour) such attempts to assert the presence of a terrorist personality, or profile, are pitiful. That said, however, if such limited accounts may be dismissed more readily from the outset by today's standards, three very specific psychological characterisations of the terrorist persist.

The Frustration–Aggression Hypothesis

Friedland, clearly critical of reductionist accounts, examines factors that purport to explain firstly what dictates the conditions for movements wishing to exert social change; secondly how and why such movements then turn to violence, and thirdly why such violence often escalates. Friedland characterises the movement of minority groups towards social and political conflict, and their ensuing (not necessarily consequential) turn to violence as a result of a real or imagined underprivileged, disadvantaged status and as an aggressive response from a failure to have their grievances resolved. This model has been popular in one form or another with many researchers (e.g. Birrell, 1972; Corrado, 1981; Hassel, 1977; Heskin, 1980, 1984; Tittmar, 1992; Watzlawick, 1977).

According to Tittmar (1992), we ought to consider the Frustration–Aggression Hypothesis (FAH). Originally developed by Berkowitz (1965) this describes the response to frustration, or blockage of one's goal attainment. The response to this denial or blockage may emerge as a 'fight or flight' situation—as either an aggressive, defensive reaction, or none at all (i.e. either physically or psychologically fleeing, or attempting to ignore the problem, or at least attempting to reduce its perceived importance through dissonance). Although Friedland (1992) finds this explanation 'compelling' (p. 83), several limitations of the model do exist. Ferracuti (1982) criticised this psychological approach, as well as derivatives of the FAH, as potential explanations of terrorist and other political violence on the grounds that: 'this moves the problem from the social universe to the idioverse, and motives and countermotives are superficially handled' (p. 139).

The adaptation of the FAH in understanding terrorism was, it seems, '... done by various authors with little apparent regard for modifications that the transition from the individual to the group might necessitate' (Friedland, 1992, p. 85). Merari and Friedland (1985) argue that even if one has identified 'correlates of [social] destabilization', this can only go so far in actually explaining terrorism, and 'the process whereby destabilization generates terrorism remains undetermined' (p. 187). As Friedland also remarks, several authors criticised the practice of applying the FAH explanation not only on the grounds of questionable validity (in the individual context), but furthermore from the inappropriate transfer of the FAH from individual to group and collective contexts. According to Friedland, one particular social scientist claims that the persistent popularity of the FAH may be due to its inherent simplicity (p. 86). Bizarrely, Tittmar (1992) attempts to validate the theory's applicability by examining one case history of a 'failed' terrorist.

The FAH and its derivatives (e.g. the Relative Deprivation hypothesis—initially proposed by Gurr (1970) (see also Birrell, 1972; Friedland, 1992 and Heskin, 1980, 1984)) must remain seriously limited analytical tools in the context of explaining terrorism, both on individual and collective bases. Even Friedland's (1992) own discussion of the FAH and Relative Deprivation theories arrives at the same question that led to the discussion in the first place: given the supposed influence that the frustrating conditions give to particular 'privileged members of society' (the exception to the 'terrorists as deprived citizens' rule), 'why is it [still] that so very few undertake terrorism?' (p. 85). In response to this Friedland suggests presumed individual differences.

Kampf (1990) offered similar hypotheses emphasising the attractiveness of terrorism and extreme violence to 'intellectuals' and 'affluent youth', and their 'drive' to change their societies, based on the frustrating conditions of conflicting social climates which, according to Kampf, give rise to terrorism and extremism (see also Hassel, 1977, and Watzlawick, 1977). Again, although the explanation appears attractive (certainly at least in the context of revolutionary notions), the level of integration is weak, not only from being rather too context-specific, but also because the ideological control is not considered within a developmental process of involvement. A similar argument emerged from work by Fields (1979, 1980). Fields examined children who grew up within proximal exposure to Northern Ireland's terrorism. She proposed that familial modelling processes strongly influenced the decisions of individuals to become terrorists. Fields fails to clarify, however, whether her references to the types of relative deprivation constitute causal explanations or otherwise: involvement in terrorism is a process that is portrayed as a rather simple, non-complex series of events with a linear set of family influences presumed to shape 'future' terrorists' behaviour (for a critique see Taylor, 1988, pp. 141–42).

In conclusion, amid the persistence of ill-informed discussion and second-hand analyses and interpretations of (what amounts to unsystematic and unreliable findings from) psychological research on individual terrorists, it is fair to say that it is not good enough to be satisfied that, in explaining the movement of groups to terrorism (and the move of the individual to the terrorist group, and subsequently to terrorist violence), an explanation such as the FAH might suffice for a certain proportion of terrorists, i.e. the 'have-nots', which might broadly capture the spirit of re-emergent violence in late-1960s Northern Ireland. Further, if for the exceptions to this rule, the 'have-a-lots' (e.g. West German students—some of whom came from wealthy backgrounds—who joined the RAF) or the 'intellectuals', we are simply forced at some stage to revert to internal predispositions, as is implied, then such an inconclusive theoretical framework as this does not suggest much optimism. We are back in psychodynamic territory with no escape from circular reasoning, having been misled by plausibility. Another issue emerging here is that the limits of individual research are being pressed beyond their explanatory power. Boundaries must be made explicit, and in particular secondary and tertiary discussions extrapolating findings to broader contexts (below) should not be uncritically encouraged.

Narcissism and Narcissism-Aggression

Although many of the most influential psychological studies of terrorism, as those described above, are old, newer attempts regularly surface to revive remnants of previous themes. Attempts to portray 'narcissism' as central to terrorist motivation (popular in political psychology) have been common since the original West German study that suggested it (e.g. Hassel, 1977; Lasch, 1979; Pearlstein, 1991; Post, 1984, 1986, 1987a, 1987b). According to Richard Pearlstein (1991):

> ... narcissism may be viewed as a range of psychoanalytic orientations, impulses, or behavioral patterns either wholly or overwhelmingly subject to ego concern, as opposed to object concern. Narcissism also might be seen as the manner in which an individual relates to the external, object world, either wholly or overwhelmingly upon the latter's potential capacity to provide that individual with sufficient ego reinforcement, satisfaction, or compensation ... narcissism should be defined as an internal, intrapsychic, regulatory 'tool' that enables the individual to defend the self from damage and harm (p. 7).

Pearlstein regards a theory of narcissism-aggression as a worthy successor to the FAH, and cites 15 references to narcissism as a supportive theme in explaining why people turn to terrorism (p. 28). Although several of Pearlstein's citations (e.g. three chapters by Post) are in themselves simply reiterating the work of others (i.e. the West German research),

Pearlstein does not consider the literature critically enough, and several of his references (he later admits) merely contain 'cursory suggestions of this interrelationship' (p. 28). Further, Pearlstein's own chapter 'The Psychology of the Political Terrorist' (pp. 15–31) contains no references to any of the empirical studies that firmly indicate the lack of traits such as narcissism (e.g. even when established clinically—e.g. by Rasch) or the conceptual and other critiques of studies that suggest narcissism (e.g. Corrado). Nor does Pearlstein seek to address, for instance, Post's apparent unwillingness to commit to the idea that terrorists are narcissistic, and that their behaviour simply displays transitory similarities, as Post argues. Pearlstein is clearer in his own conclusions: 'the external psychological determinants or sources of political terrorism appear to lie in what are termed narcissistic injury and narcissistic disappointment' (p. 171); '...in 90 percent of political terrorist case studies, narcissistic disappointment plays a critical psychobiographical role' (p. 7). In support of this declaration, Pearlstein presents 'nine case studies of individuals who dealt with the decision to become a political terrorist' (p. 46). However, the study was not based on any first-hand interviews with people involved in terrorism, and relies on select sources to give us the terrorists' own explanation of their decisions. These derive from citations and 'interpretations' of autobiographical memoirs (p. 53), one of which, according to Pearlstein (Susan Stern's account of her involvement in *The Weathermen*), involves the terrorist intimating to us her 'personal life and the nature of her psychological and psychopolitical evolution' (p. 53). Pearlstein argues that Stern '*honestly* and *successfully* attempts to unify her personal life and political beliefs' (ibid; emphasis added). Other cases are based on similar sources, including letters sent by terrorists to judges (p. 76), government and journalistic reports (p. 89) and other secondary and tertiary data. One might be forgiven for assuming that such specifically psychological 'diagnoses' might at least merit interviewing at least a few actual participants.

Pearlstein's subjects include Carlos the Jackal and several other very high-profile oddities, unrepresentative of the heterogeneic 'unknown' rank-and-file members of terrorist organisations around the world—a simple problem of too skewed a view of the subject matter (as with Kampf). Although Pearlstein argues that his decision to select nine terrorists from different contexts and situations illustrates the need to recognise this heterogeneity (p. 170), he does not admit that these nine terrorists have already received a substantial amount of attention from authors and journalists (especially Carlos, Ulrike Meinhof (of the Baader–Meinhof group) and the leader of the Symbionese Liberation Army). This only contributes to the rather distorted set of assertions made from what can only be described as both an equally skewed and faulty long-distance 'psychological analysis' of the kind currently (at the time of writing) once again plaguing contemporary analyses.

Despite the limitations in his assertions, Pearlstein's views, as with Tittmar's rather peculiar conclusions, remain relatively well accepted from the psychoanalytic perspective. Perhaps this is partly because there has not been a substantial critique (in scope as well as nature) of this literature in recent times, or perhaps because little is really understood of the processes and concepts to which such accounts allude (particularly across disciplines). It is easy to see why characterising individual terrorists as narcissistic might remain a popular and attractive explanation more generally, but also why such traits might form the basis of even more confusing partial explanations—essentially filling the gaps where other explanations are too general.

Psychodynamic Accounts

Although according to Taylor (1988) psychodynamic (or psychoanalytic) theories of human behaviour appear to have somewhat of 'a waning role in psychology, and generally speaking, have been supplanted by more empirically-orientated approaches' (p. 140), this is not the case within psychological analyses of terrorism. The origins of psychodynamic psychology lie in the work of Sigmund Freud, and essentially view human behaviour as heavily influenced by latent, unconscious desires, the origins of which are argued to have developed as a result of real or imagined unresolved childhood conflicts. In his 1988 review, Taylor strongly criticised a variety of psychodynamically orientated theories of what implicitly amounts to explanations based on terrorist Oedipal and Electra complexes. He therefore criticises what has been, and continues to be, a long-standing and the most popular approach to understanding the terrorist personality (e.g. Bartalotta, 1981; Brunet, 1989; Ferracuti and Bruno, 1981; Johnson and Feldmann, 1992; Kent and Nicholls, 1977; Olsson, 1988; Pearlstein, 1991; Turco, 1987; Vinar, 1988).

Konrad Kellen (1982) was one of the first to emphasise the applicability of psychodynamic theory, and in examining the case of former West German terrorist Hans-Joachim Klein, asserts:

> ... unbeknownst to himself, he was engaging in a struggle with authority because unconsciously he was struggling against his father. Klein quite consciously hated his father (he says, 'I would never talk about that man as "father"'), but he may not have been aware of the fact that his rampage against the established order and those defending it may have been a continuum and extension of that struggle (p. 17).

In support of his argument, Kellen points to Klein's later disillusionment and subsequent renunciation of the brutality of the group's violence, and his exit from the movement. Kellen argues that Klein is probably not a good example of a 'true terrorist', describing him as not 'profoundly fanatical in a political sense. He seems like a man who acted all along from the unconscious motives of merely inflicting pain and destruction on the hated enemy—in his case, persons of the establishment, i.e. "father figures"' (p. 18). Kellen argues the same with respect to Carlos the Jackal, although, as Kellen admits at the outset, it is not 'apparent from [Carlos'] words' that a similar sense of 'unconscious patricidal impulses' (ascribed to Klein) exists (p. 18). It appears that Carlos had once described his father as 'cruel and powerful'.

Others have incorporated one or more elements of psychodynamic theory within their research in other ways (e.g. Kaplan, 1981; Lacqueur, 1977), some subtle, others not, but an attractive (and somewhat less contentious) focus for several researchers has been on 'identification' or 'identity', still rooted in psychodynamic theory (with less emphasis on stricter Freudian notions). Erikson's (1968) personality theory suggests that the formation of an 'identity' (and soon after, 'negative' identity) is crucial to personality development. Erikson argued that children's development is characterised by a series of crises, each to be overcome in succession so that the personality becomes wholly integrated. Failure to resolve these early childhood conflicts manifests itself in later life, according to Erikson, via various psychological problems. In this respect, Post, like Kaplan, argues that terrorist motivation is overwhelmingly and inseparably linked to a need to 'belong' to the group and hence the group becomes central to identity formation in the terrorist (see also Cairns, 1981, 1989). According to Post's hypothesis, this is further developed by interpersonal relations within the structure, as well as the ideology and strategies used by the terrorists. Both Crenshaw (1986) and Taylor (1988) consider the process of identification as it might apply to terrorism. In interpreting Erikson's theory with special regard for terrorist motivation, Crenshaw describes how:

> At the stage of identity formation, individuals seek both meaning and a sense of wholeness or completeness as well as what Erikson...terms 'fidelity', a need to have faith in something or someone outside oneself as well as to be trustworthy in its service. Ideologies then are guardians of identity. Erikson further suggests that political undergrounds utilize youth's need for fidelity as well as the 'store of wrath' held by those deprived of something in which to have faith. A crisis of identity (when the individual who finds self-definition difficult is suffering from ambiguity, fragmentation, and contradiction) makes some adolescents susceptible to 'totalism' or to totalistic collective identities that promise certainty. In such collectivities the troubled young finds not only an identity but an explanation for their difficulties and a promise for the future (pp. 391–92).

This type of explanation squarely rests within a psychodynamic framework. It has also been applied by the West German research team's analysis of the German terrorists, and further by Knutson (1981). However, the process of identification (in its present incarnations) will remain a very limited tool for several reasons, not least due to accounts of terrorists' involvement that easily contradict suggestions about generalising from such an approach. A more sophisticated model of identity, one aware of the need to integrate levels of analysis, might prove beneficial particularly in understanding how a terrorist's own sense of identity forms and develops in response not only to his or her 'own' world but to external change. However, the more practical issues of relevance to any critique of psychodynamic perspectives relate to the unfalsifiability and circular logic of psychodynamic theories, their claim to 'special' knowledge, and characteristic reluctance to share in the rigorous scientific demands of contemporary psychology as far as theoretical development and hypothesis testing is concerned. Undeniably there are some cases that in retrospect (especially through looking at autobiographical sources) quite easily seem to fit the identity model in which family influence serves as a factor for terrorist involvement in many cases. Although this approach might draw greater attention to the role of the family, its limited applicability to understanding terrorists in general, and the equally limited conceptual utility of psychodynamic explanations altogether, serves only to confuse the clarity of our knowledge of terrorist psychology.

EVIDENCE SUPPORTING TERRORIST 'NORMALITY'

In a helpful review, Silke (1998) argued that 'most serious researchers in the field at least *nominally* agree with the position that terrorists are essentially normal individuals' (p. 53) (emphasis added). In general, his assertion can be strengthened with research supporting evidence for lack of abnormality, research supporting evidence for normality for various reasons (not exactly the same as the first point), and developments in the context of alternative explanations for abnormal (including violent) behaviour. This last point refers to an increasingly prevalent tendency in criminology and forensic psychology to use the findings of well-established research in social psychology in explaining the influence of situational factors upon violent behaviour (e.g. McCauley, 1991; McCauley and Segal, 1987; Taylor, 1988).

Firstly, one can identify evidence in support of the position that terrorists are not necessarily characterised by distinct personality traits. Some of the important contributions in this area are summarised below.

Gustav Morf (1970), in one of the very first studies to inform terrorist psychology, neither observed nor recorded distinct personality traits in his analysis of the *Front de Libération du Québec* (FLQ) in Canada. Rasch (1979), a German psychiatrist, studied 11 male and female members of the Baader–Meinhof group, his conclusions revealing a complete absence of any indications of paranoia, psychopathy, fanaticism, or any other psychotic or neurotic illness in his subjects. Significantly, Rasch also emphasised the need to illustrate the presence of such 'illnesses' (if they were indicated) within the rigours of academic research and analysis. As McCauley (1991) precisely emphasises: 'that is not to say that there is no pathology among terrorists, but the rate of diagnosable pathology, at least, does not differ significantly from control groups of the same age and background' (p. 132).

Corrado (1981) could find no reliable, systematic evidence in support of such claims, and the Italian Red Brigades were also unlikely candidates for psychological abnormality. On the contrary, as Jamieson (1989) argued: 'those who have confronted Italian terrorism directly are the first who discredit the notion of the bloodthirsty desperado...' (p. 48). Instead we observe: 'a person whose ideas are meticulously worked out through careful analysis and serious reflection, for whom everything is seen in terms of politics, someone who above all is "well-prepared"...', characterised by 'great intelligence, great openness and great generosity, with sometimes a bit of exhibitionism'. Jamieson reminds us of the complete failure to fit the Italian terrorist into a 'particular sociological or psychological group', and given her repeated interactions over time with such subjects, her observations are significantly strengthened.

In the Irish context, psychiatrists Lyons and Harbinson (1986) found that in a study to compare 47 'political murderers' with 59 'non-political murderers', the politically motivated killers generally came from more stable backgrounds and the incidence of psychological disturbance was much less than in the 'ordinary criminals'. Indeed Lyons (cited by Ryder, 2000) said recently:

> The political killers tended to be normal in intelligence and mental stability, didn't have significant psychiatric problems or mental illness and didn't abuse alcohol. They didn't show remorse because they rationalised it very successfully, believing that they were fighting for a cause. The politicals, generally speaking, did not want to be seen by a psychiatrist; they feel there is nothing wrong with them, but they did co-operate. Some of them were probably quite bright... (p. xiii).

Elliott and Lockhart (cited in Heskin, 1980) demonstrated in their own study that 'despite remarkably matching socio-economic backgrounds, juvenile scheduled offenders (broadly, those found guilty of terrorist-related offences)... were more intelligent, had higher educational attainments, showed less evidence of early developmental problems and had fewer court appearances than "ordinary" juvenile delinquents' (p. 78).

Indeed, one of the earliest analyses to emphasise the rationality and functionality (in logical and strategic contexts) of terrorist activity on the whole was presented by Margolin (1977), asserting that we ought to be aware of the 'rewards' of terrorism. These tend to be expressed in terms of more diffuse political and ideological benefits than immediate financial or other material rewards. To this day, analysts frequently fail to appreciate this dimension of involvement in terrorism (see also Crenshaw, 1986, 2001).

To conclude this section, if the elements of psychopathy and other psychological abnormalities can be dismissed as too simplistic explanations of complex phenomena, and often through some rudimentary logic (as in the case of the psychopathy model), the reader may well wonder why such explanations have proved to be so persistent in the literature, and why such apparently 'simplistic' characterisations of terrorists have proceeded largely unchallenged?

PERSISTENCE WITH INCONSISTENCY: A CLOSER LOOK AT THE LITERATURE

Despite the persistence of evidence to suggest terrorist normality (as well as the poor quality of research indicating the contrary and the lack of alternative explanations), a general claim of psychological 'normality' does not permeate the individual psychological literature and current analyses as much as one would expect. And despite the concerns expressed here so far, explanations in terms of blatant psychological 'abnormality' clearly persist in some relatively modern accounts (Johnson and Feldmann, 1992; Pearlstein, 1991). A number of brief examples illustrate this confusion.

Ferracuti (1982) argued that predominant explanations of terrorist motivation relate to the 'generally accepted characteristics... [of] violence and death wishes...' (p. 129), but of his observations of Italian left- and right-wing terrorists, he noted that they:

> ... rarely suffer from *serious* personality abnormalities. Generally, they demonstrate a good capacity to stand stress, both in clandestinity and in long term imprisonment, and an ability to organize themselves in groups, to sustain each other and to carry out adequate actions aimed at propaganda and dissemination of their principles [italics added].

Although Ferracuti's findings are frequently used to support the lack of abnormality of terrorists, they need closer examination. Kellen (1982), who himself does not appear to address the inconsistency, cited Ferracuti as describing the psychology of right-wing terrorists thus: 'Even when they do not suffer from a clear psychopathological condition, their basic psychological traits reflect an authoritarian-extremist personality', characterised by behaviours such as an 'ambivalence towards authority', 'poor and defective insight', 'emotional detachment from the consequences of their actions', 'destructiveness', and 'adherence to violent subcultural values', among others (p. 15). Ferracuti (1982) argued that the implications of his findings were 'self-evident' in that: 'right-wing terrorism can be very dangerous not only mainly because of its ideology, but because of its general unpredictability and because of its destructiveness often resulting from psychopathology' (see pp. 3–6). In other words, while terrorists are not suffering from a 'clear psychopathological condition', they are 'not normal': they are distinctive in psychological terms by being characterised by a specific, finite set of trait behaviours. Ferracuti's ideas about the psychology of the terrorist appear anchored in an unclear conceptual argument.

Firstly Ferracuti demonstrates a reluctance to describe the terrorists as either wholly 'normal' (i.e. as not being distinctly characterisable—due to the lack of a terrorist personality) or on the other hand as wholly 'abnormal'. So as far as being psychologically characterised in terms of personality attribution, the Italian terrorist apparently lies in some grey area between the two—something slightly less than the stated 'serious' personality disorder. Ferracuti argues that the behavioural patterns of the Italian terrorists reflect a personality type, but not that the terrorists are characterised by 'authoritarian-extremist' personalities. This is not a pedantic criticism, but reflects conceptual confusion within the theoretical parameters Ferracuti has adopted. The issue emerging here appears to be that such research is all too willing to ascribe positivist explanations of behaviour, yet simultaneously stresses that this still does not either characterise 'abnormality' or set the terrorist aside from the non-terrorist. The terrorist is simply quite 'different', or 'special', but not 'abnormal'. Furthermore, in arguing that the implications of his results were 'self-evident' on the basis of the 'ideology', 'unpredictability' and 'destructiveness' associated with terrorism, Ferracuti seems to be suggesting that the existence of some 'psychopathology' is an inevitable consequence of becoming a right-wing terrorist per se. Again, this needs to be very carefully qualified with respect to what he appears to be hinting at as a form of increasing brutalisation occurring as membership is prolonged and commitment to the group ideals increases. This obviously then calls into question the predictive utility of assessing the personalities of terrorists after the event, particularly when the measured 'traits' (actually measured, and not implied) are used in arguments about why people become involved in terrorism in the first place.

Although Ferracuti was himself responsible for earlier research that concluded that terrorists *are* psychologically different to non-terrorists, he argued that 'although mentally imbalanced individuals, in the psychiatric range, can be used by terrorist groups, what is of greater interest is, of course, the "normal" terrorist, that is the individual who is mentally sane' (p. 130). Despite this apparently implicit recognition of an equally apparent absence of convincing evidence of a distinctive terrorist personality, Ferracuti held firmly that 'the terrorist' per se was still 'only slightly altered, at most in the psychoneurotic or psychopathic range'.

Given the relatively small amount of psychological studies on terrorists, the lack of conceptual clarity in what research does exist is surprising. But using such conclusions as a basis for supporting subsequent assertions represents a pitfall: certainly this makes accurate discussion difficult, and allows for much flexibility in the interpretation of the conclusions of studies like these. Ferracuti, Kellen and Cooper together represent some of the earliest but confusing foundations of modern-day assumptions about terrorist psychology. At best, they conclude that a terrorist is either completely mad (e.g. Carlos, as Kellen argued) or 'half mad' (or mad some of the time) (e.g. the Italian terrorists in Ferracuti's study), or that they have their own distinct personality profiles. Interestingly, one observes the peculiar flaws in analyses only from examining the original works—secondhand interpretations are symptomatic of something altogether different. Sometimes the inconsistencies in the original research are quite blatant, for example while Kellen (1982) seems perfectly satisfied to describe terrorists as psychopathic, he still criticises other 'observers' because they 'never postulate that terrorists feel sorry for what they do' (p. 23).

Finally, Kellen often emphasised the lures associated with the lives of terrorists, for example quoting Carlos: 'revolution is the strongest of tonics' (p. 19), and also adding: 'I like women'. While the idea that people join terrorist groups because of some (usually not apparent) 'lures' is well documented, interpreting them as necessarily feeding personality disorder is nonsensical.

Inconsistency appears to tarnish much of the research, and again this is not clear in the literature. Further inconsistencies emerge from examining the work of Post, Heskin and others. Given that Post, a psychiatrist, represents one of the few researchers with at least some background in psychology, criticisms of his inconsistencies appear all the more salient. As if the question of 'who or what is a terrorist?' was not problematic enough, there are differing views on what constitutes 'abnormality' and what does not, as well as whether positivist explanations constitute valid means of exploration in this field given both the absence of common identifiable personality characteristics, and even the presence of similarities between terrorists and non-terrorists. Silke (1998) vociferously criticises Post: 'while on the one hand freely acknowledging the lack of "major" psychopathology, Post . . . [has] been quick to switch the search towards finding some form of minor psychopathology' (p. 64).

The unchecked tendency to reinterpret and recirculate conclusions of earlier findings will ultimately damage our progression. Although further review is necessary, examining evidence for 'abnormality' and 'normality' within the available literature might seem almost pointless because it would be easy to use arguments from the *same* studies to support *either* of both perspectives!

THEORETICAL, CONCEPTUAL AND METHODOLOGICAL DIFFICULTIES

In his highly critical review, Taylor (1988) highlighted the attractiveness of simplistic explanations as well as why they might persist: 'it might be argued that the *nature* of terrorist acts offers excellent vehicles for the expression of paranoia and other abnormalities' (emphasis added). Silke (1998) also emphasises the attractiveness of using terms such as 'antisocial, narcissistic and paranoid personality types', which portray the terrorist's behaviour as characteristic of an abnormal personality since 'observers cannot but fail to notice the striking parallels between the two' (p. 56).

Perhaps the relevance of these issues becomes clearer in examining interpretations of the usefulness of traits, if and when they can be rigorously recorded and verified. In contemporary psychology, psychometric evaluation systematically assesses personality characteristics by questioning individuals—reducing the intricacies of behavioural observations into more easily categorical 'classes of behaviour', i.e. traits (Blackburn, 1989). An important issue here, and one that Blackburn reminds us of, relates to the predictive utility of trait measures as used by psychologists— particularly given suggestions that some individuals are more likely to become terrorists than others. It is clear within contemporary psychology that traits are weak predictors of behaviour in specific situations, and responses that are, as Blackburn suggests, 'supposedly indicative of the same trait' do not inter-correlate at significant levels (p. 63). One cannot expect trait measures to predict single occurrences, and traits cannot be inferred from single behavioural responses; instead we assume that stability exists over time and situation (ibid). This simple assumption does not translate well into psychological analyses of terrorism, the small number of empirical analyses being over-generalised, and the issue of predictive utility confused.

Many have developed individual or broader taxonomies or typologies of terrorists, what in today's climate might be referred to as the terrorist profile. These include categorisation systems derived from 'commonly held motivations that...move individuals and groups to use terrorist techniques for political change' (Handler, 1990). In arguing for the development of improved terrorist profiles of American left- and right-wing terrorists, Handler notes that while 'evidence is available...[and] comes from a variety of sources...none of these efforts has brought together conclusively a definitive sense of how membership in these two extremist political groups differed' (p. 198). In 1990, Handler offered a socioeconomic profile of American left- and right-wing terrorists, arguing that the West German study was previously the most significant (p. 199). According to Handler, efforts at developing such profiles would eventually allow for greater insights into organisation and leader–follower differences (p. 199).

Attempts to produce individual terrorist profiles include that by Russell and Miller (cited in Taylor, 1988, p. 124), who describe the 'typical terrorist' as: 'likely to be single, male, aged between twenty-two and twenty-four with some university experience, probably in the humanities. He is likely to come from a middle- or upper-class family, and was probably recruited to terrorism at University, where he was first exposed to Marxist or other revolutionary ideas' (p. 127). Strentz (1988) gives a very detailed demographic profile of 1960s and 1970s left-wing 'American and international terrorist groups', and gives profiles of Middle Eastern and right-wing terrorists. He is quick to remind us, however, that the data presented in his analysis should be regarded as historically beneficial, 'which presents what terrorists groups *were*' (emphasis added). At the risk of sounding pedantic, rather this statement could be rephrased to: '... which presents how *specific* members of *specific* groups were at *specific* times of *specific* stages in their own *specific* types of terrorist campaign'. As Cooper (1985) notes: 'terrorism is not a discrete topic that might be conveniently examined apart from the political, social and economic context in which it takes place...Terrorism is a creature of its own time and place.'

But what practical use can we possibly derive from any attempt at terrorist profiles, assuming uniformity not only between various groups but even within the same group across time and place? Blackburn (1993) reminds us also that the issues surrounding the utility of traits for understanding behaviour are 'as much conceptual as they are empirical' (p. 63), but Friedland (1992, p. 83) concludes: 'The critique of the attribution of terrorist behaviour to individual idiosyncrasy or pathology is not meant to imply that individual predispositions play no role whatsoever in the emergence of terrorist groups and in eruptions of terrorist action' (McCauley expressing the same sentiment). Perhaps psychological motives influence the particular form taken by terrorist campaign tactics as opposed to relating to some supposed conscious decision to become a terrorist (Crenshaw, 1986, p. 387). Terrorists are not always necessarily 'psychologically compelled' (in Post's words) to conduct terrorism, and the strategic logic needs attention to discern which factors (e.g. psychological or strategic, if either) appear to determine terrorism more. The debate need not necessarily be a 'polar' one either: terrorism, from both a psychological, personal and group/organisational strategic perspective, often appears to follow logically bounded processes. These views only comple-ment other disciplines, rather than oppose them.

A crucial implication of the heterogeneity of terrorism is that there is, again: '. . . no sound, a priori reason to assume much in common between different terrorist groups' (Merari and Friedland, 1985, p. 187; Merari, 1978). This may also be responsible for the failure to arrive at a psycholog-ical theory of the causes of 'terrorism' per se (Merari and Friedland, 1985, p. 187). In this light the other obvious conceptual problems of definition do not help either, but efforts to arrive at formulating a theory of terrorist be-haviour must accommodate the heterogeneity of the phenomenon as well as the wide diversity of individual motivations that terrorist members might themselves push as explanatory factors. Heterogeneity is a very pervasive emergent theme, across and within movements, and this is a useful reason to study historical and biographical accounts of terrorism within psychological contexts.

CONCLUSION—AND A FRESH START?

The rigour of research pointing to either explicit or implicit abnormality, or to the existence of a 'terrorist personality', is such that its propositions are built on unsteady empirical, theoretical and conceptual foundations. Nevertheless, for many this still does not mitigate against the possibility that terrorists remain psychologically distinctive, and unfortunately it will probably remain difficult to challenge forthright this view in the absence of empirical data—now a major problem.

It is pessimistic that one of the few certainties about this issue is probably the lack of conceptual and practical clarity with which psy-chological terminology is used. However, it is significant that psycho-logical researchers have not systematically addressed conceptual issues surrounding the utility of trait measures. The relevant literature should be cognisant of the concerns raised by Blackburn if psychologists are to outline and describe the relevance and utility of personality traits and more generally the role of any 'individual psychology of terrorism' that might advance our efforts.

The purpose of the assertions made in this chapter is not to attempt to comment on the nature of psychological theories of personality or motiva-tion, but to hopefully generate some consideration of the utility of certain types of psychological research on terrorists. If such research continues it cannot naively ignore earlier limitations. As psychologists studying ter-rorist behaviour, we are responsible for improving our own contributions at least. We otherwise run the risk of not only disservicing efforts at un-derstanding terrorism, but also how psychology's true contribution to this complex problem might be perceived.

REFERENCES

Anderson, S. (1994). Making a killing. *Harper's Magazine*, **288**(1725), 45.

Baeyer-Katte, W., Claessens, D., Feger, H. and Neidhart, F. (Eds) (1982). *Analyzen zum Terrorismus 3: Gruppeprozesse*. Opladen: Westdeutscher Verlag.

Bartalotta, G. (1981). Psicologia analitica e terrorismo politico. *Rivista di Psicologia Analitica*, **12**(24), 21–30.

Berkowitz, L. (1965). The concept of aggressive drive. In L. Berkowitz (Ed.), *Advances in Experimental Social Psychology*, Vol. 2. New York: Academic Press.

Birrell, D. (1972). Relative deprivation as a factor in conflict in Northern Ireland. *Sociopolitical Review*, **20**, 317–43.

Blackburn, R. (1989). Psychopathy and personality disorder in relation to violence. In K. Howells and C.R. Hollin (Eds), *Clinical Approaches to Violence* (pp. 58–78). Chichester, UK: John Wiley & Sons.

Bowyer-Bell, J. (1979). *The Secret Army: the IRA 1916–1979*. Dublin: Academy Press.

Bowyer-Bell, J. (2000). *The IRA 1968–2000: An Analysis of a Secret Army*. London: Frank Cass and Co.

Brunet, L. (1989). Le phénomène terroriste et ses effets sur les objets internes. *Revue Québécoise de Psychologie*, **10**(1), 2–15.

Brunet, L. and Casoni, D. (1991). Terrorism: attack on internal objects. *Melanie Klein and Object Relations*, **9**(1), 1–15.

Burton, F. (1978). *The Politics of Legitimacy: Struggles in a Belfast Community*. London: Routledge and Kegan Paul.

Cairns, E. (1981). Intergroup conflict in Northern Ireland. In H. Tajfel (Ed.), *Social Identity and Intergroup Relations* (pp. 277–98). Cambridge: Cambridge University Press.

Cairns, E. (1989). Social identity and intergroup conflict: a developmental perspective. In J. Harbinson (Ed.), *Growing Up in Northern Ireland* (pp. 115–30). Belfast: Stranmillis College.

Coogan, T.P. (1995). *The IRA*. London: HarperCollins.

Cooper, H.H.A. (1976). The terrorist and the victim. *Victimology: An International Journal*, **1**(2), 229–39.

Cooper, H.H.A. (1977). What is a terrorist: a psychological perspective. *Legal Medical Quarterly*, **1**, 16–32.

Cooper, H.H.A. (1978). Psychopath as terrorist. *Legal Medical Quarterly*, **2**, 253–62.

Cooper, H.H.A. (1985). Voices from Troy: what are we hearing? Outthinking the terrorist: an international challenge. *Proceedings of the 10th Annual Symposium on the Role of Behavioural Science in Physical Security*. Washington, DC: Defence Nuclear Agency.

Corrado, R. (1981). A critique of the mental disorder perspective of political terrorism. *International Journal of Law and Psychiatry*, **4**(3–4), 293–309.

Crenshaw, M. (1986). The psychology of political terrorism. In M.G. Hermann (Ed.), *Political Psychology: Contemporary Problems and Issues* (pp. 379–413). London: Josey-Bass.

Crenshaw, M. (1990). Questions to be answered, research to be done, knowledge to be applied. In W. Reich (Ed.), *Origins of Terrorism: Psychologies, Ideologies, Theologies, States of Mind* (pp. 247–60). New York: Cambridge University Press.

Crenshaw, M. (2001). The psychology of terrorism: an agenda for the 21st century. *Political Psychology*, **21**(2), 405–20.

Erikson, E.H. (1968). *Identity, Youth and Crisis*. London: Faber and Faber.

Ferracuti, F. (1982). A sociopsychiatric interpretation of terrorism. In M.E. Wolfgang (Ed.), *International Terrorism: the Annals of the American Academy AAPSS Vol. 463* (pp. 129–40). Beverly Hills, CA: Sage.

Ferracuti, F. and Bruno, F. (1981). Psychiatric aspects of terrorism in Italy. In I.L. Barak-Glantz and C.R. Huff (Eds), *The Mad, the Bad, and the Different: Essays in Honour of Simon Dinitz* (pp. 199–213). Lexington, MA: Heath.

Fields, R.A. (1979). Child terror victims and adult terrorists. *Journal of Psychohistory*, **7**(1), 71–75.

Fields, R.A. (1980). *Northern Ireland: Society Under Siege*. New Brunswick, NJ: Penguin.

Friedland, N. (1992). Becoming a terrorist: social and individual antecedents. In L. Howard (Ed.), *Terrorism: Roots, Impacts, Responses* (pp. 81–93). New York: Praeger.

Gurr, T.R. (1970). *Why Men Rebel*. Princeton, NJ: Princeton University Press.

Hacker, F.J. (1976). *Crusaders, Criminals, Crazies: Terror and Terrorism in our Time*. New York: W.W. Norton.

Handler, J.S. (1990). Socioeconomic profile of an American terrorist: 1960s and 1970s. *Terrorism*, **13**, 195–213.

Hassel, C. (1977). Terror: the crime of the privileged—an examination and prognosis. *Terrorism*, **1**, 1–16.

Heskin, K. (1980). *Northern Ireland: A Psychological Analysis*. Dublin: Gill and Macmillan.

Heskin, K. (1984). The psychology of terrorism in Northern Ireland. In Y. Alexander and A. O'Day (Eds), *Terrorism in Ireland* (pp. 85–105). Kent: Croom Helm.

Heskin, K. (1994). Terrorism in Ireland: the past and the future. *Irish Journal of Psychology*, **15**, 469–79.

Horgan, J. (2000). *Terrorism and Political Violence: a Psychological Perspective*. PhD dissertation, Department of Applied Psychology, University College, Cork.

Jäger, H., Schmidtchen, G. and Sullwold, L. (Eds) (1982). *Analyzen zum Terrorismus 2: Lebenslauf-analyzen*. Opladen: Westdeutcher Verlag.

Jamieson, A. (1989). *The Heart Attacked: Terrorism and Conflict in the Italian State*. London: Marian Boyers.

Jamieson, A. (1990a). Entry, discipline and exit in the Italian Red Brigades. *Terrorism and Political Violence*, **2**(1), 1–20.

Jamieson, A. (1990b). Identity and morality in the Red Brigades. *Terrorism and Political Violence*, **2**(4), 508–20.

Johnson, P.W. and Feldmann, T.B. (1992). Personality types and terrorism: self-psychology perspectives. *Forensic Reports*, **5**(4), 293–303.

Kampf, H.A. (1990). Terrorism, the left-wing, and the intellectuals. *Terrorism*, **13**(1), 23–51.

Kaplan, A. (1981). The psychodynamics of terrorism. In Y. Alexander and J.M. Gleason (Eds), *Behavioral and Quantitative Perspectives on Terrorism* (pp. 35–51). New York: Pergamon.

Kellen, K. (1979). *Terrorists—What are They Like? How Some Terrorists Describe Their World and Actions: RAND publication N-1300-SL*. Santa Monica, CA: RAND.

Kellen, K. (1982). *On Terrorists and Terrorism: A RAND Note N-1942-RC*. Santa Monica, CA: RAND.

Kent, I. and Nicholls, W. (1977). The psychodynamics of terrorism. *Mental Health and Society*, **1**(2), 1–8.

Knutson, J.N. (1981). Social and psychodynamic pressures toward a negative identity: the case of an American revolutionary terrorist. In Y. Alexander and

J.M. Gleason (Eds), *Behavioural and Quantitative Perspectives on Terrorism* (pp. 105–50). New York: Pergamon.

Lacqueur, W. (1977). *Terrorism*. London: Weidenfeld and Nicolson.

Lanceley, F.J. (1981). The anti-social personality as hostage-taker. *Journal of Police Science and Administration*, **9**, 28.

Lasch, C. (1979). *The Culture of Narcissism*. New York: W.W. Norton.

Lyons, H.A. and Harbinson, H.J. (1986). A comparison of political and non-political murderers in Northern Ireland, 1974–1984. *Medicine, Science and the Law*, **26**, 193–98.

Margolin, J. (1977). Psychological perspectives in terrorism. In Y. Alexander and S.M. Finger (Eds), *Terrorism: Interdisciplinary Perspectives* (pp. 270–82). New York: John Jay Press.

McCauley, C.R. (1991). Terrorism, research and public policy: an overview. *Terrorism and Political Violence*, **3**(1), 126–44.

McCauley, C.R. and Segal, M.E. (1987). Social psychology of terrorist groups. In C. Hendrick (Ed.), *Review of Personality and Social Psychology*, Vol. 9 (pp. 231–356). Beverly Hills, CA: Sage.

Merari, A. (1978). A classification of terrorist groups. *Terrorism*, **1**(3–4), 331–46.

Merari, A. (2000). Terrorism as a strategy of struggle: past and future. In M. Taylor and J. Horgan (Eds), *The Future of Terrorism* (pp. 52–65). London: Frank Cass and Co.

Merari, A. and Friedland, N. (1985). Social psychological aspects of political terrorism. In S. Oskamp (Ed.), *Applied Social Psychology Annual (Vol. 6): International Conflict and National Public Policy Issues* (pp. 185–205). London: Sage.

Morf, G. (1970). *Terror in Quebec—Case Studies of the FLQ*. Toronto: Clark, Irwin.

Olsson, P.A. (1988). The terrorist and the terrorized: some psychoanalytic consideration. *Journal of Psychohistory*, **16**(1), 47–60.

Pearce, K.I. (1977). Police negotiations. *Canadian Psychiatric Association Journal*, **22**, 171–74.

Pearlstein, R.M. (1991). *The Mind of the Political Terrorist*. Wilmington: Scholarly Resources.

Post, J.M. (1984). Notes on a psychodynamic theory of terrorist behaviour. *Terrorism*, **7**, 241–56.

Post, J.M. (1986). Hostilite, conformite, fraternite: the group dynamics of terrorist behaviour. *International Journal of Group Psychotherapy*, **36**(2), 211–24.

Post, J.M. (1987a). Group and organisational dynamics of political terrorism: implications for counterterrorist policy. In P. Wilkinson and A.M. Stewart (Eds), *Contemporary Research on Terrorism* (pp. 307–17). Aberdeen: Aberdeen University Press.

Post, J.M. (1987b). 'It's us against them': the group dynamics of political terrorism. *Terrorism*, **10**, 23–35.

Post, J.M. (1990). Terrorist psycho-logic: terrorist behaviour as a product of psychological forces. In W. Reich (Ed.), *Origins of Terrorism: Psychologies, Ideologies, Theologies, States of Mind* (pp. 25–40). New York: Cambridge University Press.

Rasch, W. (1979). Psychological dimensions of political terrorism in the Federal Republic of Germany. *International Journal of Law and Psychiatry*, **2**, 79–85.

Reich, W. (1990). Understanding terrorist behaviour: the limits and opportunities of psychological inquiry. In W. Reich (Ed.), *Origins of Terrorism: Psychologies, Ideologies, Theologies, States of Mind* (pp. 261–79). New York: Cambridge University Press.

Ryder, C. (2000). *Inside the Maze: the Untold Story of the Northern Ireland Prison Service*. London: Methuen.

Silke, A.P. (1998). Cheshire-Cat logic: the recurring theme of terrorist abnormality in psychological research. *Psychology, Crime and Law*, **4**, 51–69.

Strentz, T. (1988). A terrorist psychosocial profile: past and present. *FBI Law Enforcement Bulletin*, April, 13–19.

Taylor, M. (1988). *The Terrorist*. London: Brassey's.

Taylor, M. and Quayle, E. (1994). *Terrorist Lives*. London: Brassey's.

Tittmar, H.G. (1992). Urban terrorism: a psychological interpretation. *Terrorism and Political Violence*, **4**(3), 64–71.

Turco, R.M. (1987). Psychiatric contributions to the understanding of international terrorism. *International Journal of Offender Therapy and Comparative Criminology*, **3**(1–2), 153–61.

Vinar, M.N. (1988). La terreur, le politique, la place d'un psychanalyste. *Patio*, **11**, 43–51.

Wardlaw, G. (1989). *Political Terrorism: Theory, Tactics and Counter-Measures*, 2nd edn. Cambridge: Cambridge University Press.

Watzlawick, P. (1977). The pathologies of perfectionism. *Et Cetera*, **34**(1), 12–18.

CHAPTER 2

Becoming a Terrorist

ANDREW SILKE

University of Leicester, UK

INTRODUCTION

Many myths surround terrorists and terrorism, but surely one of the most widely held is that terrorists are crazed fanatics: psychopaths who are completely immune to the suffering of their victims and who always remain ruthlessly committed to their cause. Like many myths, this one is easy to believe yet is almost always completely untrue. Terrorism is a very emotive subject and terrorist groups have carried out atrocities of appalling scale and horror. The actors themselves can display a formidable commitment to their cause and are often willing to make enormous personal sacrifices as well as to inflict suffering on others. Extreme behaviour, of any sort, invites extreme speculation as to the individuals who carry it out. As a result, it has become dangerously easy for society to dismiss terrorists as deranged fanatics. James Gilligan (2000) in a thought-provoking book on the psychology of violence noted that:

> Labels like bad or mad, 'guilty' or 'insane,' may or may not serve a useful function for legal purposes. But if our purpose is to learn about the causes and prevention of violence, then the labels simply enable us to close the door on someone, lock him away and never have to listen to him, understand him, or think further about him. In fact, these labels serve as substitutes for psychological understanding (p. 258).

Why do people become terrorists? Too often labels have replaced serious efforts to provide an accurate answer to this question. A common belief

---

Terrorists, Victims and Society: Psychological Perspectives on Terrorism and its Consequences.
Edited by Andrew Silke. © 2003 John Wiley & Sons, Ltd.

held about those few individuals who carry out terrorist attacks is that they are people who have a pathological attraction for violence and for inflicting harm on others. It is often said that such people are severely lacking in their ability to empathise with others (thus explaining their ability to inflict great harm and suffering on innocent civilians and bystanders). For some psychologists and psychiatrists, such expectations have given rise to beliefs that terrorists are much more likely to suffer from personality disorders of an antisocial, paranoid or narcissistic nature and that they are likely to have had the damaging and abusive childhoods often seen in other dangerously violent groups such as sadistic sexual murderers.

As John Horgan pointed out in the previous chapter, much of the psychological research and analysis on terrorists of the past four decades has revolved around the search for a terrorist personality. In the early 1970s in particular it was widely believed that terrorists suffered from personality disorders and that there would be an exceptionally high number of clinical psychopaths, narcissists and paranoids in the ranks of the average terrorist group. The belief was that only people who were mentally ill or who possessed these deviant personalities would be capable of committing the often horrific acts sometimes carried out by terrorist groups.

This line of thought has endured since the early 1970s, and a steady stream of psychologists and psychiatrists have pushed the idea that terrorists suffer from mental illness, damaged psyches and deviant personalities. In the wake of the dreadful events of September 11, 2001, such opinions were again expressed in a number of journals and books. For example, Walter Laqueur (2001), an experienced writer on the subject of terrorism, wrote in the weeks after the September 11 attacks that:

> Madness, especially paranoia, plays a role in contemporary terrorism. Not all paranoiacs are terrorists, but all terrorists believe in conspiracies by the powerful, hostile forces and suffer from some form of delusion and persecution mania...The element of ... madness plays an important role [in terrorism], even if many are reluctant to acknowledge it (p. 80).

Among the 'many' Lacquer is referring to in his parting comment are those researchers and writers who have argued against seeing terrorists as madmen (and women) and who have said that psychopathology simply is not a key to understanding their minds and motivations. As John Horgan pointed out in detail in the previous chapter, the idea that terrorists are crazy or psychologically deviant simply is not supported by the findings of four decades of scientific research. Though good research on the psychology of terrorists can hardly be described as plentiful, the more reliable studies have always concluded that terrorists are essentially 'ordinary' individuals.

An important question here is what exactly is meant by 'more reliable studies'? This is a vital point because if one wishes to find papers in academic journals and books to support the view that terrorists are in some way 'different' or 'crazy', one can find them. A steady stream of psychologists have argued this case. The result has been that a number of honest outsiders who want to review the field come away thinking that 'terrorist experts are divided in their opinions about the terrorist psyche' (Vohryzek-Bolden, Olson-Raymer and Whamond, 2001, p. 15) and because of this division, we must continue to wait for a clear answer to emerge. But this is not the case at all. While the divide certainly exists, the evidence supporting the two sides is greatly mismatched.

Consider for example the case of Andreas Baader, the West German who was one of the leading figures of the infamous Baader–Meinhoff Gang, the group that evolved into the Red Army Faction (RAF). In 1977, while Baader languished in Stannheim prison, a psychologist published a paper describing Baader as a 'sociopath' (Cooper, 1977). Cooper went on to say that the German terrorist was 'extremely manipulative . . . a pathological liar . . . Baader displays characteristics of a marked psychopathic order'. Two years later—and some 18 months after Baader committed suicide in prison—a paper with a rather different view of his psychology was published. This was written by Wilfried Rasch, a German psychiatry professor. Rasch (1979) wrote of Baader (and other captured RAF members) that 'nothing was found which could justify their classification as psychotics, neurotics, fanatics or psychopaths'. Despite the fact that Baader and the others would go on to commit suicide in prison, Rasch claimed that he could not even diagnose these individuals as 'paranoid' and that this was particularly true of Baader.

How had Cooper and Rasch arrived at such startlingly different conclusions about the same man? The methods they used to get their answers are certainly revealing. Rasch had extensive, personal contact with the captured terrorists, who he met and assessed while they were serving their sentences in prison. Cooper, on the other hand, never actually met Baader. Rather he came to his conclusions entirely through reading second-hand reports of the German terrorist, such as stories from newspapers and magazines.

This is a disappointingly common trend in the research on terrorism and terrorists. For example, Lasch (1979) wrote that members of the Canadian terrorist group the *Front de Libération du Québec* (FLQ) suffered from narcissistic personality disorder. This opinion contradicted entirely the views of Morf (1970) who had failed to find any clinical evidence for the presence of narcissistic personality disorder (or any other personality disorder for that matter) among captured FLQ terrorists. Yet again, Lasch had based his conclusion solely on a study of secondary sources, whereas Morf's judgement was again the result of personal interviews with the terrorists.

Overall, writers who suggest that terrorists are psychologically abnormal tend to be those with the least amount of contact with actual terrorists. This is a very important point as they are by and large making this inference from research only on secondary sources. Rasch (1979) commented that this widespread habit was a scientific travesty, and that any explanation not backed by direct examination of terrorists amounted to little more than 'idle speculation'.

In contrast, those researchers who say that terrorists are not abnormal tend to be the ones who have had direct contact and experience with actual terrorists. The reality of close contact has displaced any comfortable notions of aberration that may have been harboured. They have learned that terrorism cannot be dismissed in such terms. Yet this seems to have been a remarkably slow lesson for others to learn.

It is important to remember that the above research is not saying that mentally unbalanced or pathological personalities are *never* present in terrorist organisations. On the contrary, researchers such as Rasch (1979) and Lyons and Harbinson (1986) did find such individuals in their samples. However, these individuals were a rarity, being the exception rather than the rule, a finding supported by work in other countries (e.g. Ferracuti and Bruno's (1981) study of Italian terrorists). Further, the research also indicated that when they do appear, such personalities tend to be fringe members of the terrorist group, rather than central characters. Quite simply, the best of the empirical work does not suggest, and never has suggested, that terrorists possess a distinct personality or that their psychology is somehow deviant from that of 'normal' people. As far back as 1981, Martha Crenshaw was able to conclude that 'what limited data we have on individual terrorists... suggest that the outstanding common characteristic of terrorists is their normality'.

Sadly, however, even today many psychologists and psychiatrists who write about terrorists seem unaware of the work of people like Morf, Rasch, and Lyons and Harbinson. Neither do they seem to have read any of the informed reviews of this research which clearly spell out how mistaken is the view that terrorists are in some way psychologically abnormal or deviant (e.g. Corrado, 1981; Crenshaw, 1983; Silke, 1998). Instead, a steady stream of psychologists continue to diagnose at a distance and not surprisingly keep coming to the same extreme conclusions. Even being aware of the perils of such assessment does not seem to help. Pomerantz (2001), for example, wrote an assessment of the psychology of al-Qaeda leaders after the September 11 attacks. His assessment began with a hint of promise but soon fell foul of the same mistakes of the past:

> At the very start, I need to make clear that I do not believe in evaluating persons whom I have not personally interviewed, especially when they come from a different culture. However, Osama bin Laden and other terrorist

leaders may fit into some broad diagnostic categories that we would like to review . . . Whatever the diagnosis, we should not minimise terrorist leaders' disordered thinking. Although it may be tempting to normalise terrorist behaviour by trying to understand terrorist grievances and follow their logic, there is danger in such an approach as well. Mental disorders such as paranoia, and certainly character disorders, such as pathologic narcissism and sociopathy, do not yield to logic and placation. [Terrorism is] the byproduct of a group mental disorder—an extreme example of destructive cult behaviour in which paranoid/narcissistic/sociopathic leaders convince vulnerable individuals to follow their megalomaniac 'logic' . . . My vote [in explaining terrorism] is clearly for . . . emphasising mental difficulties as opposed to legitimate economic, political, and religious grievances (pp. 2–3).

There is no sign that the claims of the type made here by Pomerantz will ever completely cease. Indeed, even though one could argue that by 1981—when a number of thorough reviews of the matter were published— we had already enough evidence to clearly establish that the vast majority of terrorists are not crazy or abnormal, a number of psychologists have persisted in saying otherwise and yet have failed entirely to provide reliable evidence to support such claims. Suffice to say here that terrorists are very rarely crazy or disordered, and any explanation for why people become involved in terrorism will have to look elsewhere for answers.

ELSEWHERE

Ultimately, even 'popular' terrorist groups such as the Provisional IRA or Hamas represent a violent and extreme minority within the immediate social group that shares the terrorists' beliefs and backgrounds. While the terrorists (and in particular the larger ethnic groups) may be largely tolerated within their communities, the number of individuals actively involved in the campaign of violence is always relatively low. Very few individuals of aggrieved minorities go on to become active terrorists. The question has always been, why did these particular individuals engage in terrorism when most of their compatriots did not? While individual terrorists may possess normal personalities and do not appear to be significantly different at least in psychological terms from the rest of the population, terrorism as an activity is most certainly abnormal. The extreme violence that terrorism often entails, combined with the fact that active terrorists tend to live isolated and stressful lives, raises questions about why and how anyone would get involved in such an activity.

A number of important issues need to be stressed here. The first is that terrorists are a very heterogeneous group. The range of people who become involved in terrorist groups is vast. They can vary hugely in terms of education, family background, age, gender, intelligence, economic class, etc. Consequently the manner in which they become a terrorist can also vary, and factors which played a pivotal role in one person's decision to engage in terrorist violence can play a peripheral role in the decision-making of others, or indeed may have played no part whatsoever.

Likewise, terrorist groups themselves are very varied and can differ dramatically from each other. There is a great deal of heated debate about what 'terrorism' actually is and there is no sign that a clear and widely agreed consensus on this will be achieved any time soon (if ever). 'Terrorist' is a political term, not a neat, clearly defined psychological label, and governments and security agencies are extremely quick to try to label their enemies as terrorists in the hope that this will undermine international sympathy for the organisation and deflect criticism away from any policies used to fight the group. Groups vary too in their ideology—some are secular, others are religious. Secular groups can be motivated by nationalist, separatist, ethnic, Marxist or communist agendas (among others). Groups with religious motivations currently come from Christian, Islamic, Jewish, Sikh, Buddhist and Hindu backgrounds (not to mention more obscure cultist offshoots of the major faiths). Some terrorist groups have less than 10 active members while others boast over 20 000. Some have massive resources at their disposal with budgets and assets estimated in millions or even billions of pounds, while others struggle to raise more than a few thousand pounds a year. Tactics and methods also vary between groups. Some favour hijackings and hostage-taking, others bombings and assassinations. Some will be willing to kill hundreds and even thousands in single attacks, others deliberately try to keep casualties to a minimum. Some use suicide tactics, most do not. Some will use drug-trafficking to raise money, others abhor the activity. In short, on these and a vast range of other variables and measures, it is possible to find major differences between groups who are labelled by someone, somewhere, as 'terrorists'.

In order to understand the psychology of 'terrorists', one must expect considerable variation between the people involved. There is no one path into terrorism. That said, after nearly four decades of research it is now appreciated that there are a number of relatively common factors in the backgrounds of terrorists. Although all of these factors will not necessarily be present in the experience of every terrorist, most will be there at least to some degree. Neither are their boundaries exclusive: they interact and mesh together in a complex manner that can often be very difficult to disentangle or differentiate in the case of any one person. Ultimately, it is the combined impact of a number of factors that pushes and pulls someone into becoming a terrorist, and these factors will vary depending on the culture, social context, terrorist group and individual involved.

Becoming a terrorist is for most people a process. It is not usually something that happens quickly or easily. Considering the factors in the following sections will help to gain an understanding and insight into this process.

BIOLOGICAL FACTORS

As yet there is no scientific evidence of any genetic role in determining why certain people become involved in terrorism, and specific biological approaches to explaining terrorism have tended to be flawed. Consider, for example, the work of Hubbard (1978) who examined 80 imprisoned terrorists in 11 countries. Hubbard wrote that nearly 90 per cent of these terrorists had defective vestibular functions of the middle ear. In addition to causing poor balance and co-ordination, Hubbard claimed this impairment was linked with antisocial behaviour designed to gain attention and an inability to relate to other people. In essence, these individuals had become terrorists because of an ear problem. An unorthodox hypothesis to begin with, Hubbard's argument was fatally undermined by serious doubts over the validity and reliability of his work. He never released detailed descriptions of the data he gathered or of his analysis procedures, and there have been no replications of his very unusual findings since.

When we consider biological factors here, we are not looking at such applied theories as those of Hubbard, but instead we are considering more general factors. It is important to stress again that neither are these single-issue explanations of why people become terrorists. Rather each factor works in combination with other factors, and the more factors present, and the more pronounced each factor is, then the more likely it is that the individual could become a terrorist.

The most important biological factors associated with joining a terrorist group are age and gender. While a causative role for these factors is not entirely unambiguous, there is certainly a correlation between the two factors and most recruits to terrorist organisations. Most people who join a terrorist group are young, and by young here we are referring to teenagers and people in their early twenties, and most new recruits are male.

It is already well established in other spheres that young males are associated with a multitude of dangerous and high-risk statistics. Statistics on violent crime across the world consistently show that the perpetrators of violent crimes are most likely to be males aged between 15 and 25 years of age. This is a very robust finding that is remarkably stable across cultures and regions. More crime in general is committed by teenagers and young adults than by any other age category. Adolescence brings with it a dramatic increase in the number of people who are willing to offend, and in Western societies the peak age for male offending has generally been between 15 and 18 years of age, tailoring off quickly for most individuals as they grow older.

Research studies have found that between 54 per cent and 96 per cent of young men have been involved in some form of delinquent behaviour, and there is considerable international agreement on this finding. For example, Junger-Tas (1994) compared delinquency rates in five countries and found that between 64 per cent and 90 per cent of all young men surveyed admitted to having committed a criminal offence (with between 45 per cent and 50 per cent having committed at least one offence in the previous 12 months). These rates are astronomically higher than those seen for any other age groups. As Moffitt (1993) noted: 'actual rates of illegal behavior soar so high during adolescence that participation in delinquency appears to be a normal part of teen life' (p. 675).

There is also widespread agreement that young men are far worse offenders than young women, both in terms of the quantity of crime and the severity of the offences. Studies on violent crime, for example, show that the ratio of male offenders to female offenders varies by at least 2:1 to 4:1 in Western cultures, with this ratio generally climbing higher the more serious the offences become (Rutter, Giller and Hagell, 1998).

Explaining why young men are so inclined to get involved in deviant behaviour is not straightforward. While there has been a great deal of research on juvenile delinquency, most of this has focused on examining persistent life-course offenders—the small minority of adolescents who continue to offend at significant levels into their adult life. These individuals normally comprise no more than 4 to 7 per cent of all juvenile offenders, and a range of factors have been found to predict these persistent offenders, such as family criminality, poor school performance, family poverty, poor housing, high impulsivity, etc (Hollin, Browne and Palmer, 2002). Yet in focusing so much attention on the persistent life-course offenders, surprisingly little effort has been devoted to the majority who cease deviant activity in their twenties.

Nevertheless, there is widespread recognition that most young men get involved in some form of criminal activity and deviancy during their teenage years in particular. This involvement tapers off dramatically as individuals get older, having all but vanished for most by the time they reach 28. With terrorism, the same factors that attract young men to deviant activity in other spheres can also play at least a partial role in the attraction terrorism holds for a few. Higher impulsivity, higher confidence, greater attraction to risk-taking and needs for status can all work to give life as a terrorist a certain appeal for some young males. As shall be discussed later, a desire for revenge and retribution is an extremely common motive for joining terrorist groups, and again research indicates that young men hold the most positive attitudes towards vengeance and are most likely to exhibit and approve of vengeful behaviour (Cota-McKinley, Woody and Bell, 2001; Stuckless and Goranson, 1992).

When we examine the membership of terrorist groups, it is generally the case that it is the younger members who carry out most of the violent attacks. For example, in a study of 89 loyalist paramilitaries in Northern Ireland, Silke (1999) found that it was the youngest members who were responsible for carrying out the most high-risk military operations—the assassinations and bombings. The median age of these individuals was 23 years old, compared to a median of 28 years for those involved with the low-risk vigilante activities of the group, and a median age of 39 for those involved in the very low-risk fund-raising operations.

While young men make up the majority of terrorist recruits, some recruits are female and a few are much older. Further, it is also very evident that even in troubled regions like Northern Ireland, the vast majority of young males living in the affected communities do not in fact become terrorists. The unavoidable conclusion is that other factors besides age and gender must be playing crucial roles in the process and decision to become a terrorist.

SOCIAL IDENTIFICATION AND MARGINALISATION

Before an individual will be prepared to join a terrorist group, he or she first needs to belong to that section of society which supports or shares the aims, grievances and ambitions of the terrorist group. Terrorist groups with nationalist/separatist agendas tend to have a relatively large social grouping to draw upon. For example, the IRA's social grouping is primarily the Catholic population of Northern Ireland. Not all Catholics will be nationalists, and many—if not most—of those who are nationalists will still be opposed to political violence. But most Catholics will share many of the same opinions, views and experiences of the average IRA member. For some of these communities young people joining a terrorist group is seen in a similar light to people enlisting in the military of larger or more peaceful societies. As one Palestinian terrorist put it: 'Enlistment was for me the natural and done thing . . . In a way, it can be compared to a young Israeli from a nationalist Zionist family who wants to fulfil himself through army service' (Post and Denny, 2002). Often there is widespread acceptance in communities that not only is becoming a member of a terrorist group not simply unremarkable, but it is actually something to be supported and encouraged. Another Palestinian terrorist expressed this view well when he commented that: 'My motivation in joining Fatah was both ideological and personal. It was a question of self-fulfilment, of honour and a feeling of independence . . . The goal of every young Palestinian was to be a fighter' (Post and Denny, 2002).

Indeed during especially unsettled periods, some communities can actually view not supporting or not being prepared to join a terrorist group as aberrant! During the first intifada (uprising) against Israeli occupation, the various Palestinian terrorist groups were deluged with recruits (the same thing has happened again for the more violent second intifada which began in 2000). Hassan (2002) noted that within the Palestinian communities it was entirely normal for young men to flock to groups like Hamas and Fatah during the intifada. Indeed those individuals who did not join stood out and were considered unusual. One recruit noted simply that 'anyone who didn't enlist during that period would have been ostracized' (Post and Denny, 2002).

Examples are readily found in other cultures and regions. Northern Ireland also provides examples of a number of nationalistic terrorist groups. How these groups can recruit is demonstrated by the case of Gerry Adams. Though now more widely known for his role as leader of the republican political party Sinn Fein, Gerry Adams joined the IRA as a teenager in the 1960s (Sharrock and Devenport, 1997). His motivation for joining at this time—when the IRA campaign was largely dormant—was due to his family background. Adams came from a strongly republican family: his father was in the IRA and had been shot and wounded by the Royal Ulster Constabulary (RUC) in 1940. His uncle was another IRA member and had been involved in a bombing campaign in Britain. For the young Gerry Adams, joining the IRA was simply following a well-established family tradition. He was brought up in a family that strongly supported the aims, ambitions and methods of the terrorist group, and the teenager would have been taught and encouraged to share those views.

Thus it is often surprisingly easy for nationalistic and ethnic terrorist groups to find recruits and support. However, it can be more difficult for terrorist groups with other backgrounds and agendas to attract members. Contrast, for example, Gerry Adams' smooth path into terrorism with that of the West German terrorist Michael Baumman who was a key figure in the Red Army Faction. Baumman came from an apparently normal working-class background, and there was no sense from his childhood that he may end up in a terrorist organisation. In 1965, at the age of 18, he quit his job as a builder's apprentice and took on a series of odd-jobs. He became increasingly absorbed by the emerging rock culture of the time. His interest in popular culture—and the rebellious values it entailed at that time—combined with the fact that he was moving constantly from one temporary job to another, meant that Baumman became increasingly isolated from mainstream society and more and more exposed to an alternate underground culture (Taylor, 1988, p. 148). Many of his friends came from this alternate culture and Baumman found himself increasingly exposed to the political ideologies popular in the underground. In short, Baumman's story is one of gradual marginalisation from mainstream society and increasing exposure to alternate political ideologies.

A common theme in the experiences of both Adams and Baumann though was the manner in which they were marginalised from mainstream society and exposed to the ideology that drove their particular terrorist groups. Some terrorists, like Gerry Adams and the Palestinian terrorists quoted above, are born members of a minority group and hence can literally be marginalised at birth. Others, like Baumman, come from essentially mainstream backgrounds but later become marginalised as a result of general life experiences.

If such marginalised groups are discriminated against or internal sections believe that there is discrimination, there will always be those within such communities who will be receptive to radical ideologies advocating changing or reforming the established, mainstream social system. The intent of these changes will be to improve the lot of the disadvantaged group. People on the margins have less to lose if the current social order is maintained and conceivably a great deal to gain if it is radically changed. As a result, most Catholics in Northern Ireland had relatively little to gain by supporting the status quo of Protestant-controlled government which ran the province until 1972, and potentially a great deal to gain if they could substantially reform or abolish that system of government. Among a discriminated Catholic population, ideologies that advocated changing the regime would always be popular, and in the face of continuing discrimination, ideologies that advocated violent action to change the status quo attracted significant support from some quarters.

Once an individual has become marginalised from mainstream society—and thus has lost most of the vested interest in maintaining that society—and has then been exposed favourably to the ideology shared by a given terrorist group, an important step towards becoming an active terrorist has been passed. However, while many people are politically committed to a variety of causes, few are willing to commit acts of violence to further these ideals. The move into terrorism still requires something more.

THE PSYCHOLOGY OF VENGEANCE

One of the most important keys to understanding the psychology of why people become terrorists is to understand the psychology of vengeance. Sadly, this is a topic that has been largely ignored by psychological research, and much is unclear and uncertain. Nevertheless, it has long been recognised that for most terrorists a key motivation for joining a terrorist organisation revolves around a desire for revenge (Schmid and Jongman, 1988). Humans certainly have an incredibly strong sense of justice, and a desire for vengeance represents a persistent darker side to this. And it is not just humans who can feel this way. Research on our nearest primate relatives reveals similar patterns. For example, Jennifer Scott at the Wesleyan University in Connecticut has found comparable behaviour in gorillas. Physically massive alpha males can still be given a hard time by their subordinates if they appear to behave unjustly (Tudge, 2002).

Cota-McKinley, Woody and Bell (2001) define vengeance as 'the infliction of harm in return for perceived injury or insult or as simply getting back at another person' (p. 343). These researchers carried out one of the few psychological studies on vengeance and revenge in recent years and their thoughts on the subject are worth considering in more detail.

One important element of the desire for vengeance is the surprising willingness of individuals to sacrifice and suffer in order to carry out an act of revenge. As Cota-McKinley, Woody and Bell (2001) comment: 'vengeance can have many irrational and destructive consequences for the person seeking vengeance as well as for the target. The person seeking vengeance will often compromise his or her own integrity, social standing, and personal safety for the sake of revenge' (p. 343). This observation is supported by a number of research studies. For example, in one Swiss study, researchers gave students a co-operative task of the 'prisoner's dilemma' kind: all students in the study benefit provided each behaves honourably, but those who cheat will benefit more provided they are not caught. The students were rewarded with real money if they did well and fined if they did not. They were also able to punish fellow players by imposing fines, but could do this only by forfeiting money themselves. This meant that those who punished others frequently would end up with considerably less than those who punished others only a little. Despite this, the research found that the participants tended to punish cheats severely, even though they lost out by doing so. People seem to hate cheats so much that they are prepared to incur significant losses themselves in order to inflict some punishment on the transgressors (Tudge, 2002).

This principle goes well beyond gorillas and university students. James Gilligan (2000), a prison psychiatrist who encountered some incredibly violent and dangerous individuals during his career, judged that:

> I have yet to see a serious act of violence that was not provoked by the experience of feeling shamed and humiliated, disrespected and ridiculed, and that did not represent the attempt to prevent or undo this 'loss of face'— no matter how severe the punishment, even if it includes death. For we misunderstand these men, at our peril, if we do not realise they mean it literally when they say they would rather kill or mutilate others, be killed or mutilated themselves, than live without pride, dignity and self-respect (p. 110).

Yet why are people willing to pay such costs? What ends are served by a process that brings such cost to oneself? Cota-McKinley, Woody and Bell (2001) highlight that revenge can fulfil a range of goals, including righting perceived injustice, restoring the self-worth of the vengeful individual and deterring future injustice. Lying at the heart of the whole process are perceptions of personal harm, unfairness and injustice, and the 'anger, indignation, and hatred' associated with the perceived injustice (Kim and Smith, 1993, p. 38).

Ultimately, the desire for revenge and the willingness to carry it out violently are tied both to the self-worth of the originally offended individual and also to a deterrent role against future unjust treatment. The vengeful individual 'sends the message that harmful acts will not go unanswered' (Kim and Smith, 1993, p. 40). Not only is the goal to stop this particular form of maltreatment in the future, it is to deter the transgressor from wanting to commit similar crimes; additionally, vengeance may stop other potential offenders from committing similar crimes or even from considering similar crimes.

Not everyone, though, is equally content with the idea of vengeance or equally prepared to act in a vengeful manner. As indicated earlier in this chapter, what little research there is indicates that some groups are more vengeance-prone than others. Men hold more positive attitudes towards vengeance than women, and young people are much more prepared to act in a vengeful manner than older individuals (Cota-McKinley, Woody and Bell, 2001). It is not surprising to find, then, that most recruits to terrorist groups are both young and male. Some evidence exists too to suggest that religious belief also affects one's attitude to vengeance, with more secular individuals showing less approval to vengeful attitudes.

The personal histories of terrorists frequently contain encounters with members of the security forces or rival groups where the individual, friends or family members were threatened, harassed, assaulted or even killed, and such catalyst events leave the potential terrorists (usually teenagers or in their early twenties at the time) with a powerful desire for vengeance. Consider the case of Eamon Collins who joined the IRA in the late 1970s. Collins had not grown up in a republican family and as a child and teenager had no particular sympathy for the IRA's campaign of violence and certainly no interest in joining the organisation. However, that was to change. In his autobiography he recounts a pivotal experience he and his family suffered at the hands of the British Army one summer when he was home from university. His father had been stopped at a checkpoint, and during a search of his car a dog trained to smell explosives became very agitated due to spilt creosote in the vehicle. He was allowed to proceed but late that night British soldiers arrived at the family home. Two of them grabbed Collins outside of his house:

> They began to beat me with their rifle butts. Others appeared and started to kick and punch me all over my body . . . They kicked my legs further and further apart until I fell to the ground. They spread-eagled me in the dirt . . . A soldier walked over to me and shoved his SLR rifle in my mouth, cracking my

front left tooth. I could feel the cold of the steel upon my throat. I remember the taste of gun-oil. I began to choke (Collins, 1997, p. 50).

Collins, his father and his 15-year-old brother John were all arrested as suspected terrorists and loaded into two jeeps to be taken for questioning to a nearby military barracks:

> They told me to lie on the floor as three soldiers got in on either side of me. They began to hit me with their rifle butts on my arms, legs, back and buttocks. I could hear my mother screaming hysterically... During the journey the soldiers spat on my head continuously. I felt a hand move up my trouser leg to pull hairs from my calf. All the time they kicked me in the ribs on both sides of my body. One soldier pulled me by the hair and began to bang my forehead against the radio on the floor of the jeep. A rifle barrel was twisted around the area of my anus, then two of them put their guns to my head, clicked off the safety-catches and ordered me to sing 'The Sash'—the Orange Order's supremacist marching song.... I prayed that I would survive the journey.... [After reaching the barracks] they pushed me into a room where I was forced to stand in a corner against the wall with my fingertips supporting the full weight of my body. I could see my brother John in the same position to my left, and my father to my right. I shall never forget the sight of my father standing there so humiliated (pp. 51–52).

After extensive questioning, they were released the next afternoon when forensic tests confirmed that there had indeed been no explosives in the car. The three were released from custody and returned to the family house:

> At home we discovered that soldiers had been there all night, keeping my mother and young children under armed guard while they tore the house to pieces. They had pulled up the carpets, torn out all the floorboards, and drilled into the bricked-up fireplaces. One of our ceilings had collapsed. ... I returned to [university] a different man... (p. 53).

A remarkable feature of this experience is not that Collins joined the IRA in the aftermath of it, but rather that it would take two more years before he joined the terrorist group. Incidents like this are extremely common in the lives of terrorists. Some experience far worse, both in terms of personal physical suffering and also in terms of what happens to friends and family. Yet it is important to remember that many people experience such events but do not become terrorists. For example, consider the case of Paul Morrissey who was 17 when loyalist terrorists abducted, tortured and killed his father in Belfast. While rage and a desire for revenge played a strong role in his thoughts and emotions afterwards, he did not join the IRA:

> The frustration—I could have killed somebody in the frustration. I think I was very, very close to taking revenge, very close to it.... Although the

anger got less, the bitterness and hatred started to take over and instead of actually wanting to go out and physically take revenge, I found myself wishing it on them and hoping that the paramilitaries on our side would go and plant a bomb and kill so many. I found myself going towards that mentality of it (Morrissey, 2000, pp. 105–106).

For some, though, the need to strike back becomes too strong. William Temple, a Protestant father in Northern Ireland, recounted how his eldest son joined the Ulster Defence Association (UDA), the largest of the loyalist terrorist groups:

My children were being attacked constantly on their way to and from school. When they became older, the attacks became more vicious. I have two sons and one of them was hospitalised twice through beatings and the other, once. The eldest boy, he was in hospital twice. And after two relations were shot by the IRA, he became mixed up with the UDA (Temple, 2000, p. 67).

Joining a terrorist group in the aftermath of acts of violence against either oneself, loved ones or others strongly identified with is a common theme for more ideological terrorist groups as well. Michael Baumman joined the Red Army Faction only after a friend of his was killed by a policeman during a student protest. Up until that point, even though he had been exposed to and was very sympathetic towards the philosophies and beliefs underlining the terrorist group, he had not felt motivated to join the group or to engage in political violence. However, the violent death of his friend—what he perceived as an extremely unjust act—created for him a strong personal motivation to join.

This is a central dynamic to the need for revenge. Many recruits report that 'It was the feeling that I was striking back' which motivated them to join, and this is a very pervasive theme in the lives of most terrorists. They have witnessed or experienced an act (or many acts) of injustice and this provides the catalyst motivation for them to begin life as an active terrorist. Another German terrorist, Hans-Joachin Klein, for example, became involved in political violence only after he witnessed a girl being savagely beaten by a police officer during a student protest. He did not know the girl, but he identified strongly with her. From his perspective it could just as well have been himself who was attacked by the police officer. Engaging in terrorism against the state was a way to redress this injustice. The girl had suffered because of the state, and by engaging in terrorism Klein was making sure that the state also suffered. In short, from Klein's perspective, by becoming a terrorist he was ensuring that justice was done.

Importantly, one does not need to experience unjust events first-hand in order to feel sufficiently motivated to become a terrorist. For example, many terrorists report that they first joined the organisation after witnessing events on television. They did not come from the area where the events occurred, nor did they know the people who lived there, but at some level they identified with the victims. This identification—combined with the perceived injustice of the event—compelled the individual to join a terrorist group in order to redress the balance. In Northern Ireland, after atrocities such as the Enniskillen bombing or the Shankill bombing, where large numbers of Protestant civilians were killed by IRA bombs, the loyalist terrorist groups throughout the Province, which normally struggle to find recruits, reported that they were deluged with requests from people wanting to join.

A collective sense of unjust persecution can quickly build up in aggrieved communities, and this provides the motivation that even extreme violence in response is warranted and justified. Interviewed in prison, one Palestinian terrorist was very clear on this wider sense of injustice:

> You Israelis are Nazis in your souls and in your conduct. In your occupation you never distinguish between men and women, or between old people and children. You adopted methods of collective punishment, you uprooted people from their homeland and from their homes and chased them into exile. You fired live ammunition at women and children. You smashed the skulls of defenceless civilians. You set up detention camps for thousands of people in sub-human conditions. You destroyed homes and turned children into orphans. You prevented people from making a living, you stole their property, you trampled on their honour. Given that kind of conduct, there is no choice but to strike at you without mercy in every possible way (Post and Denny, 2002).

The need for revenge is a wretchedly stable aspect of human nature. In the face of apparent injustice, and the absence of external redress, a personal motivation for vengeance is very common. For many, this motivation will not be acted on, but for some individuals, and in some circumstances, this motivation will give rise to violence in response. There is, however, nothing strange or bizarre about this. It is important to remember that to all intents and purposes the desire for violent revenge and a willingness to act on it are expected human reactions to certain situations.

STATUS AND PERSONAL REWARDS

Though the terrorist group provides a potent outlet for desires for vengeance, membership of such groups offers other inducements and rewards to outsiders. There are considerable dangers in becoming a terrorist—it can be an isolated, stressful and extremely perilous existence. Recruits to the IRA are warned that they can expect only one of two things for certain from joining the organisation: a lengthy prison sentence or a violent death. Hardship and suffering are seen as inseparable aspects of life as a terrorist, still there are often benefits and advantages to being in a terrorist group. For example, in many communities and societies, terrorist groups and their members are regarded as courageous, honourable and important. As one Palestinian terrorist described it:

> Recruits were treated with great respect. A youngster who belonged to Hamas or Fatah was regarded more highly than one who didn't belong to a group, and got better treatment than unaffiliated kids (Post and Denny, 2002).

The generally positive perception some communities can hold with regard to joining a terrorist group has already been mentioned. It helps to remember that the communities do not see the organisations as 'terrorists' but rather in such terms as 'freedom fighters', 'rebels', 'the resistance', etc. One cannot avoid the fact that applying the label 'terrorist' is often a value judgement (and a negative one) and is often a label imposed from outside of the communities and culture to which the terrorists belong. Those within that culture reject the term or else reject such a clumsy effort to describe the actors in black and white terms. Ultimately, in many communities, joining a terrorist group considerably increases the standing of a teenager or youth. As another Palestinian terrorist described the impact: 'After recruitment, my social status was greatly enhanced. I got a lot of respect from my acquaintances, and from the young people in my village' (Post and Denny, 2002).

Such perceptions are not isolated, and increased status among one's community or social network is something that can be found across the globe. In Northern Ireland, IRA members have a keen awareness of the many benefits to be gained in joining the group. As one member put it:

> In the nationalist community, in republican circles anyway, IRA men have considerable status, and for those Provos who look for sexual advantages from it, there is no shortage of women willing to give more than the time of day to IRA volunteers (Collins, 1997, pp. 164–65).

As well as providing increased status and standing for recruits, terrorist groups can also offer a degree of protection for members. In the communities of Northern Ireland, it is well recognised that it is unwise to come into conflict with paramilitary members. Entirely personal disputes can escalate if one party is 'involved' with a paramilitary group. Journalist David Smith described one encounter he had with a woman living on an estate off the Shankill Road. He was there because her son and her nephew—both 16—had been targeted by the UDA. The boys had a history of trouble with the group, but after the two were involved in a fight with other teenagers, the local UDA commander arrived at the woman's house. The other teenagers had been members of the UDA's youth wing. The woman related what the commander had to say:

> He says, 'I'm up to tell you that any time those lads are ever seen out, they're getting their bollix knocked in.' He says they're just gonna be killed any time they're seen. In other words, get them out or they're dead. And the two of them aren't getting into any bother at all (Smith, 1996, p. 17).

Thus the incentives for a potential recruit can be quite potent. Increased standing and respect among their peers and community, combined with the support of the organisation in personal disputes and other spheres, can be very attractive to individuals who often have limited opportunities to achieve success and recognition. Even for individuals who are motivated primarily by other reasons, such perks can smooth and reward the decision to join.

PRESS-GANGING AND CONSCRIPTION

While most of this chapter has looked at the question of the individual's motivation to become a terrorist, an important factor to consider is the outlook of the terrorist organisation. Terrorist groups vary hugely in their approach to recruiting new members and the strategies they use. Even the same organisation can vary its policy and approaches across time and regions. Some groups will be extremely keen to attract new members and will invest enormous effort in identifying potential recruits and in highlighting the rewards and benefits of joining. Other terrorist groups will be staid in outlook. This applies particularly to many of the ethnic terrorist groups who are sometimes deluged with requests from young people wishing to join. In the 1980s, for example, the IRA turned away far more people than it actually accepted into its ranks. Thus it is mistaken to think that a terrorist group will always be desperate to increase its size and to recruit everyone it possibly can.

That said, some groups will resort to extreme measures to gain new members. While most terrorist recruits are volunteers, people who have actively solicited entry into the group or who have willingly accepted an offer to join, some groups occasionally coerce and threaten individuals in order to get them to join. In Northern Ireland, for example, the largest loyalist terrorist group, the UDA, has often been accused of coercing young people into becoming members. Bruce (1992) has correctly pointed out that as pro-state terrorists, the loyalists are perpetually in competition with the State security forces for recruits. However, unable to offer the same incentives and security as the State's forces, the loyalists have occasionally been forced into press-ganging as a way to recruit. Consider the following comments from one local in a loyalist area:

> The UDA press-gangs seventeen-year-olds into their organization. If you get in trouble, they tell you to join the UDA. Last year one of my son's mates, who was seventeen, joined. Now he can't get out. He daren't speak out about it. Mostly you know that if you don't join, you're history. And the police don't help (Human Rights Watch/Helsinki, 1992, p. 44).

The paramilitaries can certainly make life extremely difficult for teenagers who refuse to join them when approached. An illustrative case is provided by the experiences of Raymond McCord and his family. McCord refused to join the UDA as a teenager and thus became embroiled in a long-running feud with the organisation:

> The UDA rules by terror in Protestant areas. I refused to join them when I was seventeen, and over the years they decided to make me an example. Now they are going after my son, too. Last year, when he was sixteen, UDA lads punched and kicked him. Now he's in the Air Force. When he was home on leave at Christmas, he was in a local video shop. A man called out to him and then hit him on the chin. He said, 'That's for your father. The UDA won't miss your Dad next time.' They have told me, 'If your son wants to be a big lad, tell him to join the paramilitaries.' The beating they gave me in February was the worst beating in my area in twenty years . . . They attacked me outside a bar with flagstones. They dropped flagstones on my arms and legs and kicked my face while I was lying on the ground. Their usual weapons are baseball bats (Human Rights Watch/Helsinki, 1992, pp. 43–44).

It is clear that considerable pressure can be levied against young individuals to make them join terrorist organisations. Of course threatening someone with a beating or shooting in order to force them to enlist is a double-edged sword. It can backfire in that the individual instead joins a rival terrorist group, or else goes to the security forces in order to get some protection.

OPPORTUNITY

One factor that is so obvious it is often overlooked is opportunity. One cannot become an active terrorist unless one can find a terrorist group that is willing to let you join. For the potential terrorist, there are two problems to be overcome here. First, the individual—now located in the appropriate social grouping and motivated by a desire for retribution—needs to identify an accessible avenue into a terrorist group. He or she is hampered in this task because terrorist groups are nearly always illegal, and membership is a punishable crime. This presents difficulties for the potential terrorist, as he or she must try to identify current members in order to facilitate entry into the organisation, yet the individual risks exposing him- or herself to the security forces if he or she approaches the wrong person at the wrong time.

For ethnic terrorist groups such as Hamas or the IRA, this problem is largely overcome by the use of legal political-front organisations. Hamas, for example, is a very large group and many elements of it are engaged in non-violent legitimate activity. The organisation is associated with many schools, hospitals, charities, businesses and mosques. For individuals interested in joining it is not at all difficult to make enquiries about doing so and for these to be directed to the appropriate people. Similar situations exist elsewhere, particularly in the case of nationalist and ethnic conflicts. In Northern Ireland, many IRA men first joined by contacting individuals who were publicly and openly active in the republican political party Sinn Fein. The applicant had no guarantee that the Sinn Fein member was in the IRA, but could be confident that because of the extremely close links between the two organisations a serious request to join the IRA would eventually be passed on to an IRA member.

Approaching legal groups associated with a terrorist cause is a common and generally efficient route into a terrorist group. The potential terrorist will already share the social grouping of the active terrorists and their supporters. For example, an individual who is considering joining the UK-based Animal Liberation Front (ALF) will probably have a history of involvement in other animal rights groups—most of which operate in an entirely legal fashion. Such involvement means that the individual will have learned about individuals or groups considered to be extremists by those active in the more mainstream organisations. When the individual eventually decides to join, he or she can simply approach such extremists, or their spokespeople, and make a direct request.

There are some terrorist groups that will accept almost any individual who wishes to join, but the vast majority of groups closely vet all applicants. For example, the IRA usually spends weeks or months checking the background of an applicant. Lawrence McKeown recalls his own experience of joining the organisation:

> I came to a decision to join the IRA . . . a couple of months later . . . someone approached me one night. . . . they said they had heard that I was interested in joining the IRA and that the IRA was interested in forming a unit in the area I lived in. I said I definitely was, and that took a procedure which took probably seven to eight months, to the point where I was getting exasperated, thinking that somebody had forgotten about me, that I wasn't moving ahead. But then I was taken in and asked again by others in a more formal situation had I thought it out and was I aware of the consequences and to rethink my position, the fears of imprisonment, of being shot or killed or whatever. I

said that I had thought of a lot of those issues that they had raised, that I didn't think I was going to change my mind. So, they said to give it some more thought but I didn't change my mind. Shortly after that I ended up in the IRA (McKeown, 2000, pp. 51–53).

Other groups will first arrange for the applicant to carry out some minor illegal acts to test their commitment. If the candidate carries these out successfully (and any other tasks which are set for him or her) he or she is formally accepted into the terrorist group. Some groups, however, will not accept a new member regardless of the person's background or how motivated he or she may be. As stated earlier, for the past two decades the IRA has deliberately rejected hundreds (and probably thousands) of applications due to a leadership decision in the late 1970s that a generally small size for the organisation would improve its internal security and leave it better able to resist and detect infiltration by informers and undercover agents.

For the individual who cannot identify a route into an established terrorist group, or is refused membership after applying, the remaining option is to form his or her own group. Nezar Hindawi formed his own terrorist group, the Jordanian Revolutionary Movement, with two family members, and later convinced Syria to supply this tiny group with weapons and funds. In what has been described as one of the most callous acts of attempted terrorism ever, Hindawi duped his pregnant girlfriend into taking a flight on an El-Al plane, hiding, unknown to her, a bomb in her suitcase that was set to detonate mid-flight. To the girlfriend's understandable horror and shock, an airport security check discovered the hidden bomb, and Hindawi was arrested and imprisoned (Taylor and Quayle, 1994).

In extreme cases, it is also possible for an individual to wage a one-person terrorist campaign. The question of whether these so-called 'lone-wolf' extremists should be regarded as terrorists is contentious. Brian Jenkins (2000) memorably said that 'flaming bananas' and not 'lone wolves' was a much better description for such isolated actors. Hidden within Jenkins' assessment though is the conclusion that the lack of a group is a sign that the person is in some way psychologically impaired or deviant. But the evidence to support this view is not clear-cut. Bearing in mind the widespread errors made in judging terrorist psychology elsewhere, one should be very cautious in assuming that lone-actor terrorism is the work of 'crazies' rather than of people who are genuinely politically motivated. The fact that many ideologies actually encourage the emergence of lone-actor campaigns of violence should add even further caution to assumptions of abnormality. For example, the American far-right's concept of 'leaderless resistance' explicitly endorses a philosophy of individuals (or small groups) mounting operationally independent campaigns of violence for ideologically similar reasons. The concept was first pushed in books such as *The Turner Diaries* but has now been taken up and advocated very strongly on the Internet as well (Silke, in press). As a result of this, the far-right has a particular potential to produce lone-actor terrorism, as was demonstrated by Timothy McVeigh's devastating attack on the Murrah building in Oklahoma City in 1995, or David Copeland's one-man racist nail-bombing campaign in London in 1999.

Fortunately, such individuals are currently a rarity. The enormous risks and demands of engaging in a terrorist campaign present formidable obstacles. Failure to be accepted into an existing terrorist group will for most individuals witness the end of their ambition to become a terrorist. Though their desire for revenge may lead to a few crude attacks against the perceived persecutor, one or two acts of retributive violence are usually sufficient to resolve the dissonance of the catalyst event, and the lack of a formal group to support and encourage the effort will usually see a lone individual's motivation and commitment quickly peter out.

CONCLUSION

> Both moral value judgements and psychiatric diagnoses can serve as excuses with which to justify the unwillingness to listen to, and take seriously on its own terms, what another person says, to think what it means to that person, and to do the difficult and often emotionally painful work that genuine understanding requires (Gilligan, 2000, p. 258).

Closeted as we are in our generally stable and peaceful societies, joining a terrorist group for most of us is seen as a dramatic, alien and highly deviant decision. Yet many communities view such decisions in the same way that Western society views the decision of a young person to join the police or the military. It is not a choice most young people will make, but neither is it seen as especially strange or bizarre (even though these jobs can be dangerous, unpleasant and difficult). For terrorists, their supporters and the communities around them, becoming a terrorist is not a deviant or aberrant act. Rather, terrorist recruits are often seen entirely as normal, transparent and unremarkable members of their communities, and the decision to join—while not always endorsed—can still be seen in sympathetic and understanding terms.

When terrorist violence erupts within our more placid world, we can struggle to gain an accurate grasp of where the perpetrators are coming from. As Gilligan noted, it can take truly emotionally painful work to reach a genuine understanding of terrorists and their motivations. Abhorrent condemnation is so much easier than the search for open understanding. The realisation that terrorist psychology is not significantly different from anyone else's is a cause for both hope and despair. It gives hope because it highlights the crucial role the environment plays in determining whether people become terrorists or not. If a combination of belonging to an aggrieved group and the experience of violent injustice are such common factors in the backgrounds of terrorists, then there are two clear ways to tackle the problem. First, the genuine grievances of minorities should be tackled in a fair and balanced manner. Second, the authorities should take clear action to prevent catalyst events from happening. Many terrorists report that it was violence committed by police officers or soldiers that acted as the final push for them to approach and join a terrorist group. If the security forces can show disciplined restraint when dealing with aggrieved groups, then they can help reduce the level of hostility emerging from disputes.

The despair in recognising that terrorist psychology is just like that of everyone else is the realisation that in the wrong circumstances most people could either come to support a terrorist group or possibly even consider joining one. If you, your loved ones and your community were discriminated against, persecuted by the authorities, intimidated, injured or killed, then terrorism may seem an appropriate and justified response. As Cota-McKinley, Woody and Bell (2001) sombrely observed: 'The motives of deterrence, restoration of self-worth, and elimination of perceived injustice are persistent human motives, surviving despite social taboo and legal denial, and are unlikely to fade into social obscurity' (p. 344). Happily, most of us will never live in such circumstances and will never have to face such choices.

Terrorism is a very old and very persistent problem. It emerges again and again simply because human nature is what it is, and the circumstances that produce it continue to occur across time and geography. Usually terrorist violence is a symptom of other more fundamental problems. A good appreciation of the psychology of terrorists, though, can open up genuine avenues for lasting peace. One can only hope that events like September 11 will encourage a wider appreciation of the knowledge that we currently have, rather than simply ingrain further the myths and innuendo that have dominated for so long.

REFERENCES

Bruce, S. (1992). *The Red Hand: Protestant Paramilitaries in Northern Ireland.* Oxford: Oxford University Press.

Collins, E. (with McGovern, M.) (1997). *Killing Rage.* London: Granta Books.

Cooper, H.H.A. (1977). What is a terrorist: a psychological perspective. *Legal Medical Quarterly*, **1**, 16–32.

Corrado, R.R. (1981). A critique of the mental disorder perspective of political terrorism. *International Journal of Law and Psychiatry*, **4**, 293–309.

Cota-McKinley, A., Woody, W. and Bell, P. (2001). Vengeance: effects of gender, age and religious background. *Aggressive Behavior*, **27**, 343–50.

Crenshaw, M. (1981). The causes of terrorism. *Comparative Politics*, **13**, 379–99.

Crenshaw, M. (1983). The psychology of political terrorism. In M.G. Hermann (Ed.), *Political Psychology: Contemporary Problems and Issues*. London: Jossey-Bass.

Ferracuti, F. and Bruno, F. (1981). Psychiatric aspects of terrorism in Italy. In I.L. Barak-Glantz and C.R. Huff (Eds), *The Mad, the Bad and the Different: Essays in Honor of Simon Dinitz* (pp. 199–213). Lexington, MA: Heath.

Gilligan, J. (2000). *Violence: Reflections on Our Deadliest Epidemic*. London: Jessica Kingsley.

Hassan, N. (2002). An arsenal of believers: talking to the 'human bombs'. Paper presented at the International Society of Political Psychology Conference, 16–19 July, Berlin, Germany.

Hollin, C., Browne, D. and Palmer, E. (2002). *Delinquency and Young Offenders*. Oxford: BPS Blackwell.

Hubbard, D. (1978). Terrorism and protest. *Legal Medical Quarterly*, **2**, 188–97.

Human Rights Watch/Helsinki (1992). *Children in Northern Ireland: Abused by Security Forces and Paramilitaries*. London: Human Rights Watch.

Jenkins, B. (2000). Opening address. Paper presented at the Terrorism and Beyond Conference, 17 April, Oklahoma City, USA.

Junger-Tas, J. (1994). *Delinquent Behaviour Among Young People in the Western World*. Amsterdam: Kugler.

Kim, S. and Smith, R. (1993). Revenge and conflict escalation. *Negotiation Journal*, **9**, 37–43.

Laqueur, W. (2001). Left, right and beyond: the changing face of terror. In J. Hoge, Jr, and G. Rose (Eds), *How Did This Happen? Terrorism and the New War* (pp. 71–82). Oxford: Public Affairs.

Lasch, C. (1979). *The Culture of Narcissism*. New York: W.W. Norton.

Lyons, H.A. and Harbinson, H.J. (1986). A comparison of political and non-political murderers in Northern Ireland, 1974–84. *Medicine, Science and the Law*, **26**, 193–98.

McKeown, L. (2000). Taking up arms. In M. Smyth and M. Fay (Eds), *Personal Accounts from Northern Ireland's Troubles* (pp. 51–62). London: Pluto Press.

Moffitt, T. (1993). Adolescence-limited and life-course-persistent antisocial behaviour: a developmental taxonomy. *Psychological Review*, **100**(4), 674–701.

Morf, G. (1970). *Terror in Quebec—Case Studies of the FLQ*. Toronto: Clark, Irwin.

Morrissey, P. (2000). That was the last time I seen him. In M. Smyth and M. Fay (Eds), *Personal Accounts from Northern Ireland's Troubles* (pp. 103–10). London: Pluto Press.

Pomerantz, J. (2001). Analyzing the terrorist mind. *Drug Benefit Trends*, **13/12**, 2–3.

Post, J. and Denny, L. (2002). The terrorists in their own words. Paper presented at the International Society of Political Psychology Conference, 16–19 July, Berlin, Germany.

Rasch, W. (1979). Psychological dimensions of political terrorism in the Federal Republic of Germany. *International Journal of Law and Psychiatry*, **2**, 79–85.

Rutter, M., Giller, H. and Hagell, A. (1998). *Antisocial Behavior by Young People*. Cambridge: Cambridge University Press.

Schmid, A.P. and Jongman, A.J. (1988). *Political Terrorism*, 2nd edn. Oxford: North-Holland Publishing Company.

Sharrock, D. and Devenport, M. (1997). *Man of War, Man of Peace? The Unauthorised Biography of Gerry Adams*. London: Macmillan.

Silke, A. (1998). Cheshire-Cat Logic: the recurring theme of terrorist abnormality in psychological research. *Psychology, Crime, and Law*, **4**(1), 51–69.

Silke, A. (1999). Ragged justice: loyalist vigilantism in Northern Ireland. *Terrorism and Political Violence*, **11**(3), 1–31.

Silke, A. (in press). Here be dragons? Assessing the true nature of the cyber-terrorist threat. *International Review of Law, Computers & Technology*.

Smith, D. (1996). Unholy Peace, *Sunday Times*, 7 January 1996, p. 17.

Stuckless, N. and Goranson, R. (1992). The vengeance scale: development of a measure of attitudes toward revenge. *Journal of Social Behaviour and Personality*, **7**, 25–42.

Taylor, M. (1988). *The Terrorist*. London: Brassey's.

Taylor, M. and Quayle, E. (1994). *Terrorist Lives*. London: Brassey's.

Temple, W. (2000). In the minority. In M. Smyth and M. Fay (Eds), *Personal Accounts from Northern Ireland's Troubles* (pp. 63–73). London: Pluto Press.

Tudge, C. (2002). Natural born killers. *New Scientist*, **174**(2342), 36–39.

Vohryzek-Bolden, M., Olson-Raymer, G. and Whamond, J. (2001). *Domestic Terrorism and Incident Management: Issues and Tactics*. Springfield, IL: Charles C. Thomas.

CHAPTER 3

The Psychology of Hostage-Taking

MARGARET WILSON

University of Kent at Canterbury, UK

INTRODUCTION

This chapter provides an overview of the areas in which psychological research can contribute to understanding terrorist hostage-taking. The study of hostage-taking, as with terrorism in general, has been cross-disciplinary and therefore this review includes a variety of material relating to psychological issues, whether written by psychologists or not. It sets out the scope of research directions, rather than attempting to analyse any one area in depth.

Figure 3.1 provides a summary model of the stages of hostage-taking following the temporal frame of the incident (down the page). The three main parties involved in the process are represented by three columns across the page. The psychological issues that arise at each stage are summarised within the model, and the principal phases of interaction between the parties are indicated with arrows. The chapter reviews the areas where psychology is relevant at each phase of the incident, some of which are covered in more depth in other chapters of this book.

For the purposes of the present review, an incident is described as 'hostage-taking' where the abduction takes place in order to extract some form of concession in return for the safe release of the hostages. Thus, the capture of the hostages is taken to be planned, rather than resorted to when another form of action has failed, for example where hostages are

Terrorists, Victims and Society: Psychological Perspectives on Terrorism and its Consequences.
Edited by Andrew Silke. © 2003 John Wiley & Sons, Ltd.

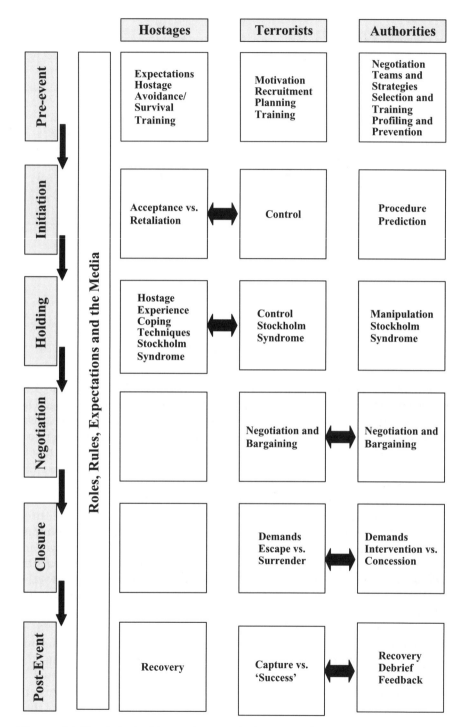

Figure 3.1 Psychological issues in terrorist hostage-taking

taken to exact a means of escape. Thus, a taxi driver hijacked for the use of his or her car, or indeed the passengers on board the planes crashed on September 11, would not be considered hostages in the current definition, although some of the issues raised here may well be equally relevant.

There are three forms of hostage-taking: hijacking, barricade-siege and kidnapping. Following Corsi (1981), Wilson and Smith (1999) summarise the distinguishing features of each strategy in terms of the number of hostages, whether or not they are targeted (named) individuals, the mobility of the event and whether or not the location of the hostages is known to the authorities. On occasion, the strategies may be mixed, for example where hostages are successfully removed from a building under siege and taken to an unknown location. However, generally the strategy chosen remains stable. It also seems to be the case that many terrorist organisations choose (or avoid) either hostage-taking as a strategy in general, or the type of hostage-taking chosen in particular (Wilson, Canter and Smith, 1995).

PRIOR TO THE INCIDENT

Hostages Prepare: Hostage Avoidance/Survival Training

Before the event takes place the hostages will, of course, be unaware of their forthcoming role. However, there are those who are known to be 'at risk' of capture by the nature of their job or location, for example embassy staff, military personnel and prominent figures visiting high-risk destinations. It might be argued that anyone who gets on a plane could consider themselves at risk. Little is known about the extent to which such considerations feature in people's decisions to fly, however Gray and Wilson (under review) show the deterrent effect of the events of September 11, 2001 on people's intentions to travel. The role of expectations on people's behaviour is considered more fully at the end of this chapter.

Those considered to be at risk by virtue of their position may be offered hostage avoidance/survival training. This will include advice about varying everyday routines and frequently travelled routes to avoid easy targeting. They may also receive training in coping techniques and may take part in sometimes highly stressful simulations. Kentsmith (1982) highlights the training value of learning about the experiences of ex-hostages. He sets out the qualities of those most likely to survive lengthy capture in a military context, from which he extrapolates to other types of hostage. Good physical health is an important prerequisite, and a strong sense of identity helps to preserve a sense of self-worth. Kentsmith claims that people who have experienced success, with purpose and meaning in their lives, and have lived a rich, full and satisfying life, stand up better to the hostage experience, where isolation leads to reflection on previous successes and failures.

Hostage training may also involve techniques of 'personalisation' based on the idea that identification with a 'person' will make it more difficult for hostage-takers to carry out any threats against the hostage's life. For this reason, potential hostages may be trained in techniques such as constructive interaction with the hostage-takers. Another example is the recommendation that potential hostages carry photographs of their family (whether or not they have one) that can be produced and talked about with their captors (see 'The Stockholm Syndrome', pp. 63–66). Whilst these techniques may prove valuable, hostage-taking incidents vary tremendously in terms of the nature of the interaction between hostages and hostage-takers, and as Hillman (1981) points out with respect to hostages' experiences of a violent and chaotic prison riot incident, there are occasions where the recommendation to relate to the captor is just 'impractical'.

Authorities Prepare: Training and Intelligence-Gathering

Negotiation Teams and Strategies

Being prepared in the event of a hostage-taking incident is clearly very important to the authorities. Training in readiness for terrorist attacks of all sorts will have been undertaken and procedures will be in place to deal with a potential hostage-taking incident. Those who will be responsible in the event of an incident will have already been determined, as will the command structure and the likely negotiators. Whilst the involvement of psychologists or psychiatrists is commonplace, the exact role that they should play has been controversial. Many authors caution against the assumption that because the psychologist is an expert in other forms of 'aberrant behaviour', he or she will have any special knowledge about those who take hostages (Wardlaw, 1983). Indeed, some have gone as far as to say that psychologists could even be harmful in a hostage-taking situation (Powitzky, 1979).

Wardlaw (1983) points out the difficulty psychologists have in predicting the dangerousness of their own patients in hospital, and since there is no scientific data on which to make their predictions, psychologists must rely on their own experience. If that is the case, then Wardlaw (1983) states that the team might as well rely on law-enforcement personnel who have more experience of being confronted by threatening and possibly violent individuals. Ebert (1986, 1988), however, sees no reason why psychologists should not be involved in negotiation, provided they have received proper training, and points out that it is probably cheaper to train psychologists as negotiators than law-enforcement personnel as psychologists.

Wardlaw (1983) further states that bad consultations with psychologists may make decision-makers more reluctant to use psychologists in more appropriate roles. These he outlines as, for example, counselling the participants following the event, developing decision-support systems, monitoring the stress levels of the negotiation team, evaluating the procedures, training and preparedness of the authorities, training hostage negotiators, gathering information from hostages, perpetrators and other contacts, and of course doing background research that can contribute to the knowledge base for decision-makers in the future. Davidson (1981), Fuselier (1981) and Soskis (1983) all agree with Wardlaw, arguing for roles other than simply in direct negotiation.

The negotiation literature is extensive and a thorough review is beyond the scope of the present chapter. Aside from the vast social psychological literature on decision-making and consensus in general, research specific to hostage-taking has ranged from analysis of participants' behaviour using computer-based hostage-incident simulations (Kraus and Wilkenfeld, 1993; Kraus *et al.*, 1992; Santmire *et al.*, 1998), to the analysis of actual negotiation behaviour in training simulations (Donohue and Roberto, 1993) and to the analysis of transcripts of negotiations during genuine incidents (Donohue and Roberto, 1996). Researchers who have tested theoretical models against actual transcripts conclude that there are important differences between the interactions of simulated and genuine incidents (Donohue and Roberto, 1996; Holmes, 1997). Further, even where transcripts of genuine incidents are used, these are typically criminal and domestic incidents rather than those involving terrorists, and as Donohue, Ramesh and Borchgrevink (1991) point out, different communication strategies appear to be characteristic of different types of hostage-taker.

Several authors have developed frameworks for defining the success of the negotiation interaction (e.g. Fowler, De Vivo and Fowler, 1985; Noesier, 1999) and researchers have established that there is an empirical link between various types of communicative behaviour and outcome (e.g. Donohue and Roberto, 1993; Olekalns and Smith, 2000). Recent research by Taylor (2002; under review) integrates the approaches of the past into models based on empirical data from genuine incidents with easily identifiable practical implications.

Profiling and Prediction

The idea that terrorists can be profiled is one that has been very popular for many years and continues to be seen as a role for forensic psychologists (see Chapter 1 for more on this). Numerous attempts have been made to set out the characteristics of terrorists in general and those that engage in various forms of action, for example left-wing versus right-wing. However, there are a number of problems with this type of approach, most of which apply to offender profiling in general.

First of all, profiles may be speculative rather than based on empirical data, typically being based on the clinical experience of the profiler, and as such as open to the usual cognitive biases (Tversky and Kahneman, 1973, 1974). Canter (2000) has proposed an empirical approach whereby data is gathered on the background characteristics of known offenders along with data on behaviour at the scene. This enables statistical relationships between offender behaviour and offender background to be derived allowing for prediction.

Secondly, profiles can be criticised for containing information that is not useful to investigators. For example, profiles may provide information that appears to be useful, but which is simply 'base-line'. Consider the following 'profile' of the possible characteristics of a rapist:

> *He is likely to be aged 20 to 35, with a record of low-status jobs and periods of unemployment. He is probably separated or divorced, and living in rented accommodation. He is likely to be sexually promiscuous and is prone to heavy drinking and / or drug use.*

Initially this profile may sound valuable to investigators. However, in reality, this information comes from Farrington's (1990) influential longitudinal study of those involved in crime, and describes the likely characteristics of all offenders. It is simply base-line information and adds no new information about the likely characteristics of this particular offender.

Generally, attempts have been made to derive common characteristics of terrorists from data drawn from interviews with those captured. Psychologists might interview known terrorists about their background and motivations, or assess their psychological make-up through clinical interviews. For example, in one of the earliest attempts to profile 'skyjackers', Hubbard (1971) draws his conclusions from interviews with known offenders. The commonalities he noted included a violent, often alcoholic father, a deeply religious mother, first sexual encounters with older women, protective attitudes towards younger sister/s and poor achievement, financial failure and limited earning potential.

However, the base-line problem is easily identifiable in this profile. Clearly there may be very many people who have these characteristics and do not become hijackers. It would be more valuable to identify why these particular people felt they had no alternative but to take a plane in order to advance their cause. A third criticism of profiles is that they can include information that is neither useful nor testable, for example the offender's likely fantasies or the nature of relationships with others.

Strentz is well known for his work on hostage-taking and presents quite detailed profiles of left- and right-wing terrorists, considering how the characteristics of the individuals involved have changed over a period of some 20 years (Strentz, 1988). The advantage of Strentz's approach is that rather than trying to generalise across many types, he breaks down the types into 'leaders' and 'followers' and those promoting left- and right-wing causes. He also concentrates on 'tangible' information rather than oblique psychological qualities that are hard to measure and can make no real contribution to detection.

Here, however, the difference between profiling a terrorist and profiling a rapist, for example, is important. The rapist profile is used to prioritise suspects where the offender is unknown. In most hostage-taking incidents the perpetrator is not only known, but present. Perhaps the most convincing argument for profiling terrorists is so that a better understanding can be gained of the likely perpetrators, in order that effective negotiation strategies can be employed. But here again there is little convincing scientific basis for matching strategies to perpetrator types, unless clearly mentally ill (Strentz, 1986). It seems unlikely that knowing the socio-demographic background, fantasies and so on of the 'typical' hostage-taker will really have any merit in the limited interaction of the negotiation. Instead, efforts would seem to be much better employed by focusing on techniques that would develop a good rapport with the particular individual at the time.

Finally, what speculative profiles might be used for must be considered. The idea of profiling terrorists is also open to the rather sinister implication of predicting who might become involved in terrorist action. If generalised base-line profiles are employed, this may put many innocent people under considerable suspicion. The way in which governments handle suspected terrorists has been shown to relate directly to the incidence of terrorist action. Hayes and Schiller (1983) report that there is indeed an empirical link between tough treatment of terrorist suspects and an increase in terrorism. In contrast to the 'tough measures' talked of by many of today's governments, Hayes (1991) reports on the success that some governments have had in employing amnesty and leniency strategies in getting less committed members to co-operate with the authorities, resulting in an overall decrease in terrorist action. Furthermore, whilst many governments have a no-concessions policy with respect to hostage-taking, some claim that this does not serve as a deterrent (Jenkins, Johnson and Ronfeldt, 1977).

Hostage-Takers Prepare

The starting point for considering terrorist preparation is in the motivation to become involved in terrorist action and the processes through which recruitment takes place. However, this applies to terrorist action in general, rather than to hostage-taking per se, and is covered elsewhere in this book. Nevertheless, it may be considered that taking part in hostage-taking missions requires more commitment to the cause, as the likelihood of capture is greater than in actions such as bombings and shootings. Evasion of capture is more likely in kidnapping incidents than the other two strategies and Corsi (1981) estimates that 83 per cent of kidnappers have escape plans.

Most of the pre-event behaviour of the terrorists is unknown, but Wilson and Smith (1999) claim that much can be inferred from their subsequent behaviour, for example motivations relating to the nature of the target and the demands issued, and planning in terms of how well organised the group is. The level of resources in terms of manpower, intelligence and weaponry have also been related to planning (Overgaard, 1994; Wilson and Smith, 1999) although in practice Wilson (2000) demonstrates that, with respect to incidents of barricade-siege, there are a limited number of combinations of resource that are actually employed.

Finally, behavioural data on the way incidents are actually carried out may prove useful for intelligence-gathering. For example, Wilson (2000) demonstrated that behavioural similarities exist in barricade-siege incidents carried out by groups known to have been training together in the 1970s.

DURING THE INCIDENT

Initiation

During the opening stages of the incident, the hostage-takers must assert control to ensure the compliance of the hostages. It is at this stage that injuries and fatalities within the hostage group are the most likely to occur at the hands of the hostage-takers. The way that the hostages behave at this point may therefore play the most important role in determining their fate. It has been argued that the most 'professional' groups will try to avoid any kind of harm to the hostages as this will deter public sympathy for the cause (Rubin and Friedland, 1986). Empirical analysis shows that it is indeed rare for hostages in hijacking incidents, for example, to be harmed by the hostage-takers, particularly in operations conducted by the larger and more established terrorist groups. Instead, the most likely time for hostage death or injury is during any kind of rescue attempt or intervention on the part of the authorities (Wilson, Canter and Smith, 1995).

At the onset of the incident, the authorities must initiate their set procedures and put training into practice. Any intelligence on the group must be gathered and predictions made about how dangerous the perpetrators are likely to be, as compared to their readiness to negotiate. From here onwards, models that predict the escalation or outcome of hostage-taking incidents could play a vital role in developing decision-support systems.

Prediction of Outcome

In addition to models of negotiation process and outcome discussed earlier, several attempts have been made to predict the outcome of hostage-taking incidents from facets known about the events surrounding the incidents themselves. Most of the empirical research into the prediction of outcome has relied, at least initially, on the influential ITERATE data set (Mickolus, 1982). For example, Sandler and his colleagues (Atkinson, Sandler and Tschirhart, 1987; Lapan and Sandler, 1988; Sandler and Scott, 1987) have successfully modelled the interaction between the hostage-takers and the authorities in terms of an economic bargaining framework (see 'Demands and Concessions', pp. 68–69). Similarly, Friedland and Merari (1992) analysed 69 incidents of hostage-taking and examined the factors that had a greater association with violent versus non-violent endings. They found that the factors most associated with violent endings were major international incidents where the strategy chosen was non-mobile, the presence of explosives or grenades, deliberate hostage execution, and the availability of a trained rescue team.

These models have been criticised, however, first for combining all three forms of hostage-taking (Hayes, 1991; Wilson, 2000), second for assuming that what the terrorists asked for was what they actually wanted (Mickolus, 1987), and thirdly, in Friedland and Merari's (1992) case, for combining violent outcomes that were initiated by the terrorists with those that were initiated by the authorities (Wilson, 2000).

Wilson (2000), again working initially from the ITERATE data and related publications, set out to overcome some of these problems. Her approach involved modelling aspects of the terrorists' behaviour, such as access to resources and demands, and using the resulting structures to develop potential models for prediction (again see 'Demands and Concessions', pp. 68–69). However, Wilson's (2000) work highlights one of the greatest problems for this type of work. Whilst the ITERATE data sets have undoubtedly been a great asset to researchers for development and modelling, and quality news coverage as used by Wilson (2000) can be helpful in adding detailed behavioural information, the fact remains that the resulting models are always based on incomplete data, since access to the fullest accounts available has not been possible for security reasons.

Holding

The Stockholm Syndrome

Very little is actually known about the Stockholm Syndrome though much has been written on the subject. Also known as Hostage Identification Syndrome (HIS), it is characterised by a 'bond' that sometimes develops during the holding phase of hostage-taking, whether unidirectional or reciprocated. The Stockholm Syndrome was named following a bank robbery that occurred in Stockholm, Sweden, on 23 August 1973, where four bank employees were held hostage for 131 hours (Strentz, 1979). The employees were found to fear the police more than the hostage-takers, and on release felt no negative feelings towards their captors.

The existence of the Stockholm Syndrome has become so ingrained in beliefs about hostage-taking that it has filtered through to public consciousness and made several appearances in film over recent years, from *The Crying Game* to *A Perfect World*, and is explicitly incorporated into the plot of a recent James Bond film, *The World is Not Enough*. I have published elsewhere my disbelief in this phenomenon as a clinical 'syndrome' in hostage-taking, preferring a social psychological interpretation in terms of 'script breakdown' and a return to ordinary scripts of social interaction (Wilson and Smith, 1999). Nevertheless, whatever HIS represents, it is seen as a real effect and is widely believed in and acted upon by the authorities. Perhaps the reason that HIS has been the focus of so much debate is because it has tangible implications for all concerned.

Much of what has been written on HIS is drawn from the experiences of negotiators (e.g. Kuleshnyk, 1984) and reports from and observations of hostages following their release. However, some attempts have been made to measure the effects of HIS in controlled simulations. For example, Auerbach *et al.* (1994) report the results of six simulated hostage incidents where (volunteer) airline employees were held hostage by FBI agents role-playing terrorists for some four days. Both parties were asked to complete measures of the perceived dominance and affiliation in the other at various stages in the simulation. Whilst the ecological validity of this simulation is clearly a problem, the authors report that those trained in emotion-focused (compared to problem-focused) coping strategies seemed to fare better overall.

Speculation as to the roots of HIS have focused on a variety of clinical interpretations, including psychodynamic theories of attachment. Turner (1985) states that the pressure of the uncertainty of life or death, along with 'helplessness and loss of control, leads to a variety of coping mechanisms including denial, repression, and identification' (p. 707).

Turner (1985) has set out the seven factors that he believes influence the development of the syndrome. The first two relate to the nature of the interaction between the hostages and the hostage-takers. First, he states that there must be face-to-face contact between the parties involved. Secondly, the hostages and hostage-takers must share a language. In support of this he cites the 1977 Japanese Red Army hijacking where only those who spoke Japanese were affected by HIS. These factors, then, account for the necessary basis of communication between the parties involved. The third factor concerns the nature of the pre-existing belief systems of those involved with respect to one another. Thus, where there are pre-existing prejudicial stereotypes the syndrome is unlikely to develop.

Turner also highlights the nature of any violence on the part of the hostage-takers. Some may assume that any kind of violence towards the hostages would prevent the bond from developing. However, Turner hypothesises that rather than the occurrence of violence per se, it is the nature and reason for any violence that is important in determining the outcome. For example, he claims that violence during the initiation of the incident is not preventative of HIS as it is a necessary means of establishing control. On the other hand, any unwarranted violence, such as the deliberate mistreatment of the hostages, may result in no attachment developing. For example, on occasion where a hostage is killed, the other hostages have reported that they 'deserved it' as they had attempted to destabilise the situation.

It is often assumed that it is the hostages that identify with the captors, and indeed attempts to explain the syndrome in terms of dependency may require this to be the case. However, as Turner points out, it is also possible not only for both sides to develop a bond with one another, but for the attachment to be solely in the direction of the hostage. Turner (1985) cites examples of captured diplomats, where guards were seen to develop HIS. He states that identification 'will move in the direction of the person who has strong beliefs and can articulate them in a nonhostile fashion' (p. 709). This of course makes sense where the guards are usually 'followers', and possibly are less likely to be as committed to or as articulate about the cause (Strentz, 1988).

Turner points out that whether or not the syndrome develops can be determined by the parties' knowledge of and intention to allow or prevent its occurrence. The hostage preparedness training techniques discussed earlier illustrate how the hostages themselves may attempt to encourage the bond to form in order to improve their own chances of survival. Likewise, there are measures that the authorities may adopt in order to achieve these same ends. For example, the authorities may manipulate interaction between the parties by sending in food that has to be divided up and shared between them. For the hostage-takers, there are less clear-cut pros and cons to the development of HIS. On the one hand, its development ensures that the hostages are easily controlled and unlikely to attempt to subvert the operation. On the other hand, HIS may prevent the hostage-takers from carrying out any threat against the hostages' lives. There is a negative side for the authorities too; the development of HIS may well mean that hostages cannot be relied upon to co-operate with the authorities in any intervention plans. The development of HIS has also been suggested to affect the response of the hostages on release, and has been cited as the reason that some hostages report positive feelings towards the hostage-takers' cause. This can be seen as an advantage in terms of publicity for the hostage-takers themselves, and, of course, on occasion as a disadvantage to the authorities.

Related to the notion of manipulation is Turner's final factor: time. It is widely believed that the longer the siege goes on the more likely the syndrome is to develop, perhaps because of the increased chances of positive interaction. This is a principle that may tempt negotiation teams to let the incident run a little longer in order that the syndrome develops. However, Turner points out that whether time acts as a contributory factor depends on the other factors present. For example, if positive communication structures exist with the group, then time may increase the likelihood of HIS developing, whereas where negative structures are in place then extra time can have little, or even an adverse, affect. Clearly this caveat should be taken into account by authorities which plan to manipulate HIS to their advantage.

Turner's account, though unsubstantiated by empirical evidence, appears the most logical perspective on HIS and is not at odds with Wilson's and Smith's (1999) interpretation in terms of 'script breakdown'. The factors cited would also determine the likelihood of a return to normal scripted social interaction in the event of hostage script breakdown.

The Hostages' Experience

Allodi (1994) characterises the experiences of those taken hostage as sensory deprivation, fear of death, powerlessness, worthlessness, dehumanisation, conflicts and feelings of ambivalence towards the other parties. Kentsmith (1982) provides a detailed breakdown of the likely experiences of hostages, although his analysis is based on hostages kept in solitary confinement for lengthy periods of time. He claims that the first stage is characterised by feelings of isolation, which is followed by a search for meaning in terms of why the hostage has been taken captive. Analysis of 'why me?' issues may be accompanied by feelings that the hostage has deserved this in some way. Furthermore, hostages may reflect on their life to date and wish that they had spent the time more productively. During the ensuing loneliness and boredom, the captive will be likely to recall everyday information and facts learnt (and thought forgotten) in detail, and experience vivid dreams and fantasies. It is at this stage that Kentsmith (1982) claims that the hostage will come to terms with his or her loss of freedom and the real possibility of death. In the subsequent stages, ritual behaviours may emerge in an attempt to impose organisation on the world and to mark the passing of time. Finally, the hostage enters a more positive stage where, through analysis of life events and experiences, an 'inventory' of assets and responsibilities is produced and detailed plans for life after release are formed, bringing with them hope for the future.

The Role of the Media

A great deal has been written about the role of the media in terrorist activity and it applies as much, if not more, to hostage-taking incidents. Hostage-taking incidents usually take place over an extended timescale in comparison to incidents such as bombings and shootings, and therefore provide better opportunity for media involvement. Some have claimed that the media play a role in encouraging incidents to take place and without media coverage hostage-takers' desire for publicity would not be met (e.g. Martin, 1985; Rubin and Friedland, 1986).

Rubin and Friedland (1986) cite the example of the hijacking of the *Achille Lauro* off the Mediterranean coast where the inaccessibility of media coverage led to the mission being, for the terrorists, a 'flop on the high seas' (p. 26). They claim that far more attention can be attracted with plane hijackings, since the media can have live access and there is often 'drama' brought about by changing locations and countries.

In addition to actually fuelling terrorists' desire for publicity, the media may influence future actions, in terms of 'contagion'. Not only may 'successful' tactics be re-employed by the same groups (Hayes, 1982), but these tactics may be imitated by others (Oots, 1986). In this way, then, the media have been criticised for supporting the terrorists' needs through extensive coverage of their actions. Whilst much research has been directed towards the electronic media, the print media have been equally criticised with, for example, Nacos, Fan and Young (1989) illustrating the high proportion of coverage devoted to the 1985 TWA hijacking in leading US newspapers.

If the media really do encourage terrorist action, this has clear policy implications in terms of news blackouts. However, some would argue that according to the laws of 'substitution', when one strategy fails terrorists will simply switch to one that is more effective in terms of their aims. For example, Landes (1978) demonstrates the decline in hijacking in the US following the installation of metal detectors in airports, whilst Lacquer (1987) demonstrates the subsequent increase in embassy sieges corresponding to this decline.

This debate centres on the publicity resulting from the actions of terrorists. However, the media are sometimes used quite directly in hostage-taking incidents, where the hostage-takers' demands involve publicity via the media, for example the publication of manifestos or statements in the press, or the delivery of statements on television. Bahn and Louden (1999) urge caution in the way that journalists are allowed to interact with the hostage scene. They claim that some journalists, 'in their naivete or in response to their professional duties, could make serious mistakes' (Bahn and Louden, 1999, p. 81). Furthermore, it is possible that reporters broadcasting events from outside the hostage incident may inadvertently alert hostage-takers to preparations for intervention.

Finally, a further area relating to the media has also received attention; the *way* in which incidents are reported. Much of this concerns the terminology employed by the press when referring to various actions taken by various parties. Numerous authors have pointed out the difference in terminology used when the writer is supportive or not supportive of the action (Clutterbuck, 1977; O'Brien, 1977; Schmidt and de Graaf, 1982) and some claim that this can influence the audience's response (Crenshaw, 1983). In terms of empirical studies, researchers have performed content analyses of media coverage and identified the terms employed. For example, Simmons (1991) examined coverage of terrorist events in US news magazines and found support for the hypothesis that more negative terminology is employed when the actions of terrorists are directed against US citizens.

Closure

Demands and Concessions

The close of the incident presents choices for the authorities and terrorists alike. The authorities must decide whether and when to intervene if they believe that the hostages are in danger. It has already been noted that the most dangerous stage of the hostage-taking incident in terms of loss of lives in general, and those of the hostages in particular, is when intervention takes place. The authorities must weigh up whether they can risk the negative publicity of not 'saving' the hostages, or risk the negative publicity of people being killed or injured during a 'bungled' rescue attempt.

Where no concessions are being granted by the authorities, the terrorists must decide whether to surrender or carry out their threats. On occasion terrorists have been known to be prepared to die with the hostages, for example by blowing up the plane or building with themselves inside as well as the hostages. This is, however, considered to be very rare. Corsi (1981) estimates that only 1 per cent of terrorists are actually suicidal and that whilst many claim to be prepared to die, few actually are (see also Strentz, 1988).

Perhaps the ideal outcome for the terrorists is to obtain concessions and negotiate a 'Bangkok Solution', that is, safe passage in return for the release of the hostages. Despite the number of governments who issue no-concessions statements, a surprising number of hostage-taking incidents do end with some concessions being made, although this varies by region. Some demands are met more frequently than others. Release of prisoners is frequently requested but rarely granted, whereas money, publicity and travel (safe passage) are more likely to result in concessions (Waugh, 1982).

Sandler and his colleagues (Atkinson, Sandler and Tschirhart, 1987; Lapan and Sandler, 1988; Sandler and Scott, 1987) have cast the hostage negotiation in an economic bargaining framework in order to test predictions as to whether the demands of the hostage-takers are met. They found that concessions were more frequently granted when hostage-takers had issued two or more demands and where no hostages had been killed. Whilst it seems reasonable that the more demands issued, the more likely some are to be met, it depends on what those demands are. It may be the case that only minor demands are met. Also of interest were the factors that had no influence on the concessions granted. Allowing deadlines to pass, holding US hostages, the number of hostages held and hostage release and substitution did not appear to impact on the authorities' decision to concede (at least in part) to the terrorists' demands.

Whilst predicting the response of authorities is of interest, as discussed earlier in this chapter, predicting what the hostage-takers will do is of more operational value. With this in mind, Wilson (2000) set out to examine whether there was any structure to what hostage-takers ask for. Wilson examined the demands issued in 100 instances of international hijackings, occurring worldwide over three decades. She found five core demands that were most frequently issued. Firstly, demands were regularly made concerning the release of prisoners. Two types are distinguished: the demand for the release of specific named prisoners, usually members of the organisation who had been captured in earlier operations, and the release of general sets of unnamed prisoners, for example all Palestinians held in Israeli jails. Publicity was also a frequent demand, whether in the form of published manifestos or broadcast statements, as was travel, for its own sake rather than for purposes of evading capture on surrender (safe passage). Finally, the demand for money was also central, that is, money for the hostage-takers themselves rather than the more infrequent 'Robin Hood ransom' of money for others.

Wilson (2000) analysed the overlap between the demands in terms of which were most likely to be issued in conjunction with one another. She found that there was remarkable consistency in the pattern of demands issued. For example, it was very rare for both the release of general and specific prisoners to be demanded, as was the combination of travel and publicity. Using these two dimensions Wilson proposed a model whereby incidents can be classified as 'global' (general prisoners) vs. 'strategic' (specific prisoners) and 'internally' (travel) or 'externally' (publicity) motivated. The remarkably structured pattern to the demands issued is hypothesised to relate to underlying psychological dimensions, and Wilson suggested that it may be possible to use such structures to help predict the outcome of hostage events. However, research to test this idea has not yet been published.

AFTER THE INCIDENT

Hostage Recovery

Clinicians have written about how to deal with released hostages, both in the periods immediately following release and in the coming weeks of therapy. McDuff (1992) reports on his own experiences of providing support to victims of terrorist hostage-taking incidents from the large and fragmented group released from Pan Am Flight 73 in 1986, through the US hostages on board the *Achille Lauro* in 1985, to a single Beirut hostage released in 1986. McDuff (1992) stresses the importance of trying to maintain a cohesive support group around the hostages and briefing them on the possibility of a phenomena termed 'Symond's second injury' whereby victims are subjected to rejection and isolation on their return to normal society. Winther and Petersen (1988) stress the importance of keeping the hostage group together and of providing immediate physical comfort as they will be in shock. They report that the hostages have strong needs immediately after release for physical contact and talking through their experiences with one another. In the following days they observed that the hostages had a marked need to construct justifications for their behaviours to one another, and that there was fear of not having done enough to attempt to secure the group's release.

Research on the long-term aftermath of hostage-taking incidents has mainly focused on the recovery patterns of the hostages, rather than the other players. Allodi (1994) describes the stages of recovery as: denial and avoidance of recalling the experience, acceptance with experience of grief and depression, and finally recovery and integration.

Studies of actual hostages are rare, with implications frequently being drawn from the experiences of those held captive as prisoners of war or victims of the holocaust. Ex-hostages who have been studied include those used as 'human shields' in Kuwait (Bisson, Searle and Srinivasan, 1998), prison officers held hostage during a riot by inmates (Hillman, 1981), victims of a hostage-taking incident carried out by Lebanese refugees in Denmark (Winther and Petersen, 1988), and adolescent high-school pupils held hostage by Palestinian gunmen in Israel (Desivilya, Gal and Ayalon, 1996). Studies where measurements of hostage recovery are employed have focused on follow-up assessments of post-traumatic stress disorder (PTSD) symptoms, indicating that most hostages still experience some symptoms many years after the event. Desivilya, Gal and Ayalon (1996) found that the majority of the 59 victims who participated in their study were still experiencing some PTSD symptoms 17 years after the incident took place. They found that exposure to the incident in terms of the stage at which they were released had no effect on the severity of symptoms at follow-up, but that the severity of the injuries they had sustained did in fact affect this.

Whilst all agree on the negative consequences, there are some references to positive outcomes. For example Van der Ploeg (1989) reported that in addition to the usual symptoms of PTSD, almost half of the hostages and their families could see positive value in the experience. Similarly, Bisson, Searle and Srinivasan (1998) report that among the negative symptoms of the British Military hostages held in Kuwait, 14 per cent reported better family relations and 57 per cent a more positive outlook, claiming that the experience had helped them to gain a better perspective on things or get their priorities right. This accords with Kentsmith's (1982) analysis of the stages of hostage experience, where a detailed analysis of life's achievements and priorities is frequently undertaken.

Definitions of Success

There has been some debate about what constitutes a successful operation on the part of the terrorists. Sandler and Scott (1987) distinguish between 'logistic success' and 'strategic success'. Logistic success is easily measured as it depends on the mission being carried out according to plan. However, strategic success is a more difficult concept, relying as it does on knowing what it is that the terrorists hoped to achieve. There has been some debate over what the demands actually mean to the terrorist hostage-taker. If the demands are met, are we to see the operation as a success? Conversely, if the demands are not met, does this really mean that the terrorists regard the event as a failure? Mickolus (1987) cautions against taking the demands as indicative of what the hostage-takers actually want, and Hayes (1991) agrees that rather than looking at the success of single incidents we must consider the bigger picture in terms of the overall campaign.

As previously discussed, many claim that the publicity surrounding the event is the primary aim for many hostage-takers (e.g. Martin, 1985; Rubin and Friedland, 1986). Some also claim that the goal of terrorist action is to create fear, and at the very least disruption. Friedland and Merari (1985) take the stance that whilst terrorist actions do create fear, they do not change attitudes to the cause. Illustrating their point through studies of attitudes in Israel, they demonstrate that despite years of living with the threat of terrorism, many Israelis do not sanction concessions over the Palestinian issue. For example, in the study, 75 per cent believed that the Palestine Liberation Organization (PLO) should not be recognised as the official Palestinian representative, and 68 per cent did not believe the Palestinians should have an independent state. Furthermore, support for counter measures was high with, for example, 71 per cent of university-educated respondents supporting demolition of houses, rising to 86 per cent of those educated to elementary-school level. However, this study is now quite old and a great deal has happened in the region since.

COMMON THEMES AND CONCLUSIONS

Throughout this review two principal areas of psychology have emerged: clinical and social psychology. Whilst researchers from both fields should be working towards developing our background knowledge of psychological issues in hostage-taking, only clinical psychologists seem able to present a case for active involvement in terrorist incidents. For example, clinical psychologists have a clear role to play in training both hostages and hostage negotiators in techniques for coping under pressure and threat. Furthermore, clinical contributions can be seen as invaluable in dealing with the aftermath of hostage-taking events, working with all three parties in coming to terms with what has happened. On the other hand, social psychology has a great deal to offer in providing an understanding of hostage-taking incidents in terms of the behaviour of all of the participants.

On the whole, the respective research contributions from these disciplines are complementary. However, there are areas where clinical and social psychologists may have competing theories on hostage behaviour. This should not be seen as disadvantageous; different interpretations lead to debate, and debate can lead to advancement of our understanding. The Stockholm Syndrome is one such area for debate. Wilson and Smith (1999) propose that like other social interactions, hostage-taking conforms to scripted behaviour patterns (Abelson, 1981), with associated role and rule structures. They claim that since it is rare to have actually taken part in a hostage-taking incident, people's hostage-taking scripts must be socially constructed. Furthermore, when these social constructions break down for some reason, Wilson and Smith (1999) describe the outcome as a return to normal principles of social interaction, and hence on occasion the unexpected positive interactions associated with the Stockholm Syndrome.

However, if people at least attempt to adhere to socially constructed scripts for hostage-taking incidents, the issue arises of how they come by these scripts. Here again some themes emerge from the present review. Those at risk of hostage-taking and those responsible for managing the incident (and possibly the hostage-takers themselves) are exposed to others' previous experiences and therefore given ready-made scripts from the trainers' perspective. But the role played by the media, through both journalistic and fictional accounts of hostage-taking incidents, must not be overlooked. For example, examining passenger behaviour in hijacking incidents, Wilson (in press) questions how the events of September 11 may have changed hostage-taking scripts for everyone concerned, and analyses the possible implications for future incidents.

In summary, the present review has set out the range of research directions that have developed with respect to terrorist hostage-taking. However, there still remain very many questions only partially answered and some completely unanswered, leaving plenty of scope for future research with important implications.

REFERENCES

Abelson, R.P. (1981). Psychological status of the script concept. *American Psychologist*, **36**, 715–29.

Allodi, F.A. (1994). Post traumatic stress disorder in hostages and victims of torture. *Psychiatric Clinics of North America*, **17**(2), 279–88.

Atkinson, S.E., Sandler, T. and Tschirhart, J. (1987). Terrorism in a bargaining framework. *Journal of Law and Economics*, **30**, 1–21.

Auerbach, S.M., Kiesler, D.J., Strentz, T. and Schmidt, J.A. (1994). Interpersonal impacts and adjustment to the stress of simulated captivity: an empirical test of the Stockholm Syndrome. *Journal of Social and Clinical Psychology*, **13**(2), 207–21.

Bahn, C. and Louden, R.J. (1999). Hostage negotiation as a team enterprise. *Group*, **23**(2), 77–85.

Bisson, J.I., Searle, M.M. and Srinivasan, M. (1998). Follow-up study of British Military hostages and their families held in Kuwait during the Gulf War. *British Journal of Medical Psychology*, **71**(3), 247–52.

Canter, D. (2000). Offender profiling and criminal differentiation. *Legal and Criminological Psychology*, **5**, 23–46.

Clutterbuck, R. (1977). *Guerrillas and Terrorists*. Athens: Ohio University Press.

Corsi, J.R. (1981). Terrorism as a desperate game: fear, bargaining and communication in the terrorist event. *Journal of Conflict Resolution*, **25**(1), 47–85.

Crenshaw, M. (Ed.) (1983). *Terrorism, Legitimacy and Power*. Middletown, CT: Wesleyan University Press.

Davidson, G.P. (1981). Anxiety and authority: psychological aspects for police in hostage negotiation situations. *Journal of Police Science and Administration*, **9**, 35–38.

Desivilya, H.S., Gal, R. and Ayalon, O. (1996). Extent of victimization, traumatic stress symptoms, and adjustment of terrorist assault survivors: a long-term follow-up. *Journal of Traumatic Stress*, **9**(4), 881–89.

Donohue, W.A. and Roberto, A.J. (1993). Relational development as negotiated order in hostage negotiation. *Human Communication Research*, **20**(2), 175–98.

Donohue, W.A. and Roberto, A.J. (1996). An empirical examination of three models of integrative and distributive bargaining. *International Journal of Conflict Management*, **7**(3), 209–29.

Donohue, W.A., Ramesh, C. and Borchgrevink, C. (1991). Crisis bargaining: tracking relational paradox in hostage negotiation. *International Journal of Conflict Management*, **2**(4), 257–74.

Ebert, B.W. (1986). The mental health response team: an expanding role for psychologists. *Professional Psychology Research and Practice*, **17**(6), 580–85.

Ebert, B.W. (1988). The Mental Health Response Team for hostage situations. In P.A. Keller and S.R. Heyman (Eds), *Innovations in Clinical Practice: A Source Book*, Vol. 7. Sarasota, FL: Professional Resource Exchange, Inc.

Farrington, D.P. (1990). Implications of criminal career research for the prevention of offending. *Journal of Adolescence*, **13**, 93–113.

Fowler, R., De Vivo, P.P. and Fowler, D. (1985). Analyzing police hostage nego-
tiations: the Verbal Interactional Analysis Technique. *Emotional First Aid: A
Journal of Crisis Intervention*, **2**(2), 16–28.
Friedland, N. and Merari, A. (1985). The psychological impact of terrorism: a
double-edged sword. *Political Psychology*, **6**(4), 591–604.
Friedland, N. and Merari, A. (1992). Hostage events: descriptive profile and anal-
ysis of outcomes. *Journal of Applied Social Psychology*, **22**(2), 134–56.
Fuselier, G.D. (1991). Hostage negotiation: issues and applications. In R. Gal, A.
Mangelsdorff and A. David (Eds), *Handbook of Military Psychology*. New York:
John Wiley & Sons.
Gray, J.M. and Wilson, M.A. (under review). The deterrent effect of September
11th 2001 on decisions to travel.
Hayes, R.E. (1982). *The Impact of Government Activity on the Frequency, Type and
Targets of Terrorist Group Activity*. McLean, VA: Defense Systems, Inc.
Hayes, R.E. (1991). Negotiations with terrorists. In V.A. Kremenyuk (Ed.), *Interna-
tional Negotiation: Analysis, Approaches, Issues*. San Francisco, CA: Jossey-Bass
Inc.
Hayes, R.E. and Schiller, T. (1983). *The Impact of Government Activity on the
Frequency, Type and Targets of Terrorist Group Activity: The Italian Experience,
1968–1982*. McLean, VA: Defense Systems, Inc.
Hillman, R.G. (1981). The psychopathology of being held hostage. *American Jour-
nal of Psychiatry*, **138**(9), 1193–97.
Holmes, M.E. (1997). Optimal matching analysis of negotiation phase sequences in
simulated and authentic hostage negotiations. *Communication Reports*, **10**(1),
1–8.
Hubbard, D.G. (1971). *The Skyjacker: His Flights of Fantasy*. New York:
Macmillan.
Jenkins, B.M., Johnston, J. and Ronfeldt, D. (1977). *Numbered Lives: Some Statis-
tical Observations From 77 International Hostage Episodes*. Santa Monica, CA:
Rand Corporation.
Kentsmith, D.K. (1982). Hostages and other prisoners of war. *Military Medicine*,
147(11), 969–72.
Kraus, S. and Wilkenfeld, J. (1993). A strategic negotiations model with
applications to an international crisis. *IEEE Transactions on Systems, Man and
Cybernetics*, **23**(1), 313–23.
Kraus, S., Wilkenfeld, J., Harris, M.A. and Blake, E. (1992). The hostage crisis
simulation. *Simulation and Gaming*, **23**(4), 398–416.
Kuleshnyk, I. (1984). The Stockholm Syndrome: toward an understanding. *Social
Action and the Law*, **10**(2), 37–42.
Landes, W.M. (1978). An economic study of US aircraft hijackings, 1961–1976.
Journal of Law and Economics, **21**, 1–31.
Lapan, H.E. and Sandler, T. (1988). The political economy of terrorism: to bargain
or not to bargain: that is the question. *AEA Papers and Proceedings*, **78**(2),
16–21.
Lacquer, W. (1987). *The Age of Terrorism*. Boston, MA: Little, Brown.
Martin, L.J. (1985). The media's role in international terrorism. *Terrorism: An
International Journal*, **8**(2), 127–46.
McDuff, D.R. (1992). Social issues in the management of released hostages.
Hospital and Community Psychiatry, **43**(8), 825–28.
Merari, A. and Friedland, N. (1985). Social psychological aspects of political terror-
ism. In S. Oskamp (Ed.), *International Conflict and Public Policy Issues: Applied
Social Psychology Annual*. Beverly Hills, CA: Sage.

Mickolus, E.F. (1982). *International Terrorism: Attributes of Terrorist Events, 1968–1977 (ITERATE 2)*. Ann Arbor, MI: Inter-University Consortium for Political and Social Research.

Mickolus, E.F. (1987). Comment-terrorists, governments, and numbers: counting things versus things that count. *Journal of Conflict Resolution*, **31**(1), 54–62.

Nacos, B., Fan, D.P. and Young, J.T. (1989). Terrorism and the print media: the 1985 TWA hostage crisis. *Terrorism*, **12**(2), 107–15.

Noesier, G.W. (1999). Negotiation concepts for commanders. *FBI Law Enforcement Bulletin*, **68**, 6–14.

O'Brien, C.C. (1977). Liberty and terrorism. *International Security*, **2**, 56–57.

Olekalns, M. and Smith, P.L. (2000). Understanding optimal outcomes: the role of strategy sequences in competitive negotiations. *Human Communication Research*, **26**, 527–57.

Oots, K.L. (1986). *A Political Organisation Approach to Transnational Terrorism*. Westport, CT: Greenwood Press.

Overgaard, P.B. (1994). The scale of terrorist attacks as a signal of resources. *Journal of Conflict Resolution*, **38**(3), 452–78.

Powitzky, R.J. (1979). The use and misuse of psychologists in a hostage situation: optimizing the use of psychological data. *Police Chief*, **47**, 28–31.

Rubin, J.Z. and Friedland, N. (1986). Theater of terror. *Psychology Today*, **20**(3), 18–28.

Sandler, T. and Scott, J.L. (1987). Terrorist success in hostage taking incidents: an empirical study. *Journal of Conflict Resolution*, **31**(1), 35–53.

Santmire, T.E., Wilkenfeld, J., Kraus, S., Holley, K., Santmire, T.E. and Gleditsch, K.S. (1998). The impact of cognitive diversity on crisis negotiations. *Political Psychology*, **19**(4), 721–48.

Schmidt, A. and de Graaf, J. (1982). *Violence as Communication*. Beverly Hills, CA: Sage.

Simmons, B.K. (1991). US newsmagazines' labeling of terrorists. In A.O. Alali and K.K. Eke (Eds), *Media Coverage of Terrorism: Methods of Diffusion*. Thousand Oaks, CA: Sage Publications, Inc.

Soskis, D.A. (1983). Behavioural scientists and law enforcement personnel: working together on the problem of terrorism. *Behavioural Sciences and the Law*, **1**(2), 47–58.

Strentz, T. (1979). The Stockholm Syndrome: law enforcement policy and ego defenses of the hostage. *FBI Law Enforcement Bulletin*, **48**, 2–12.

Strentz, T. (1986). Negotiating with the hostage-taker exhibiting paranoid schizophrenic symptoms. *Journal of Police Science and Administration*, **14**(1), 12–16.

Strentz, T. (1988). A terrorist psychosocial profile: past and present. *FBI Law Enforcement Bulletin*, **57**(4), 13–18.

Taylor, P.J. (2002). A cylindrical model of behavior in crisis negotiations. *Human Communication Research*, **28**(1), 7–48.

Taylor, P.J. (under review). A partial order of communication behavior with the prognosis of outcome.

Turner, J.T. (1985). Factors influencing the development of Hostage Identification Syndrome. *Political Psychology*, **6**(4), 705–11.

Tversky, A. and Kahneman, D. (1973). Availability: a heuristic for judging frequency and probability. *Cognitive Psychology*, **5**, 207–32.

Tversky, A. and Kahneman, D. (1974). Judgement under uncertainty: heuristics and biases. *Science*, **125**, 1124–31.

Van der Ploeg, H.M. (1989). Being held hostage in the Netherlands: a study of the long term effects. In J. Groebel and J.H. Goldstein (Eds), *Terrorism: Psychological Perspectives*. Sevilla, Spain: Publicaciones de la Universidad de Sevilla.

Wardlaw, G. (1983). Psychology and the resolution of terrorist incidents. *Australian Psychologist*, **18**, 179–90.

Waugh, W.L. (1982). *International Terrorism*. Salisbury, NC: Documentary Publications.

Wilson, M.A. (2000). Toward a model of terrorist behavior in hostage-taking incidents. *Journal of Conflict Resolution*, **44**, 403–24.

Wilson, M.A. (in press). Hostage behaviour in aircraft hijacking: a script-based analysis of resistance strategies. In R. Bor (Ed.), *Passenger Behaviour*. Ashgate: Aldershot.

Wilson, M.A. and Smith, A. (1999). Roles and rules in terrorist hostage taking. In D. Canter and L. Alison (Eds), *The Social Psychology of Crime: Groups, Teams and Networks*. Ashgate: Aldershot.

Wilson, M.A., Canter, D. and Smith, A. (1995). *Modelling Terrorist Behaviour*. Final Report to the US Army Research Institute. Alexandra, VA: ARI.

Winther, G. and Petersen, G.O. (1988). Group psychotherapy of terror victims. *Nordisk Psykiatrisk Tidsskrift*, **42**(1), 55–59.

CHAPTER 4

The Psychology of Cyber-Terrorism

MARC ROGERS

University of Manitoba, Canada

INTRODUCTION

The September 11, 2001 attack on the US has brought about a renewed interest in terrorism. However, terrorism is not a new phenomenon, or even a product of the twentieth century. It is important to understand that terrorism has been a part of society and the political landscape in one form or another for hundreds of years (e.g. thugs, assassins) (Crenshaw, 1990a; Hoffman, 1999; St John, 1991a). Terrorist activities have, out of necessity, evolved and adapted to accommodate changes in society (Lomasky, 1991). At the beginning of the twenty-first century, society is again evolving and changing. The latter portion of the twentieth century saw the rise of the information revolution. This information revolution has led not only to advances in technology, and to the creation of the Internet and cyberspace, but also to the phenomenon of what is now being called the 'virtual society' or the 'global community'. This community is having a large impact on our lives and is being populated by business, government, military and the public (North, 2000). As cyberspace evolves, terrorists are becoming increasingly aware of and interested in this new medium (Denning, 1999). Several factors, including the availability of targets, group ideology, the intended audience and the psychological make-up of the group and its members, influence the terrorist's interest in cyberspace (Clutterbuck, 1975).

Terrorists, Victims and Society: Psychological Perspectives on Terrorism and its Consequences.
Edited by Andrew Silke. © 2003 John Wiley & Sons, Ltd.

Although the primary focus of most discussions on cyber-terrorism are focused on attacks, this discussion, while including that element, will also examine other issues surrounding the terrorist's use of the Internet and technology. These issues include the general appeal of the technology, media attention and propaganda, communications, recruitment, justification and rationalisation, anonymity and target selection. An operational definition of cyber-terrorism will be introduced, to act as an anchor of sorts for the subsequent discussion. The chapter will conclude with a brief look at the potential impact of cyber-terrorist activity.

OPERATIONAL DEFINITION

To discuss cyber-terrorism it is necessary to define what the term means. An operational definition of a cyber-terrorist can be derived from combining the definitions used by the US Federal Bureau of Investigation (FBI) for a traditional terrorist with the components that make up cyberspace. For the purposes of this chapter, a cyber-terrorist will be defined as an individual who uses computer/network technology to control, dominate or coerce through the use of terror in furtherance of political or social objectives. From this definition it is apparent that cyber-terrorism incorporates elements of traditional terrorism with technology. With cyber-terrorism, the motivation for the attack is the same as that for traditional terrorism, but the medium for the attacks and the choice of victims shifts to technology, networks and computer systems.

Unfortunately, the popular media are guilty of misusing the term 'cyber-terrorism'. Cyber-terrorism is not merely the act of attacking some military or government information system. These attacks constitute a criminal act and as such the perpetrators are computer or cyber criminals. For the attack to be classified as terrorism it must have been orchestrated not only to cause fear and terror, but also to influence the opinions of both the public and government (Bandura, 1990b; Crenshaw, 1990a; Glover, 1991). To date, the majority of the documented attacks on government and military sites have been perpetrated by criminals with no real political motives (Rogers, 2000).

THE NATURE OF CYBER-TERRORISM

To understand the attraction of cyberspace for the terrorist, we need to understand the nature of traditional terrorism. Terrorism has been described as the deliberate use of violence or threat of violence designed to influence public and government opinion on political or societal issues (Hoffman, 1999; Lomasky, 1991; Rogers 1999a). The terrorist act traditionally incorporates violence and fear, and is designed to attract as much media attention as possible, thus allowing the terrorist's 'message' to be distributed to a large audience (Bandura, 1990b; Lomasky, 1991). Violence is a key component of traditional terrorism, so much so in fact that terrorism can be thought of as the deliberate and planned use of violence (Hoffman, 1999; Post, 1990). Despite this deliberate use of violence, the terrorist is generally not a deranged psychopath, but is more likely to be 'normal', calculating, and rational (Crenshaw, 1990a; Post, 1990). Terrorism is not based on ill-planned indiscriminate acts. The terrorist group's choice of targets, methods of attack and choice of weapons is a function of that particular group's dynamics, ideology and often the personalities of key individuals (Hoffman, 1999; Post, 1990). Terrorism is a very detailed and planned activity.

If the terrorists are not some deranged individuals, then who are they, and what motivates them to engage in such extreme behaviour? There have been various studies designed to identify a common terrorist psychological profile, however there does not seem to be any consensus on a single profile (Crenshaw, 1990a; Hoffman, 1999; Post, 1990). Studies have found that the motivation for becoming a terrorist, and for ultimately engaging in violent acts, seems to vary as much as the personalities of the terrorists themselves (Lomasky, 1991; Reich, 1990). Some studies suggest that among terrorists there is an over-representation of action-oriented, aggressive people who are stimulus hungry and seek excitement (Hoffman, 1999; Post, 1990). These individuals, when dealing with the world, tend to rely on the psychological mechanisms of externalisation and splitting. Externalisation refers to the concept of looking outside oneself for the source problems. Splitting refers to the splitting out and projecting onto other people the weaknesses they dislike within themselves (Post, 1990).[1]

Terrorist groups are also heavily motivated by the future outcomes of their acts (i.e. changing government policies, releasing political prisoners, sovereign independence). They look to the future as opposed to the past or the present for their reinforcement. This may be partially due to the fact that the present is often a time of conflict and turmoil for the group. This future orientation is illustrated in many of their manifestos and rhetoric.

Appeal of the Internet

In light of the 'war' on terrorism that resulted from the September 11 attacks, the threat of cyber-terrorism has set off alarm bells within governments and the counter-terrorism community. An 'electronic Pearl Harbour' and an 'electronic Waterloo' are just some of the terms that have been used to refer to the potential impact of a cyber-terrorist attack (Rogers, 1999b; Schwartau, 2000; Webster, 1999). Most analysts and to some extent governments recognise the fact that technology and its

---

[1] Chapters 1 and 2 in this volume tackle these issues in greater detail.

infrastructures are strategic and symbolic targets for criminals, terrorists and information warfare (Willemssen, 2001). In documents released by the US National Commission on Terrorism and by the US General Accounting Office, cyber attacks were considered in the same context as chemical, biological, radiological and nuclear attacks (CBRN). The US and other countries are spending millions of dollars increasing the security of their information technology infrastructure, and creating entities designed to specifically oversee cyber security.

It should come as no surprise that terrorist groups would embrace new technology and the advantages of the digitised global economy and community. The very benefits that the Internet brings to the business world, academia and society (anonymity, connectivity, the sharing of information and so on) fit the needs of terrorist organisations well (Denning, 1999). Criminals are already using the Internet as either a new medium to carry out their more traditional crimes (e.g. fraud, child pornography) or as a new target for criminal activity (e.g. denial of service attacks, web page defacements). Several aspects of the Internet are specifically suited to terrorism, and include the attention the media place on the Internet and information systems, the public relations and advertising capabilities, the anonymity of users, the ability to attack diverse targets globally, less violent types of attacks, and the potential impact due to the inherent vulnerabilities of the infrastructure.

MEDIA ATTENTION

The media play a significant role in terrorism. This fact was emphasised as the world witnessed the constant replaying of the videos showing the two planes striking the World Trade Center towers, and the massive media attention afforded Osama bin Laden and al-Qaeda. Terrorists use the media to deliver their message to a wide audience, thus increasing the fear or terror factor of the attack (Lomasky, 1991; Post, 1990; Reich, 1991). Both the public and the media give terrorist acts special attention. If a violent or destructive outcome is the result of some general criminal activity it does not get that much attention. However, if the outcome is the result of an act labelled as terrorism, it becomes the focus of attention. As Lomasky (1991) stated, the significance and attention given to terrorist acts is disproportionate to any measurable effect of these acts. Historically, few people are killed annually as the direct or indirect result of terrorist acts (Bandura, 1990b; Lomasky, 1991). Despite the attacks on New York, natural disasters and accidents still account for a more significant loss of life.

The media also pay a disproportionate amount of attention to attacks that use either the Internet as a medium or are targeted towards information systems. A terrorist attack directed at information systems, or using the Internet as an attack medium, would be a media bonanza. This type of attack would almost certainly assure the group responsible of a major media spotlight in which to deliver its message.[2] This fact is not lost on terrorist organisations that must come up with novel and creative acts to capture the fickle attention of the media and the public.

Arguably, the use of the Internet as a means of gaining attention is at a similar point to that of airline hijacking during the 1960s. The first terrorist groups to use airline hijackings soon found that not only could they affect several governments (due to international air travel), they could also gain incredible media attention. The role of the media in terrorism has caused much debate, and media attention has been heavily criticised as one of the factors that led to airline hijackings becoming the attack 'du jour' during the 1970s, 1980s and 1990s (Lomasky, 1991; St John, 1991b).

COMMUNICATIONS

Most modern terrorist organisations are made up of a collection of cells rather loosely networked with each other and spread out over large geographical areas. This structure, while affording a certain level of protection for the groups, results in an increased need to communicate in a non face-to-face manner. These distributed groups need to stay connected in order to plan and orchestrate attacks, obtain funding and in some instances obtain forged documents (e.g. visas, passports). The need to communicate is challenged by the need to keep the location and plans of a group secret. The very existence and success of these organisations is dependent upon good communications that do not tip off the various counter-terrorism and intelligence agencies that attempt to monitor the activities of the terrorists (Clutterbuck, 1975). The Internet and accompanying technology can meet the secure communications needs for these organisations extremely well. The use of encrypted communications, electronic funds transfers and public Internet kiosks allow members of the different cells to stay co-ordinated, funded and motivated to the cause while making detection and interception of their communications more difficult.[3]

---

[2]To date there have been few if any documented real cyber-terrorist attacks. Despite the popular media's assertions, merely attacking a government or military site does not qualify the attack as cyber-terrorism. The attack must fit into the definition of a terrorist act. This usually means the attack is motivated by the desire to influence or show support for some political or societal end.

[3]Evidence has suggested that the group responsible for the September 11 attacks made use of public kiosks in the days leading up to the attacks in order to co-ordinate the events; al-Qaeda members have been known to use encrypted email to communicate.

RECRUITMENT

For most terrorist groups to survive over extended periods of time, they must have a method of recruitment. The average life expectancy for a terrorist group is less than a year (Hoffman, 1999). Groups that hope to remain in existence for extended periods of time have an obvious need to replenish their numbers due to arrests, deaths and defections. The Internet will become an effective medium for attracting potential recruits (Silke, 2000). It has been estimated that by 2003 there will be in excess of 200 million users on the Internet (Schwartau, 2000). This provides for an extremely large pool of potential candidates to draw into the rank and file of disparate terrorist groups. The use of the Internet for recruiting purposes may also include enticing individuals into engaging in acts of individual civil disobedience or even terrorism, which for example would be in keeping with the philosophy of various far-right groups (Silke, in press).

The Internet reaches most of the world, and the demographics of the users may well fit the profile of the individuals terrorist groups are targeting for their ranks (e.g. young, middle-class and technologically savvy). The fact that the terrorist groups can appear 'hip' and leading edge by using the technology and the Internet is an added benefit in attracting candidates. In fact several terrorist groups already maintain web sites that, while designed to impart their rhetoric and solicit sympathy for their cause, also act as recruiting posters (Damphousse and Smith, 1998). A quick search for terrorist web sites using a common Internet search engine quickly throws up sites from groups such as the Ku Klux Klan (KKK), Hamas, Hezbollah, the Liberation Tigers for Tamil Eelam and others. Groups promoting civil disobedience, such as those involved in protests against international free-trade agreements, have also recognised the recruitment potential of the Internet, and have used it to rally both support and numbers for their protests (for example the World Trade Organization demonstrations in Seattle in 1999).

As Silke (in press) indicates, the Internet is well suited not only for recruiting but also for attracting 'soft supporters'. These individuals tend not to overtly demonstrate their support for the group by direct political or economic acts, but provide sympathetic communities within which terrorist groups can operate, thus increasing the already difficult job of counter-terrorist agencies (Damphousse and Smith, 1998; Silke, in press).

JUSTIFICATION AND RATIONALISATION

Attracting sympathy to the cause as well as providing a medium to justify their actions are important exercises for terrorist groups. As

Bandura (1990b) indicated, there is a need for terrorists to justify and rationalise the violent actions they engage in. According to Bandura's social-cognitive theory, people tend to refrain from engaging in behaviour that violates their own moral standards (Bandura, 1990a). Such actions would lead to self-condemnation and possibly self-sanctions. The theory holds that moral standards play the role of regulating our behaviours (Bandura et al., 1996). However, these standards do not necessarily function as fixed internal controls of behaviour. The self-regulatory mechanisms do not operate unless they are activated, and there are several methods by which the moral reactions can be separated from the inhumane behaviour (Bandura, 1990b). Social-cognitive theory refers to these as mechanisms of moral disengagement (Bandura, 1990b; Bandura et al., 1996).

The very nature of terrorism places terrorists in situations in which they engage in activities that are inhumane. For the terrorist to function he or she must be trained to use moral disengagement (Bandura et al., 1996; Post, 1990). Social-cognitive theory identifies several techniques commonly used in moral disengagement, including vilifying the victim (the victim deserved it or brought it on him- or herself), dehumanising the victim (stereotyping), describing their actions in euphemistic language (defeating their enemies), claiming the actions serve some higher moral or societal purpose (it is the will of some deity, or will hasten the return of their homeland), misconstruing the consequences of their actions (no one innocent will be hurt) or diffusing responsibility (usually through group membership) (Bandura, 1990b). Examples of these various mechanisms can be found in the terrorist community (Bandura, 1990b). The Internet and more specifically the World Wide Web provides an excellent platform for moral disengagement. Anyone can put a web site on the Internet and place whatever information they wish on it, no matter how inaccurate or false the information may be. There is no body that regulates web page content. By creating its own web site, the terrorist group has a worldwide medium to rationalise and justify its actions and present its flavour of the truth.

Targets that can be attacked via the Internet (information systems, networks and infrastructures) also allow terrorists to rationalise their behaviour. Attacking information or computer systems is drastically different from violent attacks on people, which cause death and injury. Placing a 'logic bomb' in a computer system could have incredibly damaging effects but, unlike the bombing of a subway or plane, the violence need not be measured in the number of people killed. However, the impact of the attack could have as large an effect (if not larger) on the public than the physical bombing of a structure, yet attacking information systems and computers does not carry the same moral baggage as killing people (Rogers, 1999b).

GROUP AND INDIVIDUAL ANONYMITY

Certain types of terrorist groups shun the limelight and prefer to operate either in the shadows or in relative obscurity (e.g. anarchists, religious extremists). Due to their extremist beliefs, they require anonymity to exist and operate in a society that may not agree with their particular ideology. The anonymity offered by the Internet is very attractive for these groups (Anderson and Hearn, 1997; Rogers, 1999a; Webster, 1999). Anonymity is useful for other reasons as well. It can be used to avoid sanctions while criticising the ruling government, and provides a certain level of covertness to the group that can be used to build up its membership to the point where it has sufficient numbers to become public.

The Internet can also provide a level of anonymity within the group itself. It is common within terrorist groups to have a certain level of segmentation (St John, 1997). The segmentation can be found between certain cells or cadres, and between individuals making up the hierarchy of the group. New recruits and foot soldiers are often segmented from the leaders and key people. Segmentation serves an important function by making it difficult for captured individuals to provide too much information to the authorities (St John, 1997). It also makes it difficult for counter-terrorist agencies to infiltrate the terrorist groups. The Internet can allow individuals or cells to operate separately from each other, yet still co-ordinate efforts and maintain a feeling of membership, albeit virtually (Rogers, 1999b).

From a social-psychology perspective, the concept of virtual membership may have an interesting effect on group attitudes and opinions, group decision-making, motivations to group action and diffusion of individual responsibility. Research on traditional group membership indicates that individual opinions and attitudes become more extreme (either radical or conservative) in a group context (Pynchon and Borum, 1999). Group membership can also lead to 'group think'. This phenomenon is characterised by excessive efforts to obtain agreement and a strong need for group consensus. This need can negatively impact the group's ability to make appropriate decisions (Pynchon and Borum, 1999). Groups often tend to see their actions as better and different than those of other groups. They also tend to view their members more positively, and hold that the positive behaviour is due to factors internal to the group (Pynchon and Borum, 1999). This behaviour is more commonly referred to as 'in-group/out-group bias'. Studies have also found that individuals tend to commit more violent acts as part of a group (Bandura, 1990b; Post, 1990; Zimbardo, 1969). This may be due to the process of deindividuation, which reduces the individual's feelings of responsibility, thus increasing the potential for antisocial behaviour (Zimbardo, 1969).

The dynamics of group membership applies to virtual membership as well (Postmes, Spears and Lea, 1999). In fact, given that virtual membership allows an individual to remain anonymous or 'pseudo anonymous' (using nicknames or handles), the effects of group think can be amplified, further reducing the accountability for violence by the individual.[4] Several social-psychology studies have documented an increase in aggressive behaviour when the subjects believed their identity was anonymous to the source of the aggression as well (Bandura, 1990a; Postmes, Spears and Lea, 1999; Zimbardo, 1969). These studies concluded that identification and personal accountability acted as constraints against individuals engaging in adherent and/or aggressive behaviour. Once these constraints were reduced below a certain level or eliminated completely, the rate of aggressive behaviour increased (Bandura, 1990b). Combining the factors of anonymity and group think, cyber-terrorists should have substantially fewer constraints on their behaviour.

ANONYMITY FOR ATTACKS

The ramifications of the anonymity offered by the Internet are far reaching. Law enforcement has already struggled with the legalities and technicalities of attempting to trace criminal acts to those individuals responsible. It is conceivable that less bold, fringe-like groups might be motivated to launch attacks if the fear of retaliation and retribution is drastically reduced (Rogers, 1999b). Due to the ubiquitous nature of the Internet, there are more and different targets available to the terrorist than in the past. This fact combined with the means to obscure the source of the attack may expedite the process of moving attacks from mere rhetoric to actual occurrence (Rogers, 1999a). This ability to operate in near obscurity has been hypothesised as a contributing factor in the increase of computer crimes over the past few years (Denning, 1999; Howard, 1997; Rogers, 1999b).

The anonymity of the Internet will also allow terrorists to broaden the scope of their attacks to victims whose governments have traditionally responded with force (Stern, 1999). Some governments have relied on this threat of retaliation as a means of deterrence (e.g. Israel and the US). The threat of aggressive retaliation for terrorist attacks is greatly reduced if the source of the attack cannot be traced. This traditional method of

---

[4] Pseudo-anonymous membership is one of the attractions that the Internet has for the hacker and phreaker communities. Individuals are able to be part of a group without actually revealing who they really are (Rogers, 2000). These individuals use 'nicknames' or 'handles' to identify themselves to the group.

deterring terrorism will have to be re-thought in light of the anonymity provided by the Internet.

The inability to trace the source of Internet-based attacks has so rattled the counter-terrorist community that several think-tanks such as Rand in the US have turned their attention from scenarios involving nuclear terrorism to scenarios involving cyber-terrorism and information warfare. The prevailing conclusion derived from these scenarios is that Internet-based attacks will be extremely effective and difficult to trace back to the source.[5] The difficulty in tracing arises because of the ability of attackers to fake or 'spoof' the source address of their attacks, making it appear that they are someone or somewhere else. Attacks can be disguised to appear as simple isolated incidents, and not co-ordinated attacks, until it is almost too late to respond effectively (Anderson and Hearn, 1997; Webster, 1999). The conclusions drawn from simulations and observed criminal attacks have led several governments to re-evaluate their approach towards non-traditional computer system defences (Willemssen, 2001; Rogers, 2000).

TARGETS

With society's increasing dependence on technology and the Internet, the very nature of targets for the terrorists has changed. The incredible rush towards everything 'e' (e-business, e-commerce, e-governments) has led to a situation in which new targets will be information systems and networks. It has been estimated that in 2003, business-to-business e-commerce revenue will be in the range of one trillion US dollars per year (McCabe, 1999). Most of the major banks in the world now incorporate some form of Internet-based banking, and the use of on-line credit-card purchases is increasing exponentially. Governments are rushing to become 'wired' in an attempt to increase efficiency and provide better access to public services.

The various public and private services being placed on the Internet are attractive targets for terrorists. In the rush towards technology and the Internet, many of the systems that place these services on-line have less than adequate security controls (Boas, 2000; Denning, 1999; United Nations, 1999). These systems perform functions such as stock exchanges and banking, housing sensitive personal information, assisting in troop deployment, controlling nuclear power plants, running air-traffic control and emergency services systems, and monitoring and controlling power

---

[5]The difficulty in tracing the source of Internet attacks has been clearly illustrated in several criminal Internet attacks and is a real problem for law-enforcement agencies.

grids. Governments are beginning to recognise the vulnerability of these systems, and have defined infrastructures that are critical and as such need to be afforded better protection. Critical infrastructures are commonly divided into five sectors: information and communication, banking and finance, energy (including oil, gas and electrical), physical distribution, and vital human services (Webster, 1999). Each of these sectors is a potential terrorist target.

The Internet is the 'glue' connecting the various infrastructures. The Internet can be conceptualised as the global network of networks—it links millions of individual computers and networks together. However, the Internet is a public, academic, business and government infrastructure all at the same time. All these different sectors share the same common infrastructure and protocols despite their vastly different security needs (i.e. critical business information, public information, credit-card data, email). Just as there are no geographical borders on the Internet, there are no clear lines of demarcation between business, military, public and academic systems. The same set of protocols that were originally designed to allow different computer systems to share information in a primarily academic environment is now being asked to protect other systems from attack.[6] However, the Internet was never designed for commercial or business use, and therefore never designed to be secure.[7] The inherent vulnerabilities of the Internet make it difficult to protect key systems, and as such open the door to terrorist attacks.

The ability to launch attacks that have a large impact on the public yet do not necessarily cause a loss of life puts a new face on terrorism. Traditional terrorism has used deliberate violence to shock the public and grab the world's attention. Extreme violence has in some cases resulted in a public backlash against the terrorist groups and in some instances hurt their cause (Crenshaw, 1990a; Glover, 1991; Post, 1990). Sympathy for a group's cause can be undermined by the public's anger over the loss of life of innocent victims, and terrorist groups that require the sympathy and protection of the people to operate have learned to be very selective in their attacks so as not to alienate their supporters (Reich, 1990). Terrorist groups that survive due to the sponsorship of certain countries also need to be concerned about falling out of favour with their state sponsors, private benefactors or other non-governmental organisations.

---

[6] A protocol is a set of agreed-upon rules for communication. The Internet uses Transmission Control Protocol/Internet Protocol (TCP/IP) as the foundation for moving data from one system to another.

[7] The original Internet was developed in the late 1960s and was known as the Advanced Research Project Network (ARPNET). Only four universities and a handful of defence sites were connected.

POTENTIAL IMPACT OF CYBER-TERRORISM

Perhaps the single most important factor that makes the Internet an attractive weapon for terrorism is the impact that cyber-terrorist attacks will have on society (Boas, 2000; Denning, 1999; Rogers, 2000; Schodolski, 2000). Successful criminal and nuisance attacks on air-traffic control systems, emergency services systems, stock exchanges and banks have already been documented. Fortunately, the majority of these attacks have been perpetrated by rather unsophisticated youths with very limited skills, motivated by ego and a desire to make headlines. However, the fact that these criminals successfully breached such important systems is very troubling. If these unsophisticated criminals with only limited technical skills can get in, what damage might a highly motivated, well-funded terrorist group with state-of-the-art technology be capable of?

The impact of a successful cyber-terrorist attack will be extremely devastating not only in financial terms but also psychologically. The terror caused by such an act is due to the realisation that almost anyone can be a victim (Post, 1990). The feeling of vulnerability is amplified with the Internet, as most of the public does not understand the technology and many already mistrust it (Boni and Kovacich, 1999). Despite this mistrust, our personal information, bank accounts and credit-card numbers all exist on systems connected to the Internet. With the Internet, users are all potentially connected to one another, thus eliminating the safety of geographical distance (Denning, 1999). This fact literally confirms the fear that anyone could become a victim of an Internet-based attack in some form or another.[8]

The potential impact of cyber-terrorism is limited only by the imagination and technical skill of the terrorist wielding this new weapon. While criminals have illustrated the ease with which our critical infrastructures can be compromised, they have been reluctant to cross certain ethical boundaries (Denning, 1999; Rogers, 1999a; Schwartau, 2000). This very fact has mitigated the damage that has resulted from criminal acts in cyberspace to date. However, the terrorist ignores these ethical boundaries or dilemmas. The only real restraints are the motives and target audiences of terrorist groups (Damphousse and Smith, 1998).

A hypothetical scenario best illustrates the potential impact Internet-based attacks could have. While hypothetical, it is based on the documented, isolated breaches that each of the infrastructures have already suffered, albeit in a limited fashion. Imagine the impact of successful multiple physical and electronic attacks against the following critical infrastructure targets: a major stock exchange's information systems,

---

[8] Identity theft, when someone who has gathered enough information 'steals' your identity in order to commit some criminal act, is becoming more prevalent, and would be an effective tool for terrorists.

hydroelectric and natural gas lines and systems (during the winter), the systems of several telecommunications companies, air-traffic control systems at an international airport and the bombing of a commercial passenger plane all in the same geographic region.[9] As we have already witnessed with the September 11 disaster, simultaneous attacks are a real danger. Any one of the above attacks on its own would be devastating in terms of the potential for loss of life and economic loss, but combined they would be catastrophic as most disaster plans are developed to deal with one disaster at a time, not simultaneous occurrences.[10]

The inability to trade after an attack on the systems of a major stock exchange would cost millions of dollars to trading houses, brokers, individuals and companies. If the outage was long enough or the manipulation of prices severe enough, bankruptcies would follow, causing economic instability, possibly worldwide. The impact would be even greater if the attack was conducted during a period of economic slowdown (i.e. recession) and investor uncertainty. The disruption of hydroelectric, oil and natural gas flows either by physical attacks (e.g. bombing hydroelectric dams or high-voltage lines) or by knocking out the control and monitoring systems for a prolonged period of, say, one to two days would be disastrous. If these attacks were conducted during the cold winter months in certain parts of the world, there would exist a real danger of people freezing to death. Without telecommunications, the ability of the emergency services organisations to respond effectively if at all would be severely crippled, compounding the impact of the other attacks. The world has witnessed the effect of physical attacks on commercial airlines either through hijacking, bombings or the combination of both. If these attacks were combined with disrupting air-traffic control for even a few minutes this would be even more disastrous and multiply the loss of life. Disrupting air-traffic control would almost certainly impede the recovery process from the other attacks, as supplies and assistance could not be flown into the affected region. The total impact of such a successful compound attack would rival many of the plots found in the disaster-movie genre of Hollywood and eclipse the death toll of any terrorist incident to date.

CONCLUSION

The threat of cyber-terrorism is very real and will likely manifest itself in the next few years (Denning, 1999; Rogers 2000). As the traditional targets

---

[9] I have purposely left out nuclear power plants and bio-terrorism (anthrax, smallpox, etc.) in order not to be accused of complete fear-mongering, but these targets would be logical as well.

[10] To comprehend just how bad things could get, imagine the September 11 attacks on the US and several of the much hyped Y2K fears actually happening at the same time.

of terrorism migrate into cyberspace, so too will the terrorists. Cyberspace lends itself well to use as a weapon and medium for terrorism. We have already seen some criminal elements in society embrace the Internet as a new frontier for continuing or inventing new criminal acts (Denning, 1999; Rogers, 1999a; Schelling, 1991). Cyberspace and the Internet are well suited to the nature of terrorism and the psyche of the terrorist (i.e. the ability to cause fear and terror within the public via media attention), and their use will not be restricted to any particular category of terrorist group (for example ethno-nationalists, fundamentalists, anarchists, left-wing or right-wing), although newer groups such as eco-terrorists who are not burdened by traditional infrastructures and methods will be quicker to use these new mediums in their repertoire. The Internet can be used as a medium to reflect the ideologies and motives of the terrorist groups and to reach their target audiences. The same aspects of cyberspace that make it attractive for individuals, businesses and governments also make it attractive for terrorists (for the purposes of information sharing, global communication, anonymity and connectivity).

The ability to remain anonymous and to obscure the true source of attacks makes the Internet even more attractive. No longer will the threat of swift and exacting retaliation by governments be an effective deterrent. Terrorists are no longer bound by geographical constraints, and will have the ability to strike at any target connected to the Internet from anywhere in the world. Psychologically, the cyber-terrorist will not be fundamentally different from the traditional terrorist. What will change is the choice of medium and targets.

As society becomes ever more reliant on technology and the Internet, we are literally placing most of our eggs into one basket. Terrorists now have the unprecedented ability to disrupt our lives, hold information hostage, and/or cause widescale damage by attacking just a few non-human targets that comprise single points of failure within our technology infrastructures (Denning, 1999; National Commission on Terrorism, 2000; Rogers 1999a). The ability to have such a large impact on society without necessarily inflicting loss of life will change the nature of the terrorism of the future.

REFERENCES

Anderson, R. and Hearn, A. (1997). *An Exploration of Cyberspace Security RandD Investment Strategies for DARPA: The Day After...in Cyberspace II*. Santa Monic, CA: Rand.

Bandura, A. (1990a). Mechanisms of moral disengagement. In W. Reich (Ed.), *Origins of Terrorism: Psychologies, Ideologies, Theologies, States of Mind* (pp. 161–91). New York: Cambridge University Press.

Bandura, A. (1990b). Selective activation and disengagement of moral control. *Journal of Social Issues*, **46**, 27–46.

Bandura, A., Barbaranelli, C., Caprara, G. and Pastorelli, C. (1996). Mechanisms of moral disengagement in the exercise of moral agency. *Journal of Personality and Social Psychology*, **71**, 364–74.

Boas, T. (2000). Information warfare and cyberterrorism: combating cyber threats in the new millennium. As viewed on 3 August 2000, *www.ceip.org/programs/info/infowar.htm*.

Boni, W. and Kovacich, G. (1999). *I-way Robbery: Crime on the Internet*. Boston, MA: Butterworth-Heinemann.

Crenshaw, M. (1990a). Questions to be answered, research to be done, knowledge to be applied. In W. Reich (Ed.), *Origins of Terrorism: Psychologies, Ideologies, Theologies, States of Mind* (pp. 247–60). New York: Cambridge University Press.

Crenshaw, M. (1990b). The logic of terrorism: terrorist behaviour as a strategic choice. In W. Reich (Ed.), *Origins of Terrorism: Psychologies, Ideologies, Theologies, States of Mind* (pp. 7–24). New York: Cambridge University Press.

Clutterbuck, R. (1975). *Living with Terrorism*. New York: Arlington House Publishers.

Damphousse, K. and Smith, B. (1998). The internet: a terrorist medium of the 21st century. In H. Kushner (Ed.), *The Future of Terrorism: Violence in the New Millennium* (pp. 208–24). London: Sage Publications.

Denning, D. (1999). *Information Warfare and Security*. New York: ACM Press.

Glover, J. (1991). State terrorism. In R. Frey and C. Morris (Eds), *Violence, Terrorism and Justice* (pp. 256–75). New York: Cambridge University Press.

Hoffman, B. (1999). The mind of the terrorist: perspectives from social psychology. *Psychiatric Annals*, **29**, 337–40.

Howard, J. (1997). *Analysis of Security Incidents on the Internet*. Unpublished doctoral dissertation, Carnegie Mellon University, Pennsylvania.

Lomasky, L. (1991). The political significance of terrorism. In R. Frey and C. Morris (Eds), *Violence, Terrorism and Justice* (pp. 86–115). New York: Cambridge University Press.

McCabe, H. (1999). E-Biz Heavies Going Global. As viewed on 9 August 2000, *www.wired.com/news/business/0,1367,21731,00.html*.

National Commission on Terrorism (2000). *Countering the Changing Threat of International Terrorism*. Report of National Commission on Terrorism. Washington: National Commission on Terrorism.

North, G. (2000). Y2K and cyber-terrorism. As viewed on 7 August 2000, *www.garynorth.com/y2k/detail_.cfm/1780*.

Post, J. (1990). Terrorist psycho-logic: terrorist behaviour as a product of psychological forces. In W. Reich (Ed.), *Origins of Terrorism: Psychologies, Ideologies, Theologies, States of Mind* (pp. 25–42). New York: Cambridge University Press.

Postmes, T., Spears, R. and Lea, M. (1999). Social identity, normative content, and 'deindividuation' in computer-mediated groups. In N. Ellemers and R. Spears (Eds), *Social Identity: Context, Commitment, Content* (pp. 164–83). Oxford: Blackwell Science Ltd.

Pynchon, M. and Borum, R. (1999). Assessing threats of targeted group violence: contributions from social psychology. *Behavioral Sciences and the Law*, **17**, 339–55.

Reich, W. (1990). Understanding terrorist behaviour: the limits and opportunities of psychological inquiry. In W. Reich (Ed.), *Origins of Terrorism: Psychologies, Ideologies, Theologies, States of Mind* (pp. 261–80). New York: Cambridge University Press.

Rogers, M. (1999a). *Cybercriminals and Cyberterrorists*. Unpublished lecture notes, University of Manitoba, Winnipeg, Canada.

Rogers, M. (1999b). *Cyberterrorism and Computer Crime*. Presentation Department of National Defence Air Command, Winnipeg, Manitoba, Canada.

Rogers, M. (2000). *Information Security and Crime*. Presentation at ISACA Infosec Security Conference, Winnipeg, Manitoba, Canada.

St John, O. (1991a). *Air Piracy, Airport Security, and International Terrorism*. Westport, CT: Quorum Books.

St John, O. (1991b). Pilots and pirates: airline pilots and hijacking. In S.R. Deitz and W.E. Thoms (Eds), *Pilots, Personality, and Performance: Human Behaviour and Stress in the Skies* (pp. 167–84). New York: Quorum Books.

St John, O. (1997). *Lecture Notes: Intelligence, Espionage, and Terrorism*. Department of Political Science, University of Manitoba, Winnipeg, Canada.

Schelling, T. (1991). What purposes can international terrorism serve? In R. Frey and C. Morris (Eds), *Violence, Terrorism and Justice* (pp. 18–32). New York: Cambridge University Press.

Schodolski, V. (2000). US vulnerable to threat of cyberterrorism. As viewed on 7 August 2000, *www.freerepublic.com/forum/a36868166183b.htm*.

Schwartau, W. (2000). *Cybershock: Surviving Hackers, Phreakers, Identity Thieves, Internet Terrorists and Weapons of Mass Destruction*. New York: Thunder Mouth Press.

Silke, A. (in press). Here be Dragons? Assessing the true nature of the cyber-terrorist threat. *International Review of Law, Computers and Technology*.

Stern, J. (1999). *The Ultimate Terrorists*. London: Harvard University Press.

United Nations (1999). International review of criminal policy—United Nations manual on the prevention and control of computer-related crime. As viewed on 14 June 1999, *www.ifs.univie.ac.at/~pr2gq1*.

Webster, W. (1999). *Cybercrime, Cyberterrorism, Cyberwarfare: Averting an Electronic Waterloo*. Washington, DC: CSIS Press.

Willemssen, J. (2001). *Critical infrastructure protection: Significant challenges in protecting federal systems and developing analysis and warning capabilities*. Testimony before the Committee on Governmental Affairs, US Senate (GAO-01-1132T).

Zimbardo, P.G. (1969). The human choice: individuation, reason and order, versus deindividuation, impulse and chaos. In W.J. Arnold and D. Levine (Eds), *Nebraska Symposium on Motivation*, Vol. 17 (pp. 237–307). Lincoln, NB: University of Nebraska Press.

CHAPTER 5

The Psychology of Suicidal Terrorism

ANDREW SILKE

University of Leicester, UK

INTRODUCTION

Suicidal terrorism is not a new phenomenon. It has a history which can be traced back for thousands of years. For example, in the twelfth century an Islamic sect, the Ismal'ili Shi'ites, launched a 200-hundred-year-long campaign of terrorism using suicide attackers. Killing with daggers, lone assassins sacrificed themselves in ruthless attacks against the leaders and nobility of the age (Rapoport, 1990). Appalled at the Ismal'ilis' relentless willingness to sacrifice their own lives, observers argued that such behaviour must be unnatural. The belief quickly spread that the Ismal'ili used copious amounts of mind-altering drugs before launching their attacks, and in Arabic the sect came to be known as the *Hashiyan* ('those who eat hashish'). But the stories of drug use were untrue, and merely the malicious rumours and propaganda of enemies and onlookers who could not understand the willingness of the attackers to sacrifice their own lives in the effort to kill.

Today, rumour and innuendo still dominate public perceptions of suicide terrorists. Indeed, in Israel some elements of the popular press continue to push the idea that Palestinian suicide bombers take drugs or alcohol before they are sent to carry out the attacks. Just as with the *Hashiyan*, however, such stories are untrue. Extensive tests are carried out on the remains of suicide bombers by Israel's Institute of Forensic Medicine, and

Terrorists, Victims and Society: Psychological Perspectives on Terrorism and its Consequences.
Edited by Andrew Silke. © 2003 John Wiley & Sons, Ltd.

the Institute's director, Jehuda Hiss, has stated bluntly that the suicide terrorists are fully lucid at the moment of death. As he comments, tests show that in the bloodstream of the terrorists there is 'no alcohol, and no drugs known to us. We test them for cannabis, cocaine, amphetamines, opiates, and so on. They are motivated by some psychological motive prior to the suicide attack' (Goldenberg, 2002).

So what is the psychological motive that drives someone to become a suicide terrorist? In previous chapters we have seen that the vast majority of terrorists do not have a particular personality type. Neither do the vast majority of them suffer from mental illness. Instead, their involvement in political violence is a result of a series of understandable factors which combined result in a process of deepening involvement in violent extremism (as outlined in Chapter 2). But does this apply to suicide bombers as well? After all, extremely few terrorists take part in suicide operations. It is understandable to wonder what, then, marks these individuals out from their compatriots so that they are willing to carry out such profoundly extreme actions.

It is a little disconcerting to learn that, as with other terrorists, there is no indication that suicide bombers suffer from psychological disorders or are mentally unbalanced in other ways. In contrast, their personalities are usually quite stable and unremarkable (at least within their own cultural context). Indeed, Nasr Hassan, a researcher who lived and worked in the Palestinian territories for over four years (and who probably has had more contact with suicide bombers than any other researcher alive), commented that in her view there was very little difference between the young men who carried out suicide attacks and those who carried out shootings and other assaults where the attackers were intended to escape (Hassan, 2002).

It is increasingly recognised that it is a mistake to view suicide bombers simply as brainwashed pawns, but attempting to place all suicide terrorists into one clear category is far from easy. There is growing appreciation that just as there is wide variation in the general membership of terrorist groups, there can also be wide variation in the type of individuals who are prepared to carry out suicide attacks. Traditionally, the 'profile' of the typical suicide bomber was that he (they were almost always male) would be young, ranging in age from 16 to 28, from a poor background with a limited education. However, this stereotype has struggled to fit suicide terrorists more and more in recent years. For example, the September 11 hijackers came from generally middle-class backgrounds, were older than might have been expected, and many had third-level education. Within the Palestinian groups, the concept of the bombers being poorly educated young men from impoverished backgrounds has also been questioned. Certainly Hassan (2002) argues against such a view. She notes that while most of the suicide attackers are young men (with a few exceptions) they do not come from desperately poor backgrounds. In contrast, the majority of suicide bombers are from the Palestinian middle-classes. Most of the bombers have successfully finished second-level education and many were university students at the time of the attack (Hassan, 2002). Indeed, within Palestinian society it is the middle-class and those who have graduated from university who have generally shown the highest level of support and tolerance for suicide actions (Shiqaqi, 2001).

Stereotypical views are under pressure on the issue of gender as well. While it is true that the majority of suicide terrorists to date have been men, a surprisingly high proportion of attacks have been carried out by women. For example, roughly 15 per cent of suicide attacks in Lebanon have been carried out by women, in Sri Lanka between 30 per cent and 40 per cent of suicide terrorists have been women, while in Turkey over 66 per cent of suicide attacks involved female terrorists. This surprising prominence of women can be explained (at least partially) by operational advantages offered by females. Women arouse less suspicion than men and with strapped explosives arranged to make the woman look pregnant, female suicide terrorists can prove remarkably adept at avoiding security measures and checks (Schweitzer, 2001a).

THE QUESTION OF MOTIVATION

Why, though, would someone choose to be a suicide terrorist? It is certainly an extreme decision and it implies that rather extreme pressures were brought to bear in order to realise it. But what kind of pressures and from what direction? A simple explanation is that the terrorist groups coerce, cajole, intimidate and brainwash vulnerable members into carrying out these attacks. This explanation is often touted and is frequently offered by politicians and security personnel.

One terrorist group that does seem to have coerced members into carrying out suicide attacks is the Kurdistan Workers' Party, or PKK. The PKK has been involved in a long-running campaign of violence to create an independent Kurdish homeland, and since 1984 the group has been carrying out terrorist attacks towards this aim in Turkey. This has been a bloody conflict, resulting in over 35 000 deaths. In the 1990s, the Turkish authorities, backed by massive aid from the US, began a major and sustained crackdown on Kurdish extremists. As a result, the PKK began to struggle to maintain its campaign of attacks. In 1993, the Turkish authorities recorded 4198 'incidents' of PKK activity, including shootings, bombings, kidnappings, armed robberies and demonstrations. But by 1997 this level had fallen dramatically to only 1456 incidents, most of which were non-violent events (e.g. distributing leaflets).

In an effort to reverse this decline, a desperate leadership began to explore the possibility of using suicide tactics, and in 1995 came the group's first suicide attack. Over the following five years the group carried out 15 suicide attacks which combined killed 19 people (mainly policemen and soldiers) and injured a further 138. The PKK attempted a further six attacks but the bombers were intercepted before they could reach their targets (Schweitzer, 2001a).

It has to be said, though, that the Kurdish group's commitment to suicide attacks was always somewhat ambivalent. The organisation's leader, Abdullah Ocalan, viewed the use of suicide attacks as a high-profile warning to outsiders of the group's commitment to persevere and endure regardless of the obstacles it faced. However, the truth was that the movement's rank and file did not embrace the tactic in the same way as Palestinian and Lebanese groups to the south. Firstly, the PKK's use of suicide tactics was not especially successful. On average a PKK suicide attack would kill one person (apart from the bomber) and would injure 10 more, compared to the average Palestinian suicide attack which typically kills seven people and injures 30. Even the most successful PKK suicide attack failed to reach such a level of harm, and this poor track-record did little to increase enthusiasm for the tactics among PKK members. The return on the lives of the bombers was simply too low.

Dogu Ergil, a political psychologist based at Ankara University, has said that only one of the PKK's 21 suicide terrorists actually volunteered for the mission (Ergil, 2001). In order to get members to accept missions, he has argued that the group sometimes had to use severe measures. He describes the case of Leyla Kaplan, a young woman who carried out what was probably the PKK's most successful suicide bombing when she struck at a police building killing three officers and injuring 12 others. According to Ergil, Leyla was not a volunteer but was heavily coerced into carrying out the attack. The attack on the building had first been offered to another female PKK member, Turkan-Adiyaman, who declined. Her refusal to carry out the attack saw her executed, in front of Leyla Kaplan, who was then given the Hobson's choice of accepting the mission.

So not all suicide terrorists are volunteers. Indeed, it would be surprising if all suicide terrorists went to their deaths with equally high levels of confidence and certainty. Some variation and some doubt is to be expected, but this should not be overestimated. The practices of the PKK as described by Ergil stand very much at odds with those of the other terrorist groups that have carried out the vast majority of suicide attacks of the past decade. Such levels of coercion and intimidation are simply not a feature of how groups like Hamas, Hezbollah and the Tamil Tigers select and prepare individuals to take part in suicide operations. In most cases, the terrorist has either clearly volunteered for the mission or has accepted the task very willingly when offered the chance.

Potential bombers have nearly always had at least one relative or close friend who has been killed, maimed or abused at the hands of enemies (Kushner, 1996). These individuals join the various terrorist groups in an angry and vengeful frame of mind and already possess the intention of taking part in a suicide action. The groups do not coerce them into it. Again, Nasr Hassan's insight from her long research is valuable here. When asked about the psychology of suicide bombers she responded: 'What is frightening is not the abnormality of those who carry out the suicide attacks, but their sheer normality. They are so normal for their communities and societies' (Hassan, 2002). This is a theme reflected in the views of family members and friends. A mother of a suicide bomber said of her son: 'He seemed normal. There was nothing, and we never sensed he had such feelings. But from a religious point of view we have to accept he is a martyr and thank God' (Kushner, 1996, p. 335). It is now increasingly accepted that a spectrum of personalities is involved in suicide attacks, and there is no single easily explained personality type who is willing to volunteer for these missions.

Overall, then, almost all suicide bombers are volunteers who have chosen to carry out a suicide action even when other avenues for violence have remained open to them. Indeed, within the communities where suicide terrorists come from, the idea that they needed to be brainwashed or indoctrinated in order to carry out the attack is seen as ludicrous. On the contrary, leaders of terrorist groups are often instructed to turn away youths who wish to take part in suicide attacks. As one senior member of Islamic Jihad put it: 'Some of the youths insist they want to lead a suicide operation... My orders are to persuade them not to go, to test them. If they still insist they are chosen' (Kushner, 1996, p. 332). In the words of Nasr Hassan (2002), in order to get people to carry out suicide attacks 'you don't have to teach, you don't have to brainwash, you don't have to push, you don't have to pressure, it goes around by osmosis'.

Some sources have suggested that suicide bombers may suffer from low self-esteem and that a disproportionately high number come from broken families (Israeli, 1997). A lower self-esteem could lead to a greater willingness to contemplate making the supreme sacrifice in order to prove or redeem one's self-worth. Combined with the personal injuries and losses suffered at the hands of perceived enemies, this could provide the emotional energy and commitment to contemplate and carry through a suicide attack. Certainly, a low self-esteem among the perpetrators is something Israeli security forces sometimes describe in briefings on suicide attacks. However, the evidence for this line of thought comes mainly from a few interviews with suicide terrorists who were captured before they could carry out their operations. Nasr Hassan, who spent years meeting and talking with terrorists, including those who went on to carry out suicide operations, disagrees with the idea that suicide terrorists in general have low self-esteem. In her view, these individuals were normally 'model youth of their communities, known for being very helpful and very generous. They were invariably good students' (Hassan, 2002). Invariably, though, they also had in them a rage. Hassan recalled them saying to her: 'Do you see how we live?' They spoke frequently of the daily humiliations they endured, but Hassan saw this producing in them a great anger and a profound sense of injustice, not a diminishment in self-esteem.

The idea that they come from broken families is also debatable. Many suicide terrorists have come from stable family backgrounds and are surrounded by loving parents, siblings, spouses and children. Indeed, the treatment and suffering of family members can be a factor in encouraging people to become suicide bombers. In the words of one young Tamil man: 'I am thinking of joining [the Tamil Tigers]. The harassment that I and my parents have suffered at the hands of the army makes me want to take revenge. It is a question of Tamil pride, especially after so much sacrifice. There is no escape. One can't give it up now.' His brother had died in a suicide attack, and two other brothers had also died fighting for the Tigers. The boys' father said of the death of his sons: 'It was heartbreaking but I also knew that they had gone for a cause, for the country, for the people. I bore the sadness, with the thought that they were doing a very desirable thing' (Joshi, 2000).

This is a theme also seen in families in other regions. For example, in June 2001 Ismail al-Masawabi died carrying out a suicide attack that also killed two Israeli Army sergeants. Ismail carried out the attack just days before he was due to graduate from university. Later, in a newspaper interview, his mother said of her son's death: 'I was very happy when I heard. To be a martyr, that's something. Very few people can do it. I prayed to thank God. In the Koran it's said that a martyr does not die. I know my son is close to me. It is our belief' (Lelyveld, 2001, p. 48).

Such pride needs to be balanced with the very real grief and loss families feel in the aftermath. Though they can understand and sympathise with the suicide terrorist's decision, most loved ones would prefer to have the bomber alive rather than dead. The experience of Maha Ghandour is revealing here. Maha married her husband, Salah, in 1990, knowing he was a member of Hezbollah. In 1995, Salah drove a car packed with explosives into an Israeli convoy in Lebanon, killing himself and 12 soldiers and injuring 35 more. Maha and Salah had three young children.

> For two weeks beforehand, I'd felt that his martyrdom was imminent. On the Sunday before, he told me to take care of myself and the children. That was the last time I would see him. I felt like my heart had been ripped out. For the first time, I begged him to reconsider. 'You have always known that I would be a martyr,' he said angrily. Then he calmed down. 'The children will be well brought up and you will always be well cared for.' He said that he loved us, but that it was his dream to become a martyr. I had no choice; I

knew I could not stand in Salah's way. I tried to convince myself that to die a martyr was better than being killed in a car accident, because at least this would encourage the Israelis to pull their troops out of Lebanon. I should feel proud. When we kissed and said goodbye, I couldn't take my eyes off him. I wanted to burn his image into my mind. As he crossed the car park, my son called him from the balcony. He came back and kissed us all again. When he left the second time, my son called again, but this time Salah kept walking. I think he was crying (Taylor, 2002, pp. 103 and 105).

The final words and letters of many suicide attackers do often reflect a sense of grief and loss over the family they leave behind and concern over the impact of their death on loved ones. One suicide bomber, Hisham Ismail Abd-El Rahman Hamed, wrote in his final letter: 'Dear family and friends! I write this will with tears in my eyes and sadness in my heart. I want to tell you that I am leaving and ask for your forgiveness because I decided to see Alla' today and this meeting is by all means more important than staying alive on this earth . . .' (Ganor, 2001, p. 138). It is a sentiment that echoes some of the words of kamikaze pilots from the Second World War. Ichizo Hayashi, a 23-year-old kamikaze pilot, wrote in his final letter to his mother: 'I am pleased to have the honour of having been chosen as a member of a Special Attack Force that is on its way into battle, but I cannot help crying when I think of you, Mum. When I reflect on the hopes you had for the future . . . I feel so sad that I am going to die without doing anything to bring you joy' (Powers, 2002).

Family members are often ignorant that a loved one is seriously contemplating a suicide attack. Maha Ghandour's awareness that her husband was very close to carrying out an attack is not common. More often, family members are entirely unaware that such extreme action is near at hand. Though they can fully sympathise and understand why the groups use suicide attacks, many family members would find it extremely difficult not to attempt to intervene in some way if they knew someone close to them was going to attempt such a mission. Nasr Hassan asked one mother of a suicide bomber what she would have done had she known what her son was planning to do. The mother replied: 'I would have taken a huge knife and cut open my heart and tucked him inside to keep him safe' (Hassan, 2002).

Maha Ghandour expresses the same desire to protect her children from following in her husband Salah's footsteps. Five years after his death, and with her children getting older, she commented with worry: 'My oldest son says he wants to be a martyr like his father, and Salah told me to encourage him. But I am trying to teach him that he should go to university because education can also be a weapon' (Taylor, 2002).

However, not every family member tries to stand in the way of the potential suicide terrorist. In June 2002, Hamas released the final video of Mahmoud al-Obeid, a 23-year-old college student who had just carried out a suicide attack. Mahmoud died in the attack on a Jewish settlement in which two Israeli soldiers were killed. Unusually, Mahmoud's mother, Naima, appeared with him in the video, and was clearly fully aware of what he planned to do. In the video Naima says to her son: 'God willing you will succeed. May every bullet hit its target, and may God give you martyrdom. This is the best day of my life.' Mahmoud replied to her: 'Thank you for raising me' (Guerin, 2002).

Even though Naima encouraged and supported her son's action, one should not interpret such a willingness to see loved ones commit suicide attacks as indifference to their deaths and loss. In an interview after her son's death, Naima told a journalist: 'Nobody wants their son to be killed. I always wanted him to have a good life. But our land is occupied by the Israelis. We're sacrificing our sons to get our freedom' (Guerin, 2002).

THE ROLE OF RELIGION

Many observers have an expectation that religious belief plays a major role in suicide terrorism. This expectation is primarily the result of the links between one religion and suicide terrorism, and that religion is of course Islam. I say 'of course', but the reality is that Islamic terrorists have not been the main users of suicide tactics in recent decades. On the contrary, Hindu terrorists have carried out far more suicide attacks in the past 20 years than extremists from all of the other religions combined. Yet, particularly in the Western world there is a widespread belief that suicide terrorism is mainly an Islamic phenomenon and that the peculiar religious beliefs of the terrorists play a major role in their willingness to use suicide tactics. Why has Islam been singled out in this way?

Certainly there is a long history of Islamic extremists showing a willingness to use suicide tactics. The fact that Islam has traditionally been an exceptionally tolerant religion throughout history has sadly been rather overlooked (Armstrong, 2001). As indicated at the start of the chapter, Islamic groups were already using these measures in the twelfth century. In the eighteenth and nineteenth centuries, Islamic extremists used suicide tactics to carry out terrorist attacks in India, Indonesia and the Philippines (Dale, 1988). Indeed, long before the advent of al-Qaeda, US troops in the Philippines were embroiled in bitter fighting with suicide attacks from Islamic extremists. Starting in 1900, US control of the southern islands of the Philippines was contested by the native Moro tribes. The US forces typically won overwhelming victories in all their conventional battles with the Moros, but then faced increasing attacks from individual *amoks* and *juramentados*, Moro warriors who attacked US positions and personnel in suicidal efforts armed often only with a sword (Woolman,

2002). Moro resistance to the US tailed off in 1913, but in more recent times Islamic groups have again brought suicide tactics back to prominence in the Western psyche. In Beirut in 1983 the newly emerging Islamist terrorist group Hezbollah launched three devastating suicide attacks using trucks packed with explosives. Over the course of the year Hezbollah attacked the US embassy, the US Marine barracks, and a French military base, killing over 360 people and injuring hundreds more. In response, the US, French and Italian governments hastily pulled their military forces out of the country. In the 1990s, Islamist suicide attackers from al-Qaeda targeted US buildings and personnel in the Middle East and Africa, killing nearly 300 people and injuring more than 5000. This ensured the West remained painfully aware of the Islamist suicide threat, an awareness taken to new levels with the September 11 attacks.

In the Western mind, then, suicide terrorism became inextricably linked with Islam. The ready assumption was that there was something different about Islam as a religion that made it prone to producing suicidal extremists. It is worth noting that Ariel Merari, a veteran Israeli researcher and one of the few psychologists to have actually interviewed suicide bombers, disagreed with this view and concluded instead that religion was 'relatively unimportant in the phenomenon of terrorist suicide' (Merari, 1990, p. 206). It is true, though, that some Islamic terrorists believe that a person who dies carrying out a suicide attack becomes a martyr, a *shahid*, a term that means 'witness' and refers to someone whose existence is a living testimony, even after his or her death (Palazzi, 2001, p. 69). As a *shahid* an individual will enter into heaven as one of the most honoured (just a step below prophets such as Moses and Abraham). However, the honoured status the *shahids* enjoy in the afterlife has fuelled some lurid speculation on the characters of potential bombers. In particular, the fact that *shahids* are attended to by 72 'black-eyed' virgins when they awake in paradise has drawn much risqué attention.[1] Westerners, hearing that the young bombers expect to awaken into a paradise surrounded by virgins, fall easy prey to stories that potential bombers are sexually frustrated and obsessed adolescents and young men who have no relationships with women, and who have been lured and enticed into carrying out attacks by cynical recruiters. This makes for lurid reading, but few in the West realise that the 72 virgins in paradise are not there to engage in uninhibited sex with the *shahids*. On the contrary, the virgins remain completely chaste (Hassan, 2002). There are no wild orgies waiting for a suicide bomber in the afterlife, and potential bombers are fully aware of this.

Another point often missed by outsiders is that simply carrying out a suicide attack is not in itself enough to make a bomber a martyr. The attack

---

[1] Some accounts claim that the number of virgins is 70, others that it is 16.

has to be carried out first and foremost for Allah. Doing it for personal fame or for the other accolades and rewards given to bombers and their families undermines the value of the sacrifice. As one bomber described it: 'If one of us blows himself up for glory, his martyrdom will not be acceptable to Allah' (Hassan, 2002). Attacks carried out in order to create a Palestinian homeland or to take revenge against Israelis are considered to have been carried out for secular motives, and the action is not considered a religious one, thus the suicide terrorist would not enter paradise because of what he or she had done. This is a subtle difference but one that often marks the suicide bombers of Hamas (who traditionally have given a high priority to the religious aspects) apart from those of the al-Aqsa Martyrs Brigade who are much more secular in outlook.

Ultimately, Islam does not deserve its strong association with suicide terrorism. Centuries before Islam even emerged as a religion, Jewish extremists were launching suicide attacks against legionnaires of the Roman Empire. In the nineteenth century, Christian Russian anarchists carried out suicide attacks trying to kill the Tsar, while Shinto and Buddhist extremists in Japan sacrificed themselves in assaults against the feudal Shogunal regime and the encroaching Western powers (Silke, 1997). In the twentieth century, Sikh, Christian, Buddhist, Shinto and Hindu extremists have all carried out suicidal attacks, sometimes with religious dimensions, but more often not. For example, while the most ardent users of suicide tactics, the Tamil Tigers, come from a Hindu background, the organisation itself is a secular one. Members of the Tamil's suicide units do not believe they are religious martyrs or that they will be rewarded in the afterlife for having carried out the suicide attack. Yet even without a religious incentive to spur on volunteers, the Tamil Tigers have been able to mount the most sustained and extensive campaign of suicide attacks in recent history.

THE GROUP FACTOR

In the summer of 2000, Ariel Merari was invited to speak before a special committee of the US Congress on the subject of suicidal terrorism. As one of the few researchers to have interviewed suicide terrorists (primarily in Israeli prisons), Merari was quick to dispatch the notion that the bombers were crazy or that they carried out the attacks primarily for religious reasons. 'To put it in a nutshell,' he said early in his presentation, 'suicide terrorism is an organisational phenomenon . . . it was an organisation that decided to use this tactic, found the person or persons to carry it out, trained them, and sent them on the mission at the time and place that the organisation chose' (Merari, 2000, p. 10).

As well as providing the necessary training and outlets, the terrorist groups also try to offer additional incentives for potential suicide attackers. The groups screen potential candidates. This goes beyond simply trying to weed out those who may lack the commitment or psychological stability needed to carry out a suicide operation. Many of the organisations examine the potential impact of the death on the individual's family. Only sons, for example, are often not allowed to volunteer as the leadership judges that their death would place too great a hardship on ageing parents. Indeed, the groups in general show a keen awareness of the needs of the surviving family. Most organisations provide pensions for the families of suicide bombers. Hamas typically pays the family of a suicide bomber $300 a month, a considerable sum within the deprived areas of Gaza and the West Bank. The group also takes responsibility to build the family a new home if the Israeli military demolishes their current one in reprisal for the attack. There are donations from other sources as well. At the time of writing, Saddam Hussein, for example, currently gives a one-off donation to the families of $25 000, a fortune considering the circumstances, and a policy that has netted him considerable goodwill among the Palestinian people.

In short, then, the groups take concrete measures to ensure that the families of suicide terrorists are looked after and that they do not suffer economically. Some sources have rather cynically suggested that these economic measures have led to families encouraging members to become suicide bombers, in the hope of receiving the various pay-outs that follow. This, however, is little more than black propaganda. The grief and loss felt by the families is very real, and while they understand the bomber's decision, most would much rather have him or her back alive and safe. Maha Ghandour touched on this issue when interviewed after her husband died in his suicide attack:

> Salah's attack took place on occupied land and a hospital named after him now stands there. People view our family as special, even sacred, and I receive great respect. But I am just the same. The only difference now is that I am missing someone (Taylor, 2002, p. 105).

During the 1990s, the Palestinian groups tended to put considerable effort into preparing bombers. Outsiders often viewed this as 'brainwashing', but potential bombers, family members and others living in the communities have rejected this interpretation. Ariel Merari (2000) also rejects the idea of brainwashing. As he said before the US Congress:

> Once the ... people responsible in the organisation are convinced that the person is serious they put them usually in a training process that may last in most cases from weeks to months. This training process involves two important elements. One element is strengthening the already existing

willingness to die by giving that person additional reasons . . . in this phase of the training if the organisation is religious the trainer also speaks about the religious justifications for this kind of act, about paradise, about the right or actually the need to carry out an act like that in the name of God, in the name of religion (pp. 12–13).

It has been noted by a number of sources that the level of training Palestinian suicide terrorists receive in the current intifada (uprising) has declined compared to that of their predecessors. This has been attributed to a higher level of motivation among the candidates and a reduced concern in the organisations that the candidates' motivation and morale needs to be bolstered. However, the second critical element Merari mentions, concerning the creation of points of no return for the bomber, remains a feature of most suicide attacks. The existence of such points underlines the fact that the motivation to carry out an attack is not necessarily absolute. Though rare, there have been isolated cases where suicide attackers have changed their mind on their way to the intended target and the attack has been abandoned. The organisations create points of no return by having candidates write last letters to their family and friends and often by also videotaping the candidate saying farewell. In groups like Hamas and Islamic Jihad, from that point on the person is referred to as *al-shahid al-hai*, 'the living martyr'. This means that the individual is already dead and is only temporarily in this world. Merari (2000) noted that with such clear demarcations:

> Under such circumstances after this phase it is very, very hard for persons to change their mind. And actually there have been practically no cases of mind changing by suicide candidates in the case of Palestinians, very, very few in the case of the Tamils, as much as a very few cases in the case of Lebanese organisations (p. 13).

However, a more important question to ask about suicide terrorism, other than why people are prepared to do it, is which terrorist groups are the ones most likely to use these extreme methods and why? On average, suicide attacks cause more deaths, injuries and destruction than any other type of terrorist tactic. Combined with such lethality they are also distinctive for being notoriously difficult to defend against. While most terrorist groups are reluctant to sacrifice members in attacks, those that are willing to go this far can generally operate—at least in the short term—on a more dangerous and lethal level. The issue for governments becomes one of identifying which terrorist groups are the ones most likely to use such methods and how long current users will persist with the tactic.

What kind of terrorist group will try to develop a strategy of suicide attacks? Under what circumstances do terrorist groups feel these attacks are appropriate and feasible? Equally important, under what conditions will groups decide that such attacks should be halted? We do not yet have clear and unambiguous answers to these critical questions, though some trends are worth noting. In general, suicide attacks seem to be most likely to occur when the following factors combine:

- There is a cultural precedent for self-sacrifice in conflict.
- The conflict is long-running.
- The conflict has already involved many casualties on both sides.
- The protagonists are desperate (e.g. they have suffered a serious setback).

Importantly, the commitment of terrorist groups to using suicide attacks is not constant. In the past 20 years more than 300 suicide attacks have been carried out in 14 countries by 17 different terrorist organisations (Schweitzer, 2001b). While the number of countries witnessing suicide attacks has grown in recent years, the commitment of individual groups to the tactic has varied considerably. Even groups with a long history of using such methods have gone through periods where they have shied away from them. Hezbollah is a good example of this. Even though the dramatic impact of Hezbollah's 1983 suicide attacks encouraged a number of other terrorist groups to adopt the tactic, suicide assaults carried out in the following years by this organisation were much less successful. As a result, after 1983 Hezbollah carried out only one or two suicide attacks a year on average, and it is worth noting that even at their zenith, suicide attacks accounted for only a tiny proportion of the group's activities. Indeed, Shay (2001) indicated that suicide attacks made up less than 0.1 per cent of all terrorist attacks in Lebanon. In 1999, Hezbollah carried out some 1500 attacks in Lebanon but only one of these was a suicide operation.

Significantly, in recent years only one group, the Tamil Tigers, has consistently used suicide attacks on a regular basis. At the time of writing, the ceasefire in Sri Lanka means that the suicide assaults have for now stopped, but it is clear to all concerned that should violence erupt again the Tigers will readily go back to using suicide tactics. As a large organisation (membership was estimated at around 20 000 combatants in the early 1990s), the Tigers can readily absorb the losses caused by suicide actions. Just as important, however, have been the reinforcing effects of several spectacular successes the group has gained through using suicide tactics. These successes include the assassination of leading political and military figures (the group is the only terrorist organisation to have assassinated three heads of state), as well as the significant damage caused to important civil and military facilities. Success encourages repetition. Should the ceasefire collapse, the Tigers would probably have to go through a period of more limited impact (such as happened to Hezbollah in the mid- and late 1980s), before they would be likely to abandon a tactic that in their eyes has served them well.

The Tigers' experience, though, is an unusual one. Of the few terrorist groups that have been willing to contemplate suicide assaults, in most cases the organisation's commitment to such methods has been sporadic and isolated. The PKK is a good example here. As highlighted earlier, the PKK began using suicide assaults after suffering a series of critical setbacks against Turkish government forces. In the wake of these defeats, the movement carried out 15 attacks which resulted in a total of 19 deaths among target groups. But considering the loss among its own members, for the terrorists this was a poor return. Suicide attacks never became a mainstream tactic within the organisation, and tended only to occur during especially desperate periods (e.g. the capture and trial of the group's leader in 1999). Few were therefore surprised when the PKK abandoned suicide methods entirely within five years of the first attack.

CONCLUSION

While interest varies, suicide attacks will always hold some attraction for terrorists. The ability of the tactic to circumvent so many traditional defence and security measures means that it will inevitably hold a special appeal for groups who are struggling to harm what they perceive to be well-defended and well-prepared opponents. This will be particularly the case where the root causes of the conflict are being exacerbated, where the loss of life is already high and where the terrorist group feels its own position is growing increasingly desperate. However, once started, most groups will not remain stubbornly committed to suicide attacks. The tactic is expensive in the lives of members and unless recruits are plentiful or the attacks result in a steady stream of significant successes, terrorist organisations prove remarkably quick to abandon the suicide approach.

Ultimately, suicide terrorism can occur anywhere. If history is any guide we are not likely to ever be entirely free from its threat and no country or region is entirely immune to the risk. In the past 10 years alone, suicide attacks have taken place in both North and South America, in the Middle East, Europe, Africa and Asia. More than any other terrorist tactic, suicide assaults are most likely to result in fatalities among the terrorist's targets, and are also the most difficult for authorities to defend against. Worryingly, the experience of recent years suggests that a growing number of terrorist groups are willing to experiment with suicide tactics. In all probability this will not make these groups more successful in achieving their strategic aims, but it will substantially increase the likelihood that they will kill and maim larger numbers of people.

Understanding the psychology of suicide terrorists and the circumstances in which individual terrorist organisations turn to this extreme tactic provides us with some keys for future prevention. It also gives guidance on how to identify emerging threats, as well as an ability to assess when a group's commitment to suicide actions will waver. But one cannot fully tackle the problem of suicidal terrorism without also attempting to resolve the bigger issues that drive terrorist conflicts. In the end, suicide attacks, however dramatic and appalling, are first and foremost a symptom of wider problems. Recognising this, and applying the proper attention to more fundamental causes, is a crucial step in achieving and safeguarding peace and security for all.

REFERENCES

Armstrong, K. (2001). Was it inevitable? Islam through history. In J. Hoge, Jr and G. Rose (Eds), *How Did This Happen? Terrorism and the New War* (pp. 53–70). Oxford: Public Affairs.

Dale, S. (1988). Religious suicide in Islamic Asia: anticolonial terrorism in India, Indonesia, and the Philippines. *Journal of Conflict Resolution*, **32**(1), 37–59.

Ergil, D. (2001). Suicide terrorism in Turkey: the Workers' Party of Kurdistan. In The International Policy Institute for Counter-Terrorism (Ed.), *Countering Suicide Terrorism* (pp. 105–28). Herzliya, Israel: The International Policy Institute for Counter-Terrorism.

Ganor, B. (2001). Suicide attacks in Israel. In The International Policy Institute for Counter-Terrorism (Ed.), *Countering Suicide Terrorism* (pp. 134–45). Herzliya, Israel: The International Policy Institute for Counter-Terrorism.

Goldenberg, S. (2002). The men behind the suicide bombers. *The Guardian*, 12 June.

Guerin, O. (2002). 'Pride' of suicide attacker's mother (18 June). As viewed on 28 July 2002, *http://news.bbc.co.uk/hi/english/world/middle_east/newsid_2050000/2050414.stm.*

Hassan, N. (2002). An arsenal of believers: talking to the 'human bombs'. Paper presented at the International Society of Political Psychology Conference, 16–19 July, Berlin, Germany.

Israeli, R. (1997). Islamikaze and their significance. *Terrorism and Political Violence*, **9**(3), 96–121.

Joshi, C.L. (2000). Ultimate references. *Far Eastern Economic Review*, **163**, 64–67.

Kushner, H. (1996). Suicide bombers: business as usual. *Studies in Conflict and Terrorism*, **19**(4), 329–38.

Lelyveld, J. (2001). All suicide bombers are not alike. *The New York Times Magazine*, 28 October, p. 48.

Merari, A. (1990). The readiness to kill and die: suicidal terrorism in the Middle East. In W. Reich (Ed.), *Origins of Terrorism: Psychologies, Ideologies, Theologies, States of Mind* (pp. 192–207). Cambridge: Cambridge University Press.

Merari, A. (2000). Statement before the Special Oversight Panel on Terrorism. *Terrorism and Threats to US Interests in the Middle East [HASC No. 106–59]*. Washington, DC: US Congress.

Palazzi, A. (2001). Orthodox Islamic perceptions of jihad and martyrdom. In The International Policy Institute for Counter-Terrorism (Ed.), *Countering Suicide Terrorism* (pp. 64–74). Herzliya, Israel: The International Policy Institute for Counter-Terrorism.

Powers, D. (2002). Kamikaze. As viewed on 7 August 2002, *www.bbc.co.uk/history/war/ww.../no_surrender_05.shtml*.

Rapoport, D. (1990). Religion and terror: thugs, assassins, and zealots. In C.W. Kegley, Jr (Ed.), *International Terrorism: Characteristics, Causes, Controls* (pp. 146–57). London: MacMillan.

Schweitzer, Y. (2001a). Suicide terrorism: development and main characteristics. In The International Policy Institute for Counter-Terrorism (Ed.), *Countering Suicide Terrorism* (pp. 75–85). Herzliya, Israel: The International Policy Institute for Counter-Terrorism.

Schweitzer, Y. (2001b). Suicide bombings: the ultimate weapon? As viewed on 8 November 2001, *www.ict.org.il/articles/articledet.cfm?articleid=373*.

Shay, S. (2001). Suicide terrorism in Lebanon. In The International Policy Institute for Counter-Terrorism (Ed.), *Countering Suicide Terrorism* (pp. 129–33). Herzliya, Israel: The International Policy Institute for Counter-Terrorism.

Shiqaqi, K. (2001). The views of Palestinian society on suicide terrorism. In The International Policy Institute for Counter-Terrorism (Ed.), *Countering Suicide Terrorism* (pp. 149–58). Herzliya, Israel: The International Policy Institute for Counter-Terrorism.

Silke, A. (1997). Honour and expulsion: terrorism in nineteenth-century Japan. *Terrorism and Political Violence*, **9**(4), 58–81.

Taylor, C. (2002). My husband was a suicide bomber. *Marie Claire*, July, 103–105.

Woolman, D. (2002). Fighting Islam's fierce Moro warriors. *Military History*, **9**(1), 34–40.

CHAPTER 6

Leaving Terrorism Behind: An Individual Perspective

JOHN HORGAN[1]

University College Cork

INTRODUCTION

It is no secret that most psychologically based commentary on terrorist behaviour focuses on understanding why people become terrorists. Despite the relatively little progress we have made via a now sterile debate about terrorist personalities, it is at the expense of valuable opportunities being explored that this issue remains perceived as the forefront of 'what psychologists have to say about terrorists'. However, and although few terrorism researchers are likely to agree, the issues surrounding how and why people leave terrorism behind are as fascinating and as important as the more frequently asked questions about terrorist behaviour. Exceptionally little is known or understood about what happens to influence people to leave terrorism behind, and this chapter therefore seeks to shed light on this rarely addressed issue.

[1]I would like to thank Graeme Steven and Clark McCauley for comments on an earlier draft of this chapter. Some of the research presented here was made possible by a Faculty of Arts Research Award (2000) from University College Cork.

Terrorists, Victims and Society: Psychological Perspectives on Terrorism and its Consequences.
Edited by Andrew Silke. © 2003 John Wiley & Sons, Ltd.

LACK OF KNOWLEDGE OR JUST LACK OF INTEREST?

Like many major terrorist incidents before it, the events of September 11, 2001 exposed a number of gaps in our analyses of terrorism. In the weeks and months that followed, however, a more depressing trend emerged to confirm the fears of analysts that progressive research on terrorist behaviour remains shackled by short-term policy goals and law-enforcement needs while equally subservient to incident-driven research agendas.

It is in this context that poorly sustained research efforts have contributed to a depressingly ambivalent perception towards a plethora of issues relating to what happens when terrorism ends, or more specifically from a psychological perspective, when people stop being terrorists (voluntarily or otherwise). A dangerous assumption that must be dismissed here is that terrorists are somehow no longer 'relevant' once their involvement in terrorism has ceased, or that when the terrorist activities of an entire organisation de-escalate it is no longer deserving of study. In an analysis of the Irish peace process, Dingley (1999) suggested that academics who study terrorism would lose a vested interest if terrorist campaigns were to come to an end. If he is correct, this blinkered attitude to what our 'subject matter' ought to represent (presumably active terrorists/terrorism) precludes by default the overwhelming opportunities now available to researchers who previous to the recent peace initiatives in Ireland, for example, could barely contemplate the possibility of 'talking with terrorists'. We will return to this argument at the end of the chapter, but talking to former terrorists is now an achievable reality and our neglect of valuable research avenues will ultimately be reflected in future assessments of our knowledge of terrorist behaviour.

This has been a persistent issue since terrorism research efforts began to gain momentum in the early 1980s, but if students and scholars of terrorism heeded theoretical issues and gaps in the literature to guide their research agendas, our knowledge and understanding of the processes involved in terrorism would be more complete. In the psychological literature, our perennial preoccupation rests with tackling the question 'why (or how) do people become terrorists', and if only to attempt to broaden our subject perspective for the moment, let us remember that despite even the best of intentions, more research on the same issue does not necessarily imply greater knowledge.

WHY TERRORISM ENDS

The focus of this chapter concerns individual issues in terrorist disengagement, but we must first consider the nature of the relevant broader processes. The terrorism literature has increasingly considered the broad factors that have contributed to the slow decline of traditional forms of terrorism since both the end of the Cold War and the changing nature and direction of many of the world's most intractable terrorist campaigns. The examples of ideological and revolutionary terrorism across Europe are familiar to most as contributing to the public image of 'the terrorist', and include the Italian Red Brigades, the German Red Army Faction (RAF) and numerous other Marxist anti-imperialist groups born largely out of the spirit of revolt in the late 1960s. Europe's last 'Red terrorists' undoubtedly remain the November 17 group in Greece, but whilst ideological terror has failed to adapt to changing times and changing opinion, ethnonationalist terrorist movements, allied with increasingly adept and influential political wings, have stood the test of time more firmly.

In the case of the Provisional IRA, a popular base, tactical, strategic and organisational adaptability (often learned through harsh experience), financial backing and a successful political wing (Sinn Fein) have contributed to the remarkable persistence of this most intractable of groups: an unwavering belief in their own imminent victory and a gradual nuancing of once offensive Marxist ideology has helped to shape the Republican movement into a now effective and attractive political force in Ireland, and a gradual involvement in a wide array of activities often not usually associated with terrorism (both legal and illegal) has contributed to its survival. The recent rise of Sinn Fein across the whole of Ireland has been directly assisted by the movement's exploitation of government disorganisation and a persistent failure to truly appreciate the long-term strategic nature of Sinn Fein and the IRA.

Although the Irish Peace Process has been the subject of many, often naive, commentaries since it began in the early 1990s, some general principles can be identified to help understand the IRA's gradual de-escalation of terrorism and escalation of political activity since the early 1980s. These include:

- A realisation that terrorism alone was insufficient in achieving the movement's aspirations (leading to the increasingly tactical use of terrorism since the rise of Sinn Fein).
- A gradual willingness by the British Government to engage in secret discussions with Republicans on how to end the conflict, or at least allow for breathing space (i.e. ceasefires) through which other alternatives to violence could be encouraged.
- Successes both by counter-terrorism efforts and an increasingly belligerent loyalist terror campaign against both the Republican movement and the wider nationalist community in Northern Ireland in the early 1990s, in itself contributing to public opinion desperate for stability in the region.

Despite a breakdown in the initial IRA ceasefire (largely arising from ac-
cusations of bad faith: whether the original ceasefire was simply perceived
as a breathing period for Republicans or a genuine move towards a greater
peace settlement at the time, we do not know), in the years since the steps
towards peace in Northern Ireland began, a number of concessions granted
towards all paramilitary movements and their political wings has meant
that their increasing involvement in the political process has ultimately
contributed to the overall decline in the activity we most usually associate
with terrorism—fatal shootings and bombings.

There is no point in describing here the various ebbs and flows in the
labyrinthine peace process with concession and counter-concession carefully choreographed in secrecy, but one recent event has given great cause
for questioning what happens to the individual member of a terrorist
movement when terrorism ends. In the weeks following the al-Qaeda
attacks on New York and Washington, a press conference was called at
Sinn Fein's former Belfast headquarters at Conway Mill. The Sinn Fein
leaders, Gerry Adams and Martin McGuinness, announced that decommissioning of the IRA's weapons (according to all perceived detractors of
the Republican movement, the main obstacle to political stability in the
region) was to become not a distant aim, but a current reality. To many
non-Republicans this offered proof (if it was ever needed) that not only did
international events overshadow the mighty IRA's self-importance and unwavering demand for parity of political esteem in the continued absence
of decommissioning, they also illustrated more obviously that Sinn Fein
and the IRA do respond to pressure.

All parties welcomed the breakthrough statement and there was no
question that Sinn Fein was now on its way to finally gaining its place
in the political process. To the public the leadership portrayed the move
as the IRA having saved the peace process: the political deadlock broken
thanks to the IRA's 'courage'. The dissent within the movement was clear,
however, and illustrated to the outside world just how little detail of this
unprecedented move had been revealed to the rank-and-file supporters of
the organisation prior to this news conference. Upon leaving the meeting,
it was reported that Adams was met with shouts and jeers from his own
followers, cries of 'you sold us out Gerry' now representing the uncomfortable reality facing Republicans who had previously been facilitated in
their commitment by an unwavering promise of 'not an ounce [of explo-
sives], not a bullet'.

Although this is just a glimpse of a specific period of one terrorist campaign, the range of questions for research here is clear: What happens to
people who leave terrorism? What influences them to leave (either voluntarily or involuntarily)? What implications does this process have? Indeed,
a broader issue is perhaps what do we mean by 'leaving' at all? Does
this mean leaving behind the shared social norms, values, attitudes and

aspirations so carefully forged while a member of a terrorist group? Or does it mean keeping these but no longer engaging in actual terrorist activity? The more issues we consider, the more we will realise that to gain a fuller understanding of how and why people leave terrorism behind we need at least some understanding of the reasons why people join a terrorist group in the first place, and also why they remain in an organisation? Some of the reasons that explain a sense of 'remaining' might further be considered as reasons that possibly inhibit or block exit routes (be they psychological—e.g. through disillusionment with some aspect of the group—or physical—e.g. apprehension by the security services).

To further complicate matters, we might think of each of these as either voluntary in origin (e.g. the decision that continued membership of the group is no longer as important as some overriding personal issue) or involuntary (e.g. an individual is forced to leave in the face of some external issue such as the reality of arms decommissioning and the implications this has for organisational dissipation, possibly leading to an outright rejection of the group's ideals as a result). We now have two broad possible categories within which we can consider the influences 'forcing' or 'attracting' a person to leave terrorism behind: voluntary and involuntary disengagement.

The reasons why people *become* terrorists are often not related in character or quality to the reasons why an individual *remains* in a terrorist group, which in turn are not necessarily similar to reasons for *leaving*. An understanding of the nature of the dynamics underpinning each phase can be gained only by avoiding the assumption that they are linear, discrete and indistinct (Horgan and Taylor, 2001; Taylor and Horgan, 2001).

BECOMING

Despite being an over-researched topic bearing little fruit, analyses of why people become terrorists reveal (inadvertently or otherwise) that one of the few known factors that binds terrorist motivation across time, place, historical and/or socio-politico-economic climate is its unwavering heterogeneity. There are many reasons as to why someone would want to join a terrorist group, and there is strong diversity of personal motivation even within the same group. Another important common feature is the gradual but progressive socialisation process into terrorism. A person does not become a terrorist overnight, and even once formally accepted into a terrorist movement individuals are often not guided into an actively violent role. There is undeniably a gradual learning process that appears to typify involvement in terrorism (Horgan, 2000).

Even a cursory examination of initial supportive qualities appears to offer a more useful way of understanding the attraction of membership in a terrorist organisation, be this confirmation of a rite of passage or other perceived positive lures (not uncommon in tightly knit ethnonationalist communities) combined with an unwavering sense of injustice as a result of some real or imagined assault (e.g. a bad experience with, or family history of, victimisation at the hands of the security services or a rival paramilitary grouping), or with the gradual acquisition of values, attitudes of a close friend or role model who is involved in at least the broader movement. The point is that a variety of complex, personal and social circumstances may combine to influence the individual to move towards what in any other setting would be considered antisocial behaviour.

Usually we fail to appreciate the time involved in becoming a terrorist. Socialisation is slow and the marginalisation from mainstream society is gradual. There is rarely even an explicit 'break' from the real world (a qualitative psychological difference between the truly 'underground' movements of the ideologically based terror groups and the larger, separatist movements where community support contributes to terrorism being more accurately conceptualised as 'semi-clandestine'). Before developing the idea of the positive lures being central to becoming (and remaining) involved in a terrorist group, we must be aware of the problem of trying to develop a sense of predictive utility, e.g. 'Who is more likely to become a terrorist?' Or, 'What makes a terrorist different?' The direct answer is that we may never be able to answer these questions. Their beguiling simplicity (and assumption that these are questions that can actually be answered) is reflected in numerous attempts by psychologists and psychiatrists to focus on individual psychological qualities (such as personality traits) to help explain in very simple terms what is essentially a complex, dynamic socio-behavioural process. Despite their attractiveness (via the simplicity any potential results would imply), personality traits are useless as predictors for understanding why people become terrorists.

REMAINING (AND GETTING CLOSER TO LEAVING...)

It is at this stage that we move much closer to actually understanding why people leave. The public opinion that terrorist movements are composed of psychopathic individuals is here dealt a blow by simple logic: the qualities the leadership looks for in its members include not only the ability to withstand the psychological pressures of living an underground (or double) life, but also reliability and trustworthiness, the ability to keep one's mouth shut about even the most inconspicuous of details that might otherwise reveal one's loyalties. These qualities are then gradually reinforced and forged as a result of membership.

The first major assertion we must make here is that terrorism is a group process, and terrorist groups set the scene for intense psychological pressures. Extreme conformity and strict obedience are organisational cornerstones that leaders must put in place to enhance the smooth, effective running of what is already a difficult, secret, and above all illegal organisation. Conformity brings about the 'we' feeling that develops when groups are cohesive. Usually, having a shared purpose or sense of unity, which in itself is catalysed by having a clearly identifiable enemy, facilitates this, and higher-status members of the organisation are the ones who ultimately command obedience and play an important role in maintaining group unity.

The distinction between where one lies with respect to the 'becoming' and 'remaining' is as much a psychological issue as anything else. The major hurdle of finally having one's identity reaffirmed within the terrorist group often comes through engagement in activity considered valuable to the organisation, for example the first shooting or bombing operation. Again, though, we ought to realise that involvement in such 'front-line' activity is something that itself develops over time, and this activity is usually reserved for those who must first earn trust and respect before acquiring the operational and technical expertise to enable them to conduct operations reliably and efficiently.

Psychological Disengagement

It is in earning trust and respect that members encounter the psychological barriers that must be overcome or at least adapted to. If not, the seeds of what we might term 'psychological' disengagement will already begin to set. A variety of influences appear to directly or indirectly facilitate (or even encourage) the prospect of leaving.

McCauley and Segal (1989) refer to the various types of rewards found in nationalist-separatist groups as follows: 'increased status and admiration by family and peers . . . terrorist organisations offer mutual solidarity and feelings of comradeship which are very important, given the illegal nature of the group. Above and beyond the solidarity necessary to cope with life underground, these kinds of rewards may be particularly relevant to individuals' (p. 49). The reality is rarely so straightforward, however, and the intensity of a group is demonstrated by many accounts of members who have left the organisation and have written memoirs or autobiographies. Michael Baumann, a former member of the German 2nd June Movement (cited in Alexander and Myers, 1982, p. 174; see also Baumann, 1979), reflects on the negative influence exercised by the power of the group:

> the group becomes increasingly closed. The greater the pressure from the outside, the more you stick together, the more mistakes you make, the more pressure is turned inward . . . this crazy concentration all day long, those are all the things that come together horribly at the end, when there's no more sensibility in the group: only rigid concentration, total pressure to achieve, and it keeps going, always gets worse.

While some members acquiesce to the pressures, others do not. Though there is simply not enough reliable data on this issue, we do know that individuals do make requests to 'leave', having decided that the lifestyle is not for them. Anecdotal evidence suggests that sometimes this is not a problem given the implicit assumption that the member will 'not talk'. For many, however, it is not so easy. After all, regardless of what stage along the 'becoming' and 'remaining' continuum a person lies, terrorist leaders may seek a return on their investment and a promise to keep one's mouth shut may not be enough. The leadership of the Baader–Meinhof group did not hesitate to clarify this: 'Whoever is in the group simply has to hold out, has to be tough . . .' (Post, 1987, p. 310), later threatening that the only way out for any doubters would be 'feet first'. Similarly, Spire (1988), a former member of the French Communist Party, describes the fear of ostracisation and marginalisation if one 'challenges the ideology . . . or the fashionable beliefs', and describes his own attempts to rationalise 'breaches of faith, oppression, and political crimes' because he felt 'terrified at the thought of being marginalised by beloved fellow comrades and colleagues' (p. 150). Adriana Faranda, a former member of the Italian Red Brigades, also reflects on the pressures associated with membership and the negative social and psychological consequences of sustained membership (in Jamieson, 1989):

> choosing to enter the Red Brigades—to become clandestine and therefore to break off relations with your family, with the world in which you'd lived until the day before—is a choice so total that it involves your entire life, your daily existence. It means choosing to occupy yourself from morning till night with problems of politics, or organisation, and fighting; and no longer with normal life—culture, cinema, babies, the education of your children, with all the things that fill other people's lives. These things get put to one side, ignored, because they simply do not exist any more. And when you remove yourself from society, even from the most ordinary things, ordinary ways of relaxing, you no longer share even the most basic emotions. You become abstracted, removed. In the long run you actually begin to feel different. Why? Because you are different. You become closed off, become sad, because a whole area of life is missing, because you are aware that life is more than politics and political work (pp. 267–68).

Another significant pressure that may later catalyse the move (psychological or physical) to leave is the uncomfortable individual realisation that the initial aspirations and personal hopes expressed through seeking membership are quite removed from the day-to-day reality of what the duties and responsibilities of this new role involve. Brockner and Rubin's (1985) *psychological traps* refer to situations where an individual, having decided upon some course of action that he or she expects will return a reward (in the broadest possible sense), for example joining a terrorist group or remaining in such a group, finds that the actual process of goal attainment requires a continuing and repeated 'investment' in some form over some degree of time. This 'repeated investment', in a psychological sense, will probably be required of that individual to sustain his or her involvement, but still the eventual goal may continue to be a very distant realisation. Brockner and Rubin note that somewhere in this process is an inevitable stage when people find themselves in a 'decisional no-man's land', the realisation that he or she has made quite a substantial investment but still not yet achieved his or her expected goal. At this point, the individual experiences somewhat of a crossroads, a decisional crisis. The investment of time, energy and hope may seem too large (especially when combined with the intense pressures one must bear per se as a result of membership), given other circumstances, to continue in the absence of a readily attainable goal. On the other hand, withdrawal means the abandonment of what has gone before, and the individual may feel a commitment if only to personally justify the investment already made (Taylor, 1988). Entrapment characterises 'the spiralling of commitment, so frequently seen in members of terrorist groups' (Taylor, 1988, p. 168). Rubin (cited in Taylor, 1988, p. 168) identifies three critical qualities of traps: (a) The ability to lure or distract the trap's victim into behaviour which may be quite socially psychologically costly to him, (b) the construction of the trap allows only decisions that permit greater movement into the trap, and (c) efforts to escape serve only to increase the trap's bite.

The longing for the once-normal life with social contacts, the ability to walk the streets or to simply engage in a romantic relationship are all normal personal factors which, at any stage of the process, may become prioritised and thereby facilitate at least the beginning of psychological disengagement (probably at the moment doubt arises). What path the member chooses to follow subsequently will be subjected to all of these and further influences.

What else, from a psychological perspective, influences the efforts to escape? Post (1987) highlights the fact that the group pressures themselves have a variety of implications for decision-making within that group. Individual judgement in most decision-making groups tends to be 'suspended and subordinated to the group process' (p. 312). *Groupthink* (Janis, 1972; Post, 1987) occurs in situations where group cohesiveness is high, and the ability of the group to engage in critical decision-making processes is interfered with. Here, the attempts of group members to portray unanimity in the context of their decision-making appears to actually take precedence over their motivation to 'realistically appraise' alternative (and perhaps more effective) decisions (Post, 1987, p. 312). The group becomes blind to the possibility that its decision might not be the most effective, and in reality this may prevent the group from attaining its goal. Post (1987) notes that there is an overwhelming sense of 'wishful thinking' in groups where this occurs (Deaux and Wrightsman, 1988), but emphasises that the processes by which such faulty decision-making can occur are quite simple: when we join a group, and views become evident from discussion, we may seek approval by sharing those views in an attempt to display a greater level of commitment to the group's ideal and thereby demonstrate our loyalty (Crenshaw, 1986). There may often be a realisation, however, that the political ideals that contributed to an initial 'becoming' process often have to make way for personalities, a stifling organisational 'climate' (often a result of an individual personality) which can give rise to enormous dissent, whether expressed overtly or not. An excellent example of this comes from an interview conducted by the present author in Northern Ireland in early 1999. The interview segment, although brief, illustrates just how several factors can come into play: conformity, obedience, groupthink and the influence exerted by a minority might (eventually) lead to a change in direction for the group, and also contribute to one member's gradual disillusionment with the movement:

> The meeting was called, and we all knew there was going to be trouble. We were all told we had to be there and I'd say a lot of fellas were told they were going to be told off in front of everyone. [The leader] came in and called things to order. He went around to each of us and wanted reports. When he came to me I was last, but I had to speak up. I told him that our arms situation was in dire straits and unless we were going to do something about it quick, let alone about the lack of funds, that we were just shooting ourselves in the foot. I had the greatest faith in that man, but he had this way of not wanting to see the reality of things as they were. So I said, we need to elect a Quartermaster, and that person would have complete responsibility for the procuring of the stuff as well as managing it, you know? He wasn't pleased at that because like I said, his ideas about the organisation was that it was 'grand', 'no problem' like. When the meeting ended, one of the lads caught up with me on the steps, and I never liked the fucker anyway, but he actually shook my hand! He said 'congratulations, that needed to be said'. No one else would have said it if I didn't open up my mouth.

The importance of this interviewee's comments becomes apparent in considering other relevant issues. The organisation he belonged to was the Official IRA, a movement that became defunct in the early 1970s primarily because it was unable to develop an effective political presence. This interviewee, one of the founding members of the group, left the movement and eventually emigrated:

> I went to [country deleted] for several years I was just so pissed off with the whole thing. We were originally established to espouse socialism. And I know we offended a lot of people [laughs] especially since we were simply spouting every party line that came from Moscow, but [the leader] brought the trouble on himself by not being in touch with the mood on the ground

and I never really patched things up with him after that... It's miserable
when you... believe in it, believe in the movement and the... ah... initial
socialist ideals I suppose... I gave up my house, my car... you had people
give up their farms, and for what in the end? Arguing about fucking guns
all the time because we'd no money.

This man's disillusionment appears to have developed gradually, and
comparison with Alison Jamieson's (1989) interviews with former Italian
terrorist Adriana Faranda reveals unmistakable similarities. Faranda described her 'dissociation' from the Red Brigades as:

a process which matured very gradually... it's not a traumatic leap, it's more
a matter of a thousand little stages. It encompasses everything though; reasoning, valuations, questions which involve not just one action, not one way
of conducting the armed struggle, not one revolutionary project—everything.
It involves the revolution itself; Marxism, violence, the logic of enmity, of conflict, of one's relationship with authority, a way of working out problems, of
confronting reality and of facing the future... I haven't taken one huge traumatic leap. It's not as if I was one person one day and a different one the next.

What is significant here is that both of these accounts point to a gradual
process of 'leaving' similar to the process that characterises involvement
in terrorism in the first place for many others.

For others, however, the catalyst for psychological disengagement seems
to occur suddenly. Sean O'Callaghan, the former IRA terrorist who subsequently became the most important informer against the IRA for the
Irish and British security services, describes one of his most important
memories as a young IRA member:

I come from the South. I come from a Republican family and was heavily
influenced in 1969 by the pogroms in Belfast and loads of nationalist refugees
fleeing south. I joined the Provisional IRA at 15 and I ended up in East
Tyrone and started to become very aware that the Provisional campaign on
the ground was extremely sectarian. That began to worry me. Once in 1975
I was sitting in a flat in Monaghan, along with about eight or ten people
from the East Tyrone IRA who were on the run. A news item came on the
television. A policewoman had been killed in a bomb explosion in Bangor. A
person, who later became chief of staff at the IRA for many years, turned to
me and said, 'I hope she's pregnant and we get two for the price of one'. I'd
been brought up in a kind of romantic, nationalist background in the deep
south and I wasn't prepared or able to cope with that kind of hate and bigotry
(Clare, 1996).

O'Callaghan claims that this was the defining moment that caused him
not only to question his own involvement in the movement, but subsequently to inflict damage on the movement (by turning informer).

In summary, there are a variety of issues contributing to a move towards psychological disengagement:

1 Negative influences as a result of membership
   • e.g. the influence of unbearable group and organisational psychological pressures and, as a result;
2 Changes in priority
   • e.g. the longing for a social/psychological state which (real or imaginary) the member feels is lacking, or existed before membership; often a result of self-questioning but mostly following prolonged social/psychological investment as a member from which little return appears evident.
3 Disillusionment
   • e.g. with the political aims (as illustrated in the Official IRA interviewee example);
   • e.g. with the operational tactics and the attitudes underpinning them (as illustrated by O'Callaghan's statement).

Physical Disengagement

In many ways, reasons for what might be called 'physical' disengagement are easier to identify. Disengagement behaviour may be described as physical where there is a change in the role of an individual terrorist away from opportunities to engage in violent behaviour, but where this move may or may not result in a lessening of commitment to the group. Often there will be physical disengagement from terrorist activity per se, but no change or reduction in support. Indeed, in some cases physical disengagement from terrorism (in terms of being removed from the activity of committing terrorist violence) might involve any of the following, none of which should be considered exclusive:

1 Apprehension by the security services, perhaps with subsequent imprisonment (or if not, forced movement by the leadership of the member into a role whereby he or she is less likely to risk arrest).
2 Forced movement into another role as a result of disobeying orders: at the very least ostracisation may occur, if not outright execution, but if there is some mitigating circumstance the member may instead be pushed into another functional role.
3 An increase in 'other role' activity whereby the original role becomes displaced (e.g. an area of specialisation that relates directly to the commission of terrorist offences such as exploiting one's technical acumen by assisting in the preparation of equipment), or increased involvement in political activity (often as a result of imprisonment).

4 Being kicked out of the movement (e.g. for improper use of arms, money, etc., or some disrespectful behaviour that warrants dismissal but not execution).
5 As with psychological disengagement, a change in priorities. The crucial difference between physical and psychological disengagement in this sense, however, is that the terrorist may continue with his or her role in the movement but may later move into another role/function in order to facilitate new personal circumstances (e.g. getting married or having children, and moving into a support or ancillary role as a result). The other direction from which this role change might emerge is from the leadership, who may place a heavier emphasis on political activity in the months approaching an election. In simple practical terms, this might involve an active terrorist engaging in distributing posters or helping to organise political rallies.

A vital source from which we may be able to formulate hypotheses relating to disengagement processes is analysing the implications of organisational issues per se, as far as the terrorist leadership is concerned, both with respect to promoting engagement and inhibiting any form of, but especially psychological, disengagement.

ORGANISATIONAL ISSUES

Terrorist organisations must not only offer incentives to join, but must also prioritise 'action over talk' (Crenshaw, 1985, p. 474) to indirectly facilitate remaining. Citing Carlos Marighella, Crenshaw notes that 'action creates the vanguard'. He describes terrorists as 'often individuals who are impatient for action' (p. 474) but it is, overall, left implicit as to whether this 'characteristic' develops as a result of non-action or whether it is a theme characteristic of those who join terrorist groups for that very reason.

The paramilitary leaders in Northern Ireland have had to deal with the problem of dissuading disengagement during times of intense organisational difficulties. The present leaders of the Irish Republican movement, Gerry Adams and Martin McGuinness, were also intimately involved in the negotiations around the last substantial ceasefire in Northern Ireland in 1975. That ceasefire (or more accurately a series of small ceasefires) yielded little on the political front towards the Republican goal of a united Ireland, but did result in the emergence of serious organisational stressors and a weakening of community support (an issue upon which counterterrorist policy at the time failed to capitalise). Gerry Adams seems to have recognised these stressors: 'When the struggle was limited to armed struggle, the prolongation of the truce meant that there was no struggle at all. There was nothing but confusion, frustration, and demoralisation, arising directly from what I call "spectator politics"' (cited in Clarke, 1987, p. 29). This comment clearly indicates the problems faced by Irish Republicanism in attempting to change the focus of the organisation, but also recognises the need to refocus 'the struggle' on a broad front in such circumstances, another challenge for the IRA following the events surrounding the emergence of the Good Friday Agreement in 1998, and a problem which may have contributed to the flow of disaffected members to the radical splinter group, the Real IRA.

A lesson that stands out from this is the danger of allowing the organisation to lose its direction and operational capacity when the focus on violence and attack against a clearly defined enemy is lost. In terms of organisational psychology, this makes good sense; any organisation, terrorist or otherwise, can rapidly lose direction when the focus of its activities changes unless something is deliberately designed to sustain and control it. Debray (1967) noted that when terrorist organisations cease to have a political objective, they may continue to exist but drift towards other things that they do well, and in the case of terrorist organisations these tend to be robberies and other criminal activities. The number of Republican punishment assaults rose dramatically during the ceasefire period, and this rise was sustained after the end of the ceasefire when the IRA campaign was initially confined to the UK. Many of the assaults were savage in the extreme, resulting in serious wounding and physical damage to the people involved. Assaults were claimed to be directed against drug dealers or petty criminals, but some of those assaulted also seem to have had political connections as well. Punishment assaults, often of barbaric savagery, are used by all terrorist organisations in Northern Ireland to exercise control over recalcitrant members and to intimidate communities (Silke, 1998). It seems likely that the rise in such punishment assaults during the ceasefire (and afterwards) relate to control and maintenance factors as much as the preservation of good order in their respective communities. Punishment assaults are also a visible indication of the continuing presence of the terrorist groups as functioning organisations within their communities, and as such may well go some way to addressing the problems of lack of focus and activity.

A second way in which the IRA attempted to sustain organisational solidarity during the ceasefire was by continuing its preparations and training for terrorist attacks. Evidence suggests that throughout this period, the IRA and loyalist organisations continued to acquire arms and prepare for attacks. Indeed, a great irony of the euphoria surrounding President Clinton's visit to Northern Ireland is that detailed preparations for the Canary Wharf bombing (which signalled the end of the ceasefire) were in fact in progress at the time. By retaining and developing the capacity for violence, the IRA (and to a lesser extent the loyalist paramilitaries) seems to have sustained the capacity for violence throughout the ceasefire period. However, it might be argued that sustaining the organisation in this way necessarily jeopardised the ceasefire, and of course calls into question the claims of openness to a peace process. All of these dynamics might have important relevance for understanding the nature of prolonged ethnonationalist terrorist campaigns more generally, and why, despite reductions in high-profile violence (e.g. bombings), ongoing low-intensity conflict plays a role in sustaining the unity of the movement (see also Oots, 1989).

IMPLICATIONS OF LEAVING

The focus of this chapter so far has been on identifying influences that might lead to disengagement. However, a further illustration of just how complex the issue is considers the implications of leaving.

Terrorists who leave an organisation (for whatever reason) might not have realised the extent to which aspects of their lives will be limited thereafter. The psychological pressures that follow the ex-terrorist wherever he or she goes sometimes become so intense as to convince him or her into surrendering. Kuldip Singh, a former member of the Khalistan Liberation Force, surrendered to the police in 2000 for crimes committed in 1991. Police reports stated that Singh's confession was spurred by his wish to start a new life following his trial. Hans Joachin Klein, a former colleague in arms of Carlos the Jackal, was tried in 2000, 25 years after his role in the infamous Carlos-led attack on the Organization of Petroleum-Exporting Countries (OPEC) oil ministers' meeting in 1974 and a lifetime on the run from the authorities. Therefore, even when protection from the enemy is not enough to keep the members part of the group at the initial phase(s), there may be little to protect them from relentless law-enforcement and intelligence efforts to bring them to justice (see also Bjorgo, 1995, 1997).

Security services often attempt to recruit ex-terrorists in an effort to persuade them to provide evidence against a terrorist movement. This may even become a factor in facilitating a way out of the group for an individual in the first place. Sean O'Callaghan regularly occupies a valuable educational role in raising awareness about the Provisional IRA. Eamon Collins, another IRA informer, gave evidence (as did O'Callaghan) at the trial of an alleged IRA leader, but was found murdered near his home a number of weeks later. Government credibility is crucial if disengagement is to be promoted as a possible counter-terrorism strategy, but the tactics used by many governments have been less than tasteful in attempting to procure 'supergrasses' in Northern Ireland (Walsh, 1989) or the 'pentiti' in Italy (Evans, 1989; Jamieson, 1989).

The Irish and British governments have attempted to facilitate organisational disengagement by Irish Republicans by reiterating their view that they do not see the IRA's decommissioning as an act of 'surrender'. This in effect is a 'face-saving' strategy via which the IRA leadership can attempt to gradually de-escalate its campaign (on all levels bar political).

However, the reintegration of terrorists into society poses significant challenges. In Northern Ireland, despite the monumental progress made in the region, forgiveness does not come cheap, and while high-level terrorist violence may currently remain a thing of the past, the civil violence and naked sectarianism slowly destroying community-based peace efforts are not encouraging signs.

Even if the entire organisation begins to dissipate, the route members may take can vary enormously. Some might drift towards other illegal activity (such as organised crime; see Bruce, 1992; Horgan and Taylor, 1999), an option made easier if the individual was involved in similar activity whilst a member of the terrorist organisation (e.g. in the context of fundraising). In such circumstances, the individual may still attempt to employ the nom de guerre of the movement in the face of threats from rival groupings. Some might drift into social isolation and the psychological problems this can create (depression, substance abuse, etc.), while others might find employment and a healthy life with new relationships. Often the perceived availability of viable avenues might reflect such issues as: (a) the extent of the person's involvement in the group (e.g. very part-time, part-time, or full-time), (b) the extent to which psychological support and identity comes solely from the terrorist group itself, and (c) whether or not the terrorist feels that his or her (perhaps lifetime) commitment to the group has actually been worth it. Following the decommissioning announcement, many Irish Republicans have continued their soul-searching, and some security analysts believe that it is possibly only because the other dissident groups in Ireland are perceived as either in complete disarray (i.e. the Real IRA) or too 'ideologically motivated' (i.e. the Continuity IRA) that there has not been a mass shifting of allegiance.

WHAT SHOULD WE DO?

At this early stage, it is far too ambitious to provide a comprehensive discussion of disengagement from terrorism from an individual perspective. If anything concrete has emerged from the preceding examples it is surely that our notion of 'leaving terrorism' is probably too simplistic. As a psychologist studying terrorism, I adopt a psychological perspective in addressing the various factors and influences outlined here, but we could have also tackled disengagement from a variety of levels of analysis: in many cases, the 'ending' of terrorism is a process that for a terrorist organisation begins and progresses over a significant period of time and is often started with the realisation that terrorist violence on its own rarely, if ever, manages to achieve its aims. In the case of the Provisional IRA, the joint development of what senior Republican Danny Morrison once famously described as the 'bullet box and armalite strategy'—the pursuit of the movement's political aspirations but with an increasingly discriminate and tactical use of its 'armed struggle'—probably signalled the very beginning of the process that recently culminated in decommissioning.

It might be too obvious at this point to suggest that more research is needed, but given the lack of basic data (from which we might in the future move from the hypothetical more easily), at least the call for more research should be forgiven. The preceding discussions have attempted to illustrate some of the issues relevant to thinking about disengagement, but there are many questions to be answered and the following list of research issues might represent a modest beginning to such a process. Their common emphasis does not rest on identifying implications for law-enforcement or policy concerns, but on illustrating psychological principles inherent in thinking about disengagement as an important research topic per se:

1 Assessing and understanding the nature and extent of the roles played by individual terrorists within their organisations in terms of promoting either momentary or long-term de-escalation of tactical activity, strategic activity or indeed of an entire campaign.
2 An exploration of the measures taken (if any) within terrorist organisations in the psychological preparation of organisational de-escalation (with an impending disintegration).
3 An analysis of what terrorist documentation and training material has to say about individual disengagement.
4 An exploration of what happens to members during temporary cessations of organisational terrorist activity (e.g. during ceasefires) and the steps taken (if any) to attempt to maintain organisational unity.
5 An exploration of ex-member lives outside the terrorist structure—what are the psychological effects of increased isolation from the group? This might be considered at a variety of levels—personal, family, etc.—and explored as a function of varying pressures on the individual depending on the social, political or organisational climate.
6 An exploration of the factors that lead to partial disengagement from role-specific behaviours: for example voluntary movement away from involvement in actual operations (e.g. shootings, bombings) to voluntary involvement in other activities (e.g. political, organisational, financial, etc.).
7 An exploration of how and to what extent former terrorists express remorse, and what actions are taken (if any) to alleviate the associated stress.

8 Comparative analyses of the experiences of involuntarily disengaged
  terrorists (e.g. imprisoned terrorists or those who have been moved into
  other roles, and those affected by organisational disintegration, etc.);
  similarly, comparative analyses between different forms of political extremism (see especially Bjorgo, 1997).
9 An examination of the possibility that different roles and functions
  within terrorist organisations have varying attrition rates with respect
  to voluntary disengagement (e.g. fundraisers vs. gunmen vs. bombers
  vs. organisers vs. political actors, etc.): what are the psychological implications of performance within specific organisational functions and
  are some roles more likely than others to result in voluntary disengagement? This serves a dual function in moving the nature and direction
  of other psychological research from the profiling of 'terrorists' per se to
  the profiling of organisational roles and functions.

A NOTE ON METHODOLOGIES

The most readily available data on disengagement comes from autobiographical sources, and while more basic research using such sources ought
to be encouraged (they remain under-exploited, as does much primary
source terrorist material, which is particularly disappointing in light of
exciting new developments in grounded theory and content analysis), caution must be exercised in assessing the value of the data from such sources.

In particular, Cordes (1987) reminds us to develop an awareness of the
ways in which terrorists 'see themselves': in terrorist autobiographies,
motivation for involvement and justification for violence sometimes relate more to the organisation's propaganda and ideological control than
any 'revealing' personal account (see also Wright and Bryett, 1991). Two
particular ways in which terrorists reveal knowledge about themselves,
according to Cordes (1987), are through propaganda efforts (in an attempt
to persuade others, usually expressed at a group or organisational level
through statements or communiqués, etc.), and 'auto-propaganda' efforts
(in an attempt to 'persuade themselves') (p. 318). Let us be in no doubt that
terrorists would like to be seen in particular ways, and in this respect, for
example, caution has been drawn to Pearlstein's (1991) use of terrorists'
memoirs in his detailed inferring of motive (Rapoport, 1988; Chapter 1,
this volume).

The language of terrorists is rooted in various social-psychological concepts both to justify their activities and continued involvement in terrorism (e.g. attribution theory, the Fundamental Attribution Error, the
actor-observer effect and so on), but there is a possibility that similar issues may be used to 'justify' disengagement or present an otherwise positive and self-serving image. According to Horgan (1999), particular events

in terrorist autobiographies are usually recalled with more clarity and vivid detail than the stages of gradual movement towards involvement in terrorist-related activities. Again in accordance with Cordes' observation, it is perhaps a tendency of acquired language and ideology more generally to help push particular events as contributory factors, and thus with the benefit of hindsight attribute at least some degree of causal responsibility to external factors. How such issues translate to matters of disengagement is easy to imagine—it is as common for specific incidents to be highlighted in autobiographical sources as contributory reasons for disengagement as for engagement.

Rather than attempting to seek some 'truth' in such sources, then, a much more promising avenue is to explore the nature of the accounts presented in such texts, perhaps in an effort to identify common processes.

Reliance on autobiographical sources will always suffer from a variety of problems, perhaps the most obvious being that there is little autobiographic material available. First-hand research, primarily via interview, is necessarily limited by a number of different practical issues, not least fears for personal safety. However, such research is possible, and the experiences of a small number of researchers have demonstrated that terrorist organisations generally tend to co-operate and be facilitative of researchers' approaches (with the proviso that the researcher is assumed to play some potential role in achieving a greater audience, for instance). Horgan's (2000) experiences with Irish Republicans illustrate this, and in the context of disengagement we might be able to identify potential interviewee types as physically or psychologically disengaged, 'involuntarily disengaged' across either physical or psychological dimensions, as well as whether or not they are now to be viewed as 'repentant' or 'unrepentant' (this final dimension contains obvious implications for questioning styles and interrogative strategies on the part of the interviewer). It is at this point that we may return to the earlier mention of Dingley's sentiment about the future likelihood of research on the Northern Ireland conflict. In fact, it is in the dissolution of terrorist organisations that interviewing has become more possible than ever before, yet we continue to dismiss these opportunities as no longer pertinent to contemporary research.

CONCLUSION

The following central assertions may have emerged from this rudimentary analysis:

1 Disengagement from terrorism is not a process that necessarily begins for the individual when the overall movement faces a threat to

its survival (whether through success, failure or stalemate). The seeds
for disengagement may emerge quite early in the developmental phase
of terrorist life but not emerge more obviously until circumstances allow for its expression or more obvious relevance for the individual concerned.

2 It is important to realise that the factors that influence the decision-
making of an individual terrorist can differ significantly at various
stages of the developmental phases—the becoming, remaining and leaving phases. We should not assume that progression through a terrorist
organisation can be examined in discrete, non-dynamic terms.

3 A major stumbling block in thinking about terrorist behaviour lies in a
fundamental problem with the identification of terrorism and a skewed
focus on the violence of terrorism as being the central quality of the
broader process of political extremism. Terrorist violence is just one
aspect (the most public) of an array of complex activities, and any attempt to understand 'why people leave terrorism' must acknowledge
the broader processes as well as generating an understanding about
the array of roles, functions and behaviours (not all illegal) that either
directly or indirectly contribute to terrorism. How and why people move
into and out of roles and functions within terrorist groups is a major
area for further exploration.

4 An undeniable lack of basic knowledge on disengagement comes from
the failure to address the issue in any systematic fashion, as well as
further failure to consider first-hand research within a solid methodological framework. These problems can be further extended to the fact
that we lack a conceptual base in analysing terrorist behaviour (Horgan
and Taylor, 2001; Taylor and Horgan, 2001).

To try to answer why people leave terrorism in straightforward terms
obscures the impressive complexity of the question and the possible assumptions that underpin it. It is for this reason that the question 'Why do
people leave terrorism?' is as conceptually and pragmatically difficult to
answer as 'Why do people become terrorists?' Leaving terrorism may be the
result of circumstances outside of one's control, or just like joining a terrorist group it may even resemble a decision made from an array of personal,
social or occupational choices. If terrorism is a product of its own time
and place, this thinking can also be extended to terrorist decision-making
and to the processes influencing how terrorists see themselves (Tololyan,
1989). Leaving terrorism from an individual perspective ought to be
viewed with the same complexity as our now undeniably over-researched
issues relating to the initial phase. If at some future point there are calls
for a taxonomy of factors contributing to disengagement (some have been
suggested here), researchers will need to accept the dynamic processes

influencing individual behaviour regarding any stage, role or function of the terrorist group.

REFERENCES

Alexander, Y. and Myers, K.A. (Eds) (1982). *Terrorism in Europe*. London: Croom Helm.

Baumann, M. (1979). *Terror or Love?: Bommi Baumann's Own Story of his Life as a West German Urban Guerrilla*. New York: Grove Press.

Bjorgo, T. (Ed.) (1995). *Terror from the Extreme Right*. London: Frank Cass and Co.

Bjorgo, T. (1997). *Racist and Right Wing Violence in Scandinavia: Patterns, Perpetrators, and Responses*. Oslo: Tano Aschehoughs Fonteneserie.

Brocker, J. and Rubin, J.Z. (1985). *Entrapment in Escalating Conflicts*. New York: Springer-Verlag.

Bruce, S. (1992). *The Red Hand: Protestant Paramilitaries in Northern Ireland*. Oxford: Oxford University Press.

Clare, S. (1996). *Ceasefire was never genuine—IRA killer*. Press Association Newswire Service, London, 9 December.

Clarke, L. (1987). *Broadening the Battlefield: the H-Blocks and the Rise of Sinn Fein*. Dublin: Gill and Macmillan.

Cordes, B. (1987). Euroterrorists talk about themselves: a look at the literature. In P. Wilkinson and A.M. Stewart (Eds), *Contemporary Research on Terrorism* (pp. 318–36). Aberdeen: Aberdeen University Press.

Crenshaw, M. (1985). An organisational political approach to the analysis of political terrorism. *Orbis*, **29**(3), 465–89.

Crenshaw, M. (1986). The psychology of political terrorism. In M.G. Hermann (Ed.), *Political Psychology: Contemporary Problems and Issues* (pp. 379–413). London: Jossey-Bass.

Deaux, K. and Wrightsman, L.S. (1988). *Social Psychology*. Pacific Grove, CA: Brooks/Cole.

Debray, R. (1967). *Revolution in the Revolution?* New York: MR Press.

Dingley, J. (1999). Peace processes and Northern Ireland: squaring circles? *Terrorism and Political Violence*, **11**(3), 32–52.

Evans, R.H. (1989). Terrorism and subversion of the state: Italian legal responses. *Terrorism and Political Violence*, **1**(3), 324–52.

Horgan, J. (1997). Issues in terrorism research. *The Police Journal*, **50**(3), 193–202.

Horgan, J. (1999). *Psychology and terrorism research*. Paper presented at the Psychological Society of Ireland 30th Annual Conference, Cork, 11–14 November.

Horgan, J. (2000). *Terrorism and Political Violence: A Psychological Perspective*. PhD dissertation. Department of Applied Psychology, University College Cork.

Horgan, J. and Taylor, M. (1999). Playing the green card: financing the Provisional IRA—part 1. *Terrorism and Political Violence*, **11**(2), 1–38.

Horgan, J. and Taylor, M. (2001). The making of a terrorist. *Jane's Intelligence Review*, **13**(12), 16–18.

Jamieson, A. (1989). *The Heart Attacked: Terrorism and Conflict in the Italian State*. London: Marian Boyers.

Janis, I. (1972). *Victims of Groupthink*. Boston, MA: Houghton Mifflin.

McCauley, C.R. and Segal, M.E. (1989). Terrorist individuals and terrorist groups: the normal psychology of extreme behaviour. In J. Groebel and J.H. Goldstein

(Eds), *Terrorism: Psychological Perspectives* (pp. 41–64). Seville: Publicaciones de la Universidad de Sevilla.

Oots, K.L. (1989). Organisational perspectives on the formation and disintegration of terrorist groups. *Terrorism*, **12**, 139–52.

Pearlstein, R.M. (1991). *The Mind of the Political Terrorist*. Wilmington, DE: Scholarly Resources.

Post, J.M. (1987). Group and organisational dynamics of political terrorism: implications for counterterrorist policy. In P. Wilkinson and A.M. Stewart (Eds), *Contemporary Research on Terrorism* (pp. 307–17). Aberdeen: Aberdeen University Press.

Rapoport, D.C. (Ed.) (1988). *Inside Terrorist Organisations*. London: Frank Cass and Co.

Silke, A.P. (1998). The lords of discipline: the methods and motives of paramilitary vigilantism in Northern Ireland. *Low Intensity Conflict and Law Enforcement*, **7**(2), 121–56.

Spire, A. (1988). Le terrorisme intellectuel. *Patio*, **11**, 150–58.

Taylor, M. (1988). *The Terrorist*. London: Brassey's.

Taylor, M. and Horgan, J. (2001). The psychological and behavioural bases of Islamic fundamentalism. *Terrorism and Political Violence*, **13**(4), 37–71.

Taylor, M. and Quayle, E. (1994). *Terrorist Lives*. London: Brassey's.

Tololyan, K. (1989). Narrative culture and terrorist motivation. In J. Shotter and K.J. Gergen (Eds), *Texts of Identity—Inquiries in Social Construction Series* (pp. 99–118). London: Sage.

Walsh, D.P.J. (1989). The impact of antisubversive laws on police powers and practices in Ireland: the silent erosion of individual freedom. *Temple Law Review*, **62**(4), 1099–129.

Wright, J. and Bryett, K. (1991). Propaganda and justice administration in Northern Ireland. *Terrorism and Political Violence*, **3**(2), 25–42.

PART II

Victims of Terrorism

CHAPTER 7

The Psychological Impact of Isolated Acts of Terrorism

GINNY SPRANG

University of Kentucky, USA

INTRODUCTION

Throughout the ages, society and its members have withstood countless tragedies and acts of violence: natural disasters, plagues and acts of war, among others. To our anguish, terrorism has become one of the most destructive threats to the human condition. Each event tears at the fabric of society and raises questions about the impact of these traumas and the capacity of humans to adapt to cataclysmic events. Is there an aetiological link between the trauma experience and hypothesised outcome? Does exposure to trauma have long-term effects? Are there personal risk factors for the development and maintenance of post-trauma psychopathology? And how does treatment and the utilisation of specific coping strategies impact the post-disaster response? These questions have received considerable attention in the literature, though considerable gaps in our understanding remain. As we sift through the aftermath of tragedies, we search for answers to these questions.

The years since the Oklahoma City bombing have provided opportunities to uncover some valuable clues. On 19 April 1995, a domestic terrorist bombed the Alfred Murrah Federal Building in Oklahoma City killing 168 people and injuring hundreds more. At the time this was the most destructive act of terrorism on US soil. Tragically, however, on September 11,

Terrorists, Victims and Society: Psychological Perspectives on Terrorism and its Consequences.
Edited by Andrew Silke. © 2003 John Wiley & Sons, Ltd.

2001, terrorists turned passenger planes into weapons of mass destruction, levelling the World Trade Center in New York City and crippling the Pentagon in Washington, DC. Thousands lost their lives that day, and in the days to follow isolated acts of terrorism claimed the lives of many more throughout the world. Counting the cost of these events requires calculations beyond the extent of property damage or summing up the number of dead and injured. The lives of countless others—rescue workers, police, family members, friends and bystanders—were shattered by the psychological, emotional, physical, spiritual and financial toll of these tragedies. Words like 'bioterrorism' and 'air marshals' replace the dialogue of the naive. Gone are the days of blind trust and unbreachable security. What price tag shall we place on the loss of innocence, on the loss of freedom?

Over the years, social scientists have laboured to understand the toll terrorism takes on the individual, community and society. Ethnographic analysis, survey research and field studies are but a few ways to capture and document the impact of terrorism. While the field is rapidly changing, some notable findings have emerged from trauma studies and these provide valuable insight into the post-terrorism experience. In this chapter, the findings from studies of the post-terror response to the Oklahoma City bombing, as well as results from studies of other isolated acts of terrorism, will be used as the context to explore the psychological impact of terrorism. To enhance this discussion, evidence from the scientific literature (i.e. quasi-experiments, epidemiology, clinical and participant observation studies) will be examined.

TERRORISM, TRAUMA AND PSYCHOPATHOLOGY

Quarantelli (1985) revealed two seemingly opposing views regarding the mental-health consequences of cataclysmic events. The first view holds that acts of violence have differential rather than across-the-board effects on those exposed to them. Different perspectives, life experiences and personality characteristics might cause one individual to view the act as traumatic and develop significant distress, whereas another individual might have little or no reaction to the event. The second view holds that terroristic acts are 'traumatic' life events, yielding 'very pervasive, deeply internalized, and essentially negative psychological effects' (p. 191). Despite their apparent contradictions, Quarantelli concedes that these positions are most likely 'additional versus oppositional' (p. 190). The question is not whether or not terrorism is traumatic, but whether exposure to terrorism produces the same observable, predictable responses in those exposed.

By definition, terrorism is intended to be traumatising. Waugh (2001) in his chapter on 'Managing Terrorism as an Environmental Hazard' outlines several key components of terrorism:

- The use of threat or extraordinary violence.
- Goal-directed, intentional behaviour to harm.
- The intention to psychologically disorganise and horrify not only the immediate victims, but those around them.
- The choice of victims for their symbolic value (even their innocence).

Given these elements, it is difficult to imagine a terroristic act that would not be considered a traumatic event. Even so, it is clear from the literature that exposure rates to traumatic events far exceed prevalence rates for psychopathology, suggesting a differential response pattern across victims.

To adapt to the traumatic event, victims must cope with the meaning of the trauma and the short-term and long-term effects of the terrorist act. Figley (1985) claims that the process of recovery requires a transformation from a disorganised psychological state (as a victim) to an ordered sense of well-being (as a survivor). To accomplish this adaptation, the individual must answer some fundamental questions, such as: What happened? Why did it happen? Why did I respond the way I did? What if it happens again? How can I live in a world where these things can happen to people like me? This type of cognitive processing is crucial to post-terrorism adaptation and may be dependent on two major sets of variables: individual characteristics (e.g. risk factors) and event characteristics (e.g. type of event, scope of the event, level of exposure, proximity to the event). Research on disasters and other types of trauma tells us that the relationship between an act of terrorism and the psycho-biological response is likely mediated by these important contextual variables.

As originally described in the early trauma literature, the primacy of the trauma was long considered the primary aetiologic agent for the development of post-trauma stress. However, as early as 1984, Foy and associates had identified characteristics of the event to be of central importance. Numerous studies have also uncovered a dose–response relationship between event severity and the development of psychopathology, namely post-traumatic stress disorder (PTSD); the cause of the trauma, its scale, and whether it was anticipated (Halligan and Yehuda, 2000; Kleber and Braum, 1992; Shalev *et al.*, 1996). Since that time, many studies have uncovered individual vulnerability factors that increase the risk of post-trauma psychiatric morbidity. Table 7.1 outlines major risk factors for the development of post-terrorism psychopathology along with important citations.

Table 7.1 Risk factors for the development of post-terrorism psychopathology

Type of risk factor	Variable	Important citations
Demographics	Gender (being female) Lower levels of education Lower income Ethnic minorities	Breslau et al., 1999 Breslau et al., 1998 Norris, 1992
Cognitive	Lower IQ Increased neurological soft signs and increased developmental problems Explicit memory impairment	Macklin et al., 1998 Gurvits et al., 2000 Yehuda and McFarlane, 1995 Jenkins et al., 1998
Biological	Increased heart rate Elevated norepinephrine during event Low levels of cortisol (HPA axis abnormalities)	Shalev et al., 1998 Pittman, 1998 Resnick et al., 1995 Yehuda, McFarlane and Shalev, 1998 Yehuda et al., 2000
Familial or genetic	Familial transmission of PTSD Family history of mood, anxiety, or substance abuse	True et al., 1993 Yehuda et al., 1998 Davidson et al., 1985
Prior psychiatric history and personality dimensions	Past psychiatric disturbance Coping Adult avoidant, antisocial and neurotic personality Peritraumatic dissociation	McFarlane, 1989 Breslau et al., 1998 Schnurr and Vielhaues, 1999 Schnurr, Friedman and Rosenberg, 1993 Koopman, Classen and Spiegel, 1994 Bremner et al., 1992 Shalev et al., 1996 Spiegel, 1991
Environmental and event	History of exposure Family instability Good social support utilisation Intermediate central scope of disaster Man-made cause	Davidson et al., 1991 Breslau et al., 1999 Bremner et al., 1993 King et al., 1996 Solomon, Kulincer and Avitzur, 1998 Green et al., 1983 Sprang, 1999 Rubonis and Bickman, 1991

The majority of the studies identified in Table 7.1 specifically investigate both sub-threshold and threshold PTSD symptomatology, and to a lesser degree other anxiety disorders such as acute stress disorders and generalised anxiety disorders. Research suggests, however, that an individual's response to a terroristic event can involve a constellation of symptomatology, including mood disorders, substance misuse disorders and disorders of extreme stress not otherwise specified (DESNOS). These conditions may exist co-morbidly or as pre- or peritrauma risk factors. A description of some of these disorders is provided below.

Post-Traumatic Stress Disorder

The *Diagnostic and Statistical Manual of Mental Disorders* (fourth edition—text revision, DSM-IV TR) identifies six criterion that must be met before a diagnosis of PTSD can be made. The stressor criteria (Criteria A) describes characteristics of the event that must exist for the individual to qualify for a DSM-IV-sanctioned diagnosis. In its current form, it states that a person must have experienced, witnessed or been confronted with an event that involved actual or threatened death or serious injury, threat to physical integrity of the individual or those around them. This stressor criterion has been revised from its form in the DSM-III-R to reflect the seriousness of the event and its impact on the individual involved. It allows for inclusion of affected family members or indirect victims such as emergency-response workers or family members of terrorism victims. It also allows for PTSD to be considered if there was no threat to life but a physical danger, as in the case of rape, hostage-taking, kidnapping or child sexual abuse. Part B of Criteria A addresses the response to the event, requiring that the individual react with intense fear, helplessness and/or horror. A provision is made for young children who may be too young to clearly describe these reactions by including disordered or agitated behaviour.

The re-experiencing criteria (Criteria B) outlines five possible symptoms of distress including recurrent and distressing recollections of the event, recurrent distressing dreams, acting or feeling as if the trauma is recurring, intense psychological distress at exposure to internal or external cues that symbolise or resemble the trauma, and physiological reactivity on exposure to internal or external cues that symbolise or resemble an aspect of the trauma. The individual needs to experience only one of these symptoms to meet the re-experiencing criteria for PTSD.

The avoidance symptomatology described in Criteria C is generally conceptualised as falling into two primary categories: effortful avoidance and numbing/dissociation (Foa, Riggs and Gershuny, 1995). Three (or more) of the following symptoms must be present: efforts to avoid thoughts, feelings, conversations, or activities or people associated with the trauma; inability to recall an important aspect of the trauma; markedly diminished interest or participation in activities; feelings of detachment or estrangement from others; restricted range of affect; and a sense of a foreshortened future. Avoidance symptomatology can be mistaken for symptoms of depression if distinctions are not made between sadness (depression) and the numbing and dissociative qualities indicative of PTSD. Of course, both conditions may exist co-morbidly.

Criteria D refers to symptoms of physiological arousal, as indicated by two or more of the following: difficulty falling or staying asleep; irritability or outbursts of anger; difficulty concentrating; hypervigilance; and exaggerated startle response. According to Resnick (2001), not only do those with PTSD suffer from pronounced startled reactions, they do not appear to habituate to repeated presentations of stimuli as those without PTSD.

Finally, the fifth criteria requires that B, C and D symptoms persist for at least a month. All of these symptoms must cause an impairment in the individual's social or occupational functioning (a requirement of Criteria 6). Mild or occasional symptoms that are short-lived and/or do not interfere with the person's life should be considered as falling in the range of normal reactions to stressful events.

As stated earlier, not everyone exposed to an act of terrorism will develop PTSD. In the largest, most recognised prevalence study conducted to date, Kessler *et al.* (1995) surveyed 2812 men and 365 women and found a population lifetime prevalence of PTSD to be 8 per cent overall (10 per cent for women and 5 per cent for men). In those exposed to trauma, the prevalence rates rose to 20 per cent for women and 8 per cent for men. Although other studies provide different figures of 12 per cent (Resnick *et al.*, 1993) and 9 per cent (Breslau *et al.*, 1991), a lifetime population prevalence of 5 to 6 per cent for men and 10 to 12 per cent for women is accepted.

Disorders of Extreme Stress Not Otherwise Specified (DESNOS)

Over the past two decades, writers have documented symptomatology that correlates to various degrees with PTSD, but exceeds the symptoms outlined in the PTSD construct (Herman, 1992; Kidd, Ford and Nasby, 1996; Pelcovitz *et al.*, 1996). Herman (1992) used the term 'complex PTSD' or 'disorders of extreme stress (not otherwise specified) (DESNOS)'. Prior to the DSM-IV revision, field trials were conducted to determine whether there was a separate disorder that depicted a more complex form of PTSD. Although it is still unclear whether the symptoms of DESNOS constitute a more severe variant of PTSD (in its simplest form), or whether they constitute a separate disorder, the initial field trials suggested that DESNOS symptoms reflect a set of associated features of PTSD. Although DESNOS is not formally recognised as a diagnostic entity at this time, numerous trauma researchers have identified a constellation of symptomatology to describe the disorder.

DESNOS is conceptualised as a cluster of chronic problems with the regulation of self, consciousness and relationships that is hypothesised to occur when an extreme trauma (such as a terroristic act) compromises the individual's sense of self and his or her trust in the world. DESNOS is formally defined by Pelcovitz *et al.* (1997) as containing eight sets of criteria:

1 alternations in the regulation of impulses and affect (i.e. rage, lethality, engaging in dangerous risk-taking behaviour);
2 alterations in attention or consciousness (i.e. pathological dissociation);
3 alterations in self-perception (i.e. subjugation);
4 alterations in perception of the perpetrator (i.e. a distorted or unrealistic view of the perpetrator's power or authority);
5 alterations in relations with others (i.e. victimisation of others);
6 revictimisation, (i.e. extreme distrust and suspiciousness);
7 somatisation (i.e. exacerbated physical complaints with no known physiological cause);
8 alterations in systems of meaning (i.e. hopelessness or loss of faith).

The characterological components (i.e. relationship disruptions, changes to identity) and repetition of harm (self-destructive behaviours, lethality, victimisation of others) were included based on a theory that these are disruptions in personality based in severe, ongoing stress versus symptoms of simple PTSD (Dietrich, 1996).

Acute Stress Disorder

Acute Stress Disorder (ASD) was included in the DSM-IV to describe individuals who tend to have a short-term but clinically significant response to trauma. Not recognised in earlier versions of the DSM, ASD symptomatology was sometimes referred to as 'sub-threshold' PTSD because individuals did not have enough B, C or D symptoms or were not symptomatic long enough to meet the temporal requirement for PTSD. Emerging research from Spiegel *et al.* (1996) that individuals whose levels of dissociation increase during and immediately after a traumatic event are more likely to develop more chronic forms of PTSD prompted further consideration of this condition as a DSM-IV anxiety disorder, though some argue that the inclusion of ASD as a separate diagnostic entity was premature. For example, evidence for the role of dissociative symptoms in the manifestation of PTSD was supported primarily by the Spiegel *et al.* study, and has been challenged by other researchers (Brewin *et al.*, 1999). Even so, the inclusion of ASD is likely to spawn other studies aimed at testing the validity of the conceptual assumptions.

Based on the DSM-IV description, ASD has the same event criterion as PTSD and requires that the individual has symptomatology from each of the PTSD symptom clusters (re-experiencing, avoidance and increased arousal), though only one symptom from each cluster is compulsory. In addition, the individual must be experiencing one of the following symptoms of dissociation: (1) numbing or detachment, (2) reduced awareness of surroundings, (3) derealisation, (4) depersonalisation, or (5) dissociative amnesia. The symptoms must be evident for at least two days but for no longer than four weeks. As with PTSD, the symptomatology must be severe enough to cause functional impairment.

Uncomplicated and Complicated Bereavement

Bereavement is generally conceptualised as the process of mourning the loss of a loved one. In its uncomplicated form, it is considered a normal reaction to death, and not a psychological disorder. In fact, the DSM-IV identifies it as a condition that may be the focus of clinical attention, but not one that constitutes a psychopathological state. Moreover, researchers are recognising the role of the mode of death in predicting or influencing the course of bereavement (Rando, 1995; Sprang, 1995).

Sudden, unexpected death has been identified as a primary determining factor for the development of complicated bereavement (Parkes and Weiss, 1983; Raphael, 1983; Sprang, 1997). The shock of the unexpected loss can be so stressful that it can overwhelm the ego and the individual's capacity to cope, thus constituting a trauma. The following factors have been identified as complicating variables in the development of the grief response (Rando, 1995):

- The individual's assumptive world is violently shattered and the individual experiences a profound loss of security and confidence in the world.
- The loss is perceived as confusing and senseless.
- There was no opportunity to say goodbye or reach closure with the deceased.
- Biopsychosocial manifestations of grief are prolonged and unremitting.
- The individual tends to ruminate and reconstruct events related to the act of terrorism.
- The violent death may be accompanied by a series of secondary losses (loss of employment, privacy, relationships, etc.).

- Normative grief responses are experienced more intensely and are accompanied by associated features of victimisation (i.e. need for attribution, disorganisation or survivor guilt).
- The bereavement response is often complicated by PTSD symptomatology.

Emerging research and suggestions from clinicians make it indisputable that in the future a delineation of diagnostic criteria for complicated or pathological mourning must be made, and these classifications must be included in future revisions of the DSM-IV.

THE OKLAHOMA CITY EXPERIENCE

The Oklahoma City experience is unique in that it represents an act of terrorism in an unlikely place, in a nation that until then was naive to its vulnerabilities. Among the 168 dead were 19 children who were spending the day in a daycare centre within the Murrah Federal Building. Oklahoma was an unlikely location for a terrorist attack, a small southwest US city with no strong political presence and no identified industrial, communication, transportation, military or financial targets. Oklahoma City's proximity to the site of the Branch Davidian fire in Waco, Texas, exactly two years earlier, may have been its primary vulnerability. If the goal of terrorism is to terrorise, then the selection of Oklahoma City as the target was shrewd. The universal cry across the nation was clear: 'If it could happen in Oklahoma City, it could happen anywhere.' A meta-analysis of the disaster literature conducted by Rubonis and Bickman (1991) uncovered two important event-related variables that may affect the relationship between this terrorist act and subsequent psychopathology: the death rate and the degree of human culpability in the event.

Based on studies conducted by Gleser *et al*. (1981), Green *et al*. (1983) and Shore, Tatum and Vollmer (1986), the death rate proved to be a powerful moderator of the relationship between traumatic events and consequent psychological problems for two important reasons. High death rates mean firstly that more individuals were exposed to the threat of death, and secondly that bereavement over the loss of life becomes a confounding variable, exacerbating post-terror stress.

The degree of human responsibility for the event has been found to be predictive of variation in post-trauma psychosocial functioning, though the nature of this change is equivocal (Rubonis and Bickman, 1991). An individual's cognitive perceptions of blame and control may mediate the relationship between responsibility and psychopathology. Baum, Fleming and Davidson (1983) reviewed studies that suggested that higher levels of stress were associated with human-made disasters due to the availability of a target for blame and anger. Likewise, Davidson *et al.* (1987) found that subjects with more loss of control reported more stress-related symptomatology than comparison subjects. However, these findings are inconsistent with other literature (Abramson *et al.*, 1978) that found support for significantly lower levels of psychopathology manifestations when the cause of the event is identifiable. It may be that the inconsistency of these findings is related to the confounding of attributions regarding the cause of the event (assignment of blame) with attributions regarding the problems related to the event, a problem inherent in the collection of perceptual data.

The unexpected, human-made nature of the Oklahoma City bombing became a crucial theme in the social and professional discourse that followed, and provided opportunities to obtain crucial data about the psychological impact of isolated acts of terrorism. The following sections describe three studies that sought to further define the psychological impact of trauma and describe the differential effects of exposure, proximity, treatment and coping across populations.

Study 1

The first study sought to determine if the dose–response relationship uncovered in studies with directly exposed groups (Green *et al.*, 1983; Shore *et al.*, 1986) extends to the community as a whole, and if the occurrence and intensity of the post-disaster response resembles a linear function of the degree of indirect bombing exposure experienced by these study respondents. The following research hypotheses were examined:

1 That the occurrence and intensity of an individual's post-terror response resembles a linear function of the degree of exposure experienced by the study respondents, with the more exposed group experiencing higher levels of distress, a higher occurrence of psychopathology and more prolonged symptomatology than less exposed groups.
2 That the level of exposure can be used to differentiate the expression of symptoms (avoidance, re-experiencing and increased arousal) and associated victimisation symptomatology (DESNOS-related symptoms) in study respondents.
3 That the physical proximity of the individual to the terroristic bombing will impact the expression of distress, regardless of the amount of exposure. Individuals who live and/or work in close proximity to the event, but are not directly exposed to it, will express higher levels of distress than those who reside and work in another area.

Methods

Sample. The sample was selected from a computer-generated list of tele-phone numbers in two cities; Oklahoma City and Lexington, Kentucky. The first group consisted of 244 adult (18 years or older) residents who were interviewed six months following the bombing of the Murrah Federal Building. Census data and city plat maps were used to divide each city into six geographic regions. A systematic random sample of households using a sampling scheme designed to provide an age, race and gender distribu-tion that would approximate that of the total population was employed. Possible respondents were randomly selected from a computer-generated list of all possible telephone numbers by prefix and then sorted into six geographic regions. The proportion of the population that belonged to each subgroup was then estimated. Each interviewer was instructed to select a systematic, random sample of residents from each area and to continue interviewing until a specified number of individuals representative of gen-der, racial and income groups was obtained. The proportions were adjusted based on the demographic profile of each region compared to the demo-graphic distribution of the entire city in question. The interviews were anonymous and voluntary.

Initial contact with the potential household was guided by a protocol that required three attempts before the household was deleted from the list and replaced by the next available household. If an adult answered the phone, his or her participation in the study was solicited. If he or she agreed to participate, whether or not he or she had been exposed to another traumatic stimuli (other than the bombing) in the past five years was determined by using the Stressful Life Experiences Screening Form (Stamm, 1996). For the purposes of this study, direct victims, those who had a family member or friend killed or injured in the bombing, as well as those who had been exposed to a traumatic stimuli (as defined by the DSM-IV's depiction of a traumatic event) within the past five years, were excluded from the sample. It was impossible to complete the call for 39 of the numbers listed due to busy signals, disconnected numbers or no answer. Four respondents reported being direct victims of the bombing, six reported experiencing a traumatic stressor in the past five years, and only 13 respondents declined to participate in the study giving a response rate of 90.5 per cent.

Sample description. The mean age of the sample was 48 years with a standard deviation of 18.8. Males comprised 41.1 per cent and females represented 58.9 per cent of the sample population. The respondents were mostly married at the time of the study, with 18 per cent wid-owed, 14.4 per cent divorced or separated and 13.7 per cent single. The mean number of years of education was 12.8 with a standard deviation of 3.02. The distribution of race was 78 per cent white, 9.9 per cent African-American, 7.8 per cent Hispanic and 2.8 per cent Native American. The majority of respondents rated their overall health as good (52.1 per cent) or excellent (38.6 per cent) with only 7.6 per cent perceiving their overall health as fair, and 1.7 per cent as poor. Since validational studies and the establishment of population-specific scoring parameters necessitate the standardisation of generalisable measurement devices on diverse population groups, a second sample was selected.

A comparison group was drawn during the same time period from Lexington, Kentucky, a city of similar size to Oklahoma City, approximately 800 miles away and similar in demographic make-up. Using the same protocols described above, a random sample of 228 individuals was surveyed. Thirty-three households were excluded as unreachable, 30 individuals declined to participate and nine responded affirmatively to the victimisation question and were omitted from further analyses.

Measurement. The Traumatic Experiences Inventory (TEI) (Sprang, 1997) was used to measure each respondent's level of post-terrorism distress, in four domains; re-experiencing, increased arousal, avoidance and dissociation, and associated features of trauma. Since the cut-off ranges for the TEI have not been empirically established, the Structured Clinical Interview for the DSM-IV/PTSD (SCID) module (First *et al.*, 1996) was also used. Each respondent interviewed was given a SCID score of: 0 = PTSD symptoms absent or false, 1 = sub-threshold symptoms of PTSD (at this point, ASD was assessed), or 3 = PTSD confirmed. Additionally, a series of questions aimed at determining the existence of pre-bombing traumatic stress ('Have you ever been diagnosed with PTSD?'), the number and type of psychosocial services received ('What have you done to deal with your feelings about this event?') and general demographic questions were included.

Three single-item, global measures of distress were used to summarise the interviewer's assessment of the degree of threat experienced by the individual at the time of the bombing, the immediate experience of distress and the individual's current level of distress. These assessments were made using a five-point Likert scale with 0 equalling no perceived threat or distress and 5 signifying an extreme level of threat or distress. The following criteria were used to calculate and summarise the respondents' scores. The immediate response to trauma (IRT) was determined by taking the sum of the respondents' intensity scores as reported during the first two weeks and applying the following conversion rules: sum scores of 0 equal an IRT score of 0; a score of 1 to 25 equals an IRT score of 1; a score of 26 to 50 equals an IRT score of 2; a score of 51 to 75 equals an IRT score of 3; a score of 76 to 100 equals an IRT score of 4; and a score of 101 to 125 equals an IRT score of 5. The same conversion process was used to determine a current level of distress (CLD) score, with the same possible range of scores. An appraisal of threat (AT) rating was assigned prior to administration of the SCID or TEI interviews (so as to eliminate potential bias) by a trained, Masters-level interviewer. These assessments were made based on the interviewer's global appraisal of the amount of threat experienced using a single five-point Likert scale with lower scores indicating less perceived threat. An inter-rater reliability rating of 0.91 was established between the three interviewers in this study.

Findings

Based on their responses to survey items regarding exposure, the 472 subjects were divided into three groups; OKC1 (high exposure), OKC2 (low exposure) and the control group (Kentucky sample). Specifically, 109 subjects who reported hearing, seeing or feeling the blast were assigned to OKC1, those who resided in Oklahoma City but did not experience the blast were assigned to OKC2 (n = 145) and the control group included all 228 Kentucky respondents. The Oklahoma City sample selected was comparable (with no significant statistical differences) to the overall city population, with regards to all the demographic variables except race, with a slight under-representation of African-Americans (16 per cent in general population vs. 9.9 per cent in the sample) $(X2 (1, 458) = 6.3, p < 0.01)$. The comparison group was similar to the Oklahoma City group with regards to age, gender and marital status, and health. In terms of racial distribution, there was a significant difference, with the Kentucky sample containing fewer African-Americans (5.8 per cent vs. 94.2 per cent white) $(X2 (1, n = 472) = 9.5, p < 0.01)$ than the Oklahoma City group.

Analysis of variance revealed that threat of harm levels were higher for the OKC1 group $(F(2, 469) = 15.31, p < 0.01)$. Scheffe's post-hoc contrasts revealed that the OKC1 group (M 2.1, SD 1.2) was higher than the OKC2 group (M 1.8, SD 1.2), which exceeded that of the control group (M 1.5, SD 0.98) $(F(2, 469) = 15.31$, bonferroni adjusted p-value of 0.001). These findings support the hypothesis that the OKC2 group represents a differentially affected group versus a second control group.

In contrast, ANOVA (Analysis of Variance) indicated no significant differences in retrospective reports regarding the respondents' immediate reaction to the bombing, though significant differences are evident in the current level of distress about the event reported by the three groups $(F(2, 471) = 4.02, p < 0.05)$. Scheffe's post-hoc contrasts revealed the OKC1 and OKC2 group levels were higher than the comparison group.

The means and standard deviations for the four trauma subscales and the PTSD scale are presented in Table 7.2. Reference to the means outlined in this table shows that the more exposed group (OKC1) had higher victimisation scores and overall PTSD than the other two groups, with little difference revealed on the avoidance, re-experiencing and increased

Table 7.2 Means and standard deviations for the four trauma subscales for the three groups

	OKC1 (n = 109)		OKC2 (n = 145)		Control (n = 228)	
Measure	M	SD	M	SD	M	SD
Avoidance	2.6	0.8	2.2	0.3	2.0	1.1
Re-experiencing	3.5	0.7	3.4	0.6	2.9	0.67
Increased arousal	7.3	1.06	7.2	0.9	5.8	1.02
Victimisation	25.3	3.4	23.0	2.6	5.1	1.7
PTSD	2.6	0.4	1.6	0.03	0.6	0.01

arousal scales. ANOVA revealed the OKC1 group significantly differed from the OKC2 and the comparison group in the level of PTSD reported ($F(2, 470) = 16.73$, $p < 0.01$). With regards to the victimisation variable, there were significant differences between the two OKC groups and the comparison group ($F(2, 470) = 7.84$, $p < 0.001$). Pairwise comparison revealed no significant difference between the two OKC groups. There were no significant differences between groups with regard to avoidance ($F(2, 470) = 0.03$, $p = 0.57$), re-experiencing ($F(2, 470) = 0.08$, $p = 0.47$) and increased arousal ($F(2, 470) = 1.7$, $p = 0.09$). Using the diagnostic criteria outlined in the SCID-IV/PTSD module, 8.1 per cent of the OKC1 group, 7.8 per cent of the OKC2 group, and less than 1 per cent of the comparison group reported symptoms of PTSD. There was a significant difference between the OKC groups and the comparison group ($X2 = 10.7$, $df = 2, 468$, $p = 0.0047$).

Among those with diagnosable PTSD, there were no significant differences in the utilisation of mental-health services following the event in the three groups, with 1.26 per cent of the OKC1 group seeking services, 1.23 per cent of the OKC2 group and 0.9 per cent of the Kentucky group seeking services. The majority, 88.6 per cent of the overall sample, reported using informal interventions such as church, family and friends to cope with the tragedy. There were no significant differences in this pattern by group.

Study 2

From the initial 244 Oklahoma City respondents, two subgroups of respondents were examined in a follow-up study. First, those who reported symptoms consistent with a diagnosis of PTSD were followed for two years to determine the nature and course of the disorder. Specific attention was paid to the nature of the expression of PTSD, the development of other symptomatology, the temporal sequence and onset of pathology and the types of mental-health services used to address the disturbance. Secondly, those who reported sub-threshold symptoms were followed to determine if there was deterioration of functioning, exacerbation of symptoms over time and when or if symptoms abated. Results from the initial study indicate that of the original sample of 244 participants, 44 respondents reported symptoms consistent with PTSD (n = 20) or sub-threshold symptomatology (n = 24). These subjects were the focus of this study.

Methods

In addition to the six-month evaluation, the identified respondents were re-contacted and interviewed at nine months, 12 months, 15 months, 18 months and two years following the event. During the follow-up study, the same measurement systems were used as in the initial study, and identical decision protocols were used to determine the past incidence of a DSM-IV-sanctioned diagnosis, the existence of a new-onset disorder, and the existence of a subsyndromal disorder (i.e. two of the three symptom clusters for PTSD).

At the initial interview, the 29 females and 15 males had a mean age of 34.8 years (SD = 4.5) and a mean educational level of 13.3 years (SD = 2.1). Four of the participants were students, the rest were employed outside of the home (31) or as homemakers (9). Thirty-three subjects reported their marital status as 'married' during the evaluation period, seven were divorced or separated, one respondent had been widowed for 12 years and three were single, never married. Most reported good to excellent health with the exception of three respondents: one with Crohn's disease, one who suffered a heart attack six years prior, and one with rheumatoid arthritis. One individual reported a prior history of major depression, but was found to have been asymptomatic for three years prior to the bombing. Initially, all of the respondents reported willingness to participate in the follow-up study, but one participant with sub-threshold symptoms of PTSD became unreachable after the first follow-up (phone number disconnected) and was dropped from the study. The following results reflect the outcomes of the 43 remaining participants.

Treatment Status

When interviewed at six months, 38 per cent of these individuals had or were receiving psychological treatment for their symptoms. Following the initial evaluation, clinical intervention was recommended to all of the respondents with PTSD or subsyndromal symptoms. However, only four additional respondents followed through with the referrals, bringing the total number of respondents seeking treatment in this study to 20. The types of treatment used included outpatient psychotherapy only (n = 11), psychotherapy plus psychopharmacological intervention (n = 6), and psychosocial interventions (i.e. support groups) (n = 3).

Table 7.3 Means and standard deviations for the treatment and non-treatment groups

Treatment Group

Traumatic experiences inventory	6 months n = 16		9 months n = 20		12 months n = 20		15 months n = 20		18 months n = 20		24 months n = 20	
	M	SD	M	SD	M	SD	M	SD	M	SD	M	SD
Avoidance	22.7	0.7	12.0	1.1	14.8	1.4	13.9	0.6	13.8	1.9	12.6	0.7
Re-experiencing	9.9	0.4	8.1	0.5	8.0	0.8	8.1	0.4	7.8	0.5	7.9	0.6
Increased arousal	16.8	1.0	6.1	0.9	6.0	1.2	6.1	0.9	5.9	0.8	5.8	1.0
Victimisation	26.9	0.4	12.3	3.6	11.6	4.4	11.0	2.8	11.3	3.6	10.9	2.8

Non-treatment Group

Traumatic experiences inventory	6 months n = 28		9 months n = 23		12 months n = 23		15 months n = 23		18 months n = 23		24 months n = 23	
	M	SD	M	SD	M	SD	M	SD	M	SD	M	SD
Avoidance	22.8	0.8	12.7	0.9	12.8	1.4	11.1	0.8	11.4	0.9	12.3	0.9
Re-experiencing	14.1	1.1	9.0	1.0	8.9	1.1	8.4	0.6	8.1	0.4	8.0	0.8
Increased arousal	16.3	1.4	6.1	0.9	6.0	1.0	6.0	0.9	5.9	0.8	5.9	1.0
Victimisation	26.6	5.1	25.4	7.3	25.5	8.0	23.0	9.1	20.8	11.0	17.9	9.4

Post-Bombing Symptomatology

Using analysis of variance with repeated measures, a Treatment Group X Time Model for each TEI dimension was used. For 'victimisation', a main effect for the Treatment Group (untreated had higher scores) was found; none of the other TEI subscales showed such an effect. The means and standard deviations for each TEI subscale across time are presented in Table 7.3. A main effect for time was found for the 'avoidance', 're-experiencing' and 'increased arousal' subscales ($F(2, 43) = 12.76$, $p < 0.01$; $F(2, 42) = 7.32$; $p < 0.01$; and $F(2, 43) = 10.84$, $p < 0.01$) respectively, but the 'victimisation' was not significant ($F(2, 43) = 3.98$, $p = 0.06$). An ns result indicates a reduction in the rating of the PTSD-related symptoms over time. There was no interaction effect for any of the four subscales. A polynomial contrast indicated a significant linear trend ($p = 0.006$) in the scores over time with a significant drop in symptoms occurring between six and nine months after the bombing. Although it appears that there is another decline in scores between 18 and 24 months, these differences are not statistically significant ($p = 0.60$). A Dunnett's t indicated no statistically significant differences ($p = 0.129$) in the way the two treatment groups responded over time.

At nine months, only 12 of the 20 respondents diagnosed with PTSD still met the DSM-IV criteria for PTSD, and there were no new onset cases of co-morbid disorders, although five people reported isolated panic-like attacks (sub-threshold). Of the 23 subsyndromal respondents, one developed symptomatology that met the criteria for a new-onset DSM-IV-sanctioned diagnosis of PTSD, and one case met the criteria for new-onset panic disorder. The total number of DSM-IV psychiatric disorders decreased from 20 to 13 at nine months, and continued to decrease over the next three months. Only one respondent from the PTSD group had a DSM-IV diagnosis at 12 months. Another 15 respondents reported subsyndromal PTSD, two reported evidence of subsyndromal panic disorder (panic attacks associated with other conditions) and one respondent had symptomatology consistent with subsyndromal major depressive disorder. The remaining respondents' (n = 25) reported symptoms were absent or mild at 12 months and at every subsequent interval.

Study 3

In this study, it was hypothesised that the type of coping strategy employed would predict the respondents' levels of distress in four dimensions: their current level of distress; their perception of current and future risk; the rate of PTSD; and the level of victimisation experienced by the respondents. It was also predicted that those with high levels of avoidance-style coping would have higher levels of distress across all four dimensions than those with task- or emotion-oriented styles of coping.

Methods

Sample. The data for this research were collected as part of a two-year follow-up to Study 1. Those that participated in the first study were re-contacted two years after the bombing. Of the original sample, 402 respondents agreed to participate (216 Oklahoma City residents and 186 Lexington residents). Nineteen reported experiencing another stressful life event since the bombing and were excluded from the study, leaving a usable sample of 390 participants, or 80.9 per cent of the original respondent pool.

Measures. The measures used in the first study were repeated at the two-year interval, with the addition of a coping strategies measure. A modified version of the Multidimensional Coping Inventory (MCI) (Endler and Parker, 1990) was used to measure the coping behaviour of the respondents. The items were factor-analysed using principal component analysis with a varimax rotation. The items successfully factored (with a loading of 0.5 or above) into three subscales: task-oriented coping (five items), emotion-oriented coping (five items) and avoidance-oriented coping (five items). The alpha reliability ratings for the scales ranged from 0.89 (task-oriented) to 0.93 (avoidance). Participants were asked to rate how often they behaved in a certain manner (in response to the bombing) based on a Likert scale of potential responses that ranged from not at all (1) to very much (5). Scores on the coping measure ranged from 5 to 25 on each scale. The respondent was placed in a coping group if a predominate coping style could be established. The following criterion was used to make these determinations. Individuals were placed in a coping group if they scored above 15 on any one subscale and less than 10 on all other scales. Application of this criterion left a usable sample of 100 subjects in the avoidance group, 153 in the task-oriented group and 110 in the emotion-oriented group, giving a usable sample of 363.

Findings

Chi-square analyses and ANOVA results indicated that there were no significant differences between the three coping groups on the variables gender, marital status, self-rated health, age, education and race. A significant relationship was uncovered between the type of intervention received and the coping style of the individual, with those in the avoidance group being the least likely to have received any type of formal intervention.

There were significant differences by coping group on three of the four criterion variables: perception of future risk (F(2, 363) = 162.87, p = 0.000); victimisation (F(2, 362) = 105.25, p = 0.000); and current level of distress (CLD) (F(2, 363) = 8.27, p = 0.001). There were no significant differences by group for rates of PTSD (F(2, 363) = 0.284, p = 0.753). Post-hoc bonferronni analyses revealed that the avoidance group had higher levels of victimisation symptoms and perception of future risk than the emotion-oriented group which, in turn, exceeded the symptom levels of the task-oriented group. This pattern did not hold true for CLD symptoms. While the avoidance group reported higher levels of distress at the time the data were collected, there were no statistically significant differences between the CLD scores for the emotion-oriented and active-coping groups (see Table 7.4).

The coping strategy employed accounted for 44.9 per cent of the variance in the perception of future risk, 34.5 per cent of the variance in the level of victimisation symptoms, and 4 per cent of the variance in the current level of distress reported.

In the first study, a dose–response relationship was uncovered between the levels of disturbance and the level of exposure experienced by the respondents. In the previous study, respondents were grouped into three groups based on their proximity to and exposure to the bombing. The OKC1 group included individuals who had seen, heard or felt the blast. The OKC2 group included those who lived in Oklahoma City at the time of the bombing, but who did not hear, see or feel the blast. The final category included a comparison group of individuals who resided in a similar size

Table 7.4 Measures of dispersion and analysis of variance results by coping group for the criterion variables

Measure	Group	N	M	SD	Range	F	p
Perception of future risk	1 Avoidance	100	3.86	1.47	0–4	162.87	0.000
	2 Emotion-oriented	110	1.68	0.78			
	3 Task-oriented	153	0.92	0.93			
PTSD (SCID)	1 Avoidance	100	0.10	0.38	1–3	0.284	0.753
	2 Emotion-oriented	110	0.11	0.37			
	3 Task-oriented	153	0.06	0.34			
Victimisation	1 Avoidance	100	24.28	10.07	0–45	105.25	0.000
	2 Emotion-oriented	110	23.62	11.22			
	3 Task-oriented	153	22.20	9.25			
CLD	1 Avoidance	100	1.12	1.21	0–5	8.27	0.001
	2 Emotion-oriented	110	0.63	1.09			
	3 Task-oriented	153	0.65	0.83			

town in another part of the country and who were exposed only via media coverage of the event.

Considering the initial findings from Study 1, these same groupings (based on exposure) were used to determine the relationship between coping and the level of exposure. Interestingly, there were statistically significant differences in the type of coping strategy employed between the groups (X^2(df = 2) = 13.55, p = 0.013) though post-hoc contrast revealed no statistically significant differences in the two OKC groups. However, a significant variation in the profile of the comparison group (from another part of the US) was discovered, with these respondents reporting higher rates of avoidance than their Oklahoma City counterparts.

DISCUSSION

The three studies here provide some useful insights into the psychological impact of isolated acts of terrorism. In partial support of the proposed hypotheses, the findings indicate significant differences in the post-bombing development of PTSD among the three differentially exposed groups at six months following the disaster. The notion that proximity to the event increases the level of exposure is further supported by the differential levels of distress reported at the time of the study, between OKC2 and the Kentucky group. As expected, the two Oklahoma City groups reported higher levels of post-disaster disturbance than the comparison sample. The PTSD variable was able to differentiate between the OKC1 and OKC2 groups, whereas the victimisation variable was able to distinguish the two OKC groups from the comparison sample. This suggests that those with direct exposure to the event were more likely to develop a psychiatric disorder, though just being a member of the Oklahoma City community was enough to cause significant problems with the regulation of self, and trust in the world, that was not experienced by the comparison group. This 'victimisation' variable may act as an intervening factor in the development of post-disaster distress. Both Oklahoma City groups were experiencing higher levels of distress at the time of the initial study than the Kentucky sample, though there was surprisingly little difference in their immediate response scores. There was no evidence of a delayed onset of symptomatology in any group, suggesting that the distress experienced by the comparison group respondents was moderate and time-limited, whereas the OKC1 and OKC2 samples reported higher distress (though still in the moderate range), with their six-month levels remaining more consistent with the intensity of their immediate response. The Oklahoma City bombing monopolised the airwaves across the country for many days. The large-scale, dramatic nature of the bombing captured widespread attention and exposed the nation to the devastation imposed by the event. This may explain the geographically diverse distress reported by the comparison group as well as the OKC groups, immediately following the event. Longer-term distress may be dependent upon the individual's interpretation of the event and the degree to which the subject felt personally affected and victimised by the unpredictable, uncontrollable event.

The follow-up study indicated that respondents experienced a significant decline in symptomatology between six and nine months after the bombing. This abatement of symptoms was sustained over the remainder of the two-year period, despite the apprehension and trial of the perpetrator and the passage of the 12-month anniversary of the incident. The only exception is the level of victimisation experienced by respondents in the non-treatment group, who reported sustained symptomatology over the two-year study period. The findings are consistent with the initial study that found the victimisation dimension to be the primary differentiating factor between the level of distress experienced by differently exposed groups.

It appears that the level of victimisation is also an indicator that mental-health intervention may be needed. However, it is important to note that the respondents reported minimal symptomatology after 12 months, with or without treatment. The pattern of disturbance can best be described as a non-episodic, sustained yet time-limited response, with a decline in symptomatology from six to nine months. PTSD was the only

DSM-IV-defined diagnosis experienced by these respondents, although subsyndromal symptoms of PTSD and some depressive symptoms were noted. The panic attacks reported by the study respondents were all situationally bound and triggered by proximity to the area and/or benign auditory stimuli that were reminiscent of the blast.

The nature of this disaster and the coping strategies used by these respondents may help explain this finding. The premeditated, intentional nature of the event differentiates this experience from some of the other trauma studies of natural disasters (McFarlane, 1988). Victimisation requires the survivor to redefine personal and social norms in a meaningful way. Making meaning out of an act of terrorism that, by definition, was intentional is a deeply personal and highly idiosyncratic process that may be seen as a spiritual or otherwise existential phenomenon. Without intervention these respondents may have been less able to integrate and resolve the experience as expeditiously as their treatment-seeking counterparts.

The coping-strategies study provides us with some useful information about the types of adaptive mechanisms that were most useful in addressing the respondents' post-terrorism responses. The avoidance-coping group reported the highest level of victimisation and perception of future risk than the other two groups, yet reported seeking out services less frequently. In fact, they were two-and-a-half times less likely to seek assistance than the other groups. This finding is consistent with results from the initial study and anecdotal accounts from mental-health professionals who report that following a disaster many residents do not believe they need help and will not seek out services, despite reporting significant emotional distress (Meyer, 1991). There may be several explanations for this phenomenon. First, some may believe that others are worse off and more deserving of attention. As one woman stated: 'I am so lucky compared to others. I can't understand why I am so upset.' Pride may also prevent some from seeking assistance if they view the development of post-disaster stress as a 'failure' or 'weakness'. Finally, there may be a language or definitional issue that is confounding this finding. For example, some may not define the services they receive as intervention, especially if the support they received was unsolicited (impromptu disaster-focused lectures, sermons or discussions; increased community cohesion, community-based ceremonies and rituals). Those that did seek intervention did so informally from family, friends and religious institutions, and may not view this type of support in a conventional context. While colloquial groups of this sort can counter isolation and the myth of uniqueness and pathology that survivors may feel following a disaster (Scanlon-Schlipp and Levesque, 1981), this less formal style of intervention may not have been sufficient to address the level of distress experienced by this particular group of respondents.

While there is evidence that the bombing produced trauma in individuals outside the bounds of the 'directly effected' group, there is little evidence of collective trauma. Anecdotally, respondents reported a 'coming together' around the event. Although concern about possible future risk was evident, the respondents seemed optimistic about the viability of the community and seemed proud of the progress made towards rebuilding and the growth and cohesion that had occurred in the past four years. One respondent stated: 'This event tested our faith in God and each other, I am so proud of how we have grown as a community and how we have responded to those in need.'

There were no significant differences in coping style between the two OKC groups, though these two sets of respondents reported utilising higher levels of task and emotion-oriented coping strategies than their comparison counterparts. This suggests that the coping strategies used by the OKC groups may be more related to proximity of the individual to the event (and/or other exogenous variables) than a dose–response exposure effect. Additionally, the comparison group (which had the highest rate of avoidance-style coping) had the lowest levels of PTSD. This finding is contrary to the prediction made in this study that avoidance strategies would be maladaptive in this type of situation. In reality, the comparison-group respondents were both physically and emotionally removed from the situation. Although the initial study revealed high levels of emotional distress in this group immediately following the disaster, it seems that this group's avoidance may have been a factor of the phenomenon 'out of sight, out of mind'. The remoteness of these respondents to the event may have allowed for some natural emotional distancing and may have promoted adaptive resolution by allowing the individuals to maintain the notion that this type of event is something that happens to other people, thereby preserving the myth of invulnerability. Further research is needed to determine if the coping strategies used in this respondent pool were indeed situationally determined or if the patterns uncovered here are static coping traits of the individuals, regardless of the type of event.

Implications for Individual and Community Intervention

The challenge for mental-health professionals is in the understanding of how prevailing strategies for creating individual and social stability and change are applied in the wake of a disaster. These intervention principles, a by-product of an occasional vexing of mental-health practices and community organisation (Magill and Clark, 1975), must be adapted to address the victimisation and emotional distress that is experienced in directly affected groups, as well as indirectly impacted populations such as the one studied here.

Typical *service* approaches, designed to help individuals adjust to the immediate realities of the situation, must take into consideration the widespread feelings of vulnerability and concerns for safety experienced across the community. Additionally, specially designed services for indirectly exposed groups should consider that many distressed individuals do not seek out services. Therefore, community education regarding the possible effects of trauma on individuals should be presented in a very public yet normalising manner so as to reach as many people as possible. These services should extend beyond the first few weeks or even months following the disaster because, as demonstrated in this study, some effects may last at least two years.

Mobilising begins the process of empowerment by inviting individuals to be part of recovery efforts. High victimisation scores in this study indicate the level of powerlessness and loss of control associated with terroristic acts. Opportunities for individuals to 'take control' via task-oriented activities can counteract the effects of isolation, loss of control and avoidance that may occur.

Organising efforts that allow individuals to plan for and build permanent community infrastructures (that may reduce the likelihood of other terrorist acts or increase the community response time to acts of violence) provide individuals with ways to attenuate their perceived risk of future harm and concerns for the safety of their family and friends.

There is much to be learned from individuals in the post-terrorism period. Studies such as these, and major contributions from the fields of psychiatry, psychology, social work and public health, provide us with valuable clues on how to address the concerns of those affected. As more progress is made in the scientific study of the post-terrorism response, it may become possible to identify specific markers for recovery that will enable mental-health professionals to develop preventative and rehabilitative interventions to address these responses. This may mean dismantling current treatment technologies (to delineate the efficacy of specific techniques) and/or increasing attention to issues of co-morbidity and temporal sequencing of psychopathology. As the threat of terrorism grows, so must our resolve to meet these challenges.

REFERENCES

Abramson, L.Y., Seligman, M.E. and Teasdale, J.D. (1978). Learned helplessness in humans: critique and reformation. *Journal of Abnormal Psychology*, **87**, 49–74.

Baum, A., Fleming, R. and Davidson, L. (1983). Natural disaster and technological catastrophe. *Environment and Behavior*, **15**, 333–54.

Bremner, J.D., Southwick, S.M., Brett, E., Fontana, A., Rosenheck, R. and Charney, D.S. (1992). Dissociation and posttraumatic stress disorder in Vietnam veterans. *American Journal of Psychiatry*, **149**, 328–32.

Breslau, N., Davis, G., Andreski, P. and Peterson, E. (1991). Traumatic events and posttraumatic stress disorder in an urban population of young adults. *Archives of General Psychiatry*, **48**, 216–22.

Breslau, N., Chilcoat, H.D., Schultz, L.R., Davis, G.C. and Andreski, P. (1998). Trauma and post-traumatic stress disorder in the community: the 1996 Detroit Area Survey of Trauma. *American Journal of Psychiatry*, **55**, 626–32.

Breslau, N., Chilcoat, H.D., Kessler, R.C. and Davis, G.C. (1999). Previous exposure to trauma and PTSD effects of subsequent trauma: results from the Detroit Area Survey of Trauma. *American Journal of Psychiatry*, **156**, 902–07.

Brewin, C.R., Andrews, B., Rose, S. and Kirk, M. (1999). Acute stress disorder and posttraumatic stress disorder in victims of violent crimes. *American Journal of Psychiatry*, **156**, 360–66.

Davidson, J., Swartz, M., Storck, M., Krishnan, R.R. and Hammett, E. (1985). A diagnostic and family study of post-traumatic stress disorder. *American Journal of Psychiatry*, **142**, 90–93.

Davidson, L., Fleming, R. and Baum, A. (1987). Chronic stress, catecholamine, and sleep disturbance at Three Mile Island. *Journal of Human Stress*, **13**, 75–83.

Davidson, J.R., Hughes, D., Blazer, D. and George, L. (1991). Post-traumatic stress disorder in the community: an epidemiological study. *Psychological Medicine*, **21**, 713–21.

Dietrich, A.M. (1996). As the pendulum swings: the etiology of PTSD, complex PTSD, and revictimization. *Traumatology*, **6**(1), 2–10.

Endler, N.S. and Parker, J.D.A. (1990). Multidimensional assessment of coping: a critical evaluation. *Journal of Personality and Social Psychology*, **58**(5), 844–54.

Figley, C.R. (1985). From victim to survivor: social responsibility in the wake of catastrophe. In C.R. Figley (Ed.), *Trauma and its Wake. The Study and Treatment of Post-Traumatic Stress Disorder*. Vol. I. New York: Brunner/Mazel, pp. 398–415.

First, M., Gibbon, M., Spitzer, R. and Williams, J. (1996). *Structural Clinical Interview for DSM-IV Disorders. Non Patient Edition*. New York: Biometric Research Development.

Foa, E.B., Riggs, D. and Gershuny, B. (1994). Arousal, numbing, and intrusion. *American Journal of Psychiatry*, **152**, 116–20.

Glesser, G.C., Green, B.L. and Winget, C. (1981). *Prolonged Psychological Effects of Disaster: A Study of Buffalo Creek*. New York: Academic Press.

Green, B.L., Grace, M.C., Lindy, J.D., Titchner, J.L. and Lindy, J.C. (1983). Levels of functional impairment following a civilian disaster: the Beverly Hills Supper Club fire. *Journal of Consulting Clinical Psychology*, **51**, 573–80.

Gurvits, T.G., Gilberston, M.W., Lasko, N.B., Tarhan, A.S., Simeon, D., Macklin, M.L., Orr, S.P. and Pitman, R.K. (2000). Neurologic soft signs in chronic posttraumatic stress disorder. *Archives of General Psychiatry*, **57**, 181–86.

Halligan, S.L. and Yehuda, R. (2000). Risk factors for PTSD. *PTSD Research Quarterly*, **11**(3), 1–8.

Herman, J.L. (1992). Trauma and recovery. New York: Basic Books.

Jenkins, M.A., Langlais, P.J., Delis, D. and Cohen, R. (1998). Learning and memory in rape victims with posttraumatic stress disorder. *American Journal of Psychiatry*, **155**, 278–79.

Kessler, R., Sonnega, A., Bromet, E., Hughes, M. and Nelson, C. (1995). Posttraumatic stress disorder in the National Co-morbidity Survey. *Archives of General Psychiatry*, **52**, 1048–60.

Kidd, P.T., Ford, J.D. and Nasby, W. (1996). Early childhood trauma in veterans with chronic military-related posttraumatic stress disorder. Paper presented at the Annual Convention of the International Society for Traumatic Stress Studies, San Francisco, CA, November, 10.

King, D., King, L., Foy, D. and Gudnaowski, D. (1996). Prewar factors in combat related PTSD: structural equation modeling with a national sample of female and male Vietnam Veterans. *Journal of Consulting and Clinical Psychology*, **64**, 520–31.

Kleber, R.J. and Braum, D. (1992). *Coping with Trauma: Theory, Prevention, and Treatment*. Lisse: Swets en Zeitlinger.

Koopman, C., Classen, C. and Spiegel, D. (1994). Predictors of posttraumatic stress symptoms among survivors of the Oakland/Berkley, Calif., Firestorm. *American Journal of Psychiatry*, **151**, 888–94.

Macklin, M.L., Metzger, L.J., Litz, B.T., McNally, R.J., Lasko, N.B., Orr, S.P. and Pitman, R.K. (1998). Lower pre-combat intelligence is a risk factor for post-traumatic stress disorder. *Journal of Consulting and Clinical Psychology*, **66**, 323–26.

Magill, R.S. and Clark, T.N. (1975). Community power and decision making: recent research and its policy implications. *Social Service Review*, **49**, 33–45.

McFarlane, A. (1988). The longitudinal course of posttraumatic morbidity. *The Journal of Nervous and Mental Disease*, **176**, 30–39.

McFarlane, A. (1989). The etiology of post-traumatic morbidity: predisposing, precipitating, and perpetuating factors. *British Journal of Psychiatry*, **154**, 221–28.

Meyer, D. (1991). Emotional recovery from Loma Prieta earthquake. *Networks: Earthquake Preparedness News*, **6**(1), 6–7.

Norris, F.H. (1992). Epidemiology of trauma: frequency and impact of different potentially traumatic events on different demographic groups. *Journal of Consulting and Clinical Psychology*, **60**, 409–18.

Parkes, C.M. and Weiss, R.S. (1983). *Recovery from Bereavement*. New York: Basic Books.

Pelcovitz, D., van der Kolk, B.A., Roth, S., Mandel, F., Kaplan, S. and Resick, P. (1996). Development of a criteria set and a structured interview for disorders of extreme stress (SIDES). *Journal of Traumatic Stress*, **10**(1), 3–16.

Pelcovitz, D., van der Kolk, B.A., Roth, S., Mandel, F., Kaplan, S. and Resick, P. (1997). Development of a criteria set and a structured interview for disorders of extreme stress (SIDESNOS). *Journal of Traumatic Stress*, **10**, 3–16.

Pitman, R.K. (1998). Post-traumatic stress disorder, hormones, and memory. *Biological Psychiatry*, **26**, 221–23.

Quarantelli, E.L. (1985). An assessment of conflicting views of mental health: the consequences of traumatic events. In C.R. Figley (Ed.), *Trauma and its Wake: The Study and Treatment of PTSD*. New York: Brunner/Mazel, Inc.

Rando, T.A. (1995). *Treatment of Complicated Mourning*. Champaign, IL: Research Press.

Raphael, B. (1983). *The Anatomy of Bereavement*. New York: Basic Books.

Resnick, P.A. (2001). *Stress and Trauma*. Philadelphia, PA: Taylor & Francis.

Resnick, H.S., Kilpatrick, D.G., Dansky, B.S., Saunders, B.E. and Best, C.L. (1993). Prevalence of civilian trauma and posttraumatic stress disorder in a representative national sample of women. *Journal of Consulting and Clinical Psychology*, **61**, 984–91.

Resnick, H.S., Yehuda, R., Pitman, R.K. and Foy, D.W. (1995). Effects of previous trauma on acute plasma cortisol level following rape. *American Journal of Psychiatry*, **152**, 1675–77.

Rubinos, A. and Bickman, L. (1991). Psychological impairment in the wake of disaster: the disaster-psychopathology relationship. *Psychological Bulletin*, **109**(3), 384–99.

Scanlon-Schlipp, A.M. and Levesque, J. (1981). Helping the patient cope with the sequelae of trauma through the self-help group approach. *The Journal of Trauma*, **21**, 135–39.

Schnurr, P., Friedman, M. and Rosenberg, S. (1993). Pre military MMPI scores as predictors of combat-related PTSD symptoms. *American Journal of Psychiatry*, **150**, 479–83.

Schnurr, P. and Vielhauer, M. (1999). Personality as a risk factor for PTSD. In R. Yehuda (Ed.), *Risk Factors for Posttraumatic Stress Disorder* (pp. 191–222). Washington, DC: American Psychiatric Press.

Shalev, A.Y., Peri, T., Canetti, L. and Schreiber, S. (1996). Predictors of PTSD in injured trauma survivors: a prospective study. *American Journal of Psychiatry*, **153**, 219–25.

Shalev, A.Y., Sahar, T., Freedman, S., Peri, T., Glick, N., Brandes, D., Orr, S.P. and Pitman, R.K. (1998). A prospective study of heart rate response following trauma and the subsequent development of posttraumatic stress disorder. *Archives of General Psychiatry*, **55**, 553–59.

Shore, J.H., Tatum, E.L. and Vollmer, W.M. (1986). Psychiatric reactions to disaster: the Mount St Helens experience. *American Journal of Psychiatry*, **143**, 590–95.

Solomon, Z., Kulciner, M. and Avitzur, E. (1988). Coping, locus of control, social support, and combat-related posttraumatic stress disorder: a prospective study. *Journal of Personality and Social Psychology*, **55**, 279–85.

Spiegel, D. (1991). Dissociation and trauma. In A. Tusman and S.M. Goldfinger (Eds), *American Psychiatric Press: Review of Psychiatry*, Vol. 10 (pp. 261–75). Washington, DC: American Psychiatric Press.

Spiegel, D., Koopman, C., Cardena, E. and Classen, C. (1996). Dissociative symptoms in the diagnosis of acute stress disorder. In W.J. Ray (Ed.), *Handbook of Dissociation*. New York: Plenum Press.

Sprang, G. (1995). *The Many Faces of Bereavement: The Nature and Course of Natural, Traumatic and Stigmatized Grief*. New York: Brunner/Mazel, Inc.

Sprang, G. (1997). The traumatic experiences inventory: a test of psychometric properties. *Journal of Psychopathology and Behavioral Assessment*, **19**(3), 257–71.

Sprang, G. (1999). Post-disaster stress following the Oklahoma City bombing: an examination of three community groups. *Journal of Interpersonal Violence*, **14**, 161–75.

Sprang, G. and McNeil, J. (1995). *The Many Faces of Bereavement: The Nature and Treatment of Natural, Traumatic and Stigmatized Grief*. New York: Brunner/Mazel, Inc.

Stamm, B.H. (1996). Contextualizing death and trauma: a preliminary attempt. In C.F. Figley (Ed.), *Death and Trauma*. New York: Brunner/Mazel, Inc.

True, W.R., Rise, J., Eisch, S.A., Heath, A.C., Goldberg, J., Lyons, M.J. and Nouak, J. (1993). A twin study of genetic and environmental contributions to liability for posttraumatic stress symptoms. *Archives of General Psychiatry*, **50**, 257–64.

Waugh, W.L., Jr (2001). Managing terrorism as an environmental hazard. In A. Farazamand (Ed.), *Handbook of Crisis Energy Management* (pp. 659–76). New York: M. Dekker, Inc.

Yehuda, R. and McFarlane, A.C. (1995). Conflict between current knowledge about posttraumatic stress disorder and its original conceptual basis. *American Journal of Psychiatry*, **152**, 1705–15.

Yehuda, R., McFarlane, A.C. and Shalev, A.Y. (1998). Predicting the development of posttraumatic stress disorder from the acute response to a traumatic event. *Biological Psychiatry*, **44**, 1305–13.

Yehuda, R., Schmeidler, J., Giller, E.L., Binder-Brynes, K. and Seiver, L.J. (1998). Relationship between PTSD characteristics of Holocaust survivors and their adult offspring. *American Journal of Psychiatry*, **155**, 841–43.

Yehuda, R., Bierer, L.M., Schmeidler, J., Aferiat, D.H., Breslau, I. and Dolan, S. (2000). Low cortisol and risk for PTSD in adult offspring of Holocaust survivors. *American Journal of Psychiatry*, **157**, 1252–59.

CHAPTER 8

The Psychological Impact of Protracted Campaigns of Political Violence on Societies

ORLA MULDOON

Queen's University Belfast

INTRODUCTION

United Nations statistics indicate that during 1993 there were 32 major and 15 minor conflicts experienced across the US, Asia, Africa and Europe. It is estimated that over the past decade at least 40 countries worldwide have been affected by ongoing armed civil conflict (Macksoud and Aber, 1996). In situations where terrorist attacks occur in the context of a wider political conflict, there are problems with defining such attacks as terrorism. In areas where the conflict is related to the perceived legitimacy of the State and its actions or forces, one person's 'terrorism' is another's 'justifiable military action', and on the other hand what some view as 'law enforcement' may be viewed by other citizens as 'state terrorism'.

Whilst there are problems associated with constructing a definition of terrorism in situations of political conflict, the human cost of armed political conflict is evident. Increasingly, civilians are becoming the victims of political conflict. During the First World War, 10 per cent of all fatalities were civilian casualties, and during the Second World War civilians represented 50 per cent of all casualties. However, during all subsequent conflicts, civilian casualties have represented upwards of 80 per cent of conflict-related fatalities (Dodge, 1990). The psychological cost of exposure

Terrorists, Victims and Society: Psychological Perspectives on Terrorism and its Consequences.
Edited by Andrew Silke. © 2003 John Wiley & Sons, Ltd.

to such conflicts is more difficult to measure, but it is safe to assume that given the increased number of civilian victims in political conflicts over the last decades there has been a concomitant increase in the number of people exposed to acute and chronic traumas associated with political conflict. Identifying the psychological cost of such experiences on individuals and societies is a difficult task.

One of the major barriers to pinpointing the psychological impact of armed conflict and terrorism on society is the heterogeneous nature of modern political conflict. Experience of armed conflict and terrorism is not a unitary phenomenon. Conflicts differ in terms of their intensity, duration, nature of attacks and types of violence employed. This chapter circumscribes this problem by considering the effects of long-running or protracted armed conflicts on individuals and society.

LOW-INTENSITY PROTRACTED ARMED CONFLICTS

Low-intensity protracted armed conflicts are characterised by sporadic and highly variable levels of violence. This oscillating yet relatively low level of violence over a long period of time has two major interacting effects: it sustains yet disguises the human cost of the conflict. These effects are readily observable in Northern Ireland where political conflict has been ongoing for over 30 years. Although the annual number of deaths in Northern Ireland as a result of the conflict never exceeded the number killed in road-traffic accidents, over the 30 years of 'the troubles' some 3600 people were killed and over 35 000 physically injured in a population of only 1.6 million. The tolerance of the conflict at an individual and community level was underpinned early in the conflict when a local politician referred to 'an acceptable' level of violence in Northern Ireland (Hayes, 1995). Despite the ensuing outcry, in truth many in Northern Ireland had come to view the troubles as part of the backdrop of everyday life.

Indeed the reality for many living in areas affected by long-running low-intensity armed conflicts, like those in Northern Ireland, Palestine and the Basque Territory, is that the conflict is part of their lives at some level. Whilst many may not have direct experience of terrorist attacks or civil unrest, they have lived through or grown up in a divided society. Although considerable social polarisation tends to pre-date such conflicts (Murray, 1995), years of violence exacerbate the situation. For example, considerable demographic change tends to be associated with ongoing conflict, and may be a direct result of coercion, as is the case with ethnic cleansing, or of gradual and ostensibly voluntary relocation. Such relocation is often prompted by a desire for safety. Nonetheless, the net result is the same: areas populated by ethnically homogeneous groups and further segregation.

Social polarisation is a blight on areas affected by long-running armed conflicts. Increased experience of political conflict appears to be associated with a hardening of political attitudes. Punamäki and Suleiman (1990) in a study of Palestinian mothers found that exposure to political hardships was associated with more active coping and more political activity. Similarly, Muldoon and Wilson (2001) found an association between reported experience of political conflict and commitment to the traditional community ideologies in Northern Irish adolescents. Obviously, any such relationship has the potential to create a vicious circle, where experience of armed conflict hardens attitudes, perpetuating the conflict at a societal level and increasing the potential for further negative conflict-related experiences at an individual level.

Many protagonists to long-running terrorist campaigns argue that violence at the hands of the enemy hardened their attitudes. They often attribute their involvement in terrorist or paramilitary organisations to these experiences (Bruce, 1992; O'Doherty, 1993; Parker, 1993; see also Chapter 2, this volume). This relationship between conflict experience and ideological commitment also blurs the line between victims and perpetrators of violence in situations of political conflict. McLachlan (1981) charted the possible progress of a teenager growing up in a deprived, violent and religiously segregated area of Northern Ireland. This young person accepts the received version of his community's situation, and in subsequently experiencing political violence comes to view the other religious group as the enemy and himself becomes an active participant in the conflict. Identifying this young person as a victim or a terrorist is a complex ethical and moral task. It is doubtless, however, that he is a product of the social polarisation that is endemic in countries affected by political conflict.

SOCIAL ATTITUDES AND POLITICAL CONFLICT

Social attitudes and belief systems are another area where the effects of the conflict may be observed. Much of the current research emanating from both Europe and North America points to the centrality of social identities in causing and maintaining conflict (Cairns and Darby, 1998). Social identity theory posits that there are a number of normal psychological activities that contribute to this process, namely social categorisation, stereotyping of the out-group and social identification.

Social categorisation is a normal process whereby people are classified in terms of salient social characteristics. This categorisation may occur on the basis of attributes such as gender, race or sexuality. In situations where there is a history of political conflict, the most salient identity is often political interest or affiliation. The importance of this process to everyday life in situations of political conflict is exemplified by the 'telling' process in Northern Ireland. Here, two white Christian groups, Protestants and Roman Catholics, are the main parties to the conflict. Despite the apparent similarity of the two groups in terms of race and religion, 50 different ways of telling the religion of others in Northern Ireland have recently been documented (Kremer, 1999).

Social categorisation is a normal social-psychological process, and in itself it is unlikely to have a damaging effect. However, social categorisation facilitates the stereotyping of the other group and in so doing can maintain and/or exacerbate poor relations between groups. Stereotypes are powerful schema that influence the interpretation of our environment. A study of eyewitness accounts of paramilitary activities in Northern Ireland (Beattie and Doherty, 1995) highlights this effect. Through the use of discourse analysis, the authors show how eyewitnesses implicitly attribute blame for a terrorist attack and how in recounting their stories portray the attackers in a manner consistent with the perceptions of their communities. Further, available evidence from two quantitative studies undertaken in 1984 and 1995 suggests that social identity is related to memories of recent ethnic conflict (Cairns et al., 1998). The authors of this study, again undertaken in Northern Ireland, suggest that social identity can be strengthened or 'switched on' by recalling or priming subjects with images of ethnic conflict events. This strengthening effect appears to be greatest when the ethnic conflict memories recalled are important or meaningful events in terms of one's own group identity. Taken together these studies suggest that social identity is important to our interpretations of both the present and the past in situations of political conflict.

The importance of the final process—the social identification process—is underpinned by its key role in the development of a sense of self (Luhtanen and Crocker, 1992; Porter and Washington, 1993). Social identity theory suggests that personal self-esteem and self-image are derivatives of group processes, for example membership of a potent or valued social group can be psychologically beneficial (Thompson and Spacapan, 1991). For this reason, group members strive to preserve or defend the group, and for their group to be both distinctive from and positively valued by others. Often positively valued distinctiveness is achieved by belittling the outgroup, giving rise to conflict between groups. This is particularly the case where it is difficult or impossible to leave or switch membership of groups. These circumstances are often present in situations of political conflict, where membership of particular ethnic groups, such as Israeli or Palestinian, Irish Catholic or British Protestant, are viewed as immutable, non-overlapping and often dichotomous social groups.

Effectively, the effects of the normal psychological processes of social categorisation, stereotyping and social identification are heightened and more readily apparent in situations of political conflict. For example, emblems and cultural markers such as language and dance may take on particular significance as groups strive for increased respect and distinctiveness. In Northern Ireland, the differences between the two main communities is often writ large, literally. Studies of wall murals have highlighted the special significance of these paintings and their relationship to political violence in Northern Ireland (Finn, 1997). As well as marking territory, these murals convey messages to members of both the in-group and out-group. They emphasise the support for paramilitaries and their activities (Gallagher and Hanratty, 1989), they provide justification for political violence and commemorate and glorify the history of each group (Finn, 1997).

More traditional emblems such as flags, anthems and language also take on significance in situations of political conflict. Frequently, valuing one emblem is viewed as a devaluation of another, not least because groups are constructed as non-overlapping and dichotomous, resulting in a similar characterisation of the groups' needs and demands. This tendency constructs a win–lose mindset that can be one of the major impediments to change and conflict resolution; changes that may advantage one group are believed to disadvantage the other group. The current faltering peace processes in Northern Ireland and in Israel/Palestine illustrate this problem all too starkly.

MENTAL HEALTH AND POLITICAL CONFLICT

Much of the research that has been undertaken in this area has attempted to identify the levels of psychopathology in communities affected by long-running political violence. In general, studies that examine mental-health problems in community populations can be said to be stronger than those that have monitored the rate of psychiatric admissions, referral rates and drug-prescribing practices (Cairns, 1994; Daly, 1999). The latter are open to many different social and cultural biases and generally do not facilitate the application of the findings to other countries. However, community-wide studies are expensive, time consuming and complex. Researchers must decide how best they can measure mental health in the general population and must control for a host of social factors that are known to be related to levels of psychopathology, such as social class and gender. Finally, there are practical and ethical issues that must be addressed before researchers ask sensitive questions about participants' experiences of conflict. For this reason, a number of alternative approaches has often been used.

Clinical studies, whilst they provide little information about the effects of political violence on the population generally, do document its effect on the most vulnerable. Lyons (1974) reported on 100 people in Northern Ireland who had been directly involved in a bomb explosion. In this group of patients, many developed several symptoms. A majority (92 per cent) displayed an affective disturbance, the commonest form being anxiety or phobic symptoms. Depression and irritability were also common. Further clinical studies in Northern Ireland (Fraser, 1971, 1973; Lyons, 1979) found that a minority of children were also vulnerable to short-term effects, including acute anxiety attacks, nightmares and enuresis, as a result of the early riots and civil disturbances in Northern Ireland. Parents who communicated their own anxieties regarding the ongoing violence to their children, by expressing their fear or distress, were particularly vulnerable to these short-term disturbances in behaviour. Indeed the importance of parents' reactions to political violence for their children's management of and adjustment to the situation is a finding evident in research from many countries that have experienced political conflict (Bryce et al., 1989; Punamäki and Suleiman, 1990).

Another approach often employed to assess the impact of political violence on mental health is targeting particular groups. For example, Gidron, Gal and Zahavi (1999) targeted a sample of bus commuters in Israel following a number of fatal attacks on buses. Their study indicated that approximately one-fifth of their sample of 50 commuters had relatively high levels of anxiety associated with terrorist attacks. The similarity in levels of psychopathology reported in this group and that of the two Northern Irish samples reported below is noteworthy.

Community surveys involving random samples of the populations are doubtless the best way to examine the relationship between experience of political violence and mental health. Barker et al. (1988) completed a survey of this type with a random sample of the population in Northern Ireland: 547 people, representative of the population, completed the General Health Questionnaire (GHQ), a standard self-report measure of mental health. Approximately 22 per cent of the sample were subsequently identified as possible 'cases'—having scores that exceeded the widely accepted cut-off point that is indicative of psychopathology. Cairns and Wilson (1984) found a similar level of psychopathology in a random sample of the population of two towns in Northern Ireland. Importantly, this incidence is slightly lower than that reported in the rest of the UK during a similar period (Huppert, Roth and Gore, 1987).

In line with this evidence, the effects of political violence on the schoolgoing population of children and young people also appears to be limited. A wide variety of psychological constructs have been studied in Northern Ireland and young people appear to display few psychological symptoms as a result of 'the troubles'. Joseph, Cairns and McCollam (1993) found no difference in the level of depressive symptomatology reported by two groups of 11-year-olds, one from an area with a high level of violence and the other from an area of low violence. Similarly, Donnelly (1995), reporting on a sample of 887 adolescents, found no evidence of higher rates of depression in Northern Ireland. Murray and Clifford (1988) found that the level of anxiety reported by 15- to 16-year-olds in Northern Ireland was similar to the levels in North America. Finally, self-esteem profiles of Northern Irish children and young people have been found to be similar to the profiles of UK and US children and adolescents (Granleese, Trew and Turner, 1988; Granleese, Turner and Trew, 1989; Muldoon and Trew, 2000a).

In effect, therefore, it can be said that there is evidence to suggest that political violence has a limited effect on the psychological health of the general population in societies affected by protracted low-intensity political violence. This apparent resilience has prompted many researchers to focus on ways in which people cope with violent experiences, conflict and trauma. This approach has been particularly useful, not least because it allows a focus on people's efforts to cope with their experiences, as well as the relationship between these coping efforts and levels of psychopathology, effectively increasing the applied value of the research findings.

COPING WITH POLITICAL VIOLENCE

Paradoxically, it would appear that ideological commitment, a causative factor in many protracted conflicts, can protect psychological integrity. Commitment to a group ideology can give meaning to stress or hardship endured as a result of political conflict. Reappraisal of negative experiences in a way that emphasises the potential benefits to the group can help people adjust to their experiences. Available research evidence supports this view. Punamäki and Suleiman (1990) found that the psychological responses of Palestinian women to political violence was moderated by ideological commitment. Similarly, Punamäki (1996) found that it was only amongst the group with the weakest ideological commitment that anxiety, insecurity and depression were related to Israeli adolescents' experiences of political violence. Strong ideological commitment, on the other hand, had a positive moderating influence on psychosocial well-being. Preliminary results (Muldoon and Wilson, 2001) from Northern Ireland would also seem to suggest that ideological commitment may moderate the impact of political violence on psychosocial well-being, although further research is required.

The need for people to cope and adjust to political violence in situations where conflict is protracted is readily apparent. In situations such as these, the coping strategies employed are likely to be different to those necessitated by situations where individuals are adjusting to acute, circumscribed stressors such as an isolated terrorist attack. Indeed the ongoing nature of the violence means that for many it must be integrated into the context of their lives. For this reason, some researchers have suggested that habituation or desensitisation is likely to be a useful strategy for coping with ongoing and protracted violence.

There is some empirical evidence to support this case. For instance Klingman (1992) studied the acute stress reactions in Israeli students over the first and fourth week of the Gulf War. Over this time, self-reported levels of psychological disturbance decreased significantly. Similarly, Gidron, Gal and Zahavi (1999), in their study of Israeli bus commuters, found that commuting frequency was negatively related to anxiety about terrorist attacks, which the authors interpreted as a desensitisation effect. In Northern Ireland, a longitudinal study by McIvor (1981) again emphasises the role of habituation. McIvor asked recently arrived students about their first impressions of Northern Ireland on arrival and one year later. References to the political violence were prevalent in the accounts received following arrival but not a year later, again leading the author to conclude that these students had habituated to the conflict.

Other strategies that may be employed to cope with ongoing conflict situations are denial and/or distancing. Cairns and Wilson (1984) examined mental health and perceptions of levels of violence in two matched towns in Northern Ireland. One town had experienced relatively high levels of violence, and the second relatively low levels. Overall, levels of psychopathology appeared to be higher in the high-violence town. More importantly, however, those individuals living in the high-violence town who perceived the area, inaccurately, to have little or no violence had better mental health. In effect, denying the existence of the conflict may facilitate psychological well-being. Other studies have supported the contention that denial and distancing may be useful strategies for coping with the stress of political conflict. In a study of Israeli young people living in a violence-prone border town and a more peaceful area, Rofe and Lewin (1982) found that the group living in the border town scored higher on a repression scale, fell asleep earlier and had fewer dreams with violent themes than their counterparts in the more peaceful area. The authors concluded that the residents of the border town, having experienced more political violence, had developed strategies to avoid thinking or ruminating about violent events.

A single-strategy approach to coping is unlikely to be of use in situations of ongoing political conflict where stressors may be many and varied. Indeed available research suggests that the most psychologically resilient select the most appropriate coping strategy from their repertoire contingent on the stressor encountered (Somerfield and McCrae, 2000). Indeed the utility of habituation or distancing as a coping strategy may be limited to contexts where an attack has not been personally experienced and the threat from the conflict does not appear imminent. Some commentators have suggested that coping processes may be sensitive to the nature and salience of violent events (Cairns, 1994). For example, Wilson and Cairns (1992) found in a Northern Ireland community that had been devastated by a bomb attack that the majority of respondents did not deny the violence. Rather, positive reappraisal and the use of social support were more important forms of coping in this context.

The role of social support and wider community resources in protecting people from the impact of political violence is unclear. Often political violence can disrupt or destroy communality by damaging community relations. In other instances, a particularly violent attack can result in a convergence of the views of two normally opposing groups (Bolton, 1999). Natural responses in Northern Ireland to particularly bloody attacks, with large numbers of fatalities, has often been to turn to the church, with large solemn funerals and memorial services being visible markers. These reactions may be seen both as a community response to grief as well as a source of support for the bereaved (Wilson and McCreary, 1990).

The effect of major trauma at a community level is hard to gauge. It is, however, worth noting that there is some evidence to suggest that certain mental-health problems are lessened following particularly violent attacks. For example, Sharkey (1997) analysed the number of parasuicides in the locality of a gun attack in which seven people were killed. Whilst establishing a cause-and-effect relationship is not possible, Sharkey did observe that the number of parasuicides admitted to the local hospital that week was just one in comparison to a weekly average of between 8 and 14 for the weeks before and after the attack. Further to this, in a 10-year period after the attack, the average monthly rate of admissions for parasuicide had decreased dramatically. The exact reason for this effect is unclear; the attack may have distracted people from their own problems, provided a sense of community or lowered average alcohol consumption (a factor implicated in overdose attempts). Regardless, the finding is an interesting one and certainly worthy of further research.

A final point that must be made in relation to coping is with regard to the long-term efficacy of coping efforts. Cross-sectional and even longitudinal research may suggest that people are coping well with the situation of ongoing political violence, but such experiences may erode personal and familial psychological resources. The increased incidence of post-traumatic stress disorder identified in Israeli soldiers who are children of holocaust survivors (Solomon, 1990), together with the higher levels of behavioural disturbance observed in children of Vietnam veterans who had experienced particularly high levels of stress during that war (Rosenheck and Fontana, 1998), suggests that the effects of war, at least, may be transgenerational. In effect, therefore, it is unclear whether coping efforts that maintain psychological health in situations of political conflict also maintain the integrity of family life.

THE CONTEXT OF POLITICAL VIOLENCE

Whilst the effects of political violence on the next generation are a concern apparent in the recent literature, the effects of growing up in a situation of ongoing political violence have concerned researchers for many decades (Cairns, 1996). As stated previously, experience of violence has not been found to be related to anxiety and depression in children. However, it has frequently been suggested that such experiences are related to externalising behaviours in children and young people (Cairns, 1996). This association has been variously attributed to increased thrill-seeking behaviour because of the excitement attached to the notion of conflict, decreased parental supervision during times of conflict, normalisation of violence and social modelling as well as the anxiety and loss of control experienced by children during times of conflict (Muldoon and Cairns, 1999). Support for this position comes from a number of studies that have used standardised psychometric measures as indices of externalising behaviour problems (Fee, 1980) as well as indices of juvenile crime (Shoham, 1994).

This tendency towards increased antisocial and externalising behaviour in young people growing up in situations of political violence has prompted concern about their moral development. There is limited evidence, largely from Northern Ireland, to suggest that young people exposed to higher levels of political conflict have lower levels of moral maturity (Ferguson and Cairns, 1996). This finding is perhaps not surprising given the justification of violence and neglect of human rights that is associated with political violence. Further, the coping strategies employed and therefore modelled by adults, such as denial and habituation, indicate a tacit acceptance of the ongoing violence.

Although the effects of political violence on children have been a concern evident in the research, sectional interests are not often in evidence during protracted political conflicts (McWilliams, 1998). Issues and problems faced by women and minority groups are often marginalised. However, the marginalisation of these problems does not mean that they do not exist, rather it may exacerbate them. For example, McWilliams (1998) documents some of the problems experienced by victims of domestic violence over the course of the troubles in Northern Ireland. In her analysis she highlights the way in which violence against women can be justified and hidden in situations of political conflict.

Essentially, it is important to remember that contextual factors such as gender and socioeconomic status retain their influence in situations of political violence. Indeed it can be said that factors such as these are fundamentally related to the experience of political conflict. In relation to socioeconomic status, for example, the areas most adversely affected by political violence tend to be the most deprived (Murray, 1995). For this reason, the stress of the conflict is likely to be exacerbated by the stresses associated with deprivation (Bryce *et al.*, 1989). There is also considerable evidence to suggest that direct experience of political violence is greater amongst men and boys than women and girls (Cairns, 1996; Muldoon and Trew, 2000b), not least because males are more likely to be active protagonists to the conflict. However, the effects of political violence for girls and women and their negotiation of often highly masculine conflicts (McWilliams, 1998) may differ fundamentally from the same process in boys and men.

CONCLUSION

Identifying the psychological impact of long-running politically motivated terrorist campaigns is a difficult task. Conducting research in this area is fraught with methodological difficulties (Muldoon, Trew and Kilpatrick, 2000). Nonetheless, research to date suggests that in terms of psychological health, the majority of people are resilient to the effects of political violence. A minority tend to display some symptomatology because of their experiences, but generally resilience is thought to be facilitated by methods of coping such as habituation, denial and distancing. The effects of protracted campaigns of political violence on community relations and social attitudes more generally is, however, worrying, in part because of these same coping efforts. Social polarisation and normalisation of violence appear to be hallmarks of societies blighted by long-running periods of political violence. These problems highlight the need for researchers to address issues such as conflict resolution and reconciliation processes that can break cycles of politically motivated violence. Without work of this kind, the circumstances that maintain such conflicts are sustained, irrespective of the human costs.

REFERENCES

Barker, M., McClean, S.I., McKenna, P.G., Reid, N.G., Strain, J.J., Thompson, K.A., Williamson, A.P. and Wright M.E. (1988). *Diet, Lifestyle and Health in Northern Ireland*. Coleraine, Northern Ireland: Centre for Applied Health Studies, University of Ulster.

Beattie, G. and Doherty, K. (1995). 'I saw what really happened': the discursive construction of victims and perpetrators in firsthand accounts of paramilitary violence in Northern Ireland. *Journal of Language and Social Psychology*, 14(4), 408–33.

Bolton, D. (1999). The threat to belonging in Enniskillen: reflections on the Remembrance Day Bombing. In E.S. Zinner and M.B. Williams (Eds), *When a Community Weeps: Case Studies in Group Survivorship*. Philadelphia, PA: Brunner/ Mazel, Inc.

Bruce, S. (1992). *The Red Hand: Protestant Paramilitaries in Northern Ireland*. Oxford: Oxford University Press.

Bryce, J.W., Walker, N., Ghorayeb, F. and Kan, J.M. (1989). Life events, response styles and mental health among mothers and children in Beirut, Lebanon. *Social Science and Medicine*, **28**(7), 685–95.

Cairns, E. (1994). Understanding conflict and promoting peace in Ireland: psychology's contribution. *The Irish Journal of Psychology*, **15**(2 & 3), 480–93.

Cairns, E. (1996). *Children and Political Violence*. Oxford: Blackwell.

Cairns, E. and Darby, J. (1998). The conflict in Northern Ireland: causes, consequences and controls. *American Psychologist*, **53**(7), 754–60.

Cairns, E. and Wilson, R. (1984). The impact of political violence on mild psychiatric morbidity in Northern Ireland. *British Journal of Psychiatry*, **145**, 631.

Cairns, E., Lewis, C.A., Mumcu, O. and Waddell, N. (1998). Memories of recent ethnic conflict and their relationship to social identity. *Peace and Conflict: Journal of Peace Psychology*, **4**(1), 13–22.

Daly, O.E. (1999). Northern Ireland: the victims. *British Journal of Psychiatry*, **175**, 201–204.

Dodge, C.P. (1990). Health implication of the war in Uganda and Sudan. *Social Science and Medicine*, **31**, 691–98.

Donnelly, M. (1995). Depression among adolescents in Northern Ireland. *Adolescence*, **30**, 118 and 339–50.

Fee, F. (1980). Responses to a behavioural questionnaire of a group of Belfast children. In J. Harbison and J. Harbison (Eds), *A Society Under Stress: Children and Young People in Northern Ireland*. Somerset: Open Books.

Ferguson, N. and Cairns, E. (1996). Political violence and moral maturity in Northern Ireland. *Political Psychology*, **17**(4), 713–25.

Finn, G.P.T. (1997). Qualitative analysis of murals in Northern Ireland: paramilitary justifications for political violence. In N. Hayes (Ed.), *Doing Qualitative Analysis in Psychology* (pp. 143–86). East Sussex: Psychology Press.

Fraser, R.M. (1971). The cost of commotion: an analysis of the psychiatric sequelae of the 1969 Belfast riots. *British Journal of Psychiatry*, **118**, 257–64.

Fraser, R.M. (1973). *Children in Conflict*. London: Martin, Secker & Warburg.

Gallagher, C. and Hanratty, A. (1989). The war on the walls. *Ulster Folklife*, **35**, 100–108.

Gidron, Y., Gal, R. and Zahavi, S. (1999). Bus commuters coping strategies and anxiety from terrorism: an example of the Israeli experience. *Journal of Traumatic Stress*, **12**(1), 185–92.

Granleese, J., Trew, K. and Turner, I.F. (1988). Sex differences in perceived competence. *British Journal of Social Psychology*, **59**, 181–84.

Granleese, J., Turner, I.F. and Trew, K. (1989). Teachers' and boys' and girls' perceptions of competence in primary school: the importance of physical competence. *British Journal of Educational Psychology*, **59**, 31–37.

Hayes, M. (1995). *Minority Verdict: Experiences of a Catholic Public Servant*. Belfast: Blackstaff Press.

Huppert, F.A., Roth, M. and Gore, M. (1987). Psychosocial factors. In B.D. Cox, M. Baxter and L.J. Buckle (Eds), *The Health and Lifestyle Survey*. London: Health Promotion Trust.

Joseph, S., Cairns, E. and McCollam, P. (1993). Political violence, coping and depressive symptomatology in Northern Irish children. *Personality and Individual Differences*, **15**(4), 471–73.

Klingman, A. (1992). Stress reactions of Israeli youth during the Gulf War: a quantitative study. *Professional Psychology: Research and Practice*, **23**(6), 521–27.

Kremer, J.M.D. (1999) Combating Workplace Harassment: A Tripartite Approach. Paper presented to the Annual Conference of the British Psychological Society, Belfast.

Luhtanen, R. and Crocker, J. (1992). A collective self-esteem scale: self-evaluation of one's social identity. *Personality and Social Psychology Bulletin*, **18**, 302–18.

Lyons, H. (1974). Terrorist bombing and the psychological sequelae. *Journal of the Irish Medical Association*, **67**, 15.

Lyons, H. (1979). Civil violence—the psychological aspects. *Journal of Psychosomatic Research*, **23**, 373–93.

McIvor, M. (1981). Northern Ireland: A Preliminary Look at Environmental Awareness. Paper presented to the Biennial Conference of the International Society of Behavioural Development, Toronto, Canada.

McLachlan, P. (1981). Teenage experiences in a violent society. *Journal of Adolescence*, **4**(4), 285–94.

McWilliams, M. (1998). Violence against women in societies under stress. In R.E. Dobash and R.P. Dobash (Eds), *Rethinking Violence Against Women* (pp. 111–40). Thousand Oaks, CA: Sage.

Macksoud, M.S. and Aber, J.L. (1996). The war experiences and psychosocial development of children in Lebanon. *Child Development*, **67**, 70–88.

Muldoon, O. and Cairns, E. (1999). Children, young people and war: learning to cope. In E. Frydenburg (Ed.), *Learning to Cope* (pp. 322–37). Oxford: Oxford University Press.

Muldoon, O.T. and Trew, K. (2000a). Social group membership and self competence in Northern Irish children. *International Journal of Behavioural Development*, **24**(3), 330–37.

Muldoon, O. and Trew, K. (2000b). Children's experience and adjustment to conflict related events in Northern Ireland. *Peace Psychology: Journal of Peace and Conflict*, **6**(2), 1057–76.

Muldoon, O., Trew, K. and Kilpatrick, R. (2000). The legacy of the troubles on the development of young people. *Youth and Society*, **32**(1), 6–28.

Muldoon, O.T. and Wilson, K. (2001). Ideological commitment, experience of conflict and adjustment in Northern Irish adolescents. *Medicine, Conflict and Survival*, **17**, 112–124.

Murray, D. (1995). Culture, religion and violence in Northern Ireland. In S. Dunn (Ed.), *Facets of the Conflict in Northern Ireland* (pp. 215–29). Basingstoke: Macmillan.

Murray, M. and Clifford, S. (1988). Anxiety and aspects of health behaviour adolescents in Northern Ireland. *Adolescence*, **23**, 661–66.

O'Doherty, S. (1993). *The Volunteer: A Former IRA Man's True Story*. London: Fount Publishers.

Parker, T. (1993). *May the Lord in His Mercy be Kind to Belfast*. London: HarperCollins.

Porter, J.R. and Washington, R.E. (1993). Minority identity and self-esteem. *Annual Review of Sociology*, **19**, 139–61.

Punamäki, R.L. (1996). Can ideological commitment protect children's psychosocial well-being in situations of political violence. *Child Development*, **67**, 55–69.

Punamäki, R.L. and Suleiman, R. (1990). Predictors and effectiveness of coping with political violence among Palestinian children. *British Journal of Social Psychology*, **29**(1), 67–77.

Rofe, Y. and Lewin, I. (1982). The effect of war environment on dreams and sleep
    habits. In N.A. Milgram (Ed.), *Stress and Anxiety*, 8. New York: Hemisphere.
Rosenheck, R. and Fontana, A. (1998). Transgenerational effects of abusive vio-
    lence on the children of Vietnam combat veterans. *Journal of Traumatic Stress*,
    11(4), 731–42.
Sharkey, J. (1997). The Greysteel Massacre: the local effect on the prevalence of
    admissions with overdose. *Irish Journal of Psychological Medicine*, **14**(2), 55–56.
Shoham, E. (1994). Family characteristics of delinquent youth in time of war.
    International Journal of Offender Therapy and Comparative Criminology, **38**(3),
    247–58.
Solomon, Z. (1990). Does the war end when the shooting stops? The psychological
    toll of war. *Journal of Applied Social Psychology*, **20/21**, 1733–45.
Somerfield, M.R. and McCrae, R.R. (2000). Stress and coping research. *American
    Psychologist*, **55**(6), 620–25.
Thompson, S.C. and Spacapan, S. (1991). Perceptions of control in vulnerable pop-
    ulations. *Journal of Social Issues*, **47**, 1–27.
Wilson, R. and Cairns, E. (1992). Psychological stress and the Northern Ireland
    troubles. *The Psychologist*, **5**, 347–50.
Wilson, G. and McCreary, A. (1990). *Marie: A Story from Enniskillen*. London:
    Marshall Pickering.

CHAPTER 9

Victims of Terrorism and the Media

BETTY PFEFFERBAUM
University of Oklahoma College of Medicine

INTRODUCTION

On September 11, 2001 the attention of the world was riveted to news of a carefully orchestrated attack on the US and the Western world. Injured and alarmed victims ran for their lives through dense clouds of smoke and debris, jumped to their deaths from the highest floors of the World Trade Center, and used mobile phones to contact family members before dying in flames as the aircraft in which they were travelling crashed into the Pentagon and the countryside of Pennsylvania. The exact death toll may never be known but thousands were injured, killed or missing. Citizens from around 80 countries were among the victims. Massive property destruction occurred at the Pentagon, the centre of US military command, and at the World Trade Center, a symbol of the world's financial markets. The government scrambled to establish security both on the ground and in the air. A greatly shaken nation and world watched in horror as the media covered the events in graphic detail and then broadcast them again and again.

The goal of terrorism, evident in the word itself, is measured not only in the death and injury of direct victims, the sorrow and grief of their loved ones, the wreckage of property and the disruption of government, commerce and travel; it includes as well the fear and intimidation that accompany a new way of life. The media have a central role in realising this goal.

Terrorists, Victims and Society: Psychological Perspectives on Terrorism and its Consequences.
Edited by Andrew Silke. © 2003 John Wiley & Sons, Ltd.

Definition

While the definition of terrorism was once commonly debated, the number and magnitude of incidents in recent years have sufficiently familiarised professionals and the public to establish a consensus of understanding about the term (Jenkins, 2001) and have raised numerous other issues to occupy the time and attention of experts. Defining the term deserves some attention, however, as it influences the information that is compiled and how it is used, the response to events, and attitudes about individuals, groups and governments.

Virtually all definitions of terrorism recognise key elements: (1) the use or threat of violence, (2) to create fear and intimidation, (3) in an audience of indirect victims, and (4) to effect changes in ideology, attitudes and behaviour. Wilkinson (1990) defines terrorism as 'coercive intimidation' using violence or the threat of violence 'to create a climate of terror, to publicize a cause, and to coerce a wider target into submitting to its aims' (p. 27). Stern (1999) defines it as 'an act or threat of violence against noncombatants with the objective of exacting revenge, intimidating, or otherwise influencing an audience' (p. 11). Terrorism is further characterised as 'unpredictable' and 'indiscriminate' (Wilkinson, 1990, p. 28). It is designed to communicate (Hoffman, 1988) and uses publicity to accomplish its goals.

Terrorism is distinguished from other forms of violence by two characteristics (Stern, 1999). First, the intended target of terrorism is noncombatants, and second, violence is used for 'dramatic' purposes to instil fear (Stern, 1999, p. 11) in a larger class of indirect victims (Wilkinson, 1990). Even war is governed by rules that give immunity to civilian noncombatants, prohibit the taking of civilians as hostages, regulate the treatment of prisoners of war and recognise neutral territories (Hoffman, 1988). While specific targets are the intended victims of the acute harm inflicted, terrorism is indiscriminate with respect to indirect victims (Wilkinson, 1990). The apparent randomness of an act creates a sense of vulnerability in a larger class of indirect victims (Wilkinson, 1990) who identify with the direct victims. This 'vicarious dimension' generates and spreads apprehension and alarm (Hoffman, 1988, p. 138).

Factors Influencing Media Coverage

A host of factors influence modern news reporting. Technological advances, a demanding public and editorial convictions have shaped the content, character and timeliness of the news. Technology has meant tighter deadlines often with less informed, unedited and unscrutinised reports (Kingston, 1995). Competition is fierce as the market clamours for the dramatic and sensational. Editors who believe that the news must be reported regardless of its nature may be manipulated by individuals or groups intent on obtaining coverage (Kingston, 1995). This has led to calls for self-restraint and for legislation to curtail reporting that might glorify the terrorist cause, disseminate terrorist propaganda or inadvertently aid terrorist efforts (Kingston, 1995; Wilkinson, 1990).

THE ROLE AND RESPONSIBILITY OF THE MEDIA IN REPORTING TERRORIST ACTS

Conflict over the appropriate role and responsibility of the media in covering terrorist events is perhaps inevitable (Elmquist, 1990) and derives from the competing needs and perspectives of the terrorists, the government and the media. Media coverage is an essential weapon of terrorists. They use it in multiple ways: to convey their message; to gain recognition of their causes, demands and grievances; and to spread fear and anxiety (Nacos, 1994; Wilkinson, 1990). The portrayal of shocking events, the chaos that ensues and the inability of authorities to prevent the act, protect the citizenry and provide security (Nacos, 1994; Wilkinson, 1990) undermine confidence in our institutions and democratic way of life. At the same time, media coverage is used to attain recognition, respect and legitimacy for a cause (Nacos, 1994; Wilkinson, 1990) and to mobilise supporters, enhance recruitment, raise money and threaten and inspire additional attacks (Kingston, 1995; Wilkinson, 1990).

The government uses the media to address the public and to advance its position. Modern society relies heavily on print, broadcast and electronic media to alert, inform and educate the public, roles that intensify during an attack when warning and civil notice, such as evacuation or quarantine instructions, must be disseminated quickly. This mechanism is vital in preparing and protecting a community and in generating an effective response (Elmquist, 1990). Media coverage also alarms and incites the public, providing stimulus and support for the government's efforts to apprehend and punish the enemy (Perl, 1997). The media become part of the process, articulating and rationalising the government's position (Seaton, 1999).

From the perspective of journalists and the media, a free society means, in part at least, the unfettered ability and responsibility to report events and issues (Perl, 1997), especially those with a political message. Censoring news about terrorism, they argue, infringes on the public's right to know, potentially depriving the public of information needed to assess and react to events and trends. Ignoring an issue does not eliminate it; and reporting events and ideology, and encouraging discussion about them, are not the same as advocating terrorism (Protheroe, 1990). Furthermore, failure to report the full news might also lead to criticism. A public deprived of information might begin to question the thoroughness and accuracy of the news they do receive, decreasing confidence in a political system built on the free exchange of ideas.

Trends in Terrorism Linked to the Media

Three new trends in terrorism have been linked to the media—more violent incidents, anonymous acts and attacks on media personnel and institutions (Perl, 1997). First, the lethality of terrorist acts has increased (Dishman, 1999; Perl, 1997). This can be attributed in part to technological advances in the media that have made it easier to access information on how to develop weapons and to recruit group members and plan attacks (Stern, 1999). The use of weapons of mass destruction invites media coverage because the effects are dramatic and the randomness associated with them is 'inherently terrifying' (Stern, 1999, p. 11). In addition, policies against negotiating with terrorists or publicising their causes and acts may have unwittingly encouraged increased violence to gain the attention they sought (Nacos, 1994). Any resolve not to cover or dramatise terrorist action could not have withstood the magnitude and surprise of the September 11 attacks, which simply could not be ignored.

The second trend, anonymous terrorism, in which there are no claims of responsibility and no terrorist demands, allows the media to publicise an event and to speculate about it without incurring criticism for promoting the terrorist agenda (Hoffman, 2001; Perl, 1997). In major events, despite alleged anonymity, there is rarely doubt with respect to the origins of terror. One need not know the identity of a suicide bomber, for example, to understand the message. Furthermore, while anonymous terrorist acts do not necessarily advance the cause of a particular group, they may create chaos, instil fear and erode confidence in the government's ability to respond.

The third trend involves increased attacks on journalists and media organisations (Perl, 1997). Danger to the press and the widely publicised kidnapping and brutal killing of journalists covering the US war on terrorism deliver a chilling message to those whose profession symbolises freedom of speech. The targeting of news organisations through anthrax-contaminated mail sent a similar message and simultaneously crippled a fundamental institution in the infrastructure of modern society—the mail-delivery system.

THE MEDIA AND VICTIMS

In the face of threat, the body responds, sometimes without one's awareness. A host of physiological and neurochemical changes ensue to prepare the individual to address the threat. Encoded into us across generations, these responses promote survival of both the individual and the species. In addition to this instinctive mechanism, the subjective perception of the threat also influences the reaction (Yule, Perrin and Smith, 2001).

The threat associated with terrorism raises important issues with respect to victims. Among them are definition and classification. Disaster studies identify several categories of victims. Direct victims are those physically present at, or in close proximity to, an event. Secondary victims include the family members and close associates of direct victims and the first responders and other professionals who assist them. Indirect victims are those individuals in a community who are impacted by the secondary effects of disaster. These indirect victims are the principal targets of terrorism. Reached largely through the media, they are the audience for the terror and recognise little distinction between themselves and direct victims beyond the happenstance of time and place.

While not the only condition that occurs in response to trauma, post-traumatic stress disorder (PTSD) is the one most commonly associated with it. The essential feature of PTSD is the development of characteristic symptoms after exposure to a traumatic event that arouses 'intense fear, helplessness, or horror' (American Psychiatric Association, 1994, p. 428). These symptoms involve three clusters: persistent intrusive re-experiencing of the stressor, persistent avoidance of reminders of the event and numbing of general responsiveness, and persistent symptoms of arousal (American Psychiatric Association, 1994).

Direct Victims

The media can be problematic for direct victims in two ways. First, the intrusive re-experiencing of PTSD can be expressed as a need to tell and re-tell the trauma story. Coupled with heightened arousal, this commonly makes for dramatic coverage in the aftermath of an incident. Journalists can be aggressive in their attempts to interview and photograph victims, potentially exploiting them in the process.

Second, media coverage may constitute a source of secondary exposure for direct victims capable of retraumatising them through images which rekindle arousal linked to the attack. Pynoos and Nader (1989) have speculated that traumatic memories persist in an active state because of intrusion and arousal associated with the traumatic experience. Media exposure may maintain this state in the absence of other forms of exposure.

Secondary Victims

The impact of exposure on secondary victims such as rescue and recovery workers and other professionals working with victims has been addressed (Alexander and Wells, 1991; Epstein, Fullerton and Ursano, 1998; North *et al.*, 2002). Another group of secondary victims, comprising media personnel, is now also receiving attention. While not examining reporters of terrorism per se, Feinstein (2001) found high rates of divorce, alcohol use, depression and post-traumatic stress in war correspondents compared to journalists without this kind of experience. More work is needed in the area to document the effect of exposure and how it might influence news organisations and coverage.

Indirect Victims

Indirect exposure to trauma is recognised in the diagnostic criteria for PTSD (American Psychiatric Association, 1994), but the criteria provide little guidance about the mechanisms through which indirect exposure occurs, and little research has addressed the issue. Terr *et al.* (1999) have proposed a 'spectrum' classification to address indirect and distant exposure. The spectrum classification includes several categories that are pertinent with respect to terrorism: distant trauma, reaction to a real event observed at the time but from a distant site; indirect trauma, reaction to an event not directly observable; and vicarious trauma, reaction to a highly threatening event that was not directly observable but was nationally threatening. Media coverage serves as a conduit in these forms of indirect trauma.

The Media's Role in Victimisation

While media coverage is essential to achieving the terrorist goal, measuring its impact is not easy. Because media coverage is so integral to the process, it may be impossible to separate the impact of the media from the impact of the event itself. After all, indirect victims of terrorism do not exist until they know about the event. This is also true for other disaster situations. For example, post-traumatic stress in evacuated residents of an area threatened with a nuclear (Handford *et al.*, 1986) or technological (Breton, Valla and Lambert, 1993) accident may arise from the media notice to evacuate, from the process of evacuation itself or from the event and the fear associated with it. Fear and anxiety associated with media exposure to a terrorist incident do not necessarily impugn the media, but may instead simply reflect the degree of horror associated with the event.

Two studies have addressed the psychological impact of the September 11 attacks. In a random-digit-dial telephone survey of residents of Manhattan one to two months after the destruction of the World Trade Center, 7.5 per cent of the respondents reported symptoms consistent with PTSD and 9.7 per cent reported symptoms consistent with depression. Of those living in the vicinity of the World Trade Center, Galea *et al.* (2002) reported a 20 per cent prevalence of PTSD. While many of these individuals directly witnessed the attacks, had a friend or relative killed or were involved in the rescue effort, most were not physically on-site or in immediate danger and were not related to direct victims (Galea *et al.*, 2002). With the sights and sounds, alarm and chaos stemming from the attack evident for miles around, many instinctively turned to television, radio and the Internet to learn what had occurred. The media, so essential in providing information, became the vector of fear—a powerful weapon of the terrorists. For these direct and indirect victims, it may never be possible to tease apart the impact of the event from the impact of media coverage of it.

Schuster *et al.* (2001) also used a random-digit-dial telephone survey of a nationally representative sample to examine the immediate reactions of 560 adults to the September 11 attacks. On the day of the attacks, participants acknowledged watching television coverage for a mean of 8.1 hours. It is assumed that, for many, the media provided a primary source of exposure. Over 40 per cent of the sample reported at least one of five 'substantial stress symptoms', and 90 per cent reported at least low levels of stress symptoms. Participants who were closer to New York had the highest rates. While a positive relationship between television exposure and stress was established, television coverage that day and in the days to follow constituted a major source of information and may have been a means of coping for individuals interested in obtaining information about the situation or what to do (Schuster *et al.*, 2001).

Schuster *et al.* (2001) also assessed children's reactions to the September 11 attacks by interviewing their parents. Over one-third of the parents reported that their children had at least one of five stress reactions and almost half reported that their children had worried about their own safety or the safety of loved ones. According to parental reports, children watched television for a mean of 3.0 hours per day, with older children watching more than younger children. Approximately one-third of the parents tried to limit or prevent this viewing. Parents were more likely to limit viewing in younger children and in those perceived to be stressed. For children whose parents did not attempt to restrict viewing, there was an association between the number of hours of viewing and the number of reported stress symptoms. Many parents discussed the events with their children, especially with older children. The number of hours of discussion was associated with the number of hours of television viewing, but there was no relationship between the extent of discussion and the degree of stress symptoms in either parents or children (Schuster *et al.*, 2001).

A series of reports related to the 1995 bombing of the Alfred P. Murrah Federal Building in Oklahoma City also documented a relationship between media exposure and post-traumatic stress reactions in children (Pfefferbaum *et al.*, 1999a, 1999b, 2000, 2001). At the time, the bombing was the deadliest act of terrorism on US soil forcing the issue into the consciousness of the nation. Television coverage as an aspect of exposure was examined in a large sample of middle- and high-school students assessed seven weeks after the bombing. The bombing occurred during the morning hours when most children were in school and, while over one-third reported knowing someone killed or injured in the explosion, for most these relationships did not involve immediate family members. Therefore, the majority of the sample would be considered indirect victims. The children retrospectively reported fear and arousal at the time of the bombing, and many continued to worry about themselves and their families (Pfefferbaum *et al.*, 1999a, 1999b). The majority of the children reported that in the aftermath of the bombing, 'most' or 'all' of their television viewing was bomb related. As expected, relationship to the deceased correlated with difficulty calming down after bomb-related television exposure, but many children reported no such difficulty (Pfefferbaum *et al.*, 1999b). Television exposure correlated with post-traumatic stress symptoms at seven weeks (Pfefferbaum *et al.*, 1999a, 1999b, 2001).

Findings in the middle-school sample revealed that television exposure was a better predictor of post-traumatic stress than either sensory exposure, measured as hearing or feeling the blast, or interpersonal exposure, measured as knowing someone killed or injured. Television exposure accounted for only a small amount of the variance in post-traumatic stress reactions, however, indicating that other factors were more important correlates of stress. For children without sensory or interpersonal exposure, those with high television exposure had significantly greater post-traumatic stress symptomatology than those with low television exposure (Pfefferbaum *et al.*, 2001).

Elementary-school children enrolled in grades three to five were assessed in the next academic year, eight to ten months after the bombing. By then, media attention was focused on the criminal investigation and proceedings but also included images of the devastation and the victims. Bomb-related television exposure was associated with higher levels of post-traumatic stress response in this sample as well (Gurwitch *et al.*, 2002).

In a study of children residing a hundred miles from Oklahoma City, Pfefferbaum *et al.* (2000) assessed the relationship between media exposure and post-traumatic stress two years after the incident, just as the federal trial of Timothy McVeigh was beginning and news coverage related to the trial intensified. This sample was chosen specifically to represent indirect victims not expected to be closely related to victims or to have been in Oklahoma City on the day of the bombing. Interestingly, while both broadcast and print media exposure were related to post-traumatic reactions, print exposure was the stronger correlate (Pfefferbaum *et al.*, 2000). The findings may reflect peculiarities in the measures used in the study, but differences associated with the two forms of media may also explain the results. Children with greater interest in or more intense reactions to the bombing may have actively sought print coverage. Processing and retention of broadcast and print material may differ as may memory of information obtained through these different modalities. While televised scenes capture terror and are commonly rebroadcast, these scenes are often fleeting. Printed images may spotlight the most salient and graphic part of an experience, and they endure, allowing one to view them for any length of time and repeatedly over time. It is not uncommon for television or radio to play as background while children engage in other activities. In these instances, the child's attention may be diminished and passive. Furthermore, broadcast coverage of the bombing was so extensive that children may have discounted it or 'tuned it out'.

Imitation

Concern has been raised about the imitative effect of terrorist acts, and the media have been roundly criticised for being complicit, though there is no conclusive empirical evidence to support these claims (Nacos, 1994). This is not to say that examples of imitation are lacking. For example, four months after the September 11 attacks, a 15-year-old boy flew an aeroplane into a bank building in Tampa, Florida, in a violent imitative suicide. While this is consistent with the literature on cluster suicides in teenagers (Phillips and Carstensen, 1986; Shaffer, 1988) and is likely a reflection of the boy's mental state, we might well count him among the victims.

CLINICAL IMPLICATIONS AND FUTURE DIRECTIONS

Media coverage of major terrorist events tends to be intense, capturing acute suffering and personal vulnerability. Unlike fictional stories, it portrays actual events and is sometimes unedited. And it produces the images of death and destruction, chaos and helplessness that instil fear and intimidation in the larger public. Media attention can also evoke the intense patriotism and rage essential in support of government forces needed to combat the enemy terrorists.

What constitutes responsible reporting of terrorist events has been the subject of heated debate for decades. To some extent, that debate stems from the public reaction that results from media attention to specific incidents. For example, public reaction, if severe enough to influence political leadership and decision-making, may complicate hostage negotiations. Surely few would seriously recommend that terrorist incidents not be covered at all. Not only would the free world recoil at the thought of news being suppressed, but the political implications of an uninformed public would prevent the government from making decisions that serve the near- and long-term interests of the whole.

Recognising that coverage will and must occur, however, does not mean that it should go unscrutinised. Scrutiny should serve the goal of promoting mental health as well as national security interests, and should derive from careful clinical observation and research. Several questions arise. First, what do we know about the impact of media exposure—positive and negative—related to terrorist events, and is there sufficient knowledge to make specific recommendations related to the content or presentation of news? Second, what are the clinical implications associated with this issue and what caveats about media exposure should be provided to the public and the professionals who serve them? And finally, what are the implications with respect to future directions in research?

The Impact of Media Coverage

While tempting, there is insufficient evidence at present to implicate the media in adverse emotional reactions. First, studies of direct victims have not reported findings with respect to the media's influence. One would surmise that media exposure would pale in comparison to other factors such as physical injury and recalled emotional states, though media exposure may re-ignite the experienced trauma in direct victims.

Another interesting issue is the impact of media exposure on indirect victims. The few studies reported to date suggest that there is a relationship between television exposure and post-traumatic stress reactions in indirect victims (Schuster et al., 2001; Pfefferbaum et al., 1999a, 2000, 2001). In studies by Pfefferbaum et al. (1999b, 2001), however, television exposure accounted for only a small part of the variance in post-traumatic stress. In addition, the association does not imply a causal relationship. Media content and images associated with terrorism are likely to contribute to heightened arousal in some individuals, but those with heightened arousal may also be drawn to media coverage to obtain information or to maintain a heightened state of arousal. Furthermore, not all post-traumatic stress reactions represent pathology; they may be adaptive and, in some situations, may even promote survival.

Clinical Implications

The clinical implications associated with media coverage of terrorism are intuitive. First, while media coverage may be essential to obtain information, exposure should be monitored. The pervasiveness of the media in modern society and the potential for passive exposure in which individuals are affected without even realising it may necessitate concerted individual effort to prevent excessive exposure. Professionals should routinely assess exposure and reactions, even in those who reside outside the immediate area where an incident has occurred and in situations where exposure may not be obvious. This is especially true for children, who should be given opportunities to discuss their concerns about an incident, and media depictions of it, with parents and other adults. To that end, the public, parents, primary-care physicians, teachers and counsellors should be taught to recognise post-traumatic stress reactions.

The media also have an important role in ameliorating the detrimental effects of terrorism. Everly and Mitchell (2001) emphasise the potentially positive aspects of media coverage. They recommend that the media be used to provide information to affected populations. This should include information about clinical indicators of stress and where to obtain appropriate mental-health care. Appropriate, credible and adequate information may diminish the 'sense of chaos' (Everly and Mitchell, 2001, p. 134). Recommended steps for re-establishing a sense of safety and security should be widely publicised. Communication should be normalised as soon as possible. Symbols, such as the flag, should be used to help re-establish community cohesion. Rituals may be beneficial and can be promoted by the media (Everly and Mitchell, 2001).

Future Directions and Research

Additional research is needed to determine the impact of the media on terrorist victims—direct and indirect. Like the subject of media violence, it will take many studies across multiple samples using a variety of measures to settle the issue. It was only the weight of the evidence after decades of research that ultimately satisfied the public and policy-makers that media violence may be detrimental; yet today, the media industry remains dubious.

Research should attempt to disentangle the effects of events themselves from aspects of coverage. It should investigate the multiple media modalities, specific aspects of coverage and exposure, a range of both positive and negative outcomes, and mediating and moderating influences. Other specific issues warrant exploration. For example, certain categories and characteristics of victims may be more or less susceptible to the influence of the media. It seems reasonable to assume that direct victims, who experience multiple forms of exposure to an incident, may have different patterns of exposure and may respond differently than indirect victims. Developmental and cultural factors may influence response. In addition, the current literature has used post-traumatic stress as the primary outcome measure, but other reactions such as fear, generalised anxiety and changed attitudes and behaviour may be more salient. Finally, media coverage is only part of a complex set of influences that constitute the recovery environment following a terrorist assault, and its impact cannot be understood without placing it in the context of these other influences.

REFERENCES

Alexander, D.A. and Wells, A. (1991). Reactions of police officers to body-handling after a major disaster: a before-and-after comparison. *British Journal of Psychiatry*, **159**, 547–55.

American Psychiatric Association (1994). *Diagnostic and Statistical Manual-IV*, 4th edn. Washington, DC: American Psychiatric Association.

Breton, J.J., Valla, J.P. and Lambert, J. (1993). Industrial disaster and mental health of children and their parents. *Journal of the American Academy of Child and Adolescent Psychiatry*, **32**, 438–45.

Dishman, C. (1999). Trends in modern terrorism. *Studies in Conflict & Terrorism*, **22**, 357–62.

Elmquist, S. (1990). The scope and limits of cooperation between the media and the authorities. In Y. Alexander and R. Latter (Eds), *Terrorism and the Media*, pp. 74–80. Washington, DC: Brassey's (US), Inc.

Epstein, R., Fullerton, C. and Ursano, R. (1998). Post-traumatic stress disorder following an air disaster: a prospective study. *American Journal of Psychiatry*, **155**, 934–38.

Everly, G.S. and Mitchell, J.T. (2001). America under attack: the '10 Commandments' of responding to mass terrorist attacks. *International Journal of Emergency Mental Health*, **3**(3), 133–35.

Feinstein, A. (2001). Risking more than their lives: the effects of post-traumatic stress disorder on journalists. As viewed on 12 April 2001, *www.freedomforum.org*.

Galea, S., Ahern, J., Resnick, H., Kilpatrick, D., Bucuvalas, M., Gold, J. and Vlahov, D. (2002). Psychological sequelae of the September 11 terrorist attacks in New York City. *New England Journal of Medicine*, **346**, 982–87.

Gurwitch, R.H., Sitterle, K.S., Young, B.H. and Pfefferbaum, B. (2002). Helping children in the aftermath of terrorism. In A. La Greca, W. Silverman, E. Vernberg and M. Roberts (Eds), *Helping Children Cope with Disasters: Integrating Research and Practice*, pp. 327–57. Washington, DC: American Psychological Association Press.

Handford, H.A., Mayes, S.D., Mattison, R.E., Humphrey, F.J. II, Bagnato, S., Bixler, E.O. and Kales, J.D. (1986). Child and parent reaction to the Three Mile Island nuclear accident. *Journal of the American Academy of Child Psychiatry*, **25**(3), 346–56.

Hoffman, B. (1988). *Inside Terrorism*. New York: Columbia University Press.

Hoffman, B. (2001). Change and continuity in terrorism. *Studies in Conflict & Terrorism*, **24**, 417–28.

Jenkins, B.M. (2001). Terrorism and beyond: a 21st century perspective. *Studies in Conflict & Terrorism*, **24**, 321–27.

Kingston, S. (1995). Terrorism, the media, and the Northern Ireland conflict. *Studies in Conflict & Terrorism*, **18**, 203–31.

Nacos, B.L. (1994). *Terrorism and the Media: From the Iran Hostage Crisis to the World Trade Center Bombing*. New York: Columbia University Press.

North, C.S., Tivis, L., McMillen, J.C., Pfefferbaum, B., Spitznagel, E.L., Cox, J., Nixon, S.J., Bunch, K.P. and Smith, E.M. (2002). Psychiatric disorders in rescue workers after the Oklahoma City bombing. *American Journal of Psychiatry*, **159**, 857–59.

Perl, S. (1997). *Terrorism, the media, and the government: Perspectives, trends, and options for policymakers*. CRS Issue Brief, 22 October. As viewed at *www.fas.org / irp / crs / crs-terror.htm*.

Pfefferbaum, B., Nixon, S.J., Krug, R.S., Tivis, R.D., Moore, V.L., Brown, J.M., Pynoos, R.S., Foy, D. and Gurwitch, R.H. (1999a). Clinical needs assessment of middle and high school students following the 1995 Oklahoma City bombing. *American Journal of Psychiatry*, **156**, 1069–74.

Pfefferbaum, B., Nixon, S.J., Tucker, P.M., Tivis, R.D., Moore, V.L., Gurwitch, R.H., Pynoos, R.S. and Geis, H.K. (1999b). Post-traumatic stress responses in bereaved children after the Oklahoma City bombing. *Journal of the American Academy of Child and Adolescent Psychiatry*, **38**, 1372–79.

Pfefferbaum, B., Nixon, S.J., Tivis, R.D., Doughty, D.E., Pynoos, R.S., Gurwitch, R.H. and Foy, D.W. (2001). Television exposure in children after a terrorist incident. *Psychiatry*, **64**, 202–11.

Pfefferbaum, B., Seale, T.W., McDonald, N.B., Brandt, E.N. Jr, Rainwater, S.M., Maynard, B.T., Meierhoefer, B. and Miller, P.D. (2000). Post-traumatic stress two years after the Oklahoma City bombing in youths geographically distant from the explosion. *Psychiatry*, **63**, 358–70.

Phillips, D.P. and Carstensen, L.L. (1986). Clustering of teenage suicides after television news stories about suicide. *New England Journal of Medicine*, **315**, 685–89.

Protheroe, A.H. (1990). Terrorism, journalism, and democracy. In Y. Alexander and R. Latter (Eds), *Terrorism & the Media: Dilemmas for Government, Journalists & the Public*, pp. 64–69. Washington, DC: Brassey's (US), Inc.

Pynoos, R.S. and Nader, K. (1989). Children's memory and proximity to violence. *Journal of the American Academy of Child and Adolescent Psychiatry*, **28**, 236–41.

Schuster, M.A., Stein, B.D., Jaycox, L.H., Collins, R.L., Marshall, G.N., Elliott, M.N., Zhou, A.J., Kanouse, D.E., Morrison, J.L. and Berry, S.H. (2001). A national survey of stress reactions after the September 11, 2001, terrorist attacks. *New England Journal of Medicine*, **345**, 1507–12.

Seaton, J. (1999). The new 'ethnic' wars and the media. In T. Allen and J. Seaton (Eds), *The Media of Conflict: War Reporting and Representations of Ethnic Violence*, pp. 43–63. New York: Zed Books.

Shaffer, D. (1988). The epidemiology of teen suicide: an examination of risk factors. *Journal of Clinical Psychiatry*, **49**, 36–41.

Stern, J. (1999). *The Ultimate Terrorists*. Cambridge, MA: Harvard University Press.

Terr, L.C., Bloch, D.A., Michel, B.A., Shi, H., Reinhardt, J.A. and Metayer, S. (1999). Children's symptoms in the wake of *Challenger*: a field study of distant-traumatic effects and an outline of related conditions. *American Journal of Psychiatry*, **156**, 1536–44.

Wilkinson, P. (1990). Terrorism and propaganda. In Y. Alexander and R. Latter (Eds), *Terrorism & the Media: Dilemmas for Government, Journalists & the Public*, pp. 26–33. Washington, DC: Brassey's (US), Inc.

Yule, W., Perrin, S. and Smith, P. (2001). Traumatic events and post-traumatic stress disorder. In W.K. Silverman and P.D.A. Treffers (Eds), *Anxiety Disorders in Children and Adolescents*, pp. 212–34. Cambridge: Cambridge University Press.

CHAPTER 10

Examining the Impact of Terrorism on Children

DEBORAH BROWNE

University of Leicester

INTRODUCTION

In September 2002 Amnesty International reported that both sides of the Israeli–Palestinian conflict were increasingly targeting children. The report claimed that over 320 young people under the age of 18 (the majority Palestinians) had been killed during two years of conflict (BBC News, 2002). We are all too familiar with the defensive adage that it is unavoidable that innocent civilians will get killed in a war situation. The tragedy of terrorism and political violence is that the most innocent victims are those who are too young to have made an informed choice, if partiality is to be forced upon us, about whether they support the cause of the activist, the target or any other alternative. The statistics on the number of children killed offered by Amnesty International, UNICEF and other organisations worldwide are only an indicator of the damage that situations of violence and terror inflict on children. For every child killed it is very likely that hundreds more suffer physical and psychological damage. The purpose of this chapter is to examine how terrorism might impact on the psychological well-being of children and young people.

By and large, researchers have neglected to examine the impact of terrorism on children, which makes it very difficult indeed to draw on any lessons that have already been learned. Having said this, however, there are other areas of psychosocial development that it is possible to draw

Terrorists, Victims and Society: Psychological Perspectives on Terrorism and its Consequences.
Edited by Andrew Silke. © 2003 John Wiley & Sons, Ltd.

from when discussing the impact of terrorism on children. One is the substantial body of research on child abuse, of various forms, as this gives a good indication of the consequences of trauma. Researchers have isolated many effects of child abuse, and importantly it has been noted that different forms of abuse (sexual, physical, emotional) can result in some of the same responses in the victims (such as aggression, antisocial behaviour and post-traumatic stress reactions) (Hollin, Browne and Palmer, 2002). Additionally, researchers have found similar responses in children who are witness to abuse as those who are direct victims (e.g. Jaffe *et al.*, 1986). If it is possible to isolate potential effects of being exposed to the trauma of abuse, then it may be possible that these same responses will be noted in children and young people who have been exposed to other types of trauma, such as a terrorist attack. It is also possible to learn from the literature on loss and separation, as this gives an indication on how children will respond to loss of life in a terrorist event. This is something that is elaborated on later in this chapter. Finally, there is a growing body of research on more general responses to war conditions, and this helps to understand how children exposed to chronic situations of violence behave, particularly when the war situations are those that are most likely to include terrorist tactics or events.

While there are inherent difficulties associated with comparing and contrasting studies that use different methodologies with varying degrees of reliability and validity, at present the knowledge base is not extensive enough to be very selective. This chapter discusses findings and debate in the field rather more as a means of suggesting explanations than substantiating long-held theories.

DETERMINING WHETHER THERE IS AN IMPACT

Because of the paucity of empirical research, it is very difficult to describe with confidence what the effects of terrorism on children actually are. Indeed, some accounts indicate that children are not greatly affected by their experiences with such violent situations. Cairns and Wilson (1989), for example, could not find substantial evidence that children were affected by the ongoing situation of political violence in Northern Ireland, and this was at a time when frequent acts of terrorism were being reported. Similarly, Joseph, Cairns and McCollam (1993) reported no significant differences in depression scores between children going to school in high- and low-violence areas in Belfast. Findings such as these have led to considerable debate as to how resilient children and young people are to exposure to violence.

Having made this point, however, the situation in Northern Ireland, even at the worst of the troubles, does not compare to situations of chronic conflict in many other parts of the world. For example, in a Western country the health of children is unlikely to be affected by the sort of poverty, malnutrition and disease that characterise situations of political violence and militant attack in other regions. It is very possible that these environmental factors impact on children's capacity to cope with the situation. Additionally, in Northern Ireland only those children who have been injured, witnessed, or suffered loss through paramilitary attacks have actually been first-hand witnesses to the sort of terror that is likely to have a serious impact. While it has been estimated that the number of children who have witnessed the murder of family or friends by paramilitary attack is several hundred (Cairns, 1987), this does not represent an immense proportion of all children in the country. A United Nations Children's Fund (UNICEF) report described how in Rwanda in 1996, 96 per cent of the children interviewed had witnessed violence, 80 per cent had lost a family member and 70 per cent had seen someone injured or killed (Chauvin, Mugaju and Comlavi, 1998). It is reasonable to assume that this level of intense experience is far more likely to yield a statistically notable rate of post-event pathology.

DISTINGUISHING BETWEEN CHRONIC AND ACUTE EPISODES

As well as how the intensity of an event will influence the assessment of the potential impact of terrorism on children, the fundamental differences between chronic and acute experiences should also be considered. This distinction can be encapsulated as the difference between the plight of those who have witnessed or been victim to a single act of terrorism (such as the Oklahoma bombing or September 11), and those who are living in a situation where they are exposed to long-term terrorist activities (such as in Northern Ireland or Israel/Palestine). Garbarino and Kostelny (1993) distinguished between children's adjustment to acute and chronic danger, and this is essentially the same distinction that is being made here. They point out that exposure to acute danger may need a period of adjustment and assimilation, but basically that the child can be reassured of the return of relative safety and normality. Exposure to chronic danger, on the other hand, would require a more fundamental developmental adjustment that might include changes in behaviour and personality, as well as more persistent symptoms of post-traumatic stress disorder (PTSD) (pp. 26–27).

Child victims of an acute terrorist event such as a bombing may be exposed to a multitude of outcomes. They may need to deal with personal injury, which may take years to recover from physically, as well as to adjust to psychologically. They may also need to face the loss of a parent, which will be dealt with later in the chapter, or a sibling or friend. Besides ensuing bereavement issues, the latter two cases also tend to instigate a realisation of personal mortality as the child or young person deals with the death of a peer-group member.

Exposure to a single terrorist event can produce high levels of post-traumatic stress symptoms even when the individual is not directly exposed to the event through personal loss or injury. Pfefferbaum *et al.* (1999) demonstrated that PTSD scores were as high for local school students who experienced heavy television exposure to reporting on the Oklahoma City bombing as those who knew someone who had been killed or injured. This has significant implications for the treatment of such events by the media. While the public appetite for information and visual confirmation of incidents such as September 11 is extensive, it is clear that exposing children and young people increases the stressful impacts of the event. The Pfefferbaum *et al.* study also showed that PTSD scores were greater when the proportion of television viewing was higher at the time of the incident. While some effect from such catastrophes is inevitable, this study suggests that the impact on children and young people could almost definitely be reduced if their television exposure to the event were limited.

In the case of chronic long-term exposure to terror, the effects are inevitably different to a one-off attack. There is some evidence that children and young people adapt to these situations, which has resulted in what Cairns (1996) referred to as 'the resilience debate'. As described earlier in this chapter, many studies of children in Northern Ireland have concluded that they do not show significantly more pathological symptoms than their peers from other areas. While it has also been pointed out in this chapter that the situation in Northern Ireland is environmentally different to many other situations of chronic violence, reports of resilience in children are too common to dismiss as being entirely peculiar to an affluent and facilitative environment. There are many reasons why a child or young person may not show pathological reactions to stress, but not all of these are because they are not suffering. It has been suggested (e.g. Richman, 1993) that in situations of chronic stress it may be more adaptive to contain strong feelings than to yield to them.

Psychologist Willie McCarney, who has spent some time researching the effects of the Northern Ireland troubles on young people, commented: 'when you ask me the effects of the troubles on our young people, the short answer is that I simply do not know' (1996, p. 67). He presents many reasons for this. The situation is complicated by socioeconomic deprivation of those most likely to be victims, and by varying experiences of the troubles. Peoples' reactions to the situation may be influenced by their perception of the situation as a war or as a series of terrorist activities, and by whether or not they were directly involved with the activities. While some young people are far removed from the paramilitary activities, others are heavily involved. This involvement could be as victims, witnesses, perpetrators of rioting and other derivative activities, or as recruits to junior wings of the various paramilitary groups. It is easy to see, therefore, why it is difficult to describe with much degree of certainty exactly how multitudinous the effects of terrorism in Northern Ireland, or in any other situation where children are exposed to chronic violence, actually are.

Adding further fuel to the resilience debate, a number of studies have shown that exposure to long-term violence does influence levels of psychopathology. Al-Krenawi et al. (2001) investigated the psychological effects on adolescents of long-term exposure to the blood-vengeance culture that exists in an Arab neighbourhood in Israel. Although the 120 young people that made up the study group were continually exposed to the threat of blood vengeance, it was an integral part of their culture and was considered acceptable behaviour. The study concluded, however, that the participants showed higher levels of distress than the Israeli norm. They additionally displayed far higher levels of other pathological symptoms such as depression, anxiety, hostility and psychoticism. Despite potential intervening variables such as the Arab youths being exposed to higher levels of deprivation than their Israeli counterparts, it was concluded that the levels of the symptoms reported were significant, and comparisons were made to the effects of war.

Psychological reactions to persistent terrorism are, not surprisingly, similar to reactions of those who have experienced a war situation. The same conditions of harsh and prolonged environmental stress are endured by those who experience both. These conditions will exist irrespective of individual perspectives on whether the situation is a full-scale war, low-intensity conflict, guerrilla war or terrorism. Indeed, many modern low-intensity conflicts are by their very nature a combination of these, with terror being used on civilians in an attempt to exert social control (Summerfield, 1996).

LOSS, DISPLACEMENT AND SEPARATION

Some researchers in the area have indicated their opinion that the most serious consequence of acute or chronic terrorism for young children is the death or separation from a parent or most especially both parents. For example, Bowlby (1965) postulated that separation was the most distressing experience for refugee children during the Second World War. He also acknowledged, however, that 'the children had been submitted to such diverse and often horrifying experiences that it would have been almost impossible to have isolated the effects of separation from those of other experiences' (p. 50). This, unfortunately, is an ongoing problem in this field of research. The children who suffer most loss in violent situations are generally those who have been most exposed to the event. This makes it very difficult to distinguish the consequences of the event from particular factors such as separation from a parent.

The literature on grieving in children is fairly developed and it is established that children tend to grieve after the loss of a parent or close relative for about two years, the same as would be expected of an adult (Herbert, 1998). Bowlby (1969) argued that children's grieving ended with a sort of 'detachment' from the deceased individual, but other researchers describe this in more adaptive terms. Normal grieving processes (whether described as detachment or the normal process of bereavement) do not always account for the additional impact of loss through violence. Cairns (1996) pointed out that although it has been shown that children who have experienced the loss of a parent in situations of political violence show symptoms for many years (e.g. Dremen, 1989), it is very difficult to determine whether this is as a result of the violent loss, or the violence itself. Echoing Bowlby's earlier concerns, Cairns (1996) commented: 'This makes it difficult to decide if the impact on children of father-loss[1] as a result of political violence differs from the effects of bereavement under other circumstances' (p. 66).

In addition to the experience of loss and bereavement, it is clear that separation from parents, to which many children displaced during situations of political conflict will be exposed, may instigate stress and antisocial behaviour. Even in relatively normal circumstances children who have been separated from their families and spend time in residential or foster care tend to show pathological symptoms that include both internalising and externalising behaviour (Berridge and Cleaver, 1987; Massinga and Perry, 1994). Indeed many children in situations of chronic violence will have been exposed to the sort of pathogenic care that the *Diagnostic and Statistical Manual of Mental Disorders* (DSMIV) (APA, 1991) has noted precipitates reactive attachment disorder. Pathogenic care is characterised by persistent disregard for the child's emotional and physical needs, and repeated changes of primary carers. Whilst the children who are victims of separation through a violent event may have carers who are very caring and competent individuals, the environmental conditions are frequently such that the child is exposed to neglect by misadventure (rather than by any evident disregard on the part of the adults) and through the same mechanisms experiences changes in, or perhaps the absence of, carers. This may explain why the common symptoms of neglect, such as depression, anxiety, withdrawn behaviour and excessive clinging, have been

---

[1]Cairns pointed out that most circumstances of political violence that have been researched examine the loss of the child's father. The applicability of these findings applies more to situations of chronic violence than attacks such as the Oklahoma bombing or September 11.

observed (e.g. Bowlby, 1965, pp. 50–52) in children separated from their parents as a result of war or other violent situations.

STRESS RESPONSES TO VIOLENCE AND TERROR

Characteristic responses to stress in children and young people include anxiety, behavioural changes and sleep disturbances such as nightmares and night-terrors, and most of these have frequently been reported by those researching children who have been exposed to terrorist activities. Fraser (1974) reported that children in her study who had been exposed to a violent incident in Northern Ireland experienced fainting fits, asthma attacks and sleep disturbances. A similar study by Lyons (1974) found that children exposed to bomb explosions displayed various behaviour changes that included speech problems and bed-wetting. Somasundaram (1998) described cases of Sri Lankan children admitted to psychiatric wards after being exposed to terrifying militant attacks. Two little boys who witnessed their father being assaulted by a militant group before they killed him presented symptoms of night-terrors, frequently screaming in terror at night, and waking drenched with sweat. Another boy developed severely anxious symptoms, including school phobia, after travelling on a school bus that was strafed by helicopters. While disturbing and potentially damaging, these symptoms are well recognised and can often be treated quite effectively when they are presented as isolated disturbances. Children exposed to a traumatic event or to chronic war or terrorism can also display an array of disturbances that may be signs of the more complicated symptoms of PTSD.

PTSD has been recognised as a response to exposure to severe stress, including war and violence, for several decades, and was introduced as an official diagnosis by the American Psychiatric Association in 1980 with the publication of DSM-III. It is characterised by rather severe symptoms of trauma that last longer than a month. These symptoms include re-experienced trauma, avoidance of stimuli associated with the trauma, numbed responsiveness and persistently increased autonomic and emotional arousal (Oltmanns and Emery, 1995). It is becoming clear, however, that it may not be appropriate to look for 'adult symptoms' in children as the disorder may manifest itself in different ways depending on age and developmental aptitude. Recognised symptoms of PTSD that may be more applicable to children include changes in school performance, interpersonal relationships and mood, as well as reckless behaviour and the onset of new fears or the reoccurrence of old ones (Herbert, 1998). It has also been noted that children who have been exposed to political violence sometimes suffer symptoms of PTSD and distress even when they continue to function reasonably well socially and academically. In these cases the adults in the children's lives are not aware of the extent of their distress (see Richman, Ratilal and Aly, 1989). This is another factor that needs to be considered when children's apparent adaptability to war situations is debated. Methodological issues such as using parent/teacher versus self-report instruments will need to be examined more carefully before firm conclusions can be drawn.

There is some indication that a very pathological form of PTSD, known as malignant PTSD or 'disorders of extreme stress not otherwise specified' (DESNOS), can be seen in people whose personality development was severely distorted in childhood due to their experience of violence. These young people appear to display anger, resentment, impulsiveness and an apparent inability to control their feelings. Somasundaram (1998) described case studies of patients with this disorder who attended clinics in northern Sri Lanka between 1983 and 1987.[2] These include accounts of two teenage boys who joined militant groups after a relatively normal childhood. After some years of experiencing violent battles during which they witnessed many gruesome deaths, both boys began to show symptoms that included insomnia and aggressive outbursts. One of the boys (R) responded particularly poorly to his re-experiencing symptoms, which made him very violent; he frequently assaulted family members as well as strangers, and made several attempts at suicide. The other boy, also called R (to avoid confusion I shall refer to him as R1), became obsessed with the need to see blood and gradually began to derive pleasure from brutally killing people. Those treating him noted that he too was prone to outbursts of violence and became angry at the sight of others enjoying themselves. Both boys were very difficult to treat, and did not respond to drugs or psychotherapy. While both boys joined the military in adolescence, R1 was considerably the younger (11 years of age as opposed to R's 15) of the two when his normal life was exchanged for one where he was exposed to persistent violence and trained to carry out civilian massacres. He also remained within the situation for four years, which is twice as long as R. His arguably more pathological symptoms (obsession with blood, desire to kill people and lack of remorse) may well be due to differences in personal and environmental interactions; for example, he was at a more vulnerable age and also exposed to the violence for a longer period of time. Whatever explanation is offered or accepted, it is clear that the varying accounts of PTSD symptoms that have been reported, as well as the resilience debate, seem to indicate quite strongly that there is evidence of notable individual differences in children's responses to war and terrorism.

---

[2]The situation in these years in Sri Lanka was generally characterised by chronic, low-intensity conflict with periods of more violent guerrilla attacks and state reprisals.

EXPLAINING INDIVIDUAL REACTIONS

While a lack of validated research into children's reactions to terrorism makes it difficult to accurately predict how individual children will respond, emerging theories are beginning to synthesise models that might help to explain individual differences. It has been suggested, for example, that the magnitude of the impact on the individual will depend on how the person has interacted with the environment of the disaster. Wilson (1988) proposed a person–environment interaction that could account for why some people, including children, respond to a traumatic event more maladaptively than others. The environment in which the event occurs will react with individual characteristics to produce an individual response. This model proposes that variations in response might be determined by differences in the components of these interacting elements. Somasundaram (1998) considered these components in the context of war stress and children, and gave examples of both environmental and personal factors that interact to determine how the child responds to the situation. Parson (1995) described similar categories in risk factors for pathological reactions to the Oklahoma City bombing. He maintained that risk factors could be categorised under the broad types of 'intraself' and 'socioenvironmental'. Parson did not limit his discussion to children, and nor are the concepts described by each writer identical. Nonetheless, there are some interesting parallels that shall be elaborated during the discussion in this section.

Somasundaram (1998) considered environmental factors to include the dimensions of space, time and severity of the event, the type of event, whether indirect effects were experienced, and other post-traumatic milieu. In essence, 'space' refers to how close the individual was to the event (e.g. a bomb dropping), 'time' to how long the event lasted (which includes any anticipatory period), and of course 'severity' refers to the gravity of the event, although it needs to be acknowledged that personal perception affects this. Parson's socioenvironmental factors, although presented in a manner that places more emphasis on individual experience, include conceptually similar variables. Although he does not list space as a factor, Parson nonetheless strongly emphasises its importance. Writing shortly after the Oklahoma City bombing, he predicted that those most likely to suffer from PTSD would be those children and adults who were in closest proximity to the explosion. Parson's time variables are described in terms of whether or not there is warning and how quickly social and emergency services react to the event. He listed a number of factors that might be said to describe severity, including degree of life threat and degree of socioecological destruction.

As already mentioned, however, severity of an event will depend on personal perception. While most people will acknowledge the severity of an attack such as September 11 or the Oklahoma bombing, many individuals, including children, might appear to adapt to more chronic terrorism or low-intensity war conditions, such as seen in Northern Ireland or the Israeli–Palestinian conflict. Severity has also been referred to earlier in this chapter in reference to the difference in the level of experience between exposure to violence in Rwandan children and those in Northern Ireland. It will be recalled that it was pointed out that the intensity of the Rwandan experience would appear to be more likely to yield significant measures of pathology in the wake of the terrorist event. Future research will need to examine the impact of these factors in more depth.

Somasundaram (1998) included loss, life threat, displacement, torture and rape as 'types of event', and also included indirect effects of war such as illness, lack of food, poverty, etc. Parson also described 'type' of disaster, but distinguished more broadly between natural and man-made disasters. He suggested that different types of disaster are more likely to produce chronic disturbance and illness. He also acknowledged that further research is needed to distinguish between the consequences of natural and various man-made disasters (Parson, 1995). As most research to date has concentrated on the impact of events, including floods, earthquakes, war and terrorist attack, on the adults involved, further research is required to examine the comparative and contrasting effects on children. An important distinction in relation to type of event has already been discussed earlier in this chapter, and that is the difference between acute and chronic terrorism.

'Indirect' or secondary stressors, which Somasundaram also included under type of event, include economic and social disruption, the destruction of property, reduced availability of food and other products, etc. Parson (although not listing them as secondary effects) gave examples such as strangeness of relocation environment and degree of social network disruption, which apply more strongly to the sort of experiences that children may have to deal with following a disaster in a more developed country. A child coping with the secondary effects of a terrorist attack such as September 11 may face disruption of normal schooling, restrictions on travel, etc. Secondary effects will be more severe in situations of longer-term violence or low-intensity conflict. In these cases there is more likely to be poor availability of food and medical supplies, which will have more severe health implications for the children involved.

The final environmental factor that Somasundaram listed, 'post-traumatic milieu', refers to the surroundings, support and setting in which the victims find themselves after a traumatic event. Parson also felt that these were important issues, listing efficacy of post-disaster services, degree of strangeness in relocation environment and degree of cohesiveness of recovering environment among his socioenvironmental risk factors relevant to victims of the Oklahoma City bombing. In a situation of continuous war it is difficult to adjust 'adaptively', and indeed the futility and potential dangers of expecting children to overcome their defence mechanisms in a situation of continuing violence is broached later in this chapter. When the event is a specific act of terrorism, however, the support of family and wider social attitudes would be expected to affect the environment within which the individual is interacting. Many researchers who have spent time studying the effects of terrorism and political violence on children have indicated that a supportive environment has a considerable impact on how the child recovers from the event. For example, Richman (1993) notes: 'My personal experience is that many [children] show a gradual diminution of distress over time provided they are living in an adequate situation, i.e. with supportive adults and without the threat of violence' (p. 1297). There is also some evidence that the parents' own reactions to the event may impact on the child's response (e.g. Chimienti, Nasr and Khalifehi, 1989; Punamäki, 1989). Despite some debate on the strength of this association, a correlation between parent response and child response should not be surprising. Such a relationship is common in the developmental literature, and has been noted with antisocial behaviour and depression among other things (e.g. see Quinton and Rutter, 1985).

The personal variables that may impact on individual reactions to the event are also numerous. Somasundaram (1998) included personality, heredity, role and attitudes, past experience, age, gender and groups in his discussion on reactions to war stress. Parson (1995) listed some similar concepts under the heading 'intraself risk factors' (pp. 162–63). These included pre-existing psychiatric illness, family psychiatric history, educational attainment, prior traumatic exposure and various attitudes and psychological reactions to the event. Parson does not appear to have included factors such as age and gender, which may be related to why his account does not differentiate between the reactions of children and adults.

Somasundaram (1998) included cognitive style under the construct he named 'personality', as an important determinant of how a person responds to stress. It must be remembered, however, that the personalities and cognitive styles of children and young people are very much still developing. It is possible that traits in their as yet nascent stages will have only a limited impact on how a child reacts to the event. Rather than these variables influencing a child's reaction, therefore, the event itself may have more of an influence on a child's *emerging* personality and cognitive style. Personality has long been described as the result of biological developmental processes interacting with environmental events throughout childhood and adolescence, and even beyond (e.g. Erikson, 1965). With this in mind, it should be clear that a terrorist event might influence a child's *future* behaviour and cognitive responses quite significantly. It is also possible, however, that the evolving quality of a child's personality may allow for a greater degree of flexibility with the immediate response to a violent situation. This may go some way to explaining why it has been noted that some children appear to respond with more adaptability to a situation of terror and violence than the adults around them.

Another factor that should be considered is that it is not necessarily the case that the child's immediate response will be a reflection of his or her independent cognitive state. It has been suggested that a child's cognitive appraisal of the situation may be determined by other factors. A potential relationship between a child's response and that of his or her parents has already been mentioned, and there is certainly evidence that a child's stress response relies on parental emotional cues (Bat-Zion and Levy-Shiff, 1993). The impact of the media on children's cognitive appraisal of the event is also important, as was demonstrated earlier in relation to discussion of reactions to the Oklahoma bombing (Pfefferbaum *et al.*, 1999).

Personality may also be influenced by inherent factors that might predispose a child or young person to respond in a certain way. 'Heredity' may also influence whether stress triggers a particular mental disorder. In a very traumatic situation, however, people are more likely to show symptoms of disorders for which they do not appear to have a genetic disposition. It has been suggested, for example, that a traumatic event may trigger the onset of schizophrenia. Although this disorder appears to have a genetic aetiology (e.g. Gottesman, 1991), Somasundaram (1998) reported a number of cases that presented themselves at a Sri Lankan clinic where schizophrenic symptoms appeared in young people with no psychiatric history and no immediate family history of the disorder, but who were exposed to chronic low-intensity conflict. He also maintained, however, that people who were already predisposed were more likely to develop psychotic illness.

The response to stress will also vary depending on whether the individual had an active or passive role in the event, and their attitude to the situation. In Northern Ireland, for example, those young people who are actively involved with junior wings of the paramilitary groups will react differently to news of a bomb or punishment beating than young people who avoid such groups. The perception of these children will also differ from those who have experienced more indirect consequences of the situation, such as harassment on the way to school (see McKeon, 1973), or whether or not they feel the area they live in is 'safe' (McGrath and Wilson, 1985). Garbarino and Kostelny (1993) distinguished between 'objective' and 'subjective' dangers in children's responses to war. The fundamental difference between the two is that the former refers to actual dangers, while the latter refers to individual perception of the experience. A child who has been harassed on the way to school may continue to feel threatened by such an event even if the actual chances of it happening again are significantly diminished. The 'past experience', therefore, of the individual will also have an impact on how he or she responds. Previous experience of loss or trauma tends to make children and young people more vulnerable, and previous maladaptive coping mechanisms may reappear. As has already been discussed in relation to cognitive functioning, however, the child's perception of events will be affected by cues he or she picks up from the adults and the media around them.

'Age' is a key personal variable, with children of different ages responding in different ways as well as children and adolescents generally responding differently compared to the adults around them. As mentioned earlier in this chapter, children's symptoms of PTSD tend to differ from those 'adult symptoms' listed in diagnostic tools such as DSM-IV. They are far less likely to display symptoms of numbed responsiveness, for instance, and can often react far more adaptively to traumatic events and ongoing conflict. It would appear that younger children are more likely to respond to the fear or anxiety of the adults around them than to develop any significant responses themselves, probably because of their inability to comprehend what is going on. Adolescents in particular may be vulnerable to the accentuated forms of behaviour that are common at this stage, including moroseness and/or aggressive responses. As Garbarino and Kostelny (1993) point out, from a developmental perspective adolescents tend to be more responsive to the society around them than to their parents, which in a situation of political violence and terrorism may mean that they respond differently than their parents or young siblings. As a time of ideological appraisal of moral and political events, this may also mean a stronger and more radical response to the event than at other periods of development. Whether this is to withdraw from society or to engage actively in the event may depend on other personal and environmental factors.

In between the younger age group of children who do not fully comprehend the situation, and the adolescents who possibly spend too much time analysing it, are the older children. These older children have developed the cognitive capacity to understand the magnitude of a terrorist event but do not yet engage so closely with society that they can cope by responding to personal ideologies. It has been noted that these children may be those who are most psychologically affected by the event (e.g. Fraser, 1974), but this is very difficult to substantiate. Different aspects of the event may affect different age groups in diverse ways, and it is difficult to say objectively what the most consequential outcomes will actually be. It has been indicated, for example, that the responses of different age groups may vary with 'gender', with younger girls responding better but adolescent boys showing more resilience (Dawes, Tredoux and Feinstein, 1989). It has already been described how some researchers feel that potentially the biggest impact of a terrorist event for a younger child is the danger of loss or separation from parents and family. This is also linked to the personal factor 'groups', as the support of groups and the loss or injury of members of relevant groups (such as the family) can cause particular stress to individuals and most notably to children. Identification with groups may also impact on adolescents, and may lead to their joining a particular group as a response to their ideologies in relation to the event. As shall be discussed later, the consequences of this may be engaging in brutal behaviour themselves, and possibly death due to the activities of the group.

Besides the obvious direct application of a developmental emphasis, Somasundaram's (1998) model goes a very important step beyond Parson's in explaining the individual child's response to terror. The former model does not merely list factors, but highlights the fundamental interaction between his two groups of factors. It is not merely the presence of specific personal or environmental factors that determines a response, but the interaction between these factors. Other researchers in the field have also highlighted this importance. Bat-Zion and Levy-Shiff (1993), for example, proposed a model to explain children's responses to stress, which they tested by looking at various correlations between the factors they examined in children exposed to scud-missile attacks during the Gulf War. They found that the model explained much of the behaviour they saw, including a correlation between parent response and the coping efforts of children, and between distressing emotions and proximity. It is clear, then, that what determines the response is not merely how personal and environmental factors impact on the individual, but also how some of them might impact on each other. Figure 10.1 attempts to highlight how complicated the mediations are between the various factors that determine what the individual response of each child might be.

It is clear, then, that factors of personal predisposition or vulnerability interact with factors of the actual event to produce the individual response. What the key variables are and how they interact may then precipitate PTSD or other psychopathology. While undoubtedly showing degrees of resilience in certain situations, children and young people may be particularly vulnerable to specific factors at certain stages of development, or may be more vulnerable depending on the circumstances of the event itself.

Figure 10.1 Web of interactions: personal (shaded) and environmental influences on a child's response to a terrorist episode, and some of the interactions between the two

PARTICIPATION IN TERRORIST ACTIVITIES

Some of the most chilling images of terrorism and political violence have been those depicting child warriors or children dressed in the recognised clothes of the perpetrators of violence. While most children and young people who participate in situations of political violence engage only in the peripheral, if provocative, activities such as rioting and provoking rival groups, it must be acknowledged that a disturbing number of children become actively involved in violent activities. In Colombia alone it has been reported that there are around 6000 children fighting for rebel armies or the militias (Machel, 2001, p. 15). It is an affront to Western ideals of childhood innocence to consider the possibility, and in very many cases the probability, that these children engage in vicious acts. The tragedy is, of course, that very often children indeed *are* perpetrators of savage violence themselves, or become terrorists later, possibly due to their childhood experiences.

The case of R1 described earlier related to a 15-year-old boy who had been involved in horrendous acts of violence. This included the murder of a small child by holding him by the legs and bashing his head against a wall until his brains spattered out, while his mother watched screaming (Somasundaram, 1998). Similar acts have been carried out, sometimes against their own families, by children and young people in countries such as Colombia, Rwanda and Sierra Leone (Machel, 2001). Machel's view of such behaviour is that 'children can become desensitised to suffering as a result of their exposure to extreme violence. Often they are exposed deliberately to horrific scenes to harden them and make it easier to sever links with the rest of society' (pp. 11–12). In support of this, Cairns (1996) described how some reports suggest that governments of countries such as Iran and the Lebanon target young children, especially boys who have experienced the loss of a father, for indoctrination into programmes that glorify violence and/or self-sacrifice.

Although horrific, cases of childhood brutality exist in normal conditions (e.g. the killing of James Bulger in the UK) as well. Indeed, there is some evidence that children exposed to violence are no more violent themselves than those who are not. Lorenc and Branthwaite (1986), for example, showed that Northern Irish children were no more tolerant or accepting of violence than English children not exposed to the troubles. It has already been mentioned, however, that social and economic variables mean that the impact of terrorism on children in Northern Ireland may not be as notable as it would be on children exposed to other conflicts. It is probable, then, that specific interactions between personal factors and environmental factors cause vulnerability to engaging in violent acts, in a similar manner to how these same factors interact to precipitate PTSD or other pathological reactions.

Cairns (1996) discussed the available literature on why some young people engage in terrorism and others do not. Personality, failure to bond and external locus of control are all factors that have been used to try to explain this. Cairns (1996) also points out, however, that some researchers have noted that 'what determines that their aggressive response develops in this way is the social and political climate prevailing in their particular society during a crucial stage in their development' (p. 120), and that the opportunity to join a terrorist group must present itself. As with other behaviours, aggressive or otherwise, social learning may play an integral role in the development of a propensity to participate in terrorist activities. If young people perceive that their peers or older adults are being rewarded in some way for engaging in provocative activities such as rioting or demonstrating aggression towards another group, then they are more likely to engage in these behaviours themselves. The political climate influences not only the likelihood that these peripheral activities will happen, but also the likelihood that the opportunity to engage in more organised activities will present themselves.

The sort of traumatic events that can lead a child or young person to volunteer to participate in terrorism are discussed in more detail in Chapter 2 of this volume. The interaction of environmental and personal factors are again evident, with some predisposed (for whatever reason) young people responding to the trauma in a manner that results in extreme forms of behaviour.

While there is considerable evidence that in many countries children and young people are coerced into joining militant or terrorist groups (Machel, 2001), it is also clear that some children join out of their own free will. Adolescent ideologies, a sense of 'duty' to an identity group and the ease with which an impression can be made on children and young people are all reasons why they may choose to join a particular group. They will also join, however, because of anger and resentment against policies and/or acts of violence that have brought distress to themselves or to the people in their immediate environment. As with children who have been exposed to other forms of violence, such as child abuse, it would appear that exposure to terrorism can become a cyclical pattern whereby the victim becomes the perpetrator. For whatever reason a child or young person originally becomes involved with a militant group, he or she will generally at some point engage in acts of extreme violence him- or herself.

Whether or not it is consistent with descriptions of malignant PTSD, engaging in violent behaviour is not conducive to dealing effectively with the significant events that led to the initial desire to react in a violent manner. Somasundaram's case studies of R and R1, as described earlier, offer insight into the potential long-term risks of involvement of children and young people in terrorist and violent activities. Although it is not clear why these young people joined militant groups in the first place, it is obvious that participation in the horrific activities of the groups served, at least in part, to precipitate the development of antisocial tendencies in both boys. A similar process is found in children in many other environments of conflict and violence. Indeed it is not necessary to limit scrutiny to children exposed to terrorism or political violence. The literature on child abuse clearly demonstrates that those exposed to violence as children show an elevated risk of becoming violent themselves (e.g. Widom, 1989), and it has been suggested that early socialisation experiences, such as exposure to abuse, can significantly affect later social interactions (Cicchetti, 1989). It is very probable that the same sociodevelopmental factors apply in all cases.

Terrorist groups are not always successful in persuading members of their own side to participate, and indeed there are accounts where childhood experiences have served to turn the individual against the group. For example, Silke (2000) gives examples of individuals who took action against paramilitary groups in Northern Ireland. One example he gives is that of Raymond Gilmour who worked as a Royal Ulster Constabulary (RUC) agent and provided sensitive information on the IRA, which he joined effectively as a spy. His reason for doing this dated back to an IRA punishment attack on his brother. His account stated: 'I felt nothing but hatred for the people who'd dared to do that to my big brother...what could a kid like me do against the IRA?...I never did forget, I never will forget and in the end I found a way to take my revenge' (cited in Gilmour, 1998, pp. 38–39).

TREATMENT AND INTERVENTION

Given that it is difficult to determine the impact of terrorism on children because of a dearth of research, it is also difficult to establish the best way to treat that impact. Before therapists can decide on appropriate treatment, they need to be clear about what it is they are treating. Earlier in this chapter a lack of symptoms in children in some situations of political violence was described, and of course it first needs to be established whether the child is showing signs of resilience or whether he or she is suffering undesirable consequences of his or her experience.

Cairns and Wilson (1989) postulated that the resilience that many children in Northern Ireland showed might be due to the coping mechanisms that the children were using to deal with long-term violence. While follow-up work failed to fully support this (Joseph, Cairns and McCollam, 1993), it is clear that this is something that needs to be considered further. If 'resilience' is a coping mechanism, then does it need to be treated? As Naomi Richman (1993) points out, the Western practice of sending children who are living in stressful situations to individual therapy may be neither practicable nor beneficial in a situation of long-term political conflict. Many of the defences and coping strategies—for instance denial—necessary for the child to deal with the stressful environment may be removed in therapy. If the child is to remain in the situation, therefore, professionals need to be very careful of the type of care that is recommended. Richman pointed out, and indeed the evidence seems to support this, that children who continue to live in a conflict situation may show a gradual decrease in distress if they perceive their own situation is adequate. As with other situations where a child has been abused or exposed to violence, the most viable solution would appear to be allowing the child a period of stability in the presence of supportive adults. The context of the situation will also need to be taken into account, as young people will respond with more understanding and acceptance if they perceive the situation as normal or necessary. It has also been suggested that stress levels in situations of ongoing political violence can be influenced by the coping strategies of the parents and of their own perceptions of the situation (e.g. Punamäki, 1989).

In any social situation that a child or young person is exposed to, 'adaptive coping' depends on context (Frydenberg, 1997). Hollin, Browne and Palmer (2002) offer an illustration that explains this:

> A young person may respond to bullying by becoming aggressive in return. If this strategy results in a cessation of bullying then it could be argued that the young person coped effectively with the stressor. In such a case they identified the problem, assessed possible solutions and acted effectively on their assessment. Alternatively, however, it could also be argued that the young person responded in a manner that shows poor emotional management, which is indicative of a more dysfunctional manner of coping. In this particular example, the context leaves room for some ambiguity of interpretation. However, if the same young person responds aggressively to a nonconfrontational social situation, then it is more evident that she or he does not cope adaptively with social stresses (pp. 25–26).

In the context of a situation of chronic terrorism, or indeed in response to a single terrorist attack, a response that in normal circumstances would be indicative of dysfunction may well be the most productive coping strategy that a child or young person can respond with. In the latter case (acute terrorism) the cessation of the event may demonstrate whether behaviour returns to 'normal' or whether the child continues to respond in a way that is clearly not adaptive to other circumstances. In the former case (chronic terrorism) it may be that all that can be done is to try to enhance the coping strategies that are being demonstrated until the situation has changed.

In some situations of chronic terrorism and political violence, however, there are periods of calm and relative peace between periods of unrest. In these situations it may be possible to prepare children and young people for a possible recurrence of violence, either by enhancing and transforming their coping strategies (see Frydenberg, 1997) or by other means. The UN has used the method of stress inoculation before going into combat situations such as Operation Desert Storm. This involves exposing individuals to simulated, perhaps slightly diminished forms of the stress they would encounter, and encouraging them to experiment with and rehearse various coping strategies (Somasundaram, 1998). It is possible that such techniques could be modified to be used with children and young people in areas that are at high risk of recurring political violence.

Once a conflict has ended it is important that a child is given the opportunity to recover and deal with whatever range of experiences the situation has thrown at them. Indeed, the UN Convention on the Rights of the Child guarantees that children should be provided with psychosocial recovery and social reintegration following such experiences (Machel, 2001). Again, because the effects of terrorism on children have not been thoroughly researched it is difficult to determine how best these children should be treated. Herbert (1998) maintains that the two most important components in treating child survivors of a traumatic event include spending time with parents and family (which may involve acquiescing to requests to sleep in their parents' bed at night, etc.) and supportive re-exposure to the traumatic cues. He also recommended the use of critical incident stress debriefing, which involves a group therapy situation where feelings about the event are shared among survivors. Such techniques may be quite readily adaptable to situations where children and young people have been exposed to the trauma of terrorist activities.

CONCLUSION

While it is clear that researchers into terrorism need to spend more time studying the impact of such activities on children and young people, it is possible to draw from a number of sources to attempt to explain some of the findings that have to date been reported. It is evident that children respond in different ways to situations of extreme violence, but also that certain responses are more common than others. It would also appear that these responses are in keeping with more general findings from the developmental literature. Traumatic situations will bring about responses that indicate dysfunction or an attempt to cope (or indeed a combination of these). Individual responses will depend on interactions between personal characteristics and the nature of the environment in which the event takes place. As in other social situations, children are responsive to the adults around them, and adolescents show a heightened responsiveness to society outside their immediate family.

As with other forms of child abuse, exposure to the violence of terrorism can, and evidently very often does, have damaging and long-lasting psychological effects. The damage this causes can be seen to affect the lives of individuals and their immediate families as they try to cope with PTSD and other symptoms of their experiences. Society at large also suffers, along with new victims as the cycle of violence perpetuates from one generation to the next. Although, as with victims of child abuse or bullying, it would be a mistake to think that most victims become perpetrators, this aspect of the impact of today's acts of terror on the young needs to be carefully considered. It would be interesting for researchers in this area to reflect whether the impact of terrorism on children would receive more attention if this impact were perceived to be more at the beginning of the cycle of violence rather than merely as a victim at its culmination.

REFERENCES

Al-Krenawi, A., Slonim-Nevo, V., Maymon, Y. and Al-Krenawi, S. (2001). Psychological responses to blood vengeance among Arab adolescents. *Child Abuse & Neglect*, **25**, 457–72.

American Psychiatric Association (1980). *Diagnostic and Statistical Manual of Mental Disorders*, 3rd edn. Washington, DC: American Psychiatric Association.

American Psychiatric Association (1991). *Diagnostic and Statistical Manual of Mental Disorders*, 4th edn. Washington, DC: American Psychiatric Association.

Bat-Zion, N. and Levy-Shiff, R. (1993). Children in war: stress and coping reactions under threat of scud missile attacks and the effect of proximity. In L. Leavitt and N. Fox (Eds), *The Psychological Effects of War and Violence on Children*. Hillsdale, NJ: Lawrence Erlbaum.

BBC News (2002). Children 'bear brunt' of Mid-East conflict (30 September). As viewed at *http://news.bbc.co.uk/1/hi/world/middle_east/2288380.stm*.

Berridge, D. and Cleaver, H. (1987). *Foster Home Breakdown*. Oxford: Blackwell.

Bowlby, J. (1965). *Child Care and the Growth of Love*, 2nd edn. London: Penguin.

Bowlby, J. (1969). *Attachment and Loss: Vol 1. Attachment*. New York: Basic Books.

Cairns, E. (1987). *Caught in Crossfire: Children and the Northern Ireland Conflict*. New York: Syracuse University Press.

Cairns, E. (1996). *Children and Political Violence*. Oxford: Blackwell.

Cairns, E. and Wilson, R. (1989). Mental health aspects of political violence in Northern Ireland. *International Journal of Mental Health*, **18**, 38–56.

Chauvin, L., Mugaju, J. and Comlavi, P.J. (1998). Tackling new evaluation challenges: Rwanda Trauma Recovery Programme. *UNICEF Newsletter on Planning, Research and Education*, **2**(1).

Chimienti, G., Nasr, J. and Khalifehi, L. (1989). Children's reactions to war-related stress-affective symptoms and behaviour problems. *Social Psychiatry and Psychiatric Epidemiology*, **24**, 282–87.

Cicchetti, D. (1989). How research on child maltreatment has informed the study of child development: perspectives from developmental psychopathology. In D. Cicchetti and V. Carlson (Eds), *Child Maltreatment: Theory and Research on the Causes and Consequences of Child Abuse and Neglect* (pp. 377–431). New York: Cambridge University Press.

Dawes, A., Tredoux, C. and Feinstein, A. (1989). Political violence in South Africa: some effects on children of the violent destruction of their community. *International Journal of Mental Health*, **18**, 16–43.

Dremen, S. (1989). Children as victims of terrorism in Israel—coping and adjustment in the face of trauma. *Israel Journal of Psychiatry and Related Sciences*, **26**, 212–22.

Erikson, E. (1965). *Children and Society*. Harmondsworth: Penguin.

Fraser, M. (1974). *Children in Conflict*. Harmondsworth: Penguin.

Frydenberg, E. (1997). *Adolescent Coping: Theoretical and Research Perspectives.* London: Penguin.

Garbarino, J. and Kostelny, K. (1993). Children's responses to war: what do we know? In L.A. Leavitt and N.A. Fox (Eds), *The Psychological Effects of War and Violence on Children.* Hillsdale, NJ: Lawrence Erlbaum.

Gilmour, R. (1998). *Dead Ground: Infiltrating the IRA.* London: Little Brown.

Gottesman, I.I. (1991). *Schizophrenic Genesis: The Origins of Madness.* New York: Freeman.

Herbert, M. (1998). *Clinical Child Psychology*, 2nd edn. Chichester: Wiley.

Hollin, C., Browne, D. and Palmer, E. (2002). *Delinquency and Young Offenders.* BPS Blackwell: Oxford.

Jaffe, P., Wolf, D.A., Wilson, S. and Zak, L. (1986). Emotional and physical health problems of battered women. *Canadian Journal of Psychiatry*, **31**, 625–29.

Joseph, S., Cairns, E. and McCollam, P. (1993). Political violence, coping and depressive symptomatology in Northern Irish children. *Personality and Individual Differences*, **15**, 471–73.

Lorenc, L. and Branthwaite, A. (1986). Evaluations of political violence by English and Northern Irish school children. *British Journal of Social Psychology*, **25**, 349–52.

Lyons, H.A. (1974). Terrorist bombing and the psychological sequelae. *Journal of the Irish Medical Association*, **67**, 15.

McCarney, W. (1996). Psychological and social impact of The Troubles on young people in Northern Ireland. *Juvenile and Family Court Journal*, 67–75.

McGrath, A. and Wilson, R. (1985). *Factors which influence the prevalence and variation of psychological problems in children in Northern Ireland.* Paper presented at the Annual Conference of the Developmental Section of the BPS, Belfast.

Machel, G. (2001). *The Impact of War on Children.* UBC Press (in association with UNICEF): Vancouver.

McKeon, M. (1973). Civil unrest: Secondary School Survey. *Northern Teacher*, **1**, 39–42.

Massinga, R. and Perry, K. (1994). The Casey Family program: factors on effective management of a long-term foster care organisation. In J. Blacher (Ed.), *When There's No Place Like Home* (pp. 163–80). Baltimore, MD: Paul H. Brookes Publishing Co.

Oltmanns, T.F. and Emery, R.E. (1995). *Abnormal Psychology.* Englewood Cliffs, NJ: Prentice-Hall.

Parson, E.R. (1995). Mass traumatic terror in Oklahoma City and the phases of adaptational coping, Part I. *Journal of Contemporary Psychotherapy*, **25**, 155–84.

Pfefferbaum, B., Nixon, S.J., Krug, R.S., Tivis, R.D., Moore, V.L., Brown, J.M., Pynoos, R.S., Foy, D. and Gurwitch, R.H. (1999). Clinical needs assessment of middle and high school students following the 1995 Oklahoma City bombing. *American Journal of Psychiatry*, **156**, 1069–74.

Punamäki, R.L. (1989). Factors affecting the mental health of Palestinian children exposed to political violence. *International Journal of Mental Health*, **18**, 63–79.

Quinton, D. and Rutter, M. (1985). Family pathology and child psychiatric disorder: a four-year prospective study. In A.R. Nicol (Ed.), *Longitudinal Studies in Child Psychology and Psychiatry.* Chichester: Wiley.

Richman, N. (1993). Children in situations of political violence. *Journal of Child Psychology and Psychiatry*, **34**, 1286–302.

Richman, N., Ratilal, A. and Aly, A. (1989). *The Psychological Effects of War on Mozambican Children.* Maputo: Ministry of Education.

Silke, A. (2000). The impact of paramilitary vigilantism on victims and communities in Northern Ireland. *The International Journal of Human Rights*, **4**, 1–24.

Somasundaram, D. (1998). *Scarred Minds: The Psychological Impact of War on Sri Lankan Tamils*. New Delhi: Sage.

Summerfield, D. (1996). The impact of war and atrocity on civilian populations: basic principles for NGO interventions and a critique of psychological trauma projects. *Relief and Rehabilitation Network, Network Paper 14*. London: Overseas Development Institute.

Widom, C.S. (1989). Does violence beget violence? A critical examination of the literature. *Psychological Bulletin*, **106**, 3–28.

Wilson, J. (1988). *Trauma, Transformation and Healing*. New York: Bruner/Mazel.

PART III

Responding to Terrorism

CHAPTER 11

Retaliating Against Terrorism

Andrew Silke

University of Leicester, UK

INTRODUCTION

It is probably fair to say that Western democracies in general have not rushed to embrace military force as a standard response to terrorism. In Europe, while states have certainly been willing to use force to end hostage and siege situations, such action has usually been seen as a tactic of last resort, with first preference traditionally going to negotiated settlement. Campaigns of assassination against terrorist groups have not been favoured, at least not openly. Unofficially, the story has sometimes been very different. UK governments, for example, certainly appeared to tolerate an undisclosed 'shoot-to-kill' policy in dealing with the IRA in the 1980s. In a number of high-profile cases, IRA members were shot dead by the security forces (usually elite SAS teams) in circumstances where their non-violent arrest seemed readily achievable. These deaths were often highly controversial, for example when three unarmed IRA members were shot dead in Gibraltar in March 1988 or when one civilian was killed by the security forces in 1987 in an SAS ambush that also killed seven IRA members in Loughgall.

Other states have been far more open in their use of lethal force and indeed some nations have made violent retaliation a cornerstone of the national effort to combat and defeat terrorism. Israel certainly stands out as an example of a state that has embraced military force as a solution to terrorism. However, research on the effectiveness of military force as a response to terrorism is thin on the ground. In a familiar story with research on

Terrorists, Victims and Society: Psychological Perspectives on Terrorism and its Consequences.
Edited by Andrew Silke. © 2003 John Wiley & Sons, Ltd.

terrorism, there has been little work on this question, leaving the door open for personal opinion and biases, rather than hard facts, to influence policy.

THE QUESTION OF DETERRENCE

It is a common assumption, both in security and public spheres, that military retaliations in response to terrorism can be an effective way to deter future acts of terrorist violence. Most experts usually add two caveats to this assumption: first, that the response should be swift and take place soon after the terrorist event that provoked it; and second, that the attack should be properly focused, i.e. targets selected on the basis of accurate intelligence. However, a number of studies carried out in the early 1990s raise some serious concerns about the effectiveness of retaliation in any circumstance, though this research has been dangerously overlooked in the current rush to arms.

In 1990, as the Gulf War loomed, research programmes in the US were looking to identify the most effective ways to combat terrorism. One of the most significant efforts was that led by Walter Enders and Todd Sandler, two economists then based at the University of Iowa. They looked closely at the major tactics governments had used to respond to terrorism over the preceding 20 years. One consistent finding was that major military retaliations had never led to a reduction in terrorism. On the contrary, terrorist attacks either stubbornly remained at their original levels, or worse, increased dramatically in the months after the retaliation, before slowly returning to their original levels many months or years later.

Enders, Sandler and Cauley (1990), for example, examined the impact of a number of counter-terrorism measures on terrorism levels. The measures they examined included the implementation of metal detectors at airports, international agreements and the retaliatory bombing of Libya in 1986. The researchers based their analysis on the International Terrorism: Attributes of Terrorist Events (ITERATE) database, available through the Inter-University Consortium for Political and Social Research, at the University of Michigan, and widely regarded as the most comprehensive databank of terrorist events for academic research. Enders, Sandler and Cauley (1990) found that the metal detectors had a significant and long-lasting effect, and while technology was later developed to circumvent metal detectors, the results indicated that up to January 1989 terrorists had not been able to successfully utilise this technology.

While this was an encouraging finding, the remaining results were disheartening. First, Enders, Sandler and Cauley (1990) found that the success of metal detectors in airports led to a significant displacement into other terrorist activities, such as kidnapping. Further, of the five major international agreements tested, only one had a significant impact (and that was for the international introduction of metal detectors). Finally, it was found that the US bombing of Libya, Operation El Dorado Canyon, was not a significant deterrent to terrorism, and had actually led to a significant short-term increase in terrorism directed against the US and its close ally, the UK. Eventually the level of terrorist attacks against these two countries returned to their previous levels, and it is interesting to note that this statistical finding is in agreement with much theoretical speculation at the time that the bombing would not benefit the US (e.g. Post, 1987).

Operation El Dorado Canyon is an event worth closer examination. On 5 April 1986 a bomb was detonated at La Belle disco club in West Berlin, a popular venue with off-duty US soldiers. The explosion killed three people and wounded more than 200 others. Two of the dead and some 80 of the injured were US servicemen. Intercepted embassy messages indicated that the Libyan Government had been involved in the attack. In retaliation, the Reagan administration authorised a direct military strike on Libya, codenamed Operation El Dorado Canyon.

Ten days later, in the early morning of 15 April, more than 40 US warplanes entered Libyan airspace. Flying just over 200 feet above the ground and at speeds of around 540 miles per hour, the planes closed in on targets in Tripoli and the important port city of Benghazi. The Americans devoted special attention to attacking Libyan leader Gaddafi's personal compound at the Sidi Balal naval base, dropping 2000-pound laser-guided bombs on buildings Gaddafi was believed to use. After the raid, the Libyans claimed that 37 people had been killed and nearly 100 wounded. Among the dead was Gaddafi's adopted daughter, and two of his sons were among those seriously injured. Gaddafi himself escaped the attack unharmed.

The military strike was extremely popular in the US. Most Americans believed that the strike sent a powerful warning to states and groups who were contemplating terrorist attacks against US targets. However, the international community reacted badly to the bombings and it was condemned outright by Arab nations. In Europe, only the UK provided support for the US action. The British Government allowed the Americans to use airfields based in England to launch the attack. In contrast, other European countries, such as France and Spain, refused even to allow the US planes to fly through their airspace.

In the eyes of many experts and professionals, the raid came to be seen as having had a valuable deterrent effect on terrorist activity. For example, a research study conducted at Harvard University by Mark Kosnik, a US Navy commander, concluded that the attack 'left Qaddafi weak, vulnerable, isolated and less able to engage in terrorism ... it put Qaddafi's terrorist apparatus on the defensive, rendering it less able to focus on new terrorist activities . . . following the raid Qaddafi reduced his terrorist activity . . . [and the attack] did not trigger a new cycle of violence against America' (Kosnick, 2000). Similar views are common in the literature on terrorism, and seen in such terms the retaliation seems an unequivocal success. But is this an accurate assessment? Even before the economists, many experts had serious doubts about the claims of success surrounding El Dorado Canyon. Bruce Hoffman, the highly respected RAND expert on terrorism, commented that contrary to many claims Libyan involvement in terrorism detectably increased in the immediate years after the raid. The RAND-St Andrews database on International Terrorism showed that Libya sponsored at least 15 acts of terrorism in 1987, and a further eight in 1988, a significant increase on what they had done in the two years prior to the raid (Hoffman, 1998).

The economists working in Iowa agreed with Hoffman, and judged that the accepted view of El Dorado Canyon being a success was badly misplaced. Drawing information from the massive ITERATE database, they discovered that the retaliatory strike led to a significant short-term increase in terrorism directed against the US and the UK. In the three months after the raid, terrorist bombings and assassinations against US and UK targets nearly doubled. Significant disruption was also caused when hoax attacks increased by over 600 per cent. Libya, far from being cowed into submission, actually increased its commitment to terrorism and began to sponsor even more acts of terrorism than before. These new efforts included an attempt to launch a bomb attack in New York in 1988 (an attempt foiled only when the terrorist delivering the bombs was unlucky enough to be pulled over for a traffic offence in New Jersey). More tragically, the new terror campaign also included the bombing of Pan Am flight 103 in December 1988 over Lockerbie in Scotland, which left 270 dead.

The UK was to pay further for its support of the US. In the months after the raid, Libya secretly shipped an estimated 130 tonnes of weapons and munitions to the Provisional IRA (Bowyer-Bell, 2000). This haul included at least 5 tonnes of Semtex-H explosive (the bomb which brought down Pan Am 103 is believed to have contained just 8 ounces of Semtex-H). Such a massive injection of weaponry virtually guaranteed that the IRA would have the means to continue its terrorist campaign for decades to come if they so wished.

Enders and Sandler (1993) conducted further work looking at counterterrorism measures. Using more detailed data sets and testing a larger number of hypotheses the later findings supported the earlier work, but because of greater statistical sophistication previously undetected significant trends were also unearthed. Once again, the researchers looked at the effectiveness of various counter-terrorism measures, but this time examined the effect not on transnational terrorism in general but on specific terrorist tactics such as skyjackings, assassinations and threats. They also looked at both the short- and then long-term impact of the measures.

The results showed again that the Libyan raid (contrary to US expectations) had no long-term deterrent effect on terrorism and in the short term led to a substantial increase in terrorist incidents, though much of this increase took the form of empty threats and hoaxes rather than genuine terrorist attacks. Fortification of US embassies in 1976 reduced attacks against these buildings but led to an increase in assassinations. Worryingly for policy-makers, research showed that increased funding for embassy security in 1986 had no deterrent effect on terrorism—despite the fact that over $2.4 billion was spent on these improvements. However, other measures were more successful. In agreement with the previous work, metal detectors were found to have significantly decreased skyjackings and threats but again this was linked to increased assassinations and other kinds of hostage incidents not protected by the detectors. Overall, then, these studies were finding it difficult to identify any counter-terrorism measures that did not have unexpected downsides to their use.

'WRATH OF GOD' AND BEYOND

The massacre of 11 Israeli athletes at the 1972 Munich Olympics was one of the most high-profile terrorist incidents of the twentieth century. Israeli governments have traditionally been more open to using direct military force in response to terrorism, and their response to the massacre was predictably aggressive. Three days after the final shoot-out in Munich, Israel launched major military strikes against Lebanon and Syria. The Israeli airforce bombed ground targets in both countries and also engaged in dog-fights with Syrian jets. On the ground, Israeli troops pushed into Lebanon to confront Palestinian terrorists near the border. It was the largest military action taken by Israel since the end of the 1967 Arab–Israeli war, but it was not the only action authorised by the government in reprisal for Munich.

Behind the scenes, the government quietly authorised Operation Wrath of God. This was a deliberate and systematic campaign of assassination targeting the terrorist group Black September and all the individuals believed to be involved in the planning and carrying out of the Munich attack. Wrath of God was not about capturing or imprisoning those responsible. It was purely and simply about killing those the Israelis could find and terrorising those they could not (Hunter, 2001). In order to accomplish this task, a specialist assassination unit, known as the *kidon*, was activated, comprising of just under 40 highly trained members.

Death warrants were issued for 35 people believed to have been involved or connected with the Munich attack, and the *kidon* members were allowed enormous latitude in their operations. Less than five weeks after Munich, the first of the targets, Wael Zaitter, a cousin of Yasser Arafat and a principal organiser of Palestine Liberation Organization (PLO) terrorism in Europe, was gunned down at his apartment near Rome. Over the following months, the assassination squads killed several more people on the list, and the following year in a major operation on 10 April 1973, a large commando raid was launched against Palestinians based in Beirut. Over 100 people were killed in the attack, including a number on the Wrath of God death list.

The attacks continued as the Israelis hunted down those on the list. In July 1973, however, the campaign led to a high-profile blunder: the murder of Ahmed Bouchiki, an innocent Moroccan-born waiter living in Lillehammer, Norway. The assassination squad who killed Bouchiki mistakenly believed he was Ali Hassan Salameh, a senior PLO official and leader of Force 17, Yasser Arafat's personal bodyguards. Six members of the Israeli team were captured by Norwegian police before they could flee the country, and five were convicted for their involvement in the murder of Bouchiki.[1] However, the two shooters managed to escape safely to Israel.

Wrath of God continued until 1979, when assassins finally managed to kill the elusive Ali Hassan Salameh with a car bomb in Beirut. One hundred thousand people came to his funeral while the widow of one of the Munich athletes publicly thanked the assassins for what they had done (Taylor, 1993).

After Wrath of God, the Israelis continued to favour the use of assassination as a standard tactic in their fight against terrorism. Advocates argued that the policy was highly effective in disrupting and crippling terrorist groups. Black September, they said, had been eviscerated by 1979 and was never again a force to be reckoned with. To a degree this is true. As Wrath of God unfolded, attacks claimed by Black September did indeed plummet. But this is also misleading as well. Black September was never a stand-alone terrorist group. On the contrary it was better seen as a small branch of Fatah, the large military arm of the PLO. Between 1972 and 1979, while Wrath of God was apparently dealing body blows to Palestinian terrorism, Fatah actually increased in size and strength, and the number of attacks it carried out against Israeli targets also increased. Far from improving, the situation steadily became worse over time. Indeed, so significant did the terrorist threat become that Israel felt compelled to invade Lebanon twice in the late 1970s and early 1980s in an

---

[1] The five received very light prison sentences given the circumstances, and all were released from custody within 22 months.

effort to destroy the PLO and its bases. This was hardly, then, a movement cowed into submission by the lethal determination of Wrath of God.

Yet there was widespread belief within the Israeli security forces that the assassinations were not simply justifiable but were (and still are) a necessity. Interviewed by a British journalist in the 1990s, the originator of Wrath of God, General Aharon Yariv, defended the assassination campaign:

> I approach these problems not from a moral point of view, but, hard as it may sound, from a cost-benefit point of view. I'm not sure that assassinating a leader here or there will bring us anywhere nearer to peace. But if it is a clear case that by removing this personality you can deal a mortal blow to your enemy that will bring him to the table, that's something else. But that doesn't happen very often. If I'm very hard-headed, I can say, what is the political benefit in killing this person? Will it bring us nearer to peace? Will it bring us nearer to an understanding with the Palestinians or not? In most cases I don't think it will. But in the case of Black September we had no other choice and it worked. Is it morally acceptable? One can debate that question. Is it politically vital? It was (Taylor, 1993, p. 27).

But the claim that it worked is, as has already been indicated, extremely uncertain at best. The murder of an innocent man in Norway was a highly damaging public relations disaster for the Israeli effort and undermined much of the international sympathy focused on the country in the aftermath of Munich. Further, as time passed, it became increasingly clear that many of those who had been selected for assassination had nothing at all to do with the Munich attack. For example, Dr Mahmoud Hamshari was fatally injured at his home in Paris by *kidon* assassins when he answered his phone in December 1972. Yet there was no credible evidence to link him to Black September and none at all to link him with the events at Munich. The same applied to other victims, and even Ali Hassan Salameh, the target of so many assassination attempts, is not thought to have had any involvement in the planning or commissioning of Munich. Senior Israelis later admitted that under the rubric of retaliating for Munich they used Wrath of God as an opportunity to eliminate leading Palestinians regardless of whether they were involved in the Olympics atrocity (Taylor, 1993).

General Yariv's highlighting of the 'cost-benefit point of view' is significant too. Such a statement creates the impression that there were clear and objective benefits to the Israeli policy. In this case, he argues that the Palestinians pulled back from terrorism as a result of the assassinations. He may genuinely believe this—certainly others do—but the records of attacks carried out by Palestinian groups do not show such a decline. Indeed, if Wrath of God was so successful, why then did Israel have to also resort to two full-scale invasions of Lebanon (first in 1978 and then again in 1982) in order to deal with Palestinian terrorism?

Economists who take the 'cost-benefit analysis' approach very seriously indeed have not found evidence to support the idea that assassinations and military force are effective in these terms. Brophy-Baermann and Conybeare (1994) explored whether Israel's retaliatory policies had any discernible effect on terrorism. As already described, previous work had shown that the US retaliatory bombing of Libya had only a brief short-term effect on terrorism directed against US targets, with attacks increasing significantly on previous levels before quickly returning to their original levels. Rational expectations theory suggested that the punishment of terrorism will only cause terrorist attacks to deviate from the natural rate when the reprisals are unexpected. Brophy-Baermann and Conybeare (1994) tested this idea by examining six major Israeli retaliations against terrorism.

The first of these retaliations was prompted by a bloody terrorist attack on 11 March 1978. A team of Palestinian terrorists landed on the Israeli coast 20 miles south of Haifa. They promptly killed a US tourist, shot dead the occupants of a taxi, took the passengers of a bus hostage and then drove the bus to Tel Aviv, firing randomly at passing traffic as they went. The event ended in a violent shoot-out with the authorities. By the time it was all finished, 25 civilians were dead, as were 9 of the 11 terrorists, and over 70 people had been left injured. In response, Israel launched a massive invasion of Southern Lebanon. Over 20 000 troops poured over the border backed up by tanks and jets. In the resulting fighting the Israelis killed some 2000 people and left a further 250 000 homeless. But did all this military force have an effect on terrorism?

Brophy-Baermann and Conybeare (1994) found that the answer was a dispiriting no. Despite the ferocity of the strike-back and the massive casualties inflicted, terrorist attacks against Israel, as recorded in the ITERATE database, did not decrease in the aftermath. In the face of massive international condemnation the Israelis slowly pulled their troops back across the border. However, irked by continuing terrorist attacks, Israel invaded again a few years later in June 1982. This time they were determined to teach an even harsher lesson. In Operation Peace in Galilee, the Israelis forced their way deep into Lebanon and after four days of fighting they reached Beirut, which was put under siege. The bombardment of the city lasted for over four weeks and casualties were horrendous. More than 18 000 people—most of them civilians—were killed and at least 30 000 were injured. Yasser Arafat and the PLO, the main targets of the Israelis, fled Beirut into exile. In the aftermath, around 1000 Palestinian refugees were massacred in the city at the hands of paramilitaries allied to the Israeli army. The level of force in this second retaliation probably at least matches that so far displayed in the US campaign in Afghanistan. Yet what did all this bloodshed achieve? Did terrorist attacks against Israel decline thereafter? Despite the violence, Brophy-Baermann and Conybeare found that Peace in Galilee failed to stop or reduce terrorism: attacks continued unabated and undiminished.

Of the six major Israeli retaliations against terrorism tested, Brophy-Baermann and Conybeare (1994) found that only the first had a significant effect. Just like the Libyan attack, the first retaliation led to a dramatic short-term *increase* in terrorist attacks against Israel. This increase soon dissipated and within nine months the level of terrorist attacks had returned to pre-retaliation levels. Further, the subsequent retaliations had no significant effect whatsoever. In line with the theory, the first attack 'raised the expected level of retaliation and reduced the impact of any future retaliation' (Brophy-Baermann and Conybeare, 1994, p. 209). In short, the terrorists expected further retaliations and planned for them accordingly. They were built in to their planning and how they operated, and had no discernible long-term effect.

Even the argument that the attacks disrupted terrorist groups has been criticised. A common defence of military strikes is that regardless of the wider, long-term impact, in the short term they will certainly disrupt the terrorist network targeted and undermine the ability of that group to carry out future attacks. This line of argument follows the cold logic that if members of the terrorist organisation are killed, then the group is deprived of their effort, experience, skills and abilities. The more senior and skilled the person killed is, the more pronounced the loss. For this reason, some states make enormous effort to kill terrorist leaders and also to kill individuals who are especially skilled, such as explosive experts and bomb designers. A good example of this was Israel's assassination of Hamas' leading explosives expert, Yehiya Ayyash, in January 1996. Israeli intelligence placed a small explosive device in his mobile phone which detonated when he answered and confirmed his name. Such precision assassinations, though, contrast with far blunter strikes as that in July 2002, when Israel used an F-16 jet to drop a one-tonne bomb on the apartment block where Sheikh Salah Shahada, a founding member of Hamas, was staying. The massive bomb devastated the building, destroyed Shahada's apartment and also demolished several adjacent residences. Shahada was killed in the explosion, as were 14 other people including 9 children, and more than 140 people were injured; 300 000 Palestinians turned out for the funerals of the dead.

Indeed, the current Israeli campaign of 'targeted killing' has resulted in a disturbingly high number of innocent fatalities (Amnesty International, 2001). Since the latest round of slayings began in November 2000 it is thought that over 70 Palestinian militants and activists have been deliberately assassinated by the Israeli security services.[2] However, this

---

[2]This should be seen as a conservative estimate. Some sources place the figure as being much higher.

campaign of elimination has also resulted in the deaths of at least 40 innocent bystanders, including no fewer than 21 children.

Yet advocates of these tactics are often blind to such collateral damage and its wider impact. The fact that the current campaign results in the death of at least one bystander for every two 'militants' is generally overlooked in assessments of the policy. For advocates, the loss of assassinated members deals a steady stream of serious blows to the terrorist groups. The death of an experienced bomb-maker, for example, can disrupt planned attacks that must be postponed or abandoned until alternative sources of weaponry can be acquired. The reliability and quality of these alternative suppliers may be uncertain, however, resulting in less effective and more risky operations for the terrorists. The loss of senior leaders also necessitates internal reorganisation and again a period of adjustment for the group. The destruction of bases and training camps affects the groups in a similar manner. Such facilities must be repaired or replaced and this takes time, effort and money.

Todd Sandler remarked that 'the one thing economists know is that if you degrade someone's assets, you degrade and undermine what that someone can do' (Silke, 2002). Sandler was referring to the ongoing US effort to destroy al-Qaeda's finances, resources and support structures. In his view, the US onslaught was translating into a tangible and unavoidable weakening of al-Qaeda's overall ability to engage in terrorism. But there are downsides too. Like many, Sandler is convinced there will be a significant terrorist retaliation in response. 'That is an absolute', he noted, adding that 'long-term success against terrorism depends on long-term international co-operation'. With cracks and strains already clear in the international alliance composing the so-called 'War on Terrorism', the long-term ability of the US effort to deliver this seems uncertain.

Commenting at the same time, Brophy-Baermann was more pessimistic about the outlook of the current US campaign. Unlike Sandler, he has focused his study on the large-scale military strikes adopted by Israel, and is not as convinced that the current US effort will be significantly different. The evidence coming from the ITERATE monitoring of terrorist attacks does not support the idea that bigger is better when it comes to using military force to strike back. Brophy-Baermann concedes that the US campaign will almost certainly achieve most of its narrow military goals (e.g. the destruction of training bases in Afghanistan). But as for the long-term impact on global terrorism: 'I don't see it changing a whole lot' (Silke, 2002).

In the end, though many have continued to portray the various retaliations as successes, there is now clear evidence that they fail to deter terrorism. Worse, the retaliations often provoke a backlash of violence that can include acts of terror more destructive and more costly than those that originally goaded the governments into action.

A QUESTION OF POPULARITY

Though rarely used by most Western democracies, military retaliations have generally been widely approved of in home opinion when they have been employed. In polls and surveys carried out in the aftermath of terrorist attacks, a clear majority consistently voice approval of their government's use of military force against terrorism. In the US, for example, although the government has only rarely resorted to such methods in recent decades, each occasion has been met with warm and overwhelming domestic approval. Though condemned internationally, the US strike against Libya in 1986 was approved by 77 per cent of US citizens polled. The two strikes authorised by the Clinton administration, first against Iraq in 1993 and then against alleged al-Qaeda interests in 1998, had approval ratings of 66 and 77 per cent respectively, even though the latter occurred at a time when the president himself was embroiled in a humiliating personal scandal (Kosnick, 2000). After the terrorist attacks on September 11, the use of US military force in Afghanistan received massive domestic support, with 87 per cent of the US population expressing approval. This high level of support remained solid over the following months of fighting as the Taliban collapsed and US troops scoured the countryside for al-Qaeda remnants.

The levels of public support for these actions, from Libya to Afghanistan, have always been considerably higher than that seen for other harsh measures democracies utilise in the interests of security and law enforcement. For example, support for the use of capital punishment in the US has normally fluctuated between 59 and 75 per cent. These are comfortable majorities, but the figures are less than those seen for the various retaliations. It is interesting that there is less public support for the killing of offenders whose culpability has been established by a rigorous, overt and lengthy judicial process, compared to the swift elimination of alleged terrorist adversaries in a process that enjoys no such safeguards.

In Israel, too, support for retaliatory measures in response to terrorism has traditionally been high. Friedland and Merari (1985) found that 92 per cent of Israelis surveyed supported the assassination of terrorist leaders, 75 per cent supported the bombing of terrorist bases (even if it jeopardised civilian life), and 79 per cent supported the demolition of houses that harboured terrorists. Friedland and Merari found that males tended to support these measures more strongly than females. Also, religious respondents expressed more support for them compared to secular respondents. It is significant that these last two findings match the work from Cota-McKinley, Woody and Bell (2001) (discussed in Chapter 2) which noted that these were exactly the same groups in society most likely to show approval of vengeful attitudes.

The surveys and polls indicate again just how common vengeful attitudes are, and one does not have to be a terrorist (or support a terrorist group) to believe that the use of violence is appropriate and justified even when it incurs the loss of innocent life and bypasses non-violent means of responding to the problem. Ultimately, for any government that wishes to make a widely popular response to terrorist violence (at least among its own domestic population), aggressive military force is by far the most obvious choice.

Yet despite this, the reality is that liberal democracies in general have tended to avoid overt military retaliations. Countries that have embraced the approach more fully have tended to be states whose status sits uncomfortably with the concept of a liberal democracy. Arguably, the two most ardent users in recent decades were the already much discussed Israelis followed then by apartheid South Africa. The US, though siding with these two on many international counter-terrorism issues in the 1970s and 1980s, has been far more restrained. Between 1983 and 1998, there were some 2400 terrorism incidents directed against US citizens and interests throughout the world. More than 600 US citizens were killed in these attacks and another 1900 were injured (a casualty list that does not include the many non-US citizens killed and injured). Yet in response to these 2400 acts of terrorism the US government decided to take overt military reaction in just three cases.

The first of these three terrorist incidents was the already discussed bombing of a West German discotheque in April 1986 which led to a retaliatory strike against Libya a few weeks later. The second was the attempt by Iraqi agents to assassinate former President George Bush using a car bomb when he visited Kuwait in April 1993. The third incident was the near-simultaneous destruction of the US embassies in Kenya and Tanzania by al-Qaeda terrorists in August 1998. These attacks killed 224 people, including 12 Americans, and more than 4000 were injured.

It is revealing to ask why the US responded violently to just these three incidents? After all, during that period the country and its citizens had endured thousands of terrorist attacks, but did not use overt military force in response. What was different about these three? Malvesti (2001) argued that while governments spoke about deterring and preventing terrorism in justifying the use of retaliatory military force, the reality was that there were other factors that actually predicted when the US at least would resort to such measures. Malvesti identified six factors common to the three terrorist attacks but which were not seen in the others. She argued that it was this combination of factors that was important in leading to the use of military force. The factors she identified were:

1 Relatively immediate positive perpetrator identification—the US authorities were quickly able to identify who they thought was responsible for the attack.

2 Perpetrator repetition—this incident was not the first time the perpetrators had attacked US interests.

3 Direct targeting of a US citizen working in an official US government-related capacity—Malvesti found that attacks against government officials, military servicemen, etc., seemed to illicit a retaliatory response whereas attacks against civilians only did not.

4 The fait accompli nature of the incident—it was completed by the time the response was being contemplated. So, for example, retaliation was not used in response to sieges or kidnappings.

5 Flagrant anti-US perpetrator behaviour—the perpetrator had a history of defying and denigrating US interests in a high-profile and open manner.

6 The political and military vulnerability of the perpetrator.

The sixth factor is a particularly important one. When terrorist groups were not vulnerable in these terms, the US did not move against them. Most of these factors probably also play a major role in explaining the decisions of other states to strike back. For example, these factors appear to be present for most Israeli strikes. The anti-Israeli terrorist groups, whether in the Palestinian territories, Lebanon or further afield, are certainly militarily vulnerable to Israel's overwhelming conventional forces. This was proved in the invasions in the 1970s and 1980s and again more recently with the relative ease with which Israeli troops have been able to take control of towns and camps in the Palestinian Authority even when faced with determined opponents such as at Jenin in April 2002.

The political vulnerability of the groups is also well established. While most of the Islamic and Arab world is sympathetic to the Palestinian plight—and hostile towards Israeli military retaliations—the reality is that such states exert little political influence over Israel. The only foreign state with real political clout in Israel is the US. Israel has received more financial aid from the US than America has given to any other country in the last 40 years. It has also enjoyed a favoured (and unique) status for receipt of the latest US military hardware. With this support and aid, Israel has been able to survive and fight off threats from a barrage of hostile neighbours and internal dissidents. US governments have traditionally been very tolerant or else simply ambivalent about hard-line Israeli measures in combating terrorism. So long as this remains consistently the case, the terrorist groups themselves will remain politically vulnerable and thus one can expect Israel to feel relatively unrestrained in considering military responses to terrorism.

So while government spokespeople will make various defences of retaliatory responses to terrorism, Malvesti's research highlights that other undisclosed factors play an important role in the decision to use these measures. We have already seen, though, that retaliation does not seem to prevent or deter future acts of terrorism.

SALT IN THE WOUND

Why do military retaliations struggle to have more of an obvious detrimental impact on terrorism? Though many writers, analysts and security practitioners argue that they do work, the reality as testified by the actual records of terrorist attacks and activity is that retaliations do not have this effect. Why is this the case? The answer lies in understanding why people become terrorists and support terrorist groups to begin with. Labels like extremism, fundamentalism and fanaticism all work to help dismiss terrorism as the aberrant behaviour of an isolated few. However, Chapters 1 and 2 in this volume both clearly attacked how misguided such thinking is, and Chapter 2 instead focused attention on the importance of understanding the psychological need for vengeance.

The true irony of retaliation and military force as a tool of counter-terrorism is that it is a child of, and a father to, the cycle of vengeance and the common human desire for revenge and retribution. Social psychology has long appreciated that groups in conflict become extremely polarised in their views of each other. There is a pervasive tendency to show increased appreciation of the traits and characteristics of the in-group (the group to which you as an individual identify with) and to denigrate the members of the out-group. Such denigration includes a tendency to dehumanise members of the out-group. Their members are described as 'animals' or 'monsters' rather than as people, and their psychology is regarded in suitably similar terms.

One unfortunate result of this common phenomenon is that as well as making it easier to tolerate and support the killing, suffering and harsh treatment of the out-group, it also lulls members of the in-group into thinking that the psychological response of out-group members to events will be qualitatively different to their own. For example, if the out-group kills our members we will not surrender but will continue to struggle on and will persevere to the end. However, if we kill members of the out-group, that will teach them that they cannot win against us and that they must surrender and give in to our will.

Colin Powell, the current US Secretary of State, highlighted in his autobiography the dangers of such thinking. He made the point while discussing his reaction to the suicide attack against the Marine Barracks in Beirut in 1983 that killed 241 marines. In the weeks prior to the attack, US ships off the coast of Lebanon had fired hundreds of shells into the hills around Beirut. This massive bombardment was supposed to support US allies in the area and deter attacks against US positions. Yet as Powell (1996) commented:

> What we tend to overlook in such situations is that other people will re-act much as we would. When the shells started falling on the Shiites, they assumed the American 'referee' had taken sides against them. And since they could not reach the battleship, they found a more vulnerable target, the exposed Marines at the airport (p. 281).

Powell's point is an important one. Inevitably, both the out-group and the in-group are composed of people, and how they react to events will not escape this simple fact. As seen in Chapter 2, the human desire for justice and for vengeance is extremely common. Indeed, it is arguably a universal trait of the human condition regardless of language, culture or racial background. Thus when Jews kill Arabs, and Arabs kill Jews, both sides can be expected to be equally vulnerable to issues pertaining to the psychology of vengeance and retribution.

In-group and out-group stereotyping, however, can leave both sides de-pressingly blind to this reality. As Cota-McKinley, Woody and Bell (2001) emphasised, revenge revolves around the idea of injustice and more par-ticularly redressing injustice. However, appreciating this reality involves accepting that your in-group has behaved in an unjust manner. But in a conflict situation stereotyping does not easily allow for accepting ig-noble behaviour of the in-group. 'We are good, they are bad.' 'God is on our side.' 'Everything we do is justified, everything they do is provocative, inhumane and cruel.' 'We are innocent, they are guilty.' Or at least, 'we are more innocent than they are'.

Consider again the comments of General Aharon Yariv justifying Opera-tion Wrath of God. For him the Israelis were forced to kill the Palestinians in response to Munich. The slaughter of the athletes provoked the at-tack. If the Palestinians had not committed these murders the Israelis would not have launched the operation. Similar 'logic' defends current Israeli retaliatory measures. In 2001, Dalia Rabin-Pelossof, deputy de-fence minister of the Israeli Government, said of such measures that: 'It is a policy of self-defence. When we know of a terrorist who is a ticking bomb, it is incumbent on us to prevent it. And that is what we do' (Gilbert, 2002, p. 154). Of course such justifications, very understandable within the framework of the psychology of vengeance, are also a product of in-group short-sightedness. There is a failure to recognise that the out-group will also be afflicted with stereotypical views and will be equally vulnerable to the psychology of vengeance and retribution.

The killing of Palestinian leaders which began in Wrath of God did not lead to an improvement for the Israelis. Indeed, violence in the Middle East increased dramatically as the 1970s progressed, and as more time passed Israel eventually came under overwhelming international pressure to make profound concessions to their Palestinian terrorist foes.

Ultimately, military retribution in response to terrorism fails so often in its stated aims because it so badly misunderstands and ignores the basic psychology of the enemy and of observers. Terrorist groups can endure military strikes and 'targeted assassinations' not because the people and resources lost were not important, but because the violence works to increase the motivation of more members than it decreases, and works too to attract more support and sympathy to the group than it frightens away. During the 1980s, the apartheid regime in South Africa sanctioned an organised campaign of assassination of black activists and their prominent supporters, which resulted in scores of people being killed. The assassination campaign was intended to give the government better control over the process of change. However, as O'Brien (2001) argues, the policy in all likelihood hastened the collapse of the system as wider support for the African National Congress (ANC) and other opposition groups burgeoned in the face of the perceived injustice of the policy. When the US bombed Libya, the Libyans increased their involvement and support of terrorism rather than pulling away from it. When Israel kills Hamas members and imposes other sanctions on Palestinian communities it increases the sense of perceived injustice—particularly considering the high loss of innocent life—driving more recruits into extremist groups and facilitating increased sympathy and support for these groups not only within the West Bank and Gaza, but further afield among the nations of the world. As a result, Israel may win skirmish after skirmish in these terms but still find itself unable to establish lasting peace and stability. For similar reasons, the US, aggressively chasing down al-Qaeda and its affiliates throughout the world, may find that a lasting resolution to the chase eludes it, regardless of how much energy and military force it invests in the campaign.

CONCLUSION

Military retaliations in response to terrorism can be both justifiable and popular, and they can also successfully fulfil a number of important short-term objectives. However, if past experience is anything to go by, defeating or diminishing the overall threat of terrorism is not something that either small- or large-scale retaliations have yet been able to achieve. It is a serious concern, though, that there remains such a widespread commitment to believing otherwise.

Terrorist conflict is not the same as conventional military conflict. The destruction of an enemy's personnel and resources is not a guarantee of victory. Human psychology, however, is inclined to support and tolerate such hard-line approaches even if the policies only exacerbate and prolong the conflict (an especially likely outcome given the peculiarities of terrorist campaigns). This realisation is not a carefully guarded secret. Even within the Israeli parliament, the Knesset, there are voices who have long criticised the policy of retaliation and pre-emptive assassinations. Speaking in 2001, Naomi Chazon, the deputy speaker of the Knesset, said simply that such an approach 'is an ineffective policy. It breeds more hatred and more terrorism instead of eliminating or even reducing it' (Gilbert, 2002, p. 154). Too few, it seems, are willing to heed such a message.

REFERENCES

Amnesty International (2001). *Broken Lives: A Year of Intifada*. Rugby: Amnesty International.

Bowyer Bell, J. (2000). *The IRA 1968–2000: Analysis of a Secret Army*. London: Frank Cass.

Brophy-Baermann, B. and Conybeare, J.A.C. (1994). Retaliating against terrorism: rational expectations and the optimality of rules versus discretion. *American Journal of Political Science*, **38**(1), 196–210.

Cota-McKinley, A., Woody, W. and Bell, P. (2001). Vengeance: effects of gender, age and religious background. *Aggressive Behavior*, **27**, 343–50.

Enders, W. and Sandler, T. (1993). The effectiveness of antiterrorism policies: a vector-autoregression-intervention analysis. *American Political Science Review*, **87**(4), 829–44.

Enders, W., Sandler, T. and Cauley, J. (1990). UN conventions, technology and retaliation in the fight against terrorism: an econometric evaluation. *Terrorism and Political Violence*, **2**(1), 83–105.

Friedland, N. and Merari, A. (1985). The psychological impact of terrorism: a double-edged sword. *Political Psychology*, **6**(4), 591–604.

Gilbert, M. (2002). *The Routledge Atlas of the Arab–Israeli Conflict*, 7th edn. London: Routledge.

Hoffman, B. (1998). *Inside Terrorism*. London: Victor Gollancz.

Hunter, T. (2001). Wrath of God: the Israeli response to the 1972 Munich Olympic massacre. *Journal of Counterterrorism and Security International*, **7**(4), 16–19.

Kosnick, M. (2000). The military response to terrorism. *Naval War College Review*, **53**(2), 13–39.

Malvesti, M. (2001). Explaining the United States' decision to strike back at terrorists. *Terrorism and Political Violence*, **13**(2), 85–106.

O'Brien, K. (2001). The use of assassination as a tool of state policy: South Africa's counter-revolutionary strategy 1979–92 (Part 2). *Terrorism and Political Violence*, **13**(2), 107–42.

Post, J. (1987). Rewarding fire with fire: effects of retaliation on group dynamics. *Terrorism*, **10**(1), 23–36.

Powell, C. (with Persico, J.) (1996). *My American Journey*. New York: Ballantine.

Silke, A. (2002). Striking back at terrorism: lessons from history. *Journal of Counterterrorism and Security International*, **8**(1), 12–14.

Taylor, P. (1993). *States of Terror*. London: BBC Books.

CHAPTER 12

Terrorism and Imprisonment in Northern Ireland: A Psychological Perspective

JACQUELINE BATES-GASTON

The Northern Ireland Prison Service

INTRODUCTION

When most people think of imprisonment and terrorism in Northern Ireland they think of Long Kesh or the Maze. In fact, in the 30 years of the present 'troubles' other prisons like Magilligan, Belfast and Armagh, which held females, have also played a significant part in containing the greatest numbers of the most difficult and dangerous terrorists in the world. In his report after a mass escape at the Maze in 1983, Sir James Hennessey said that: 'It consists almost entirely of prisoners convicted of offences connected with terrorist activities, united in their determination to be treated as political prisoners, resisting prison discipline, even if it means starving themselves to death, and retaining their paramilitary structure and allegiances even when inside. Bent on escape and ready to murder to achieve their ends, they are able to call on the help of their associates and supporters in the local community and—though increasingly less frequently—to arouse the sympathy of the international community; they are able to manipulate staff and enlist the support of paramilitary organisations in the process of intimidation' (1984).

The physical conflict and terror in the community was mirrored by physical and psychological conflict and terror inside the prisons. A relationship

Terrorists, Victims and Society: Psychological Perspectives on Terrorism and its Consequences.
Edited by Andrew Silke. © 2003 John Wiley & Sons, Ltd.

that was unique to Northern Ireland developed over time, to the point
that terrorists inside prison often dictated, by their disruptive behaviour,
political concessions outside. Prisoners were used by their political mas-
ters to gain political concessions in the community. The hunger strikes
tragically demonstrated the power of that relationship. The present-day
levels of paramilitary political sophistication, negotiating skill, power and
influence were honed by trial and experimentation in the prisons. The
Maze in particular became the development site and training ground of
paramilitary political leaders, some of whom are now elected representatives and ministers in the Northern Ireland Assembly.

It is not the intention of this chapter to analyse each incident and its
impact on specific events. Rather, by retrospectively examining events in
context, and observing what was happening to staff and prisoners inside
the Maze prison, from a psychological perspective, it is hoped that the
chapter will inform a greater understanding and offer some explanation
of how specific behaviours and situations evolved and developed over time.
From this perspective, it is necessary to briefly review significant prison-
related events from 1971 to July 2000.

BACKGROUND AND CONTEXT

The prison population in Northern Ireland had been traditionally small
(below 700) until August 1971 when internment without trial was introduced to cope with an upsurge in politically motivated community unrest.
In 1971 the police recorded 1756 shooting incidents and over 150 explosions, most of which were in Belfast. Hennessey (1984) described how the
Maze grew from a small, temporary, internment centre, into a large maximum security prison, and in just over 10 years it contained the largest
concentration of terrorists in western Europe.

In 1971, the Long Kesh Detention Centre housed the first internees in
existing RAF Nissen huts separated into sectarian compounds. These compounds were largely internee managed and had a paramilitary structure
with officer commanders, formal and assigned roles and factional allegiances. In March 1972 those convicted of 'politically motivated' offences
were sent to Long Kesh, which was then renamed HM Prison Maze.

In June 1972, in a bid to halt community violence and rioting, 'special
category status' was granted to convicted prisoners who claimed that their
offence had been politically motivated, and who had been accepted by one
of the paramilitary compound leaders. Special category status meant that
convicted prisoners would be separated by paramilitary and political faction, they could wear their own clothes and receive more privileges than
conventional prisoners. The experience of being in an almost autonomous
compound structure, and the granting of special category status, had

profound and lasting effects on the prisoners' perceptions of themselves and their future behaviour, as well as on their management by the authorities. In his 1998 inspection report, Her Majesty's Chief Inspector of Prisons, Sir David Ramsbotham, said that the granting of special status was 'the first step towards official acknowledgement that the institution [Maze] was not an ordinary prison performing an ordinary function' (Ramsbotham, 1998).

In 1974, the Provisional IRA and the Official IRA, following confrontation with the authorities, burned all their accommodation at the Maze, leaving only the two huts housing the loyalist prisoners. This act was followed by disruption in other prisons and in the wider community. In 1976, the first blocks, planned to hold 700 prisoners, were constructed at the Maze and were regarded as an interim measure, consisting of temporary cellular accommodation, with each unit being built in an H-shape. Meanwhile, a new and permanent prison was to be constructed at Maghaberry.

In March 1976, the government ruled that in future, special category status would no longer be granted to any prisoner convicted of a terrorist crime. This meant that all those convicted would be put into a conventional cellular prison, and denied the special privileges that had been granted in 1972. Ramsbotham stated that the 'alteration in policy was to have a significant consequence for the new cellular institution at the Maze' (Ramsbotham, 1998). In September 1976, sentenced republican prisoners refused to accept that they were 'ordinary criminals' and refused to work or wear prison clothing. In protest, the prisoners removed their prison-issued clothing, and initially were given blankets by staff to protect their decency. Republican prisoners then began a protest by wearing only blankets instead of clothing, a move that became known as 'on the blanket'. Prisoners lost privileges and relationships with the prison authorities deteriorated over time with both sides becoming ever more intransigent.

This protest was followed in March 1978 by further action by republican prisoners, who smeared their cells with their own excreta ('the dirty protest') in an attempt to get the government to concede to their demands. This was followed by paramilitary attacks on staff and their families. Between November 1978 and December 1979, 12 prison officers and a senior member of the Maze management team had been killed by terrorists due to the republican protest.

In October 1980, seven republican prisoners refused food and began a hunger strike, a weapon that had been used in the past by republicans in various prisons in the British Isles. This hunger strike ended in December 1980, but was succeeded by a second more sustained hunger protest in March 1981. By October 1981, 10 republican prisoners had died. The strikers' families, church and community leaders persuaded the prisoners to discontinue their protest, which had been based on five demands: the right to wear civilian clothes, the right not to work, the right to free association with other prisoners, the granting of remission of 50 per cent on all sentences, and the restoration of all normal privileges such as parcels, visits, educational and leisure activities.

The hunger strikes, and the deaths in particular, provoked a huge swell of public sympathy and action for the republican cause, both at home and abroad. The campaign of protest by the paramilitary organisations, both inside and outside of the prison environment, served to bond the terrorist prisoners in their determination for their political demands and in their sense of grievance against the prison authorities. A further consequence of the protests was that the terrorists also realised that the harnessing of the media, and consequent international pressure, was a powerful weapon in their struggle against the authorities.

Another event, this time orchestrated by the loyalists in 1982, gained all factions much sought-after paramilitary segregation at the Maze. The loyalists began their own 'dirty protest' after their demands for segregation from republican prisoners were refused. They also wrecked their cells, necessitating a move to separate accommodation under punishment. As Ramsbotham (1998) states: 'This "de facto" segregation was an important milestone in the history of the Maze as it permitted the development of more clearly defined segregated prisoner communities. Both loyalist and republican prisoners could now begin to challenge the authority of staff without the distraction of a power struggle between factions.' This meant that the paramilitaries could impose total control and discipline over their own prisoners, and it gave their officers commanding the freedom to re-create a compound-style regime with the corresponding autonomy that had existed in 1971.

Thirty-eight republican prisoners escaped from the Maze in 1983. Although 19 escapees were quickly recaptured, one prison officer died while helping to prevent the breakout. Sir James Hennessey carried out a special investigation into the escape in 1984. He was very critical about the circumstances as they were then, and made many recommendations about the changes that would have to be made regarding future security at the Maze.

In 1984, another member of the senior management team at the Maze was murdered in his home by the Provisional IRA. The then governor reported concern that security procedures were not being followed by staff, who were being intimidated in the wings, and that there was a lack of control of the prisoners in many areas. Throughout the 1980s, control in the Maze remained a problem for the authorities, and in 1988 the minister responsible for prisons said that the governor's orders should be 'revised to reflect realities'. Physical measures were taken to increase security, and improvements were introduced that were intended to benefit the wing-based regimes.

By mid-1988, the Provisional IRA had begun a concerted campaign to obtain 24-hour unlock, and inter-wing association. Around the same time, another prison officer was murdered by terrorists in the community. This reinforced for staff their vulnerability in working closely with convicted terrorists while also living in a small community that sometimes sympathised with the terrorists' aims, on either the republican or loyalist sides. From a practical point of view it was often difficult for staff to find a house in a 'neutral' or safe area. It became clear that it was becoming more difficult for staff at the Maze to carry out the governor's orders. It was therefore debated whether keeping prison staff in the wings was counter-productive to their safety and to the security of the prison.

In November 1991, a bomb planted by republicans exploded inside Belfast prison. Two loyalist prisoners were killed and seven injured. Belfast prison held remand prisoners under imposed integrated conditions, although the paramilitary factions had colluded to self-segregate in a very controlled and structured manner. This segregation led to only one faction, the loyalists, being in the dining hall when the bomb exploded.

In 1993, a working party on the situation in the Maze recommended that abutting wings should be amalgamated, which, as Ramsbotham pointed out in his report, only ratified what was already happening. However, the consequences of this decision meant that in a potential disturbance, prison officers had to control around a hundred prisoners from the same faction, rather than 50 at a time, in one wing.

In 1993, two prison officers were seized, stripped and had red paint poured over their heads in two different loyalist H-blocks at almost the same time. Staff recalled their shock and horror at the sight of these men as it was thought that they had been scalped. Neither officer was able to return to duty, and both were medically retired. These humiliating events had profound effects on all staff at the Maze and fear was reinforced when shots were fired into the homes of other prison staff. Later that year, loyalist prisoners rioted and another prison officer was shot dead in the community in, it was claimed, retaliation for the subsequent lock-up following the riot. Any sanctions imposed by the authorities were met with terror tactics aimed at the staff who had to deal with them on a daily basis both at work and at home.

In July 1994, after serious disturbances in Belfast prison, all remand paramilitary prisoners were relocated to the Maze and segregation into political factions was granted. The paramilitary objective of segregation for remand prisoners who were charged with terrorist-type offences had been achieved. This step had serious effects on the morale of staff, who were transferred from Belfast with the prisoners. Staff described how in a matter of hours the regime changed from one of tight control to one where the prison officers became runners for messages at the behest of the prisoners in the blocks. Many officers found the transition very difficult to accept.

In 1994, Maze prisoners successfully negotiated, using the late-night viewing of the football world cup television coverage, to gain a 24-hour unlock in the wings. This became a permanent feature, and in return the prisoners' leaders agreed that staff should be allowed to carry out daily security checks in all parts of the wings. As later events unfolded it became clear that such security checks were not enforced.

In March 1995, around 200 prison officers were injured after loyalist prisoners rioted following a search of their H-block. The consequent lengthy periods of sick absence among staff resulted in a reduction in thorough searching for some time.

In March 1997, an escape tunnel was discovered by a dog handler outside the perimeter of H-7, a republican block. What was more remarkable was that all the soil from the tunnel had been stored inside two cells in the wing, but had not been detected by staff, search teams or the security cameras. It was also remarkable that requests for substantial amounts of additional materials, especially plywood, for handicraft purposes had not raised suspicions, especially since the proposed handicrafts never emerged from the block.

The authorities introduced increased security measures because of the tunnel, and the loyalists claimed that they were being victimised for republican actions, and, as a consequence, shortly afterwards they wrecked their accommodation. In June 1997, loyalists fire-bombed the homes of three prison officers.

It was evident that the pressures at the Maze were immense. The management at the prison suffered another blow in December 1997 when a Provisional IRA prisoner, dressed as a woman, escaped following a children's party the authorities had organised for the prisoners and their families.

The security situation was already extremely grave when on 27 December 1997 the leading Loyalist Volunteer Force (LVF) officer commanding was shot dead by three members of the republican Irish National Liberation Army (INLA) in the forecourt of a block that was shared by two factions. The victim had been on his way to a visit when the attackers broke through security fencing, climbed over the H-block roof and walked up to the van that transported prisoners to visits. The LVF prisoner was shot inside the van, at almost point-blank range, using guns that had been smuggled into the prison.

The staff and authorities were still recovering from the shock of these terrible events when an LVF prisoner, on remand for a serious crime, was killed on 16 March 1998 in the block he shared with his comrades.

In July 2000, the remaining convicted paramilitaries were released under the Belfast Agreement, a settlement negotiated with the government by elected representatives and former Maze prisoners. After 28 years, and the deaths of 30 prison staff, the closure of the Maze had begun.

HOW DID THESE EVENTS HAPPEN?

The review of these events over the years since internment highlights the extraordinary situation of a prison in the UK. Ramsbotham (1998) stated in his inspection report that events demonstrated, 'in our view, the folly of attempting, or proposing, to apportion blame or personal responsibility for what has developed at the Maze to individual Ministers, Prison Service officials, Governors or staff'. He paid tribute 'to the steadfast way in which members of the Northern Ireland Prison Service have worked, under enormous pressure, to reduce the possibility that events in the Maze might exacerbate the already fraught relationships between different factions in the Northern Ireland community'. The situation had evolved where the paramilitaries from all factions inside the Maze prison were controlling and could manipulate the internal and external environments by killing staff or attacking their families and homes. It became impossible for a governor to tighten-up the regime in order to enhance security, knowing that one of his colleagues might die as a consequence.

How can such human suffering, serious security breaches, deaths in custody, reactions of the management, behaviour of the staff and the actions of the prisoners be explained from a psychological perspective? How did these events at a prison holding such large numbers of high-risk prisoners evolve?

First of all, the situations took a long time to develop. Examination of the Hennessey Report (1984) and the Ramsbotham Report (1998) indicates that deterioration in security had been evident and ongoing from the 1970s through to the 1990s, with significant decline after the second hunger strike. Even after the 1983 escape, when additional security measures were implemented, the situation had again deteriorated to a serious level. By 1998, security breaches were common, and staff working with the paramilitary prisoners were open in expressing their feelings to the chief inspector of prisons that they felt personally and individually compromised.

The prisoners had learned how to raise the tension in an H-block in order to gain compliance on seemingly insignificant or trivial issues that had been devised and manufactured to further erode security and to gain power over the staff. On an almost daily basis prisoners would insist that they had been given short rations, even when staff knew that they had received the full allocation. The Inspection Report of 1998 cited an occasion when, within an hour of the delivery of the evening meal, 90 'extras' had been ordered.

The terrorist prisoners made everyone they came into contact with very aware that their war was personal, and that those who attempted to thwart their objectives would be held personally responsible. It was hard for individuals not to feel vulnerable, and at times they felt helpless.

Everyone had been 'conditioned' by the planned action of the prisoners, so that by manipulation and threats they could corrupt procedures as well as staff attitudes and their reactions. It was often the lowest in the hierarchy, the officer at the grill, who took the brunt of the pressure and who was most exposed. At times it appeared that the key features keeping the terrorists inside HMP Maze were the very high wall and the electronically controlled gates, although they too had been breached in the 1983 escape. Officials, staff and the public questioned how the situation could have come about.

REPORTED AND OBSERVED TECHNIQUES USED BY PRISONERS AT THE MAZE

Some of the measures developed by the prisoners were based on the academic study of psychology, in particular social, organisational and learning theories. Education classes from basic to postgraduate university levels were available and actively encouraged by the paramilitaries, especially the Provisional IRA. Prisoners learned that they could use knowledge of interpersonal skills at a very sophisticated level to manipulate the behaviour and reactions of all staff. Some strategies were discovered by serendipity, much was based on observation, analysis and by the debriefing of incidents that the prisoners had planned. They also frequently examined the impact of their behaviour on staff and other significant personnel.

Sporadic and vicious attacks by the terrorists on members of staff inside, or their families outside, the jail were influential in increasing the psychological pressure in order to gain the unconscious co-operation needed to compromise and erode security on an ongoing basis. Staff in the prison system had unknowingly absorbed a culture and adopted behaviour that they intuitively felt would keep them and their families safe from the terrorists. Survival is a strong motivating force.

The prisoners' tactics varied according to their factions, with some using more physical violence and threats while others employed more subtle psychological pressure. The objectives of the prisoners changed and developed over time depending on the wider political agenda. Their approaches and techniques evolved to meet these needs.

Following are some of the most widely used tactics.

The Murder of Staff

The sporadic murder of prison staff, some of whom had limited or no prisoner contact, was common. In one 12-month period, during the campaign for special-category status, 13 members of prison staff were murdered by terrorists. Staff were sometimes killed in their own homes in front of their family, or in a public place, for example after a church service, thus gaining maximum horror and the advantage of fear. This was the strongest of terror tactics.

Attacks on Staff at Home

There were also regular attacks on staff homes. These included petrol-bombing homes, planting under-car booby-trap devices, setting alight cars in close proximity to staff houses, firing shots at staff homes and receiving live rounds of ammunition in the post as a warning. These attacks often necessitated relocation to a different area, sometimes as much as 30 miles from their original community. Displacement for a family meant significant stress and pressure on everyone, as it entailed losing all that was familiar. Children were often most affected by having to move schools, make new friends, and having to reintegrate into a new community. Parents often concealed the fact that they worked as prison officers in case children talked about it at school, and thus, unintentionally, brought danger to the family. Such secrecy did not engender trust within the family.

Physical Violence, Threats and the Impact on Feelings of Helplessness

The sporadic physical attacks at work were varied in nature and severity. Staff suffered serious head injuries, broken limbs, scalds from boiling water and humiliation from having urine thrown over them. Additionally, verbal threats on individual members of staff in the block reminded everyone that at any time they could be next.

Ramsbotham (1998) stated that: 'Staff felt powerless when threatened by any prisoner, because they perceived that the prisoner was supported not only by his colleagues inside the establishment, but also by members of his paramilitary organisation outside, in the community in which they and their families lived.' He cited accounts of staff going sick rather than having to act as witnesses in cases where their colleagues had been attacked at work. For the individual who had been assaulted, he or she not only felt humiliated by the prisoners' violence, but also felt abandoned, badly let down by his or her friends and unsupported by management. There was little group cohesion on the staff side, as this had been eroded by the paramilitaries who increased their own cohesion by planning disruption and carrying out events knowing that they were unlikely to be held to account. A chronic state of learned helplessness set in, where staff believed, because of past negative experiences, that nothing they could do would affect or influence the outcome of events. These feelings of powerlessness and their effects on behaviour had been investigated in other contexts by Seligman (1975) who held the view that human depression was sometimes a consequence of chronic feelings of helplessness.

The mental health of staff was reflected by 50 staff suicides from the early 1970s to the late 1980s. Many took their lives using handguns issued to them for their personal protection against the terrorists. The stress and pressure experienced by staff might help to explain the high rates of absenteeism and why over half of the Maze staff had sought help from psychology services after its formation by the prison service in 1991. Avoidance of a place where there has been a fear for safety and one's life is a common coping mechanism. Some staff unknowingly experienced chronic stress over a period of time, and found it difficult to adjust to normal family routines when they went home at the end of a shift. Many resorted to self-medication with prescribed drugs and alcohol in order to get through another day. The consequences were felt in family relationships, which bore the brunt of the stress symptoms of extreme irritability, anxiety and rage over seemingly small issues. Tempers had to be contained in the work situation, but spilled out in the home environment, to the detriment of personal and family life. Ramsbotham (1998) stated: 'The staff are the real victims, many of the normal prison rules being inoperable and Prison Service Headquarters not being as understanding or supportive as one would wish.'

Social Influence and Subtle Threats

In his book on the history of the Maze, Chris Ryder (2000) described how prisoners waged constant psychological warfare against the officers, alternatively threatening and being friendly to them. Staff reported how the prisoners were always trying to get personal information to use against them. In a 'casual' conversation an officer would be asked by a prisoner about general, innocuous topics like their holidays, moving house, getting a new car or events in their neighbourhood. Some time later, parts of this information would be relayed back to the officer from a different prisoner in a manner that insinuated intimate knowledge and implied threat. There might be an additional spin, which would include other information like the mention of the colour of the new car, indicating that the information had been confirmed by paramilitaries outside. The officer would realise, too late, that his safety may have been breached by his own careless conversation, and he would spend hours trying to remember the original dialogue and how much he may have shared and exposed about his private life.

This created ongoing anxiety for the officer, as he never knew whether the security of his family really was in jeopardy, or whether he was merely being duped and deliberately unnerved by the prisoners. As Ryder (2000) said: 'It was very difficult when staff lived in a small community where everyone knows everyone else and when the links between prisoners inside and their terrorist organisations outside were so close.'

Invasion of Personal Space and the Defying of Conventional Social Interactions

Another tactic familiar to prison staff in the late 1980s and early 1990s was the surrounding of a prison officer by a group of prisoners in the wings. This was accompanied by the prisoners bombarding the officer or governor with questions and demands in quick succession, giving no time for replies before the next demand was made. This tactic was designed to disorientate and confuse the individual, and included invasion of the officer's personal space, close eye-contact, finger pointing as well as aggressive shouting, jostling and nudging to increase the tension and fear. Whilst a member of staff felt that an attack was imminent, it seldom occurred at that time.

The prisoners utilised rational, logical arguments in debates with staff about prison rules and regulations and claimed that other officers had been more reasonable in the easement of the regime. The tactic was to keep repeating the question and demanding to know why certain rules existed. The 'why' question, repeated over and over again, wore the member of staff down psychologically and made him vulnerable to conceding to the targeted demands in order to rid himself of the verbal tirade.

Even when staff were prepared for this tactic, it was hard for them to maintain an objective view of the situation and remain calm. For a member of staff who may have also been previously assaulted by prisoners, or had witnessed an attack at close hand, the anxiety it provoked was unbearable and over time contributed to absenteeism. Officers described the anticipation of work and their anxiety in travelling to work as worse than actually being in work. Many staff told how they often had to stop their cars on the way to the Maze to be physically sick.

Creation and Manipulation of the Affiliative Needs of Staff

Many social psychologists have researched the human need for affiliation, which includes the need to belong and be accepted by others. It is one of the basic human survival needs described by Maslow (1970). This strong need can help explain certain types of influence others can exert on us, such as pressure to conform. Some theories in this area of research may offer explanation of what was happening in the Maze. According to Duck (1988) and Schachter (1959) we are more affiliative and more inclined to seek out the company of others when we are anxious. Additionally, research by Festinger, Schachter and Back (1950) indicated that proximity encouraged friendliness, while Zajonc (1968) found that mere exposure and familiarity led to fondness and increased interaction between people. According to Argyle (1983), the more two people interact, the more polarised their attitudes towards each other become, usually in the direction of greater liking.

As in any setting where people meet and interact, relationships developed over time. Ramsbotham (1998) stated that staff were not rotated at work as often as may have been desirable. He noted in his inspection report that 'episodes of demands and complaints were interspersed with periods when prisoners would chat to staff at the grilles about mutual interests, such as football, politics, and even decorating, so that staff bonded with prisoners and tried to avoid any situation that would bring conflict. As a result goods, even meals from the prison kitchen, coming into the blocks were not checked by block staff. Prisoners were not given a rub down search on entering or leaving the block for activities, or if they crossed the circle to visit the other side of the H-block. Teachers and other visitors were not checked on entering or leaving the block. If a search took place it was with the agreement of the OC . . .' (Ramsbotham, 1998). Indeed, he went on: 'wings were controlled by prisoners, routine access to a wing was almost only after permission had been granted by the prisoner designated as "Officer in Command" (OC). This meant that even routine tasks, such as counting prisoners twice a day, could only be achieved with the prisoners' co-operation.' The development of social relationships between staff and prisoners through close contact led over time to a relaxation of security vigilance in the prison.

The Role of Cognitive Dissonance

When an inmate has befriended an officer in a hostile environment and offered him protection from the other 'threatening prisoners' it is very difficult not to reciprocate in some manner with a 'favour', especially if the officer could persuade himself that the 'favour' was not really important. This unconscious rationalising process could be explained by Festinger's (1957) Theory of Cognitive Dissonance in which he suggested that cognitive dissonance arises for the individual when there is a conflict between attitudes and behaviour, and when someone has found him- or herself compromised by another person, or by a situation, and consequently is made to feel very uncomfortable by his or her own actions. Festinger proposes that when such conflict occurs it creates a state of 'dissonance', which an individual seeks to reduce in order to eliminate the feelings of conflict and guilt. The reduction in dissonance can be resolved in a number of ways, including changes in attitude and behaviour or by minimising the importance of the elements involved in the dissonant situation.

This psychological process became apparent in the Maze situation when an officer found that he had unwittingly become too familiar with a prisoner who called him by his first name, knew what cars he liked, and what music he preferred. He may have been reminded by the prisoner that the two shared the same cultural and religious background, and may even have grown up in the same neighbourhood. Familiarity and social affiliation thereby developed and consequently the officer would become ready to be manipulated.

Unconsciously, an officer then had to reconcile his compromised behaviour (relaxation of security) and his social affiliation for the prisoner (liking and familiarity) with the contrary security demands of his training, work environment and the expectations of management. Therefore, for the officer to feel more comfortable with his emotional state, it became possible, and even necessary, to believe that he had done nothing wrong, because, he rationalised, his colleagues were not carrying out the governor's orders either. The prisoners reinforced this rationalisation process by repeatedly pointing out that no one else carried out the governor's orders.

This rationalising of an individual's behaviour and beliefs is not difficult to understand because staff knew that colleagues and families had been attacked and often murdered. Carrying out the governor's orders to the letter would mean that the officer would incur the wrath of particular prisoners and would be disowned and ostracised by those who had 'befriended' him. Even more worryingly, the focus of the next assault could be on that particular officer as he would no longer be in the 'accepted group', and consequently would not merit 'protection'.

It therefore became imperative for staff to keep the prisoners content, as management and the authorities were unlikely to extract physical retribution for non-compliance. The development, manipulation and maintenance of the social affiliation needs of staff and the exploitation of the process of cognitive dissonance were therefore very powerful weapons in the paramilitary armoury. These approaches were subtle and invidious, and staff found such behaviour confusing and difficult to counter because these tactics exploited and manipulated familiar and conventional social norms and relationships.

The Stockholm Syndrome

Taylor (1988), in his analysis of aspects of terrorism, described a phenomenon known as the Stockholm Syndrome, which has been observed in different hostage situations. He stated that the critical general feature in the development of the syndrome is the mutual dependency of the captor and hostage in circumstances of extreme tension and stress. Taylor (1988) suggests that: 'The hostage is, in a very obvious sense, dependent on the captor, and is in his or her power; the hostage taker, however, is also in a sense dependent on the hostage, for it presumably is the presence of the hostage that inhibits the observing security forces from all-out attack. This complex interrelationship seems to create between them a bond of some form, where initial acquiescence of the hostage turns to submission... Similarly, the captor is necessarily physically close to the hostage, and in a sense dependent on the hostage for achieving his ends. Both share danger (albeit created by the hostage incident), and that sharing, and the consequent development of group cohesion seems to change the relationship of dependency to one of, if not affection, at least tolerance.'

There have been some very serious individual and group hostage situations in the Maze over the years. However, in a general but real sense staff felt as though they were hostages in their work environment every day. If the prisoners decided to create a disturbance over food, visits, exercise, etc., then an emergency would be called and staff would not be allowed home until the situation was settled. Additionally, works/maintenance and other staff were sometimes held against their will in the wings until some small domestic concessions, like additional curtains or shelving, were installed in cells. After such incidents it was noticeable that staff anger was always directed at management for not preventing it, rather than towards the prisoners who had caused the event. The potential to become a hostage at any time was always real. Staff had expressed their fears about being taken hostage and the potential for physical violence and rape was often in their thoughts. Officers described their feelings by explaining that although they went home at the end of the day, they often felt more captive than their charges.

Bullying and Alienation Tactics

A sinister yet infrequent development emerged over time where staff became abused by both prisoners and inadvertently, or unintentionally, by their own colleagues. The terror tactics developed by the prisoners meant that all were constantly afraid that they would become the next focus for negative attention. Staff unconsciously developed strategies to avoid attention at all costs, and learned to avert their eyes in case eye contact with a prisoner was interpreted as assertive or confrontational. Officers, however, found themselves being drawn into situations that had been devised by the prisoners to divide the staff and thereby conquer by breaking down staff cohesion. These incidents were some of the most difficult and shameful for staff. There are powerful emotional and often long-lasting negative consequences for the person subjected to feelings of shame, even though an event was not their fault or of their making. Situations similar to bullying in the school playground were engineered by prisoners, whereby staff found it was safer to take the bully's point of view than side with the victim, their colleague, and thus risk becoming the next victim.

Ramsbotham (1998) reported that 'there was little evidence of the normal confidence in their own authority that we look for in prison staff. We observed a prisoner walking into a Principal Officer's office without knocking or waiting to be invited in. The prisoner demanded to know why the usual number of milk cartons had not been delivered, and wanted the name of the officer who had accepted the milk delivery onto the block. The Officer to whom he was speaking noticeably tried to distance himself from the problem by blaming the kitchen: his colleagues in the room did nothing to support him as the prisoner persisted. The outcome of this was that the prisoner virtually ordered the Officer to get more milk, and the Officer complied by telephoning the kitchen. The tension in the room during this exchange was palpable.' Those not directly involved in the exchange kept quiet in case they too incurred the attention and wrath of the prisoner. It is not difficult to imagine how lonely, unsupported and alienated the officer felt.

On other occasions, a member of staff sometimes found himself selected by the prisoners for a challenge, such as lifting extremely heavy weights in front of a group of prisoners and staff while his credibility as a 'real man' was called into public question. The chosen officer, not usually selected because of his large build, felt that he could not refuse the challenge, and colleagues knew that if they went to his assistance they too would become the focus for bullying. The task was usually designed to be unachievable so that the officer would fail, and therefore feel humiliated. Officers who experienced this treatment reported that what hurt most was the fact that their colleagues joined in with the prisoners' derision of the member of staff.

It is also understandable how difficult it must have been for all staff involved in such situations to feel comfortable with their colleagues afterwards. As a terrorist tactic these challenges were successful in that they decreased staff morale, reduced individual self-esteem and negatively impacted on the cohesion of the group.

ORGANISATIONAL AND MANAGEMENT ISSUES

Many organisational and management practices contributed to the observed behaviours in the Maze. Most managers suffered the same intimidation and conditioning endured by the block staff. The prisoners encouraged the staff to conform to their demands for increased relaxation of the rules, and openly conspired with the uniformed staff to 'protect' them from the block governor's disapproval. They created a 'them and us' environment where the prisoners let it be known that compliant staff would be under their personal protection but, it was implicitly understood, that they would be obliged to them in the future. Role reversal had allowed power to be taken from the staff by the prisoners, allowing the prisoners to control the staff against the management.

At the same time, prisoners undermined staff authority by bypassing wing staff and taking up matters directly with the block governor. The block governor's status and position was, in turn, usurped by the prisoners' demands to be attended to by the number one governor. The number one governor was also undermined by the prisoners' demands or issues being raised at headquarters or Secretary of State level. The authority's chain of command was constantly undermined by the prisoners, who in turn insisted that they would communicate only through their official channels, which meant recognising their officers' commanding and political status. In a bid to get anything agreed, management found that they had no choice but to talk to the officer commanding in each faction. Ramsbotham (1998) mentioned that: 'In the eyes of many staff the lack of clear rules for the operation of the prison, the lack of consultation and communication, and the alleged undermining of the management line by the Governor's practice of negotiating policy by direct consultation with officers commanding, had reduced the staff on the blocks to mere go-betweens or runners of errands for prisoners.' As one officer put it in the chief inspector's report: 'staff felt humiliation and degradation by being managed by prisoners'. It seemed that the prisoners had little to lose by standing firm, while management had reached a point where they could not win without retribution being delivered, either inside or out, as a consequence.

Hennessey (1984) and Ramsbotham (1998) both highlighted failures on the side of the management. According to Hennessey: 'The human failures were many. Staff had become complacent about the dangers, and lazy practices had been allowed to develop. There were examples of security grilles being left unlocked, orderlies allowed too much freedom, vehicles unchecked, posts left unattended, alarms not properly answered—and so on, the list is long.' The report also identified terrorist pressures as increasing this tendency for staff to turn a blind eye to such security threats. It stated that: 'It was the responsibility of the Governor and his senior staff to ensure that such procedures were both adequate and effective, this they failed to do.' Hennessey did acknowledge that the work at the Maze was also mundane and boring, which did not assist staff in their general state of alertness or help to raise their self-esteem.

The Ramsbotham Report highlighted the series of events between the 1983 Maze escape up to 1997, which indicated all was not well: 'It was quite clear that the degree of fear and intimidation, which pervaded throughout the prison, had made it understandably difficult for clear rules to be drawn up and enforced. This pressure extended to senior managers and senior members of the Northern Ireland Prison Service who had also been openly and publicly threatened.' Ramsbotham stated that: 'There was an urgent need for managers and staff to define realistic protocols and procedures which could be enforced by staff.' His report drew attention to the gaps in normal security expectations with the following in observation: 'During the evening roll check at approximately 20:00 hours, prisoners were supposed to gather in the dining area to be counted. We were told that this rarely happened. It was left to the officers to arrive at a successful count by glancing around the wing for about ten minutes.' It would be difficult to suppose that subordinate staff would behave any differently to their managers whose leadership was constantly being diverted to dealing with prisoner requests and demands. The fact that the prisoners usually achieved their demands meant that management had very few sanctions to impose when behaviour was violent, antisocial or unacceptable.

The prisoners knew that threats and assaults worked in gaining concessions, and management had found itself in a position of inadvertently reinforcing bad behaviour as a consequence. This contributed to control problems, as staff felt that if they did try to hold the line on an issue they were likely to be undermined by a manager, who, under great personal pressure, would concede to the prisoners' demands, often in order to protect the staff who he had just countermanded. In the process, respect for management was further eroded, which further enhanced the power of the prisoners.

ADDITIONAL FEATURES AFFECTING BEHAVIOUR IN THE MAZE

The Management Structure

The many layers in the prison management structure led to communication, role and accountability difficulties. There were eight levels, from Basic Grade Officer to Governor 1, in the management structure of the Maze. This allowed staff to pass responsibility from one level to another, and encouraged prisoners to exploit the situation when they were in dispute. A favoured tactic of the prisoners was to threaten individual members of staff and hold them personally responsible for their non-compliance or lack of co-operation with prisoner demands. They would also remind all staff that their colleagues were always more reasonable and tolerant than them, and that their lack of sympathy would be remembered. It was little wonder that some governors found it difficult to spend time in their respective blocks when they knew that the uniformed staff would be expecting them to relieve them of the daily pressure from the prisoners. Avoidance of the prisoners became an attractive proposition for staff and managers alike.

Communication

As staff became less resilient over time, communication between staff and between management and staff deteriorated. There were few formal or structured debriefs between managers and groups on each shift, and therefore vital information and important intelligence was often lost. It may have been possible to prevent some of the negative events like riots, assaults and security breaches by the sharing of information and ongoing experiences when staff were changing shifts. However, the desire for staff to get out of the Maze before something happened at the end of their shift was extremely compelling and, therefore, staff could be observed leaving the blocks almost before the next shift was in place.

It also became noticeable over time that many of the important security issues that worried everyone at every level began to be ignored and accepted as how things were. In concluding his report, Ramsbotham (1998) stated: 'many of the normal statutory Prison Rules were not being applied'. There was an avoidance of reality and, in an environment of learned help-lessness, everyone avoided talking about the important security issues and seemed less anxious if they ignored certain irregularities. One member of staff said that 'it was as though everyone connected with the management of the prisoners was living a lie'. Reality became blocked out, and denial set in as a corporate coping mechanism.

THE DILEMMA OF THE PRISONERS

Containment of republican and loyalist internees in the compound structures in 1971 created an environment where group cohesion thrived. Shared political idealism, common goals, the endurance of physical hardships due to the basic Nissen hut, open-plan accommodation with very limited facilities instilled in the various paramilitary factions a sense of purpose and group loyalty. This was perpetuated in the blocks over the years by the maintenance of military titles (officer commanding, quartermaster, adjutant, and other 'officers' who were responsible for administration, supplies, welfare and education). Rules, discipline, assigned roles and organisational structures, enhanced the power and control of the paramilitary leaders.

All issues and problems, including mental health, were contained in the blocks and dealt with by the group. While psychological support was available to all prisoners in the Maze from the late 1980s, few requested the service. Complete obedience to the group needs was essential and there would have been limited approval for seeking psychological support outside of the block, in case the confessional aspects of therapy might allow disclosure of terrorist activities. Strong support from colleagues was a very positive mechanism for helping the paramilitary prisoners to cope.

Some of the tactics that kept staff controlled by the prisoners also kept prisoners in control. There were noticeable cultural differences between the factions in the prisoners' adherence to conformity and discipline, but generally the commanding officer's authority was absolute and they ensured that discipline was enforced. Conformity and obedience to the imposed group norms was essential to the survival of the group, and few prisoners rebelled as the punishment was severe. Ryder (2000) cites several instances of punishment in the compounds: 'One man had his nipples badly burnt with a cigarette lighter, another had tram lines burnt on his back with the bars of an electric fire and another received severe body and head bruising when he was beaten with a wet, knotted towel.'

There is no doubt that the stress of being imprisoned within very tightly knit factional groups was considerable. Requests for medication for stress-related complaints greatly increased towards the latter part of the existence of the Maze. Taylor (1988), in an analysis of terrorism and mental health, suggests that 'the nature of the terrorist life has implications for the terrorist's mental health'. He says that 'whilst his mental health might not be in question, when he becomes a terrorist, terrorism itself impinges on his mental state and brutalises the individual involved'. Taylor expands this view by suggesting that: 'the covert context of terrorism supplies an important difference, as does the fact that the terrorist does not usually "go to war" but conducts his activities in his own environment. The supportive context of terrorism extends to maintaining terrorist behaviour, rather than offering counselling or more explicit intervention to deal with these problems.' Taylor also says that it seems reasonable to conclude that 'whilst mental illness may not be a particularly helpful way of conceptualising terrorism, the acts of terrorism, and membership of a terrorist organisation, may well have implications for the terrorist's mental health'. This is perhaps more particularly evident on release, when the tight support of the group becomes fragmented.

In a typical prison environment the range of personalities and offences of the inmates are varied. In the Maze prison this diversity would have been limited. At the time of the Ramsbotham inspection in 1998, 82 per cent of the 525 prisoners in the Maze were between 20 and 39 years old, 62 per cent were serving over 10 years with 21 per cent on life sentences; 98 per cent were categorised as medium and high risk, while loyalist and republican affiliation was equally divided. There was strength in belonging to the paramilitary factions, but freedom to deviate from the interests and direction of the group was discouraged and would have been dangerous to the individual and to the paramilitary group. The paramilitary discipline was all-consuming, and groupthink was demanded. Acting in unison meant strength of discipline and achieved results. There was no room for independent or divergent thinkers.

As in any conflict situation where people get killed, it assisted terrorist prisoners and their families in coping with their offences and imprisonment if they constantly reinforced the belief that they were prisoners of war, and that their cause was just. Another coping mechanism adopted by some prisoners was religious conversion, especially among the loyalist factions.

WAS THE MAZE UNIQUE IN THE USE OF PSYCHOLOGICAL TACTICS?

All those who worked in the Maze felt it was unique, but could the situation, behaviour and events happen in other places where groups of terrorists or like-minded people are detained together? Certainly the large numbers of terrorists held at the Maze made it different, and the numbers contributed greatly to the problems of management and control. However, research into the escapes of six and three high-risk prisoners from Whitemoor and Parkhurst prisons, respectively, indicate that what happened in the Maze, over a long period of time, also happened in these other two prisons but in a comparatively short time-span. The prisoners were from the Provisional IRA and their behaviour and utilisation of sophisticated interpersonal skills to influence staff mirrored those of the same faction in the Maze around that time.

The Report of the Woodcock Enquiry 1994 (Whitemoor prison) and the Learmont Inquiry 1995 (Parkhurst prison) had made many similar observations to those reflected in the Hennessey and Ramsbotham reports. The reports into the escapes from the English prisons highlighted extreme breaches in security and reported extraordinary behaviour of prison staff and prisoners. The Woodcock Report concluded: 'The findings of the Enquiry describe an awful story where it appears that everything which could have gone wrong has in fact done so' (Woodcock, 1994).

The Woodcock Report found that there was evidence of bad practice, including apparent examples of lax security, ineffective searching routines and an extraordinary catalogue of unearned privileges for the special segregation unit (SSU) inmates. The inspection team noted that equipment used to effect the escape had been manufactured or adapted on-site, yet went unnoticed by staff. The hobbies room was described as 'an Aladdin's cave of equipment'.

Security cameras had been obscured and extra privacy had been demanded by the prisoners, and this had been accommodated by the staff. 'The reduced ability of staff to monitor visually activities in the communal room, and in particular the workshop, was nothing short of scandalous' (Woodcock, 1994). There was evidence of 'no go' areas, and that visits to cells and patrolling of wings was not encouraged without permission from the prisoners. Officers summed up the ethos within the SSU as 'don't upset the inmates and don't rock the boat'.

Additional materials for handicrafts were provided without audit. Prisoners had amassed large quantities of property which had filled unoccupied cells, and dozens of transit boxes of possessions had spilled over into the corridors and communal areas and included a bicycle belonging to an inmate. Such overcrowding made searching a cursory exercise. Two inmates had 82 boxes of property on transfer to Maghaberry prison in Northern Ireland.

Prison officers were intimidated by inmates when any search was attempted, and some searches were discontinued rather than risk escalation of prisoner reaction. Two guns, eight rounds of ammunition, Semtex explosive, fuses and detonators were found in a false base of an artist's paint box. Visitors objected strongly to 'rub down' searches and staff were untrained as to how to deal with the opposition and the procedures. In the light of threats from the prisoners, the governor suspended the 'rub down' searches for the SSU in March 1992. Prisoners put forward the argument that the non-searching of prisoners had never been abused, and this was accepted by all staff. When visits were in progress, staff had learned not to be too vigilant, and to 'sit down and not move about, as the prisoners don't like it'. The string of concessions to inmates had all combined to produce a sense of resignation amongst SSU staff and a feeling that it was not worth confronting any abuses.

The prisoners set up security diversionary tactics intended to distract and divert the attention of staff away from important, relevant security activities. Woodcock (1994) also stated that 'the lack of vigilance generally displayed by staff owed much to the intimidation, conditioning and underlying desire to avoid any confrontation'.

Prisoners encroached on staff areas as though it was an entitlement. Inmates at the SSU had systematically added to their privileges by finding areas where other establishments had allowed greater concessions. They then challenged the absence of such privileges and demanded parity. Officers found that their role was demeaning, as illustrated by the fact that prisoners routinely sent two officers to purchase, over 20 miles away, special foodstuffs for their meals. This diverted these staff from security duties and the supervision of inmates.

The security situation at Parkhurst prison in 1995 was very similar to that found at Whitemoor SSU and the Maze. Learmont's (1995) report into the escape in 1995 stated that: 'The fact that all the basic weaknesses of Whitemoor, which had been so clearly identified by the Woodcock Enquiry, reappeared at Parkhurst, with other failings, makes the escape inexcusable.' The report revealed 'a chapter of errors at every level and a naivety that defies belief'. Learmont went on to say that there 'has been a failure to meet basic security requirements of searching, locks, bolts and bars and "rub down" searching'. The report also indicated lack of supervision and checking by middle management, excessive property storage beyond normal guidelines, evidence of the conditioning of staff by prisoners, and that staff had become stale and complacent due to the length of time served on the SSU. Additionally, Learmont found that staff morale was extremely low due to little or no management support, hastily made decisions by managers in order to appease prisoners' demands, failure to communicate between staff and their managers, and that limited training had been provided to address the difficulties that staff encountered.

The numbers and the length of time that inmates were held in high-security conditions at both Whitemoor and Parkhurst were limited in comparison to the numbers of prisoners and time served at HMP Maze. The English prisons were located in a larger, more anonymous community and staff were therefore less vulnerable to personal and local intimidation tactics favoured by terrorists. It is to the credit of the staff who served at the Maze that there was only one escape since 1983, even though the normal conditions expected of prisons in the UK were not in evidence.

CONCLUSION

It would seem that given a particular set of circumstances and a grouping of extremely determined and ruthless people, the situation that evolved at the Maze could be replicated in other prison situations. There have been several reports of various terrorist factions sharing information, training and intelligence. The paramilitary prisoners of all factions in the Maze learned much from each other, and the authorities have since gained considerable knowledge and experience. Some of the personally difficult situations suffered by Maze staff have been reported by security personnel in other jurisdictions. The understanding of terrorists and terrorist behaviour has increased greatly in recent years, and terrorism is now a global problem.

With hindsight many lessons have been learned about the management and containment of dedicated terrorists through the Northern Ireland experiences. Prison officers who are trained to take a rehabilitative and personal approach to prisoners would find their skills counterproductive in a terrorist context. Guards who are constantly rotated to avoid the development of close interpersonal relationships with prisoners would be less vulnerable to the various kinds of manipulation and conditioning described above. Staff who have no family connections in the community are less likely to be compromised by threats and intimidation. Further, the physical layout and design of the accommodation can determine and contribute to the safety of security personnel and the prisoners themselves. Systems that reward and reinforce positive behaviour can be developed to enhance co-operation and safety, and it is essential that policies and rules must be visible and enforceable, and communication continually reviewed. A 'no blame' culture that engenders trust between staff and management has to be developed, and the management style needs to be supportive but firm. Training must address an awareness of the intricacies, complexities and impact of interpersonal skills on human behaviour. It is important that staff understand non-verbal communication at a micro level to ensure that the potential for terrorists to generate stress and fear and to intimidate those with whom they come into contact can be reduced. Finally, individual prisoners who feel trapped by fellow terrorists within their own factions need a mechanism to allow them to leave the group safely.

It would be compelling to leave behind the painful experiences over the last 30 years of dealing with dedicated terrorists in a small prison service and community. However, the traumatic events of September 11, 2001 remind us that terrorism is a major concern and that containment of dangerous groups and individuals will become a necessary issue for more countries. Learning from previous experiences could be beneficial in reducing the victimisation of security personnel in the future.

REFERENCES

Argyle, M. (1983). *The Psychology of Interpersonal Behaviour*, 4th edn. Harmondsworth: Penguin.

Duck, S. (1988). *Relating To Others*. Milton Keynes: Open University Press.

Festinger, L. (1957). *A Theory of Cognitive Dissonance*. New York: Harper and Row.

Festinger, L., Schachter, S. and Back, K. (1950). *Social Pressures in Informal Groups: A Study of Human Factors in Housing*. Stanford, CA: Stanford University Press.

Hennessey, J. (1984). *The Hennessey Report: A Report of an Inquiry by HM Chief Inspector of Prisons into the Security Arrangements at HMP Maze*. Cmnd 203. London: HMSO.

Learmont, J. (1995). *Review of Prison Service Security in England and Wales and the Escape from Parkhurst Prison on Tuesday 3rd January 1995*. London: HMSO.

Maslow, A. (1970). *Motivation and Personality*, 2nd edn. New York: Harper and Row.

Ramsbotham, D. (1998). *HM Prison Maze (Northern Ireland), Report of a Full Inspection 23 March–3 April 1998*. Home Office, London.

Ryder, C. (2000). *Inside The Maze: The Untold Story of the Northern Ireland Prison Service*. London: Methuen.

Schachter, S. (1959). *The Psychology of Affiliation: Experimental Studies of the Sources of Gregariousness*. Stanford, CA: Stanford University Press.

Seligman, M.E.P. (1975). *Helplessness: On Depression, Development and Death*. San Francisco, CA: W.H. Freeman.

Taylor, M. (1988). *The Terrorist*. London:Brassey's.

Woodcock, J. (1994). *Report of the Enquiry into the Escape of Six Prisoners from the Special Security Unit at Whitemoor Prison, Cambridgeshire, on Friday 9th September 1994*. London: HMSO.

Zajonc, R.B. (1968). Attitudinal effects of mere exposure. *Journal of Personality and Social Psychology*, **9**(2), 1–27.

CHAPTER 13

Deterring Terrorists

KARL A. SEGER
Associated Corporate Consultants, Inc.

UNDERSTANDING THE CURRENT THREAT

The US Federal Bureau of Investigation (FBI) defines terrorism as: 'the unlawful use of force or violence against persons or property to intimidate or coerce a government, the civilian population, or any segment thereof, in furtherance of political or social objectives'. The US Department of Defense (DoD) has a similar definition in its Directive 0-2000.12H: 'Terrorism is the calculated use of violence or threat of violence to instill fear, intended to coerce or try to intimidate governments or societies in the pursuit of goals that are generally political, religious or ideological.'

The DoD, though, differentiates between the three components of its Combating Terrorism Program: (1) anti-terrorism, (2) counter-terrorism, and (3) terrorism consequence management. Anti-terrorism refers to defensive measures used to reduce the vulnerability of individuals and property to terrorist attack. Counter-terrorism refers to offensive measures to deter, resolve and mitigate a terrorist act. Consequent management refers to measures used to minimise loss of life and property damages following a terrorist incident (Ralston, 1999).

Psychology plays a role in all three of these components. Within the anti-terrorism component psychological warfare and other defensive measures may be used to convince the terrorist that attempting to target a specific asset or person has a low probability of success, or that the action would not achieve the terrorist's objective. An important aspect of psychological anti-terrorism is the need to create awareness among the targeted population.

Terrorists, Victims and Society: Psychological Perspectives on Terrorism and its Consequences.
Edited by Andrew Silke. © 2003 John Wiley & Sons, Ltd.

People within this population then become the additional eyes and ears for the law-enforcement and intelligence communities. When Europe was experiencing heightened levels of terrorism during the 1980s, governments used television and other media to enlist civilian awareness and participation in combating terrorism with 'Stop the Terror' campaigns. As a result of the increased awareness, citizens were alert to persons who left suspicious packages or briefcases behind or who appeared to be gathering intelligence on targets. Many of these activities were reported and terrorist incidents were prevented.

An effective counter-terrorism psychology programme will convince the terrorist that even if he or she is successful in an attack, the consequences could be devastating. For example, while the September 11 attacks were certainly an operational success from al-Qaeda's perspective, they resulted in a massive backlash against the organisation. The US' campaign against the group has brought about the collapse of the Taliban regime in Afghanistan, the deaths and capture of hundreds (if not thousands) of al-Qaeda members, and the destruction of much of al-Qaeda's infrastructure (e.g. the training camps in Afghanistan). A year after the New York and Washington attacks, the surviving elements of the terrorist group are still being relentlessly pursued. Even so, it remains risky to assume too much deterrent value will come from even this formidable clampdown on the group. The massive international military and political response to the September 2001 attacks may only add resolve to the network created by al-Qaeda and validate the misguided beliefs of the individuals associated with that network.

Psychology plays a major role in terrorism consequence management. Within an hour of the attacks on September 11, the American Psychological Association's Disaster Response Network (DRN) was in contact with the American Red Cross. By noon the DRN members met by conference call and within hours the Association had sent DRN co-ordinators to the disaster sites (APA responds to terrorist attacks, 2001). Long after incident sites are cleared and buildings restored there will still be psychological wounds, many of which will never heal. The need for psychological intervention within this component continues for years after the event.

Deterring terrorism is an anti-terrorism activity. The objective is to prevent incidents from occurring and to make it difficult for the terrorist organisation to function or even to exist. The first step in developing an anti-terrorism programme is to understand the problem and the specific terrorist threats to the assets being protected. This awareness must then be communicated to the general population. The final step to an anti-terrorism programme is to initiate actions that will make it more difficult for terrorists to target interests.

To understand terrorism we should first examine the general categories of terrorist organisations and then explore the specific motivating behaviours of each group and its members. Only then can psychological approaches (that must be used in conjunction with other anti-terrorism measures) to deter terrorists be developed. There are currently five categories of terrorist threats that should be considered:

- International groups.
- Regional groups.
- Domestic threats.
- Special interest extremists.
- Lone terrorists who practise leaderless warfare.

Al-Qaeda is the most well-known international terrorist organisation. But it is important to note that al-Qaeda is actually a network of terrorists and terrorist organisations. Some of these organisations are highly structured while others operate as loosely knit cells. The behaviour of highly structured organisations is somewhat predictable. The behaviour of networks and loose cells, however, is more difficult to predict, in part because the strong leadership that contributes to the predictability of structured organisations is missing. International organisations are transnational, striking at targets around the world.

There are international terrorist organisations that limit their terrorist operations within a specific region. Several of the groups operating in the Middle East have cells and supporters across Europe and North America but they do not commit terrorist acts in these locations. This is where they draw much of the money and support needed to attack Israel, and they do not want to create a backlash that would jeopardise these activities by bombing Israeli or other targets in the US, Europe or elsewhere.

Regional groups may also have a transnational reach but it is limited to one part of the world. For example, the Abu Sayyaf operates primarily in the Philippines but has kidnapped hostages from other countries in the region. The hostages it targets are from around the world.

The motivation of domestic terrorist groups differs according to the state in which they exist. The objective of the Real IRA is to continue the struggle to unite all of Ireland. The objective of its loyalist counterparts is to use terrorism to prevent that from occurring. In the US there are groups that want to form separate nations within the US based on ethnic or racial identity. There are other groups whose objective is to overthrow the entire US government and create a new nation based on their beliefs.

Special interest extremists also operate internationally but their activities are more predictable because they have a narrow focus of interest. To understand the interests and mindset of groups such as the Animal Liberation Front or the Earth Liberation Front, one need only visit their web sites. Here they brag about their past accomplishments, present their views, provide the reader with information on the tactics they use, and may even suggest targets. Groups associated with the anti-globalisation movement such as the J18 use their web sites to achieve the same objectives.

The lone terrorist is the most difficult to predict. The Unabomber operated in the US for years until members of his family contacted law enforcement. He expressed his anti-industrialisation views by building and detonating a number of explosive devices. The lone operator doesn't make contact with other terrorists and is more difficult to identify than terrorists operating within a group. As a result, this terrorist is harder to identify, predict and deter.

Traditionally, terrorists have relied on the old saying, 'Kill one and frighten ten thousand'. Today's terrorists understand that with the impact of the media they can kill thousands and frighten millions. This is certainly what happened on September 11, 2001. The report of the United States National Commission on Terrorism (2000) noted that the terrorist threat is changing in ways that make it more difficult to counter. The report included the following findings:

- *'International terrorism once threatened Americans only when they were outside the country. Today international terrorists attack us on our own soil.'* While this is a new phenomenon in the view of the Commission, it is hardly new in dealing with international terrorism. International terrorists have been responsible for a number of attacks in Europe and elsewhere for the past several decades. The 1993 bombing of the World Trade Center in New York City was an international terrorist event, and terrorists representing the government of Libya and the IRA committed acts in the US prior to the World Trade Center bombing.
- *'Terrorist attacks are becoming more lethal.'* Terrorism during the 1980s and 1990s was motivated by ideological and nationalistic goals. Thus, the leaders were mindful of the potential consequences and backlash of a major loss of life as a result of an incident. Today, terrorism is increasingly associated with an abomination of a religion or an ideal, and there is an increase in the number of terrorists who want to achieve martyrdom during their attack.
- *'Now a growing number of terrorist attacks are designed to kill as many people as possible.'* This is related to the increased hatred of terrorists towards their targets and the apocalyptic vision of many groups.

If the dynamics of terrorism are to be understood and used to deter future acts, the psychological dynamics of this threat must be explored. Kurt Salzingerm, the American Psychological Association's executive director for science, when speaking on the events of September 11, 2001, said that: 'This event was a function of behavior—it wasn't a function of airplanes or buildings, or technology. Given that, we have to be concerned with how to prevent it through people's behavior' (Carpenter, 2001). Can we really understand the psychology of this threat and develop psychological approaches to deterring terrorists?

THE PSYCHOLOGY OF TERRORISM AND COMBATING TERRORISM

Terrorism is the result of the interaction between real-world issues and psychological dynamics (Bertelson, 1995). The terrorist group must share a common set of beliefs, experiences and goals. Within the terrorist organisation the group forms a cohesive community where loyalty to the group often becomes more cohesive than the cause. Members become psychologically dependent on the organisation, surrendering their personal concept of the self.

The leadership and culture of the terrorist group seeks to dehumanise the enemy and to make the point of attack an omnipotent act where the terrorist achieves ultimate identification with the group and, to some degree, its cause. Many terrorists are filled with rage and their acts allow them to vent these feelings by inflicting maximum horror and shock on their enemies. They feel that they are entitled to kill in order to survive. The enemy is the ultimate evil and hence there is no guilt for the consequences of their acts.

Previous chapters in this volume have looked at the question of terrorist motivation (see Chapters 1 and 2 in particular) but it is important to touch on this subject again here. Overall, the psychological motivation for terrorism derives from the individual's personal dissatisfaction with life and accomplishments. While there is no standard psychopathology that fits all terrorists, most of them can be described as true believers. True believers cannot conceive that their views or beliefs are not absolute, and they are unable to even consider that the views of others may have some merit. They project their antisocial motivations onto an 'us versus them' outlook, demonising their enemy. They have a great psychological need to belong to and be accepted by the group, and they define their social status by group acceptance. The dynamics within the group do not allow for dissent or compromise. Those who attempt to depart from the group's norms or decisions are not only ousted from the group, but often murdered.

Fanatical terrorists have three extreme elements to their being; a state of mind, a type of behaviour, and a goal, all three exclusive and extreme, all driven by destructive and often deadly instincts (Haynal, Molnar and de Puymege, 1983). However, the distinction between fanaticism and belief and conviction needs to be defined. Belief is more or less a vague adhesion to ideas or images, which can be neither confirmed nor denied. Conviction is certitude of an emotional nature, sometimes involving the overestimation of certain truths. Fanaticism is a mentality that appears and recedes in historical circumstances (Haynal, Molnar and de Puymege, 1983).

In his classic study on true believers, Eric Hoffer (1951) described the ideal fanatical terrorist group member: 'To ripen this person for self-sacrifice he must be stripped of his individual identity and distinctiveness. He must cease to be George, Hans, Ivan or Tado—a human atom with an existence bound by birth and death. The most drastic way to achieve this end is by the complete assimilation of the individual into the collective body. The fully assimilated individual does not see himself or others as human beings ... He has no purpose, worth or destiny apart from his collective body; as long as that body lives he cannot really die' (p. 61).

To understand terrorist movements one must also understand their cultural motivation. This is especially difficult for people in the West, who emphasise to some degree the separation of church and state, when attempting to understand the East where religion is more an all-encompassing way of life. Americans in particular are reluctant to appreciate the intense effect of history and culture on behaviour, and many of them believe in the myth that secular rational behaviour guides human actions. They have difficulty understanding such things as vendettas and martyrdom, concepts that are part of the culture of the East.

In societies where the group is more important than the individual there is a greater willingness for self-sacrifice. In the West the basic unit of human organisation is usually one's nationality, which is then subdivided in a number of ways including religion and ethnicity. In the East, and particularly in Islam, the basic unit is religion, which is then subdivided into nationality, ethnicity, etc. This was exemplified in the words of Calif Omar, Second in Succession to the Prophet Muhammad, who is quoted as saying: 'Learn your genealogy, and do not be like the local peasant who, when asked who you are reply; "I am from such-and-such a place".' Calif Omar encouraged his followers to remember their religious heritage, culture and history above all other aspects of their identity.

The current foundation for the movement towards Islamic fundamentalism did not begin with the Ayatollah Ruhollah Khomeini in Iran but with the birth of Wahhabism in Arabia in 1744. Founded by Muhammad ibn Add al-Wahhab (1703–87) Wahhabism rejects all facets of modern life and strives to return to the pure Islam of the Prophet. It attempts to demonise all those who oppose a strict interpretation of Islam, and is not only a threat to the West but to Islamic nations as well. To counter this threat the president of Uzbekistan recently signed a pact with the presidents of Russia and Tajik, vowing co-operation to fight the militant followers of the movement in their countries (Central Asia: The crusade against the Wahhabis, 1998).

What makes the Islamic terrorist threat particularly viable is the great sense of history and awareness of community within the Islamic world. An animal rights activist does not have a sense of history that goes back for centuries. The anti-government terrorist in the US has only a few hundred years of history to protest. Even an Irish republican's history is limited to less than half that of the Islamic terrorist. The greater the sense of history, the greater the commitment to the group and the cause. According to Hoffer (1951): 'A historical awareness also imparts a sense of continuity. Possessed of a vivid vision of the past and future, the true believer sees himself part of something that stretches backward and forward— something eternal.' The deeper the sense of history, the more passionate the sense of the future, the greater the commitment of the terrorist to the group to which he or she belongs.

Perhaps the most difficult aspect of terrorism for the Western mind to comprehend is the concept of martyrdom.[1] The terrorists who died on September 11, 2001 did not commit suicide, they willingly became martyrs. In Islam, suicide is a mortal sin but to die as a martyr is a great honour that results in heavenly rewards. In most cases terrorists who are willing to be martyred for the cause are acting as part of a group. They are carefully prepared, spiritually, mentally and physically. This is not a matter of an individual whim. An organisation picks the people for the mission, trains them, decides on the target, arranges the logistics and then sends them on their mission (Vedantam, 2001).

The martyred terrorist is the last actor in a long chain of events. Once a decision is made to launch a suicide attack, its implementation requires at least six different operations: target selection, intelligence gathering, recruitment, physical and spiritual training, preparation of the explosives and transportation to the target area (Sprinzak, 2001).

So can a suicide terrorist committed to becoming a martyr be stopped? Not according to Mousa Adu Marzook, a leader of Hamas: 'When one decides to die, I don't know how you can stop him.' Marzook claims that the Palestinian members of Hamas are without hope, a future, work or a homeland. According to him, there is no shortage of volunteers willing to be martyred (Phelps, 1996).

As stressed earlier in Chapter 5, martyrdom and suicide attacks are not limited to Islamic or Palestinian groups. Tamils and Kurds are among the other groups that have committed suicide attacks. Further, in the US two anti-government terrorists decided to die in separate confrontations with law-enforcement officers instead of surrendering. In both of these cases they made conscious decisions to die for their cause.

DETERRING TERRORISTS

Terrorist organisations incorporate psychological warfare within their overall strategy and use it to great effect. Their acts are designed to strike

---

[1] See Chapter 5 in this volume, which examines the psychology of suicidal terrorism in detail.

fear into the minds of the target population and to weaken confidence in their government. They also use psychological warfare to recruit members and to control their behaviour once they join the group. Hamas, as an example, uses photographs and videotaped interviews of suicide bombers as well as video footage of the actual attacks to praise those who choose to become martyrs. They use threats, such as claims that they have 10 suicide bombers ready and waiting, as part of their psychological warfare campaign against their perceived enemy (Rudge, 2001).

The anti-terrorism planner must learn first to think like the adversary. The planner must understand the culture, history and mindset of the terrorist. The planner must possess intelligence on the capabilities, organisation and motivation of terrorist groups. Ultimately, an effective anti-terrorism planner must learn to think like a terrorist. Since we all have our ethnocentric limitations, that is the set of values and beliefs we develop as we mature in our own cultural setting, developing a terrorist mindset is a challenge. This challenge is magnified by the fact that major terrorist groups around the world have different sets of motivations, beliefs and values (Seger, 1990).

However, once an individual develops the ability to think like a terrorist, he or she can begin to think like an anti-terrorism planner, and is then prepared to assess the degree of threat to his or her assets and to develop proactive approaches to manage that threat. These approaches include appropriate security measures, awareness among the targeted population, operations security and psychological methods for deterring terrorists.

The physical protection of potential targets is an essential anti-terrorism tactic and results in two psychological advantages. First, it increases the apparent risk to the terrorist group. Either the group will not be able to get to its target, or it will be unable to plan the attack with the assurance that it will be successful. The second psychological advantage to improved security is that it reassures the public. Terrorism is a form of psychological warfare where the terrorist seeks to undermine a government in the minds of its people, and improved security measures can help to counter that goal (Sprinzak, 2001).

In addition to knowing that their government is doing everything it can to protect them, targeted populations must also be educated to the fact that terrorism is a form of psychological warfare. A population that knows it is being subjected to psychological manipulation may develop strong terrorism antibodies (Sprinzak, 2001). For example, cash rewards for information on terrorists and their activities are an effective psychological weapon. Not only do rewards result in an increase in intelligence, they also put the terrorist on the defensive because he or she does not know who he or she can trust (Rudge, 2001).

Operations security (OPSEC) is defined by US Army Regulation AR-530-1 (15 October 1985) as: 'the process of denying adversaries information about friendly capabilities and intentions by identifying, controlling, and predicting indicators associated with the planning and conducting of military operations and other activities'. The basic objective of an operations security programme is to deny terrorists the opportunity to collect information on your activity and prevent them from developing the intelligence that would allow them to predict your actions (Seger 1990). Again, psychology plays an important role in OPSEC.

Consider, for example, the three 'Ds' of OPSEC: denial, disguise and deception. If we understand the mindset and capability of the adversary, we can institute psychological measures to apply each of these approaches. We can deny the terrorist the information needed to plan an event by creating an awareness of the threat in the targeted population, who will then be more likely to guard this information and to report attempts to compromise it.

We can also play mind games with the enemy using disguise and deception. If plain-clothes security personnel are used in place of uniformed guards, the terrorist will be unable to identify the size of the force or the persons associated with it. Deception is often used when transporting sensitive materials. Some vehicles will actually contain the material but others will be empty or may contain a harmless substance. The terrorist is unable to predict which vehicles hold the sensitive material and the probability of success in trying to attack or obtain it is decreased substantially.

An effective approach to deterring some domestic extremists has been to meet with them. Law-enforcement officers visit them at their homes and encourage them to discuss their concerns and views. The officers are non-judgemental and do not argue or attempt to correct the views expressed. When the meeting concludes, the officers provide the extremists with a business card and encourage them to contact the officers if they have additional concerns. This approach provides a 'face' to the faceless government the extremist had confronted in the past. It also removes some of the paranoia that law enforcement is simply out to get the extremist because of his or her views, and often results in the extremist providing intelligence to his or her new friend.

Reaching out to extremists works best if it is coupled with an aggressive response to terrorist activities. Planned activities must be disrupted and the persons responsible prosecuted. If a terrorist attack has taken place, those responsible must be brought to justice. By combining these activities the extremist who is on the edge of becoming a terrorist learns that the government he or she perceives as the enemy is not demonic but that there is a price to pay for those who plan or engage in terrorist activities.

In the eyes of many, reaching out is not an option with international extremists and terrorists. The new breed of terrorists are carefully programmed to destroy their enemy at all costs. They are likely to be educated, well trained, blindly obedient to authority and totally dedicated to the group and its ideology. They are trained to remain faceless with nothing to lose except sacrificing their lives for a higher cause (Zimbardo, 2001).

This new breed of terrorists embodies creative evil at its worst. The attacks of September 11, 2001 were the product of extensive planning, training and professional expertise. They required financial resources and networks of co-conspirators living among the targeted population. These acts were not senseless, mindless or insane. They were acts that had a clearly defined purpose that must be understood if future attacks of this nature are to be prevented (Zimbardo, 2001).

Unfortunately, history and research both find that normal people can be convinced to commit aggressive and evil acts. Research has indicated that Nazi concentration camp guards were 'ordinary men' before and following their years of working in the camps. Laboratory experiments conducted by Stanley Milgram, Albert Bandura and others have showed that intelligent students were willing to become extremely aggressive towards other groups of students given the right circumstances (Zimbardo, 2001).

So how do we deter fanatical terrorists who are willing to die for the cause? How do we deter individuals who offer themselves for martyrdom? To such a terrorist, 'dying and killing seem easy when they are part of a ritual, ceremonial, dramatic performance or game' (Hoffer, 1951). We must remember that suicide terrorists are not lone zealots. They are instruments of the terrorist leaders who expect to achieve tangible results from this tactic. The key to countering martyrs is to make terrorist organisations aware that they will incur painful costs if this tactic is used. Security forces and the military must strike against the commanders who recruit and train suicide terrorists and then plan the attacks.[2] It is essential to put these leaders on the defensive (Sprinzak, 2000). This was the response to the September 11 attacks. Today the al-Qaeda network is in shambles and the Taliban government that supported it is history.

These events demonstrate the Achilles' heal of suicide terrorists in that they are part of a large operational infrastructure. While it may not be possible to profile and apprehend would-be suicide terrorists, it is possible to target and destroy the groups that support them. When a group implements suicide terrorism systematically within its community, that community must be targeted. The military and law-enforcement agencies have an important role in this response, but the diplomatic and financial communities also play a key role. This is not an easy response to coordinate (Sprinzak, 2001).

In September 2001 the US Department of State had several nations on its list of states which sponsor terrorism. Afghanistan was not one of them.

---

[2]Though there are problems and drawbacks to this approach as well, as discussed in Chapter 11 of this volume.

Afghanistan could not be listed because the US did not recognise the Taliban as a legitimate government. If a government is not recognised, it cannot be designated a sponsor of terrorism, and the sanctions imposed on other terrorism state sponsors cannot be implemented. Implementing financial restraints on terrorist organisations and their sponsors requires international co-operation, and this was certainly something that was lacking before September 11, 2001.

Though security measures are in place to prevent the fanatical terrorist bomber from becoming a martyr for the group and its cause, terrorists are inventive and ingenious, and martyrs will constantly be looking for ways to thwart security measures and impose a great price on our failure to be equally inventive. The terrorists on September 11 did not attempt to bring explosives or guns on to the aircraft. They brought box cutters that were legal at the time. Instead of blowing up the aircraft they used them as weapons, killing thousands of victims instead of hundreds. Again, the effective anti-terrorism planner must learn to think like the adversary and try to anticipate future tactics and targets.

Does using a massive force against the terrorist infrastructure have a catch-22 effect? There are two concerns here. First, the use of military force confirms the terrorists' self-image as heroic warriors and martyrs to the cause. It also reinforces the image of the target of their aggression to be an evil enemy and enhances their status with supporters and followers. A major military response may result in additional recruits to the cause of the terrorist organisation to fight what they perceive as the evil aggressor (Crenshaw, 2001). In addition, large-scale military action may increase the demands for revenge, not just from the terrorist organisation but from others who identify with the cause, and this can result in a spiral of revenge and counter-revenge (Crenshaw, 2001).

The dilemma is this. States that are attacked by international or regional suicide terrorists believe they must strike back, seeking to destroy the culture and group that instigates the attacks and prepares and trains its martyrs. In doing so, however, the government may motivate additional attacks by other terrorists and supporters sympathetic to the cause. There are many terrorists who are willing, and may even desire, to die for the cause. There are also defenders of civilised societies who are prepared to die in the protection of their causes—the law-enforcement officers and the armed forces (A violent sacrifice, 2001). Is the psychology of preparing these individuals for their roles really any different? Terrorists define their enemies as evil. As Hoffer (1951) suggests: 'mass movements can rise and spread without belief in God, but never without a devil' (p. 89).

In describing Osama bin Laden, President Bush has repeatedly used the word 'evil'. We have identified the enemy as demonic, just as the enemy has defined us. History is replete with examples of the need to identify the adversary in negative terms so as to justify actions against them.

The British have a negative word used to describe Arabs and others from the East. In the US there is a host of words that have been used to refer to minorities. In wartime we have had a number of terms to refer to Japanese, Germans, Chinese, North Koreans, North Vietnamese, and Arabs sympathetic to Iraq. The demonisation of the adversary makes it easier for both terrorist and for counter-terrorist forces to conduct their respective missions. Take away the humanity of the enemy and one is justified in destroying him.

CONCLUSION

Terrorists cannot be deterred solely via psychological approaches. These must be used in combination with practical security measures, intelligence collection and effective law-enforcement investigation and prosecution. Individual terrorists must believe that the probability of their completing their mission is minimal, and terrorist organisations must understand that their actions will result in a prompt and appropriate military and/or law-enforcement response. Individuals must be apprehended and incarcerated for long periods of time, and the organisations that support them must be destroyed.

However, these combined measures will not prevent future terrorist organisations from emerging or major attacks from occurring. Terrorism is a constantly evolving phenomena that the West is just beginning to understand. Following the bombing of the Khobar Towers in 1996, Osama bin Laden declared war on the US. In an interview with a television reporter he said: 'We believe that the biggest thieves in the world are Americans and the biggest terrorists are Americans. The only way for us to defend off these assaults is by using similar means. We do not differentiate between . . . uniforms and civilians.' Following this declaration, al-Qaeda bombed the USS *Cole*, killing 19 people and injuring more than 300 others. They then detonated two bombs at US embassies in Africa, killing 224 people and injuring more than 5000. But the US did not take the declaration of war seriously until September 11, 2001.

The civilised world is facing a new terrorist threat. Rather than confronting structured groups we are dealing with loosely interconnected networks. We are not dealing with political or nationalistic ideas, we are facing fanatical religionists with deep roots in the past and a unique perspective of the future. The adversary is willing to be martyred for the cause of the group to which he or she belongs: 'Faith organizes and equips man's soul for action. To be in possession of the one and only truth and never doubt one's righteousness; to feel that one's opponents are the incarnation of evil and must be crushed; to exult in self-denial and devotion to duty—these are admirable qualifications for resolute and ruthless action in any field' (Hoffer, 1951, p. 119).

Future challenges in the deterrence of terrorism are formidable.

REFERENCES

A violent sacrifice (2001). *The Washington Post*, 22 December, A21.

APA responds to terrorist attacks (2001). *Monitor on Psychology*, **32**(10).

Bertelson, C. (1995). How could anyone do that? Expert gives an answer. *St Louis Post-Dispatch*, 22 April, 1B.

Carpenter, S. (2001). Behavioral science gears up to combat terrorism. *Monitor on Psychology*, **32**(10).

Central Asia: the crusade against the Wahhabis (1998). *The Economist*, **348** (4 August).

Crenshaw, M. (2001). The attack on America/Know the enemy mind. *Newsday*, 15 September, B05.

Haynal, A., Molnar, M. and de Puymege, G. (1983). *Fanaticism: A Historical and Psychoanalytical Study*. New York: Schocken Books.

Hoffer, E. (1951). *The True Believer*. New York: Harper and Row.

National Commission on Terrorism (2000). *Countering the Changing Threat of International Terrorism*. Washington, DC: National Commission on Terrorism.

Phelps, T.M. (1996). Insight into terror/Can't stop bombers, jailed Palestinian warns. *Newsday*, 17 May, A04.

Ralston, J.W. (1999). *Combating Terrorism*. Congressional Testimony, 9 March 1999.

Rudge, D. (2001). Psychological warfare needed for terror—expert. *Jerusalem Post*, 20 August, p. 3.

Seger, K. (1990). *The Antiterrorism Handbook*. Novato, CA: Presidio Press.

Sprinzak, E. (2000). Outsmarting suicide terrorists. *The Christian Science Monitor*, 24 October, p. 9.

Sprinzak, E. (2001). Rational fanatics. *Foreign Policy*, September–October.

US Army Regulation AR-530-1 (1985). *Operations Security*. US Army, 15 October.

Vedantam, S. (2001). Peer pressure spurs terrorists, psychologists say: attackers unlike usual suicide bombers. *The Washington Post*, 16 October, A16.

Zimbardo, P. (2001). Opposing terrorism by understanding the human capacity for evil. *Monitor on Psychology*, **32**(10).

Index